The Cambridge Companion to Medieval Logic

This volume, the first dedicated and comprehensive Companion to Medieval Logic, covers both the Latin and the Arabic traditions and shows that they were in fact sister traditions, which both arose against the background of a Hellenistic heritage and which influenced one another over the centuries. A series of chapters by both established and younger scholars covers the whole period including early and late developments, and offers new insights into this extremely rich period in the history of logic. The volume is divided into two parts, 'Periods and Traditions' and 'Themes', allowing readers to engage with the subject from both historical and more systematic perspectives. It will be a must-read for students and scholars of medieval philosophy, the history of logic, and the history of ideas.

CATARINA DUTILH NOVAES is professor and Rosalind Franklin Fellow in the Faculty of Philosophy of the University of Groningen (the Netherlands). She is the author of *Formalizing Medieval Logical Theories* (Springer, 2007) and *Formal Languages in Logic* (Cambridge University Press, 2012), as well as many articles on the history and philosophy of logic.

STEPHEN READ is Professor Emeritus of History and Philosophy of Logic at the University of St Andrews (Scotland). He is the author of *Relevant Logic* (Blackwell, 1988) and *Thinking about Logic* (Oxford University Press, 1995), editor of *Sophisms in Medieval Logic and Grammar* (Springer, 1993), editor and translator of *Thomas Bradwardine: Insolubilia* (Peeters, 2010), translator of *John Buridan: Treatise on Consequences* (Fordham University Press, 2015), as well as the author many articles on contemporary and medieval philosophy of logic and language.

D1570593

Other Volumes in The Series of Cambridge Companions

The Cambridge Companion to *Medieval Logic*

Edited by
CATARINA DUTILH NOVAES
AND
STEPHEN READ

CAMBRIDGE
UNIVERSITY PRESS

CAMBRIDGE
UNIVERSITY PRESS

University Printing House, Cambridge CB2 8BS, United Kingdom

One Liberty Plaza, 20th Floor, New York, NY 10006, USA

477 Williamstown Road, Port Melbourne, VIC 3207, Australia

4843/24, 2nd Floor, Ansari Road, Daryaganj, Delhi - 110002, India

79 Anson Road, #06-04/06, Singapore 079906

Cambridge University Press is part of the University of Cambridge.

It furthers the University's mission by disseminating knowledge in the pursuit of
education, learning and research at the highest international levels of excellence.

www.cambridge.org
Information on this title: www.cambridge.org/9781107656673

© Cambridge University Press 2016

First published 2016

A catalogue record for this publication is available from the British Library

Library of Congress Cataloging in Publication data
Names: Novaes, Catarina Dutilh, editor.
Title: The Cambridge companion to medieval logic /
edited by Catarina Dutilh Novaes and Stephen Read.
Description: New York : Cambridge University Press, 2016. |
Series: Cambridge companions | Includes bibliographical
references and index.
Identifiers: LCCN 2016026605 | ISBN 9781107062313 (hardback) |
ISBN 9781107656673 (paperback)
Subjects: LCSH: Logic, Medieval.
Classification: LCC BC34.C36 2016 | DDC 160.9/02–dc23
LC record available at https://lccn.loc.gov/2016026605

ISBN 978-1-107-06231-3 Hardback
ISBN 978-1-107-65667-3 Paperback

Contents

Contributors

E. JENNIFER ASHWORTH is Distinguished Professor Emerita at the University of Waterloo (Canada). She is the author of *Language and Logic in the Post-Medieval Period* (Reidel, 1974) and the editor and translator of Paul of Venice's *Logica Magna* Part II.8 (Oxford University Press, 1988).

JULIE BRUMBERG-CHAUMONT is a researcher at the Centre National de la Recherche Scientifique in Paris (France). She is the editor of *Ad notitiam ignoti, L'Organon dans la translatio studiorum à l'époque d'Albert le Grand* (Brepols, 2013).

MARGARET CAMERON is the Canada Research Council Chair in the Aristotelian Tradition and associate professor in the Department of Philosophy at the University of Victoria (Canada). She is the editor of *Methods and Methodologies: Aristotelian Logic East and West 500–1500* (Brill, 2010) and *Linguistic Content: New Essays on the History of the Philosophy of Language* (Oxford University Press, 2014).

LAURENT CESALLI is professor of medieval philosophy at the Département de philosophie, Université de Genève (Switzerland). He is the author of *Le réalisme propositionnel: Sémantique et ontologie des propositions chez Jean Duns Scot, Gauthier Burley, Richard Brinkley et Jean Wyclif* (Vrin, 2007).

ELIZABETH COPPOCK is a fellow at the Swedish Collegium for Advanced Study and a researcher at the Department of Philosophy, Linguistics and Theory of Science, University of Gothenburg

(Sweden). She has published articles in journals such as *Linguistics and Philosophy* and the *Journal of Semantics*.

CATARINA DUTILH NOVAES is professor at the Faculty of Philosophy, University of Groningen (the Netherlands). She is the author of *Formalizing Medieval Logical Theories* (Springer, 2007) and *Formal Languages in Logic* (Cambridge University Press, 2012).

KHALED EL-ROUAYHEB is James Richard Jewett Professor of Arabic and Islamic Intellectual History at the Department of Near Eastern Languages and Civilizations, Harvard University (USA). He is the author of *Relational Syllogisms and the History of Arabic Logic, 900–1900* (Brill, 2010).

AHMAD HASNAWI is director of research at the Centre National de la Recherche Scientifique in Paris. He is the author of articles in venues such as *Arabic Sciences and Philosophy* and *L.E.U.S.* and the editor of *La lumière de l'ntellect: La pensée scientifique et philosophique d'Averroès dans son temps* (Peeters, 2011).

WILFRID HODGES is a fellow of the British Academy and Emeritus Professor at Queen Mary, University of London (England). He is the author of *Logic* (Penguin, 1977) and *Building Models by Games* (Dover, 2006).

CHRISTOPH KANN is professor at the Institute of Philosophy, University of Düsseldorf (Germany). He edited and translated William of Sherwood's *Introduction to Logic* (Meiner, 1995) as well as his *Syncategoremata* (Meiner, 2012) and is the author of *Die Eigenschaften der Termini. Eine Untersuchung zur 'Perutilis logica' Alberts von Sachsen* (Brill, 1994).

GYULA KLIMA is professor at the Department of Philosophy, Fordham University (USA). He is the author of *John Buridan* (Oxford University

Press, 2009) and the translator of John Buridan's *Summulae de Dialectica* (2001).

HENRIK LAGERLUND is professor and chair at the Department of Philosophy of the University of Western Ontario (Canada). He is the author of *Modal Syllogistics in the Middle Ages* (Brill, 2000) and the editor of the *Encyclopedia of Medieval Philosophy* (Springer, 2011).

STEPHEN READ is Professor Emeritus of History and Philosophy of Logic at the University of St Andrews and researcher at the Arché Research Centre (Scotland). He is the author of *Thinking about Logic* (Oxford University Press, 1995), and the editor and translator of Bradwardine's *Treatise on Insolubles* (Peeters, 2010) and Buridan's *Treatise on Consequences* (Fordham University Press, 2015).

RICCARDO STROBINO is Mellon Bridge Assistant Professor at the Department of Classics of Tufts University (USA). He has published articles in journals such as *Vivarium, Oriens, and the British Journal for the History of Philosophy*.

PAUL THOM is Honorary Visiting Professor at the School of Philosophical and Historical Inquiry, University of Sydney (Australia). He is the author of *The Syllogism* (Philosophia, 1981), *Medieval Modal Systems* (Ashgate, 2003), and *Logic and Ontology in the Syllogistic of Robert Kilwardby* (Brill, 2007).

SARA L. UCKELMAN is a lecturer at the Department of Philosophy, Durham University (England). She has published articles in journals such as *Synthese, Vivarium,* and the *Journal of Philosophical Logic.*

IAN WILKS is professor and chair at the Department of Philosophy, Acadia University (Canada). He has published articles in journals such as the *Journal of the History of Philosophy* and the *Review of Metaphysics.*

MIKKO YRJÖNSUURI is professor at the Department of Social Sciences and Philosophy, University of Jyvaskyla (Finland). He is the editor of *Medieval Formal Logic* (Kluwer, 2001) and author of *Obligationes: 14th Century Logic of Disputational Duties* (Acta philosophica Fennica, 1994).

Introduction

Catarina Dutilh Novaes and Stephen Read

O.I THE SCOPE OF MEDIEVAL LOGIC (IN THIS VOLUME)

What counts as "medieval logic"? The Middle Ages is traditionally conceived as the period between the fall of the Roman Empire in 410 and the fall of the Byzantine Empire in 1453 (alternative end dates are Columbus' first trip to the Americas in 1492 or the Protestant Reformation in 1517).[1] So technically, logical theories and traditions of roughly between AD 500 and 1500 could all qualify as belonging to the realm of "medieval logic". In practice, however, this is not what most of us have in mind when we speak of medieval logic; we tend to think specifically of textual material in Latin, produced within Europe, and typically from the twelfth century onwards. Moreover, there is the issue of delineating what is to count as "logic" among the different theories and topics, as the borders between logic, grammar, metaphysics, theology, etc. were then rather fluid.

For this volume, we have chosen to adopt geographical borders going beyond the usual Eurocentric narrative, even if only slightly, and this has meant in particular including the rich Arabic tradition (more on this choice shortly) alongside the Latin tradition. We also sought to be more inclusive on the temporal dimension by taking into account developments in the so-called Early Middle Ages, though the focus remains on later developments.

The inclusion of the Arabic tradition is a very natural choice, for a number of reasons. First, the Latin and the Arabic medieval logical traditions[2] are strongly connected thanks to the prodigious

---

[1] Naturally, this is a Eurocentric periodisation that does not necessarily reflect historical turning points in other parts of the world.

[2] Notice that, in both cases, the criterion is essentially linguistic: we are concerned with logic produced in Arabic in the Islamic World (though not necessarily by ethnic Arabs, nor necessarily by Islamic authors); and with logic produced in Latin in the Christian World (in the latter case, most if not all authors are indeed Christians).

1

influence of one author, namely Aristotle. Indeed, these two traditions are best studied in tandem, as they originate against the background of the same authoritative texts (especially Aristotle's logical works), and as cross-fertilisation (especially the influence of Arabic logic on the Latin tradition) regularly occurred. Second, in recent years, scholarship on Arabic medieval logic has attained a level of maturity that allows for detailed analysis at an accessible level, even if it is not yet as thoroughly studied as the Latin tradition.

These two kinds of consideration also motivate the choice to exclude a number of traditions we might have included in the volume. In particular, the Chinese and Indian traditions do not share the same general Hellenistic (especially Aristotelian) background (and do not seem to have been in close, regular contact with the Latin and Arabic traditions); thus, it seems that they are best studied separately. (Perhaps a more accurate title for this volume would have been something like *The Cambridge Companion to Medieval Aristotelian Logic*.) But if belonging to the Aristotelian tradition, broadly construed, were the only criterion, then we would have had to take into account also the Byzantine tradition, which remained active, albeit to a lesser extent, in later centuries (Ierodiakonou 2011), and the Hebrew tradition, which developed in close proximity with the Arabic as well as the Latin traditions (Manekin 2011). However, current scholarship on these two traditions is still incipient, and so it seemed prudent to focus specifically on the two Aristotelian traditions for which we could rely on extensive existing scholarly work: the Latin tradition and the Arabic tradition. This choice also provided a solution to the issue of what to count as "logic": given the pivotal place of Aristotle's logical texts in both traditions, delineating logic as a discipline in this period then becomes by and large a matter of focusing on responses to these texts and on new theories emerging within these contexts.

We, the editors, are the first to admit that the volume as a whole is still very much skewed towards the Latin tradition, which is more thoroughly covered (in number of pages and in the choice of themes) than the Arabic tradition. But we hope that the volume will constitute a further step (following in the footsteps of pioneering work by, e.g., John Marenbon and Tony Street with their project 'Aristotelian Logic East and West, 500–1500', among others) towards a systematic, integrated study of these two sister traditions.

In short: this volume covers developments in logic (understood predominantly, but not exclusively, as material related to Aristotle's canonical texts) in the period ranging roughly from the eighth to the fifteenth centuries, as produced in Christian Europe (in Latin) and in the Islamic World (in Arabic). This choice of scope is not arbitrary (indeed, it is motivated by the reasons just discussed), but it could well have been a different one (in particular by the inclusion of the Byzantine and Hebrew traditions).

0.2   STRUCTURE AND CONTENT OF THE VOLUME

However, even with these restrictions in place, there remains a formidable amount of material that asks to be included. Given the general goal of accessibility for a *Companion* volume, some difficult choices had to be made on what to include and what not.

We opted for a bipartite structure. The first part is dedicated to periods and traditions, focusing on developments considered diachronically within each period. The key question for these chapters was how logical doctrines evolved within the relevant period, what were the main trends, concepts, authors, etc. The first chapter lays down the basis for the subsequent chapters by providing an overview of the ancient, Hellenistic background against which each of the two traditions went on to develop, and the reception of the different texts. We then have two chapters on the development of the Arabic tradition, and four chapters on the Latin tradition; in both cases, we looked for somewhat natural cut-off points. (As it so happens, the Latin tradition has very natural cut-off points by century, and for the Arabic tradition we took the pivotal figure of Avicenna to represent a natural cut-off point.)

The second part focuses on themes and concepts; here the emphasis is predominantly (and perhaps disproportionately) on the

Latin material, as many of the themes receiving full chapters are crucial within the Latin tradition but absent within the Arabic tradition (e.g. properties of terms, *obligationes*). Here, too, difficult choices had to be made, and in order to respect the standard length for a *Companion* volume, we had to restrict ourselves to eight general themes, which collectively cover much but naturally not all of the important developments in both traditions.

Some of the important topics that were by and large excluded (albeit with somewhat brief mentions in other chapters) but which could just as well have received full chapters are: exponibilia; syncategorematic terms; the Arabic traditions of "ma'ani wa bayan" (semantics–rhetoric) and "adab al-bahth" (formal dialectics); the connections with grammarians and grammar; logic and theology. Let us comment briefly on each of them.

Exponibilia are a major focus within Latin fourteenth-century logic and beyond (Ashworth 1973); the basic idea is that of analysing the meaning of a sentence by its exposition into presumably simpler sentences. These are sentences "which need further analysis in order to lay bare their underlying logical form and to make clear under what conditions they can be said to be true or false" (Ashworth 1973, 137). Some examples of sentences requiring exposition are exceptives (e.g. 'Everyone except Socrates is running'), exclusives (e.g. 'Only Socrates is running') and reduplicatives (e.g. 'Justice is known qua good').

Syncategorematic terms (Kretzmann 1982; Spruyt 2011) are those "funny words" that typically cannot figure as subject or predicate in propositions unlike categorematic terms (predominantly nouns and adjectives) and do not straightforwardly stand for "things", but which make significant contributions to the overall meaning of propositions where they figure. Typical examples are what we now call "logical terms" such as 'not', quantifying terms such as 'all', 'some', 'no', among many others. (A glimpse of medieval discussions on syncategoremata can be found in the chapter "Sophisms and Insolubles".) They gave rise to sophisticated discussions on the nature of linguistic meaning, the semantics of propositions, and even metaphysical issues by Latin authors (Dutilh Novaes and Spruyt 2015).

Grammar and the work of grammarians was a major influence for the development of medieval logic in both traditions, Latin and Arabic. On the Latin side, while there was widespread recognition that logic and grammar were different disciplines (they were both part of the *Trivium* curriculum, more on which shortly), there were continuous close contacts between the two throughout the centuries. The work of the ancient grammarian Priscian in particular was very influential among logicians (as well as grammarians). The early stages of development of theories of the properties of terms (see Chapter 9) were strongly influenced by grammatical concepts and concerns, and at some points in the development of Latin medieval logic one can even speak of an "invasion" of the domain of logic by grammar, in particular by the *Modistae* at the end of the thirteenth century in Paris (see Chapter 5 and van der Lecq 2011).

On the Arabic side, grammar and logic were sometimes contrasted with each other as different approaches to similar questions pertaining to language and thought, as in the famous debate opposing the philosopher and logician Abu Bishr and the grammarian Sirafi in Baghdad in 937 or 938 (Adamson and Key 2015). In this particular instance, the opposition was not only between logic and grammar, but also between a "foreign, Greek" framework and an "Arabic, Islamic" one, the same opposition underlying the dispute between *"falsafa"* and *"kalam"* (more on which shortly). Nevertheless, the relations between grammar and logic in the Arabic tradition go much beyond mere opposition, and constitute an important factor for the development of Arabic logic (Black 1991; Street 2015). Indeed, the traditions of "ma'ani wa bayan" (semantics–rhetoric – Versteegh 1997, Chapter 9) and of "adab al-bahth" (formal dialectics, literally "the rules of inquiry" – Miller 1984) are illustrations of the fruitful connections between logic and other language-oriented disciplines in the Arabic tradition, including a great deal of cross-pollination.

There were also close connections as well as oppositions between **logic and theology** in both traditions. On the Latin side, and as will be discussed in more detail shortly, logic occupied a foundational position in the medieval academic curriculum, and while this meant that logic was sometimes viewed as a topic for the youth, this also meant that logic continued to provide the conceptual background for investigations in all fields, including theology. However, because theological truths often seem to defy mere "earthly" logic, a number of logical theories were developed in particular so as to allow for the discussion of difficult theological matters such as the Trinity. For example, God is the Father and God is the Son, but the conclusion by expository syllogism (see Chapter 7) that the Son is the Father is heretical (whereas, e.g., from 'Aristotle wrote the *Categories*' and 'Aristotle is the Philosopher' we can safely infer that the Philosopher wrote the *Categories*). Thus ensued, for example, Trinitarian logic (Knuuttila 2011a). Similarly, some of the main impulses for the development of theories of analogy were theological problems such as how to speak meaningfully about God at all, given that no affirmation can be appropriate to a transcendent being (Ashworth 2013b, part 2).

On the Arabic side, it is tempting to view the famous opposition between *falsafa* and *kalam* in the earlier stages as an opposition between philosophy/logic and theology. However, a more fruitful way to look at this opposition seems to be as between an Arabic, Islamic framework relying on the Koran, hadith and "indigenous" sciences like grammar, and the imported framework of the Greeks. And while some authors (Al-Farabi, Averroes) seem to suggest that there was a sharp opposition between *kalam* and *falsafa*, in practice many authors were happy to treat problems and ideas of these two traditions in a more integrative way, especially starting with Al-Ghazali and Razi.

Indeed, the early *kalam* tradition contained a great deal of sophisticated argumentation techniques (Schöck 2005), and this is why it is best described as rational, speculative theology. At later stages, however, logic and particularly Avicennan logic becomes increasingly incorporated into the training of theologians and jurists in the madrasa system (more on which shortly), just as Aristotelian logic is widely used for theological inquiry in the Latin tradition. (See El-Rouayheb 2016 for a systematic overview of the relations between logic and theology in the Arabic tradition.)

0.3   INSTITUTIONAL SETTINGS

A crucial element in truly understanding medieval logical theories, both on the Latin side and on the Arabic side, are the various institutional factors that had considerable effect on how the theories themselves developed. After all, philosophical/logical theories typically do not arise in a vacuum: they emerge as responses to particular intellectual needs felt within a given intellectual community. Throughout this volume, and in particular in the 'Periods and Traditions' section, close attention is paid to these factors as well as to more general social, historical developments (e.g. the impact of the Papal Schism in the fourteenth century for logical developments – see Chapters 6–7).

Medieval scholars, both on the Latin side and on the Arabic side, had inherited from (late) Antiquity the idea that logic played a crucial foundational role in the pursuit of knowledge; logic was generally seen as providing the very methodology to be applied in all areas of inquiry. In practical terms, the upshot was that the basics of logic were typically taught to students very early on in their education, in particular the contents of Porphyry's *Isagoge*, Aristotle's *Categories* and *On Interpretation*, and some syllogistic. But each of these traditions should not be treated as monoliths, as important transformations occurred in each of them throughout the centuries.

Another aspect of commonality between the two traditions is the challenge of harmonising the "pagan" conceptual framework inherited from Antiquity with monotheistic faith. Indeed, both in the Latin and in the Arabic traditions, we observe an uneasy but often also fruitful interplay between these two poles, when philosophical and logical concepts become appropriated to clarify and defend religious convictions. In both cases, the result is often rational, philosophical approaches to theological questions, but also clashes between essentially philosophical and essentially theological perspectives (such as between *falsafa* and *kalam* in the Arabic tradition, or between Aristotelian scholasticism and the medieval mystical Christian tradition).

On the Latin side, the noticeable differences between the philosophical and logical theories of the earlier centuries (roughly until the eleventh century) and later theories are to a great extent due to a radical shift in terms of institutional settings. With the exception of the period of the so-called Carolingian Renaissance (late eighth to early ninth centuries), the general economic stagnation in Christian Europe up to around AD 1000 is reflected in lesser (though still interesting) intellectual activity. As is well known, in this period, the pursuit of knowledge took place essentially in the context of monasteries, monastic schools and ecclesiastical centres more generally. This earlier period is not characterised by intense activity specifically on logical matters, but it certainly laid the grounds for the emergence of Latin scholasticism as we know it (see Chapter 4).

With the economic prosperity of the eleventh and twelfth centuries and the rise of towns and cities, the situation for intellectual pursuits more generally, and for logic in particular, began to change dramatically. Especially in France (though in other European countries as well, e.g. Germany, the Netherlands, Italy), this period saw the flourishing of distinguished centres of learning such as cathedral schools in Chartres, Rheims, Paris, but also the famous abbey of Bec in Normandy (where Anselm wrote many of his most remarkable works, alongside his teaching and administrative duties as the prior of the abbey). And while the cathedral schools still mostly focused on training future clergy, the urban setting, the focus not only on religious but also on some civic matters, and the closer contact with other scholars were in clear contrast with the monastic focus on "leading a pious life" as the main purpose of education. In particular, while the monastic setting was characterised by master–pupil modes of dialogical interaction (as attested, e.g., in Anselm's writings), the rise of the schools meant that more "adversarial" modes of dialogue such as debates and disputations became more prominent (Wei 2012; Novikoff 2013).

Indeed, the twelfth-century Parisian schools were positively marked by the competitiveness among individual teachers in a marketplace of learning, where attracting students through one's charisma as a teacher was a necessary condition for obtaining one's income (see Chapter 4 and Wei 2012, chapter 1). But it would be a mistake to conclude that the monastic model had been entirely surpassed by the competitive model of the schools (Wei 2012, chapter 2). Indeed, some of the most famous disputes in the twelfth century (such as the one involving Peter Abelard and Bernard of Clairvaux) can be understood as the clash between the two models, both of which remained equally vibrant. Even with the rise of the universities later on, the monastic, contemplative model did not disappear completely and lived on with authors such as Hildegard of Bingen, Master Eckhart and the mystical tradition more generally. What is clear, at any rate, is that different institutional settings (the monastery, the cathedral school, the university) greatly influence the way intellectual inquiry is pursued, having consequences in particular for the logical theories developed given the tight connections between logic and argumentation.

As is well known, with the rise of universities in the thirteenth century, most notably in Bologna, Paris and Oxford, a new system of learning emerged which was to have long-lasting consequences (see Chapter 5). In the fourteenth century, the university model was then exported from the original centres in France, Italy and England to the rest of Europe, with the foundation of universities in cities such as Prague, Vienna, Heidelberg, etc. (see Chapter 6).

Essentially, much of the current structure of higher education is to be traced back to medieval universities, in particular the division of universities into different faculties. Philosophical instruction took place for the most part in the Arts faculties, and the classical Liberal Arts curriculum was famously structured in two clusters: the *Trivium*, composed of logic (or dialectic), grammar and rhetoric; and the *Quadrivium*, composed of music, arithmetic, geometry and astronomy. The *Trivium* was taught very early on (which then gave rise to the word 'trivial', meaning 'unimportant'), and logic was to acquire increasing importance in the *Trivium* curriculum at the expense of the other two disciplines (something that humanists in the Renaissance would later criticise vehemently). The more common trajectory for a master was to start in the Arts faculty and then teach in the Arts faculty while studying in the higher faculties such as Law, Medicine and especially Theology (the notable exception being John Buridan, who spent his whole academic career at the Arts faculty in Paris). The teaching of logic in the thirteenth-century universities relied extensively on a few canonical textbooks, in particular Peter of Spain's and William of Sherwood's (see Chapter 5).

It is also with the rise of universities that Aristotle's canonical position became consolidated, as education in the Arts faculties consisted essentially in reading and commenting upon Aristotle's texts (see Chapter 5 and Hoenen 2011). Indeed, up to the rediscovery of the Aristotelian corpus in its full glory at the end of the twelfth century, the most influential author as far as logical matters were concerned was Boethius, whose logical textbooks were widely read and provided the basis for logical education (along with his translations of Aristotle's *Categories* and *On Interpretation*) (see Chapter 1).

On the Arabic side, interest in logic and philosophy more generally emerged with the advent of the Abbasid Caliphate (750–1258), which promoted a vigorous translation movement of Hellenistic texts (see Chapter 1) sponsored by the ruling elite in Baghdad, where Al-Kindi played a major role. The absorption of the Greek tradition gave rise to the Neoplatonic/Aristotelian tradition of *falsafa*; the main competing tradition in the early period was that of *kalam*, as mentioned above.

Just as in the Latin tradition the rise of universities fundamentally changed the way logic was taught and practised, in the Arabic tradition it was the emergence of the madrasa system in the eleventh century that had an equally significant impact (Makdisi 1981). In the earlier period, logic would have been pursued in the more informal setting of an intellectual group with no institutional centre, with the most obvious examples being the Al-Kindi circle and the Baghdad school, with figures such as Farabi, Ibn Adi, etc. (see Chapter 2). In this context, the key component seems to have been the patronage relations between philosophers and various potentates, including the caliphal family in Kindi's case. There were such patronage relations also in the cases of Farabi, Avicenna, and Averroes, and indeed many of the great thinkers in the Arabic tradition were never associated with formal institutions of learning. (See Reisman 2013 for Avicenna.)

Madrasas as institutions of learning flourished from the eleventh century onwards, initially in Baghdad (Makdisi 1981). As noted, the impact of the rise of madrasas can be compared to the rise of universities in Europe in terms of how it fundamentally changed the way learning and intellectual inquiry were pursued – even if, as in the case of the European universities, these events were firmly grounded in previous developments. In particular, in the earlier period learning and intellectual inquiry were for the most part pursued in the context of centres of political power (given the patronage system), but with the emergence of the madrasas it became much more widely disseminated, geographically speaking.

In the madrasas, the Arabic scholastic method became consolidated and widely disseminated, a method in which logic occupied pride of place (Street 2015). Notice, however, that if in the early stages the most influential logician was Aristotle, by the twelfth century the logic taught in the madrasas was by and large Avicennan, not Aristotelian (with a few pockets of diehard Aristotelians, in particular in Andalusia, such as Averroes).

Moreover, in the madrasa context, logic came to be divorced from the Neoplatonic/Aristotelian *falsafa* tradition and became more of an instrumental discipline deemed useful for jurists and theologians (alongside grammar and rhetoric) (see Chapter 3). This development seems to be linked to the spread of the literary genres of condensed textbook (often memorised by students), commentary and gloss (Rescher 1964). (Of these textbooks, Al-Ghazali's *Doctrines of the Philosophers* was later on very influential in the Latin tradition – Hasse 2014 – though it was not a madrasa handbook.) It is fair to say that the establishment of the madrasa system in the eleventh century gave rise to an educational tradition that continued to flourish well into the nineteenth century in the Islamic World.

It is worth noting, however, that in the later medieval period we seem to be dealing not with one but rather with two Arabic traditions: one in the East, and one in the West, in the Iberian peninsula. These two traditions developed in largely independent ways, one noticeable difference being (as noted above) that in the East, Avicenna became the canonical logician, while in the West this position was still for the most part occupied by Aristotle, at least until the fourteenth century (during which time Avicennan logic also becomes predominant in North Africa and Islamic Spain). In this volume, the focus is predominantly on the Eastern tradition, but this editorial and authorial choice should not be interpreted as a dismissal of the historical and philosophical importance of the Iberian tradition (which also had great impact on the development of Latin logic, in particular due to the influence of Averroes – Hasse 2014).

Finally, a note on another conspicuous absence from the volume: female philosophers and logicians. It is well known that in medieval times the possibilities for women to participate in intellectual, academic endeavours were rather meagre (to say the least), both in the Arabic tradition and in the Latin tradition. For example, women were usually not permitted to enrol as students in Christian universities. But it would be a mistake to conclude that women were completely excluded from medieval intellectual life (Herzenberg 2008). The Christian monastic setting in particular gave rise to remarkable figures such as Hildegard of Bingen and Heloise. On the Arabic side, there were women intellectuals who wrote on or collected hadith (reports about the prophet), poets and other scholars;

for example, some of the members of the ulama religious elite, who pronounced on matters of religion and jurisprudence, were women. But to date there is no evidence of women having been active among logicians in the so-called Islamic Golden Age.

The fact that we are only now beginning to appreciate the role and importance of some female figures in the history of philosophy is of course also a reflection of the gender bias in philosophical historiography (Witt and Shapiro 2015); it is to be hoped that future work will shed new light on the contributions of female figures. Sadly, though, at this point the available scholarship on the history of logic for this period presents a picture entirely dominated by men. Thus, the best we can do for now is to highlight this absence and to look forward to future work on medieval female thinkers.

0.4 HISTORIOGRAPHY OF MEDIEVAL LOGIC

Medieval logic began to be studied more systematically by historians of philosophy in the mid-twentieth century (at first, almost exclusively the Latin tradition), in particular with the pioneering work of scholars such as Bocheński, Moody, De Rijk, Boehner and others. Since then, medieval logic has attracted the interest of historians as well as logicians and philosophers, but it remained by and large seen as a somewhat "obscure" topic of study, perhaps still under the influence of the "Dark Ages" mythology as well as the received idea of medieval philosophy's too-close-for-comfort connections with theology. Also worth noticing is the scarce availability of medieval texts in this period, which posed limits to the generality of the conclusions that could be drawn.

Fortunately, a steady group of dedicated researchers pursued the project of producing critical editions of a wide range of logical texts that were otherwise only available in manuscript form (with a few exceptions available in Renaissance editions and some others which had received often unreliable editions). As a result, we now have a much wider range of materials available, and not only for the Latin tradition. Due to the increasing availability of modern editions of the key texts and an ever-increasing body of secondary literature, the study of medieval logic has been greatly facilitated; it is no longer viewed as an obscure topic of study, reserved for a handful of advanced graduate students and specialists.

However, the availability of materials does not in any way solve all the issues one is confronted with in the study of medieval logic. In particular, there remain various pressing methodological issues, such as the role that modern, symbolic logic has to play in the analyses. Indeed, some of the earlier, mid-twentieth-century scholarship on (Latin) medieval logic consisted in adopting modern, potentially anachronistic logical frameworks to investigate the extent to which the medieval theories anticipated modern theories, or more generally resembled them. But while there is much insight to be gained in applying modern formal frameworks to historical logical theories (and both editors as well as many contributors to this volume have engaged in such projects), a great amount of care is required given the risk of unwittingly and unduly projecting modern presuppositions and assumptions into the medieval theories (Dutilh Novaes 2007; Cameron 2011; Thom 2011).

Notice though that the fruitfulness and applicability of modern formal frameworks in the study of medieval logic is not the only issue worthy of attention. More generally, there is the question of what logic is/was to us, modern interpreters, and to them, medieval authors. General considerations on what logical frameworks were expected to accomplish for the medieval authors, i.e. the position logic occupied in the broader context of intellectual pursuits, need to be raised. (It is particularly ironic that the medieval authors themselves did not always display much care when interpreting the ancient authors they so often engaged with, Aristotle in particular – see Knuuttila 2011b.)

Given that there are such significant differences between what logic was for medieval authors and what it is for us now, it may seem that nothing much can be gained from historical analyses for the systematic questions in modern (philosophy of) logic. But here too the situation is not as grim as it may seem: while it is always advisable to avoid viewing the medieval theories as completely detached from the broader context of their production and use, this does not mean that they cannot offer new insights in modern debates, even if the broader contexts are quite dissimilar.

The main point, which in fact holds for historiography of philosophy in general, is to avoid anachronism while still potentially recognising historical theories as philosophically interesting in their own right. And thus, this *Companion* volume strives to strike the right balance between doing justice to the medieval theories in their own terms (in their own historical contexts) and outlining the systematic interest of the medieval theories as potential contributors to modern debates. Whether we have succeeded in achieving the right balance is for the reader to judge.[3]

[3] With thanks to Peter Adamson, Khaled El-Rouayheb and Wilfrid Hodges for their assistance on details concerning the Arabic tradition in the Introduction. More generally, the editors are grateful for assistance from Peter Adamson, Tony Street, John Marenbon and E. J. Ashworth at various stages of completion of this project.

PART I Periods and Traditions

1 The Legacy of Ancient Logic in the Middle Ages

Julie Brumberg-Chaumont

1.1 INTRODUCTION

Both the Latin and Arabic medieval logical traditions drew heavily on materials and ideas produced in Greek Antiquity. Among other things, they inherited from late ancient commentators on Aristotle the very notion of logic as a discipline, a set of canonical texts organised in accordance with a stable division of logical contents, an exegetical method, an epistemological orientation of logic in which the theory of demonstrative knowledge is the culmination of logical teaching, and a defined pedagogical and scientific status within the philosophical curriculum, one in which logic is both a necessary starting point and an instrument for other sciences (see Sorabji 2004, 31ff.).

Traditionally, historians of logic identify two main ancient logical traditions: one stemming from Aristotle's writings (fourth century BC), the other from the Stoics. As we know it today, Aristotle's logic, the *Organon*, contains the *Categories*, which deals with the ten types of predicates; the *Perihermeneias* (*On Interpretation*), devoted to statements and their properties; and then the treatises about argumentation: syllogistic (*Prior Analytics*), demonstrative proof (*Posterior Analytics*), topical and dialectical argumentation (*Topics*), and fallacious arguments (*Sophistical Refutations*). To these, the *Rhetoric* and *Poetics* are sometimes added in a "long Organon", which was standard in Arabic logic (see Black 1990) and was conveyed to the Latin world especially through Al-Farabi's influential *Division of the Sciences*. The long version was adopted by Thomas

I am grateful to Henri Hugonnard-Roche and John Marenbon for the very helpful suggestions they provided in the process of writing this contribution.

Aquinas in the thirteenth century, though never effective in practice (see Marmo 1990; Brumberg-Chaumont 2013a).

According to ancient testimonies, Stoic logic was divided into dialectic, concerned with dialogical argumentation, and its "counterpart", rhetoric, a continuous discourse governed by the quest for truth in public context; two other parts are also mentioned, one about definitions, the other about the criteria for true representations. Dialectic dealt, on the one hand, with "signifying expressions", in particular the parts of speech (the so-called "Stoic grammar") and linguistic ambiguity and, on the other hand, with the "meanings", especially propositions and their structure, classifications of propositions, and propositional syllogistic.

The two traditions are nevertheless not on a par from a historical point of view. Aristotle's numerous logical writings described in ancient lists had already almost been entirely lost in the next generation after Aristotle and Theophrastus. But some 'esoteric' texts, used inside Aristotle's school, were preserved and edited by Andronicus of Rhodes (first century BC): these form what is today known as the *Organon*. By contrast, the Stoics' massive logical production, as testified, for instance, in Chrysippus' ancient list of works, were not only already lost in Late Antiquity, but furthermore they have never been recovered. Even the main texts through which their theories are now reconstructed, namely those of Diogenes Laertius and Sextus Empiricus, were not transmitted to the Middle Ages (see Colish 1990 and Ebbesen 2004). As a result, only a very indirect influence can be perceived in later authors, through authors who were themselves influenced by Stoicism in Antiquity and who were read in the Middle Ages.

The study of the legacy of ancient logic in the Middle Ages can be roughly seen as an inquiry into the Latin and Arabic translations of Aristotle's *Organon* and its companions.[1] It had a vast influence in the Middle Ages, where hundreds of commentaries were

---

[1] For a justification of this choice, see my conclusions (Section 1.8).

produced and kept on being produced till the Early Modern period. But this does not entail a simple and linear history. Aristotle did not write an "Organon" as the textbook of his "logic", a word he never used in the modern sense. Theophrastus, Aristotle's immediate successor in the Lyceum, had already introduced important logical novelties into his master's teaching. Various aspects of what was included in "Aristotelian logic" in Late Antiquity and then transmitted to the Middle Ages stem from Stoic logic, but also from medio-Platonic (Apuleius), Galenic, Neoplatonic (Plotinus, Porphyry, Themistius), and Roman (Cicero, Boethius) contexts (see Marenbon 2007b), or even from technical ancient grammar, such as the famous distinction between categorematic (subject and predicate) and syncategorematic terms (see Rosier-Catach 2003b). As an illustration of the most important extensions of Aristotle's logic common both to Latin and Arabic legacies, one can mention the addition to Aristotle's categorical syllogistic of hypothetical syllogistic, or the notion of axiomatic topics, stemming from Themistius.

This legacy was not transmitted and circulated in the Middle Ages in one block. The *Posterior Analytics* and the *Prior Analytics*, after chapter 7 of the first book, were not studied by the early Syriac[2] and Arabic commentators before the tenth century, even if they were available in translation. The Latin translation of the *Posterior Analytics* dates to the twelfth century, but it was not really commented on before the 1230s. The *Topics* studied in the early Latin Middle Ages were those of Cicero, through Boethius' commentaries and textbooks, and not Aristotle's. A history of translations and transmissions thus needs to be complemented by a careful study of circulations and appropriations, where the different versions of the *Organon* are identified, taking into account the texts that were considered as a complement to or substitute for Aristotle's texts

---

[2] Syriac was a 'learned' literary language in much of the Middle East and other parts of Asia from the fourth to the tenth centuries. Attention is paid here to the Syriac texts and translations insofar as they paved the way for the later Arabic textual tradition.

in the Middle Ages, as well as the various intellectual frameworks and filters through which logical theories were understood.[3]

As a consequence, we focus on texts that belong properly to what the Middle Ages inherited from Antiquity, in order to reconstruct the state of logic in Late Antiquity that was actually transmitted to the Middle Ages – what Sten Ebbesen has labelled a 'Logical Late Ancient Standard', to be complemented point by point by a 'Grammatical Late Ancient Standard' (see Ebbesen 2007). A portion of these texts are now lost in their Greek versions, but were directly or indirectly available to medieval logicians. The exegetical context provided, on the one hand, by the Alexandrian school, for the Arabic world (see D'Ancona 2005), and, on the other hand, by Boethius' project (see Ebbesen 1990) played a crucial role here.

In what follows, the five first sections focus on the texts and doctrines indirectly and directly transmitted. A last section traces the stages of circulation of this legacy, as well as the various conceptions of logic related to these successive versions of the logical corpus; this is done by comparing Eastern and Western contexts.

I.2 ARISTOTLE: LATIN TRANSLATIONS FROM GREEK AND ARABIC, ARABIC TRANSLATIONS FROM GREEK AND SYRIAC

The main focus of this chapter will be on Aristotle (fourth century BC) and the ensuing tradition, since his logical treatises were the textbooks used for logical instruction, both in Antiquity and in the Middle Ages, and his works have been entirely transmitted to the medieval period both in the East and the West.[4]

---

[3] See the contributions gathered in Brumberg-Chaumont 2013b.

[4] Here are the main bibliographical references on which the present synthesis was based. For the various treatises of the Arabic *Organon*, see Hugonnard-Roche and Elamrani-Jamal 1989, and Aouad 2003. For the Arabic tradition, apart from Peters 1968, Madkour 1969, Badawi 1987, Gutas 1998, and, recently, El-Rouayheb 2011, much information can be gathered from the introduction to Zimmerman 1981 or from Lameer 1994. On the *Categories*, see Georr 1948; on *Poetics*, Tkatsch 1928–1932; on *Rhetoric*, Aouad 2002. The Syriac tradition of the *Organon* is extensively covered in Hugonnard-Roche 2004. For the Latin tradition the most

The modern critical editions offer a stable set of texts that give a fairly good idea of what was were actually read in the Middle Ages: the so-called *Logica Vetus*[5] and *Logica Nova* edited in the *Aristoteles Latinus* series, and the Arabic *Organon* as embodied in the famous eleventh-century Arabic manuscript Parisinus 2346 (Badawi 1948–1952).[6] It contains a medieval 'critical' edition prepared by Al-Hassan ibn-Suwar (d. 1017) in Baghdad, i.e. a revised version of the pre-existent Arabic translations, with marginal notes where the texts used for the editions are listed and described, as well as alternative translations and known Greek and Arabic commentaries (see Hugonnard-Roche 1992).

Despite the existence of stable medieval editions, one must bear in mind that the canonical versions, when they existed,[7] were not necessarily those read by medieval commentators, or, at least, not the only ones: for example, Abelard had access to the *Prior Analytics* in a poorly circulated version of Boethius' translation, not in the far more popular Florentine version; Averroes quoted the lemmata of an otherwise unknown Arabic version of the *Posterior Analytics* in his (recently recovered) Long Commentary book 1, different from the one made by Abu Bisr Matta (d. 940), preserved in the Parisinus manuscript. The same can be said of Avicenna on the *Poetics*. Another difficulty is chronological: as we shall see later on (Section 1.6), these translations were not all produced simultaneously, made accessible,

important information can be gathered in each introduction to the edition of the Latin text of the *Organon* in the *Aristoteles Latinus* series. For the Latin tradition of the *Sophistici Elenchi*, see Ebbesen 1981b and 2008. For the *Topics*, see Green-Pedersen 1984 and Biard and Zini Fosca 2009. For the *Rhetoric*, see Dahan and Rosier-Catach 1998; for *On Interpretation*, Kneepkens and Braakhuis 2003 and the special issue of *Vivarium* 48, 2010, ed. John Marenbon and Margaret Cameron (which is also concerned with the *Prior Analytics*); for the *Categories*, Newton 2008 – also interested in the Arabic tradition, Biard and Rosier-Catach 2003 and Corti and Bruun 2005; for the *Posterior Analytics*, see Corbini 2006 and De Haas et al. 2011. For the three traditions, see Burnett 2003.

[5] See Section 1.7 below for a critical discussion of this notion, and Chapter 8 of this volume on the *Logica Vetus*.

[6] See also Chapter 2, 'Arabic Logic up to Avicenna'.

[7] See the problems raised below by the Latin translations of the *Categories*.

circulated, commented upon or used as a basic text in the philosophical curriculum.

The *Categories* was translated five times into Syriac: one anonymous though previously attributed to Sergius (d. 536); one unpublished, by Jacob of Edessa (d. 708); one published, by George of the Arabs (d. 724); one lost, by an author named Jonas the Monk (unidentified); and another one, also lost, by the physician Hunayn ibn Ishaq (d. 873) – according to Ibn-Suwar's marginal notes. There is one Arabic translation by Hunayn's son, Ishaq ibn Hunayn (d. 910), from the lost Syriac version of his father: its revised version appears in the Parisinus manuscript. The marginal notes of the Parisinus manuscript of the *Categories* have been edited in Georr (1948). The text of the *Categories* was first translated into Latin by Marius Victorinus (fourth century AD) according to Cassiodorus. Boethius offered a translation in the sixth century (a few manuscripts are preserved, the first one from the ninth century). Another version was made from the Boethian text: this 'composite translation' was copied from the ninth century (few manuscripts preserved), but it was afterwards corrected and 're-contaminated' with the Boethian translation found in earlier manuscripts. It is this unstable 'contaminated composite' version that actually circulated in the Middle Ages in more than 300 manuscripts. The *Aristoteles Latinus* editors have reconstructed Boethius' text and the 'uncontaminated' text of the composite translation, but they did not edit the standard version because of its instability. In 1266, William of Moerbeke produced a new translation that was always circulated together with Simplicius' commentary that he also translated into Latin. It was rarely read (preserved in fewer than twenty manuscripts).

On Interpretation was translated into Syriac three times, once probably by Probus (sixth century AD), with a modern edition; a second one by George of the Arabs (d. 724), also edited; and a third lost one, once again attributed to Hunayn ibn Ishaq (d. 873). The Parisinus manuscript contains the Arabic translation from Ishaq ibn Hunayn, probably made, once again, from the Syriac version of his father's, with additions from previous copyists, a version of the text that corresponds to the one commented upon by Al-Farabi in his Long Commentary. The marginal glosses of the Parisinus manuscript have not been edited so far. *On Interpretation* was translated into Latin by Boethius (more than 350 manuscripts preserved, the oldest from the ninth century). The new translation made by William of Moerbeke by the time he also translated Ammonius' commentary (1268) is preserved only in four manuscripts.

Several currently lost Syriac translations of the *Topics* were made, especially one attributed to Athanasius of Balad (d. 686) and one to Hunayn ibn Ishaq. Three Arabic translations were made, one by Timotheus I (d. 823), lost, and one by Yahya ibn Adi (d. 974), also lost. The Arabic text contained in the Parisinus manuscript is by Abu Utman al-Dimasqi (d. 920) – books 1 to 7, directly from the Greek – and by his contemporary Ibrahim ibn Abd Allah (book 8) from the lost Syriac translation of Hunayn's. The *Topics* were translated into Latin three times, but by far the most read was the version made by Boethius and preserved in more than 250 manuscripts, the earliest from the twelfth century, most from the thirteenth century.

The *Prior Analytics* was first translated into Syriac, probably from Probus, but only up to chapter 7 of book 1. A complete translation was made by George of the Arabs. Several other Syriac translations, all of them lost, are mentioned in the marginal glosses of the Parisinus manuscript (edited by Badawi), among them one by Hunayn ibn Ishaq completed by his son Ishaq ibn Hunayn. The *Prior Analytics* was given its first Arabic translation by Yahya ibn al-Bitriq in the Kindian circle, known only from one quotation. The Arabic translation contained in the Parisinus manuscript was authored by Tadari ibn Basil (first half of the ninth century). Three other translations were made, all of them now lost. On the Latin side, Boethius' translation of the *Prior Analytics* as it first appeared in a twelfth-century codex is known in two versions, sometimes distinct, sometimes contaminated with each other in manuscripts, but only the 'Florentine' one was widely circulated (more than 250 manuscripts preserved). Another anonymous translation was produced in the twelfth century (two manuscripts still extant). The Boethian translation was not revised by William of Moerbeke and survived far into the Renaissance. The three Latin texts are edited in the *Aristoteles Latinus* collection.

The *Posterior Analytics* was probably translated entirely into Syriac by Athanase of Balad (text now lost), partially by Hunayn ibn Ishaq, and then again in its entirety by his son, but the text is also lost. From it, the Arabic translation by Abu Bisr Matta (d. 940) was produced, preserved in the Parisinus manuscript. Another anonymous translation is known from the lemmata quoted by Averroes in his long commentary on *Posterior Analytics* book 1, a text that might be related to Philoponus' commentary. The Latin translation made by Gerard of Cremona in the twelfth century was based upon the two Arabic translations. It did not enjoy much circulation (nine complete manuscripts still exist), nor did another translation from the Greek, the 'John' version made in the twelfth century (two manuscripts). The most popular Latin translation (from the Greek) was made by James of Venice in the twelfth century (more than 250 manuscripts preserved). It was revised in the thirteenth century by William of Moerbeke (six manuscripts preserved), but never superseded. Boethius' translation, if it ever existed, remains unknown.

No less than five Syriac translations of the *Sophistici Elenchi* are mentioned in the records, all of them lost, as well as three lost Arabic translations. The Parisinus manuscript contains three different Arabic translations of the text. The marginal notes of the Parisinus manuscripts have been edited together with the three texts. The treatise was translated into Latin by Boethius, which became the canonical version in the Middle Ages. It has been preserved in 300 manuscripts, a few from the twelfth century, most of them from the thirteenth and fourteenth centuries. Another translation was made in the twelfth century by James of Venice, known by fragments in ten manuscripts. As for the new translation made by William of

Moerbeke around 1269, it exists in one manuscript and remained entirely unknown even in the Middle Ages except to Giles of Rome.

There was at least one lost Syriac version of Aristotle's *Rhetoric*. The only Arabic translation preserved in the Parisinus manuscript is anonymous; it is probably an early translation made from the Syriac. This text has been edited (Lyons 1982). Herman the German made a Latin translation from various Arabic versions before 1256, preserved in two manuscripts, also containing translations of glosses from Arabic commentators. It was known to Giles of Rome, and has so far not received a critical edition. The *Rhetoric* was also translated from the Greek by an anonymous author in the middle of the thirteenth century, an incomplete text almost unknown in the Middle Ages (four manuscripts preserved). William of Moerbeke's translation, made in 1270, is extant in one hundred manuscripts. The two Latin translations have been edited in *Aristoteles Latinus*.

The existence of ancient Syriac translations of the *Poetics* is not certain, but quite possibly there was a translation by Ishaq ibn Hunayn (whose text is now lost). The Arabic translation by Abu Bisr Matta (d. 940) is preserved in the Parisinus manuscript. Another Arabic translation was made by Yahya ibn Adi (text now lost), which was used by Avicenna in the part of the *Shifa* devoted to *Poetics*. Aristotle's text was translated into Latin only in 1278 by William of Moerbeke, a translation preserved in two manuscripts that remained almost unknown. The knowledge of the treatise that Latin medieval authors had was essentially gathered through Herman the German's Latin translation of Averroes' *Poetria* (a paraphrased commentary on Aristotle) made in 1256, preserved in twenty-six manuscripts.

I.3   OTHER ANCIENT GREEK LOGICIANS[8]

Plato (fifth century BC) is mentioned in histories of logic for his dialectical method. Yet his status as a logician in ancient and medieval periods is unsure: Aristotle's logic is generally seen as a reflexive

---

[8] For Aristotle and commentators on Aristotle, see Sections 1.5 and 1.6.

and systematic re-elaboration of elements already present in Plato's dialogues, especially syllogisms, so that the relationship between Aristotelian logic and Platonic dialectic is presented sometimes as overlapping, sometimes as hierarchical (see Hadot 1990). Although the role and influence of Plato's philosophy for medieval philosophy is beyond doubt, there was only an extremely limited direct transmission of his texts in the Middle Ages.

Though entirely lost today, Theophrastus' logical works[9] (fourth century BC) were associated with the rediscovery and edition of Aristotle's treatises by Andronicus of Rhodes. They were known in Antiquity, commented upon by Galen (second century AD) according to his own list of works, Alexander (second–third century AD), and Porphyry (third century AD) according to Boethius (sixth century AD). He is very often referred to in Antiquity and consequently influenced medieval logic significantly. Here are some of his main innovations: the addition of five extra modes in the first figure, an alternative justification for the conversion of universal negative propositions, the rule of the mode of the conclusion following that of the minor premise in mixed syllogisms, the addition of 'hypothetical syllogism' to what will later be called the 'categorical syllogism' of Aristotle, the notion of "prosleptic" syllogisms, the idea of "indefinite propositions", a theory of modalities. All these elements are to be encountered in authors known in the Middle Ages: Apuleius (second century AD), Alexander of Aphrodisias and Themistius (fourth century AD), Ammonius (fifth century AD), Philoponus (sixth century AD), Boethius.

The main logicians of the "Dialectical school", sometimes distinguished from the "Megaric school", are Diodorus Cronus (fourth–third century BC) and Philo the logician (fourth–third century BC). No work is attributed to Diodorus in ancient records, but his logical ideas are well known and discussed, together with those of Philo,

---

[9] Recent scholarship has listed for logic more than thirty-five titles relying on ancient testimonies; the most quoted works are those on categories, affirmation and denial, analytics, and topics; see Fortenbaugh et al. 1993 and Huby 2007.

especially about conditional propositions, consequences, modalities, and the famous "Master Argument" (Bobzien 2005). The doctrines of Megaric logicians were mainly known through authors not transmitted to the Middle Ages such as Diogenes Laertius and Sextus Empiricus (in fact translated – c. 1280 – but hardly used), especially the discussion on criteria for the truth of conditionals and the notion of strict implication. But some notions are found in Cicero, Aulus-Gellius, Alexander, Themistius, Ammonius, Simplicius, Philoponus and Boethius. Nevertheless, these testimonies do not contain enough detail for medieval logicians to have been aware of the fact that Diodorus and Philo disagreed on the criterion for the truth of conditionals and on the notion of possibility. The influence of the Megaric dialectical school on ancient Stoicism, especially with the development of a propositional logic, is not to be questioned, but the transmission of this tradition to the Middle Ages is as problematic as that of Stoic logic.

The most important Stoic logicians are Zeno of Citium (fourth–third century BC), a pupil of Diodorus Cronus, Chrysippus (third century), Diogenes of Babylon (third–second century BC), and Antipater (third–second century BC). As already mentioned, their works were already lost in Late Antiquity. They had quite different logical ideas, but this was not always known to ancient and medieval authors, nor has it always been taken into account in recent scholarship. What is labelled "Stoic logic" generally mainly reflects Chrysippus' doctrines, the prince among logicians according to ancient testimonies. Stoic logic was known to the Latin Middle Ages through Cicero (first century BC), Apuleius, Martianus Capella (fifth century AD), Aulus-Gellius (fourth century AD), Cassiodorus (sixth century AD) and Boethius, who all give descriptions of the theory of the indemonstrables, i.e. basic argumentative schemata such as *modus ponens* and *modus tollens* (up to seven in the Latin tradition instead of five). Augustine (fourth century AD) and Priscian (sixth century AD) also played an important part. In the Arabic world, it was probably essentially known through Galen (second century AD) and Alexander of Aphrodisias (second–third century AD). Some important aspects of their logical theories, such as the criterion of truth for conditionals (strict implication) were not available in the Middle Ages, though maybe independently "rediscovered" by Latin logicians (see Ebbesen 2004). But the very idea of a propositional logic, where the nature of propositions is governed by the typology of the logical particles (propositional operators), rather than by their semantic content, was transmitted in such a blurred way that one can doubt if the specificities of Stoic logic were ever recognised as such by medieval logicians, even by those who developed a theory of consequence based upon molecular propositions where 'syncategorematic' terms played a key role. This is especially visible in the hypothetical syllogistic transmitted by Boethius, a Peripatetic theory based on semantic criteria for the division of propositions and where letters (generally) represent terms and not propositions. Stoic ideas were not identified as such by Boethius, even when he commented upon the description of the indemonstrables in Cicero's *Topica* (see Speca 2001). The same can be said for the Arabic context. Yet the possible impact of Augustine's accurate testimonies contained in his *De dialectica* – about the role of propositional operators, negation included, and the distinction between truth and validity – may not have been taken into account enough by recent scholarship. By contrast, the specificities of Stoic semantics, grammar, theory of language, and conception of rhetoric as reported by Augustine, but also by Priscian (sixth century AD), seems to have been better conveyed in the Latin Middle Ages.

Galen's *Logical Institutions* (now available) were not transmitted to the Latin world. His influence on Latin medieval logic comes essentially from his methodological reflections in his very influential medical treatises that circulated very early in the Middle Ages – the eleventh-century incomplete *antiqua translatio* of the *Tegni* was added in the twelfth century to the *Articella*, a well-known Salernitan medical collection. The developments at the beginning of the *Tegni* about the 'ordered method' that articulates analysis, synthesis, and demonstration were compared to Aristotle's theories in the *Posterior*

Analytics and led to very important novelties in medieval discussions about scientific method (see Ottoson 1984 for a synthesis). His logical works were transmitted to the Arabic world, through the now lost treatise *On Demonstration* (known only partially, it seems) and through the *Logical Institutions*, as well as his work on the number of syllogisms translated into Arabic by Hunayn ibn Ishaq (now lost).

1.4 ANCIENT COMPANIONS TO THE *ORGANON* AND OTHER LOGICAL TREATISES

The medieval *Organon* consisted of the logical treatises of Aristotle known at the time, together with a set of texts that were connected to it in various degrees and manners. But there were also some canonical texts intended to be used as 'companions' (i.e. introductory or explanatory texts) to the *Organon*, produced and adopted in Late Antiquity. Many of them are ancient Latin productions that have (probably) been translated or adapted from now-lost Greek treatises.

The closest companion to the *Organon* both in Eastern and Western Aristotelian traditions was Porphyry's famous *Isagoge*. The *Isagoge* is presented as a text for beginners, and can be seen as an introduction to the *Categories*, as well as to logic and to the philosophical corpus as a whole. It raises the famous problem of the status of universals, genera, and species, but does not answer it: it conjectures both a logical and an ontological answer. Its objects are the five 'predicables', i.e. types of predicates (genus, species, difference, property, accident). It was already placed first in the canonical organisation of texts in Late Antiquity and was sometimes counted as the first book of the *Organon*. It was translated into Latin twice, first by the Latin rhetorician Marius Victorinus (fourth century AD); this text was used by Boethius in the first edition of his commentary on Porphyry's text, and a reconstruction of it can be found in the *Aristoteles Latinus*. The other translation is by Boethius. It is extant in 350 manuscripts, the oldest ones from the end of the eighth or the beginning of the ninth century. It was translated three times into Syriac, once by an anonymous author (edited); we also have a revised version of it, made by Athanase of Balad in 645 (partial edition), and a lost version by Hunayn ibn Ishaq, according to the marginal notes of the Parisinus manuscript. There is a lost Arabic translation, according to the records. The Arabic translation contained in the Parisinus manuscript was made by Abu Utman al-Dimashqi (d. 920). Porphyry's *Isagoge* was immensely influential in Syriac, Arabic, and Latin contexts; hundreds of commentaries were produced by the most prominent logicians in each tradition.

Several types of 'companions' are to be considered in the Latin world. Some were logical texts dealing with the same topics as those described by not-yet-known Aristotelian treatises, so that they are presented as 'substitutes' for them by scholarship (though doubts can be raised about their being so conceived at the time). Some texts were companions to the *Organon* because of the strong links early medieval Latin authors saw between the three arts of the *Trivium*, namely grammar, rhetoric and "dialectic". i.e., "logic" by the time of Augustine, who introduced this division. Some texts are monographs on topics not directly dealt with in Aristotelian treatises known at the time.

The pseudo-Augustinian *Categories*, also known as *Paraphrasis themistiana* (or *Categoriae Decem*), belongs to the first group. It is a Latin text, probably adapted from a Greek treatise now lost, that refers to Themistius. It was attributed to Augustine by Alcuin and was a textbook in the Carolingian period when Aristotle's *Categories* were not yet read. It is preserved in forty manuscripts, most of them from the ninth, tenth, and eleventh centuries, as well as in thirty-three manuscripts of Alcuin's *Dialectica* that contains it by means of excerpts. Apuleius' *Peri Hermeneias* deals with the content of the first seven chapters of the *Prior Analytics*. It is inspired by a Greek source, now lost, where some of Theophastus' ideas previously mentioned are echoed. It is a very important text in the history of logic, since it is probably the first logical treatise on argumentation written in Latin; it contains many notions that are considered as obvious today, but which are found here for the first time, such as the famous Square of Opposition.

Boethius' two treatises on categorical syllogisms, the *Introductio ad Syllogismos Categoricos* and *De Syllogismo Categorico* (the latter being hugely influential in the Latin medieval tradition), are probably also indirectly inspired by the same lost Greek treatise on categorical syllogistic as Apuleius', but directly modelled on Porphyry's lost treatise on the same topic (see Thomsen Thörnqvist 2014). Boethius' *De Hypotheticis Syllogismis*, also inspired by a Greek source lost today but partially identified (Bobzien 2002), is a natural complement to Aristotle's own syllogistic, since hypothetical syllogistic is presented by Boethius as a branch of syllogistic only hinted at by Aristotle, and developed by his successors, Eudemus and Theophrastus (no mention is made of the Stoics). Boethius' commentary and treatises on Ciceronian topics, *In Ciceronis Topica* and *De Differentiis Topicis*, especially the latter, had an impact on the history of logic that cannot be overestimated. *De differentiis* was a universally read textbook. It contains very important notions such as the four-fold classification of argumentations, the definition of enthymemes as truncated syllogisms, the distinction between argument and argumentation, the definition of topics as the foundation for all arguments (syllogisms included), the notion of maximal propositions and of axiomatic topics, and many others. Contrary to what happened to the other texts that were the *Organon*'s companions in the High Middle Ages, its influence did not cease in the thirteenth century after the rediscovery of Aristotle's *Topics*, and its teaching was conveyed far into the late Middle Ages, since it is the main source of Peter of Spain's *Tractatus* as far as topics are concerned.

In the second group we find Cicero's *De inventione*, also known as *Rhetorica*, his *Topica*, and the *Rhetorica ad Herennium*, an anonymous treatise from the fourth century that has been attributed to him from the fifth century on. Many commentaries on *De inventione* and to the *Ad Herrenium* were produced, especially in the eleventh and the twelfth centuries. But, the interest in these was renewed before the eleventh century thanks to the rediscovery of Marius Victorinus' (fourth century AD) very popular commentary on *De inventione*. The influence of Cicero's *Topics* on medieval logic is mediated by Boethius' interpretation, especially in *De Differentiis Topicis*, which was the text directly commented upon. The transmission of Cicero's works to the Latin Middle Ages is so unproblematic that it is medieval manuscripts that have mainly guaranteed the survival of the texts. Another very important text is Priscian's *Institutiones grammaticae*, which was the standard text for the study of grammar in the Latin world from the High Middle Ages to the Renaissance. It was also much used by medieval logicians. The text is heavily dependent on the *Syntax* by the Greek grammarian Apollonius Dyscolus (second century AD), as well as on a series of monographs by Apollonius on the eight parts of speech, most of them now lost. The philosophical reception of this work is explained by the fact that grammar deals with notions common to logic – substance and accident, linguistic derivations (paronyms), nouns (proper and common), verbs, completeness of sentences, subject, predicate, etc. (see Rosier-Catach 2003b, 2009, 2010, 2012; Kneepkens 2004; Luthala 2005). It should also be mentioned that, in addition to the references to Stoic linguistic inherited from Apollonius, Priscian uses a philosophical vocabulary borrowed from the Greek authors of his time, a situation that created inescapable connexions between grammar and logic in medieval minds (see Luthala, Ebbesen, Garcea, and Brumberg-Chaumont in Holtz et al. 2009).

To the third group belong *De Definitionibus* by Marius Victorinus, and Boethius' *De divisione*, probably inspired by Porphyry's treatise on the same topic (now lost). *De divisione* was a very influential text in the Early Middle Ages, and it was still commented on, for instance by Albert the Great, in the mid-thirteenth century. It deals with various types of divisions of wholes, of differences, thereby offering important tools for medieval mereology, such as the difference between integral and universal whole and between integral and subjective parts.

The sections of encyclopaedias that deal with logic and rhetoric should also be mentioned, especially, for the High Middle Ages, Martianus Capella's (fifth century AD) *Marriage of Philology and Mercure*, and Cassiodorus' (sixth century AD) *Institutions*.

I.5 ANCIENT COMMENTARIES AND TREATISES ON THE *ORGANON*[10]

The authors and texts discussed in this section are ancient commentaries produced in Greek or directly in Latin, and Arabic medieval translations of ancient Greek commentators. Various degrees of fragmentary and indirect transmissions have been taken into account. Texts are presented in chronological order.

The writings of the ancient Peripatetics produced after the rebirth of Aristotelian studies with Andronicus of Rhodes' (first century BC) edition were only fragmentarily known in Late Antiquity, and even more in the Middle Ages, often through Simplicius (sixth century AD). Andronicus commented upon the *Categories*, and Boethos of Sidon is the author of a commentary on the *Categories* (quoted by Simplicius) and on *Prior Analytics* (quoted by Galen and Ammonius). Boethos' ideas are mentioned several times by Themistius in his treatise about the reduction of the second and the third figures. Aristo (first century BC) is mentioned by Apuleius. Among later Peripatetic philosophers, Aspasius (second century AD), the author of a commentary on the *Categories* and on *On Interpretation*, is known through some extracts quoted by Boethius in his own commentaries on *On Interpretation*. Three main steps seem to have been followed in Andronicus' edition: the location of logic at the head of the corpus,

---

[10] Though all of them have taught or written commentaries now lost on Aristotle's *Categories*, Iamblichus (second–third century AD), Dexippe (third–fourth century AD), Syrianus (fourth century AD), and Proclus (fifth century AD) have not been studied here. For the mysterious "Allinus", see Elamrani-Jamal 1989, 151–153.

i.e. as the first texts to be read, a prominence given to analytics at the expense of dialectical argumentation, and the exclusion from logic of *Rhetorics* and *Poetics* as "poietic" arts. This approach was not universally followed in the subsequent traditions, either because the *Organon* was not yet the immediate basis of logical studies, as in the early medieval Latin schools, where dialectic and rhetoric, not analytics, prevailed under the influence of Cicero, Marius Victorinus, and Boethius, or because an alternative conception of the *Organon* was chosen, as in Arabic logic, where a Long Organon was soon adopted. Nevertheless, the indirect influence of the ancient Peripatetics on medieval logic deserves to be fully recognised since it is Andronicus' conception of logic and of the Aristotelian corpus that shaped for centuries, and until now, what is known as the 'standard *Organon*' in six treatises.[11]

Most of Alexander of Aphrodisias' (second to third centuries AD) logical commentaries and treatises were not transmitted to the Latin Middle Ages, where his influence is heavy, but indirect: Alexander's logical works were mainly known through Boethius, Ammonius, and Simplicius. One treatise on the conversions of propositions is preserved today in Arabic (Badawi 1971, 55–81). The beginning of his commentary on *Prior Analytics* (up to I 7) seems to have been translated into Arabic, a text now lost; the same holds of his commentary on the *Topics*. An Arabic version of a commentary on *Categories* is referred to as a source in the marginal notes of the Parisinus manuscript, and new witnesses have been identified in Zonta (1997). A commentary on *On Interpretation* (of which a fragment has been edited in Badawi 1971, 31) was known to Al-Farabi. The lost commentary on the *Posterior Analytics* was known in Arabic only through quotations from Themistius and Philoponus.

[11] Except that *On Interpretation* was not included and the post-predicaments (chapters 11 to 14 of the *Categories*) were considered as inauthentic by Andronicus.

We have already mentioned Porphyry's *Isagoge* in the section dedicated to the *Organon*'s companions. Arabic translations of Porphyry's commentaries on the *Categories* and *On Interpretation* are mentioned in records, as well as a now-lost Arabic translation of his treatise on categorical syllogisms by Abu Utman al-Dimashqi. He may have written a commentary on *Posterior Analytics*, the Arabic version of which was known to Al-Farabi and quoted by him in a commentary, now lost, itself quoted by Albert the Great (see Chase 2007). His indirect influence was huge, especially in the Latin world, since he has been identified as the main source for Boethius' logical commentaries, as well as the author of treatises now lost that have inspired Boethius' *De divisione* and *De Syllogismo Categorico* respectively (see Section 1.6). His long commentary on the *Categories*, now lost, was known to Latin authors through Simplicius' commentary, which was translated into Latin.

The commentary on *Posterior Analytics* by Themistius was translated from Arabic into Latin by Gerard of Cremona before 1187. Some elements of his reading of the *Categories* may be conveyed by the Latin *Categoriae Decem*, also called 'Paraphrasis Themistiana' (see Section 1.4 above). Themistius' influence on Latin logicians is deep, since his division of topics and his conception of their argumentative role is reproduced in Boethius' *De Differentiis Topicis* and his commentary on Cicero's *Topics*. Themistius' treatise, now lost, on the reduction of the second and the first figures was translated into Arabic by Abu Utman al-Dimashqi.[12] His work(s) on the topics (see Hasnawi 2007 and Zonta 2011), now lost, were probably available to Arabic logicians. Fragments from his commentary on the *Prior Analytics* translated into Hebrew from a lost Arabic version made by al-Dimashqi (fl. c. 915) have been edited (Rosenberg-Manekin 1988). Knowledge of Themistius' exegesis is also conveyed by the marginal notes on the

---

[12] Edited in Badawi 1947 and translated into French in Badawi 1971.

Arabic text of *Prior Analytics* in the Parisinus manuscript and from quotations in Averroes.

Ammonius' commentary on *On Interpretation* was translated into Latin by William of Moerbeke in 1268 from the Greek. The influence of Ammonius' commentary on the *Categories* on Syriac commentators is widely acknowledged. Not much can be said about Arabic translations of his commentaries, except that his name is quoted among other philosophers in the marginal notes of the Parisinus manuscript, not yet edited. F. W. Zimmermann (1981) thinks that Al-Farabi had access to a codex that contained a medley of sources taken from ancient commentators.

Simplicius' commentary on the *Categories* was translated into Latin by William of Moerbeke in 1266. No Arabic translation is known to us, though Simplicius' influence has been established (Gätje 1982 and Chase 2008).

Boethius' commentaries were absolutely crucial for the Latin tradition. He wrote two commentaries on *Isagoge*, one on *Categories* (maybe another one, now lost, see Hadot 1959 and Marenbon 2014 for a critical discussion) and two on *On Interpretation*. Boethius' commentaries were commented upon by Abelard, for instance, rather than on Aristotle's text directly.

Philoponus (sixth century AD), mostly known in the Arabic world under the name of John the Grammarian, was very influential for the Arabic tradition. His indirect impact can be felt through the deep influence he had on Syriac logicians. His logical commentaries, all of them said to have been translated into Arabic, are now lost in their Arabic versions. (The influence of his commentary on *Prior Analytics* on Al-Farabi has been argued for in Lameer 1994.) Not only is an Arabic translation of Philoponus' commentary on *Posterior Analytics* recorded, but its influence on many Arabic commentators, among them Averroes, has been studied several times. Philoponus' logical commentaries were not translated into Latin, but his indirect influence was significant, since he is the main source for the commentaries now lost on *Sophistici Elenchi, Posterior Analytics* and *Prior Analytics* that widely circulated in the Latin Middle Ages under the name of 'Alexander' (see Ebbesen 1981b, 1996, 2008).

1.6 LOST ANCIENT TEXTBOOKS AS PROBABLE SOURCES FOR TEXTS TRANSMITTED OR PRODUCED IN THE MIDDLE AGES

According to James Shiel's hypothesis (1958, 1990) concerning Boethius' sources, the Latin philosopher had at his disposal a medley of quotations from various Greek commentators copied in the marginalia of a series of logical treatises by Aristotle. His hypothesis has been labelled by Sten Ebbesen the 'One Source no Thinking' thesis (Ebbesen 1990). Shiel's arguments are not generally accepted among scholars (Barnes 1981); but this does not mean that such manuals did not exist.

As mentioned, a lost Greek textbook on categorical syllogisms is a common source for Apuleius and Boethius (through Porphyry), and it was translated into Arabic by Abu Utman al-Dimashqi (now lost). A lost (but partially recovered) anonymous treatise on hypothetical syllogistic has been proposed as a source of Boethius' textbook by recent scholarship (Bobzien 2002). John Magee (1998) has shown in his edition of *De divisione* that Boethius relied on a lost treatise by Porphyry on the same topic.

A lost Greek source has also been supposed to be the basis of the anonymous Arabic tract on *Isagoge, Categories, On Interpretation,* and *Prior Analytics* by Abdallah al-Muqaffa (d. 756) or by his son Muhammad ibn Abdallah al-Muqaffa (ed. Dānish Pazhūh 1978).

1.7 REDISCOVERIES, CIRCULATIONS, RECEPTIONS: WHAT WAS READ BY WHOM AND WHERE?

Several periods of rediscovery have been identified both for the Latin and Arabic Middle Ages. John Marenbon has recently distinguished two periods in the Latin Middle Ages – a 'Roman' period, which covers the Carolingian Renaissance up to 980, and a

'Boethian' period, which stretches to 1135. In the Eastern context, a "short" Syriac *Organon* is studied where the 'four books' (*Isagoge, Categories, On Interpretation, Prior Analytics* I 1–7) were privileged at the basic levels of Syriac schools. A short Arabic *Organon* matches the Syriac one in the eighth century, as can be seen in al-Muqaffa's treatise. The existence of a parallel 'short' *Organon* both in the East and in the West has long been acknowledged. The tale, stemming from Al-Farabi's (d. 950) testimony, about the theological obstacles to the study of modal syllogistic, has been discarded as historically valuable, and so much for this idea that Syriac logicians did not have access to the text of *Prior Analytics* after Book I, chapter 7 (Hugonnard-Roche 2013). Besides, Marenbon (2013) has shown that it is misleading to conflate Boethian logic with what was later known as *Logica Vetus* in the thirteenth century,[13] since the latter, not the former, was seen as a partial version of the corpus, to be complemented by *Logica Nova*. Recent scholarship has consequently established that *Organon* of these earlier periods was not a 'shortened' *Organon*, to be compared in a teleological way to the next stages of the reception: it was a corpus with a coherence of its own, in line with an alternative conception of logic, not epistemologically oriented. Furthermore, it should be noted that if the *Organon* was 'short' in an Early Latin context, logic was nevertheless 'long', since rhetoric was systematically associated to dialectic.

After the Boethian period, *Logica Nova* included first *Sophistici Elenchi*, already extensively studied by the mid-twelfth century, then *Prior Analytics, Topics,* and eventually *Posterior Analytics,* which actually entered the curriculum only with Robert Grosseteste's commentary in the 1230s. The next step corresponds to the new translations by William of Moerbeke in the 1260s.

---

[13] That included a twelfth-century anonymous tract on the six "small" categories, *De Sex principiis*.

By the time of Al-Kindi (d. 870), a long *Organon* is already considered as standard, though some texts might only have been initially known from excerpts: apart from the eighth-century compendium of the "four books", only *Prior Analytics* and *Sophistici Elenchi* were translated in the Kindian circle. A new movement of Syrio-Arabic translations in the ninth century was initiated by Tadari (first half of the ninth century), then by Hunayn ibn Ishaq (d. 876) and his son Ishaq ibn Hunayn (d. 910), as seen in Section 1.3, as well as by Abu Utman al-Dimashqi (d. 920). They produced Arabic versions of *Isagoge, Categories, On Interpretation, Topics,* and *Prior Analytics*.

The tenth century opens a new stage of translations, revisions and editions, where Abu Bisr Matta (d. 940) played a major role with his translations of *Posterior Analytics* and *Poetics*. All the texts of the *Organon* were made available in Arabic, leading to a stable teaching text as embodied in the Parisinus manuscript, a corpus that probably reflects the *Organon* as known by the time of Al-Farabi and afterwards. According to Al-Farabi, who studied under Abu Bisr Matta together with Yahya ibn Adi, the study of modal syllogistic and of *Posterior Analytics* was not yet common in the generation before him; this matches the late Latin reception of *Posterior Analytics* and the late focus on modal syllogistic despite an earlier transmission of *Prior Analytics* in the Latin world. See Table 1.1.

The above story shows that the standard *Organon* as we know it today was neither the unique nor the main version of the *Organon* in the Middle Ages: it often appeared in a "short" version, in early Syriac and Arabic and Latin contexts, in a "long" version, with *Rhetoric* and *Poetics* in Arabic logic in the classical period. Moreover, it was regularly expanded by companions that were considered as parts of "Aristotelian logic" to various degrees, among them Porphyry's famous *Isagoge*, or by logical theories which are nowhere to be found in Aristotle, but were considered as part of his teaching, such as hypothetical syllogistic or the art of divisions.

Table 1.1 *Translations of the Organon*

LATIN	SYRIAC/ARABIC
Up to 980 ("Roman" period): *Categorie Decem*, Apuleius' *Peri Hermeneias*, Isodore's *Etymologies*, Cassiodorus' *Institutions*, Boethius' first commentary on *On Interpretation* (not systematically), Porphyry's *Isagoge* (fragmentarily), Cicero's treatises on *Topics*, Victorinus' *De Definitionibus*.	**First Syriac period/first Arabic period (sixth–eighth centuries):** The "four books" (*Isagoge, Categories, On Interpretation, Prior Analytics* I 1–7) al-Muqaffa's Arabic tract (eighth century).
Up to 1135 ("Boethian" period): *Isagoge, Categories, On Interpretation*, Boethius' treatises on categorical and hypothetical syllogisms, Boethius' logical commentaries, Boethius' treatises on *Topics*, Boethius' *De divisione*.	**Al-Kindi's circle (ninth century):** Fragmentary knowledge of the whole *Organon*, Arabic translations of *Sophistici Elenchi* and *Prior Analytics*.
Second half of the twelfth century: the above list + a systematic study of *Sophistical Refutations* + a partial knowledge of *Prior* and *Posterior Analytics*. **End of the twelfth century:** first commentary on *Prior Analytics*.	**End of the ninth century:** New wave of Syriac and Arabic translations of *Isagoge, Categories, On Interpretation, Topics*, and *Prior Analytics*.
University corpus (mid-thirteenth century): Systematic study and commentary of *Isagoge, Categories, On Interpretation, De Sex principiis, Prior Analytics, Posterior Analytics, Topics, Sophistic Refutations* = *"Logica Vetus"* + *Logica Nova*.	**Tenth century:** Arabic translations of *Posterior Analytics* and *Poetics*; revision of previous translations in a stable *"Arabic Organon"* (later on edited in the Parisinus manuscript).

1.8 CONCLUSION

A justification of the methodological choices followed and the selection of materials made seems worth offering as a conclusion.

Because the history of transmissions and circulations of ancient texts in Arabic and Latin contexts is virtually finished in the Middle Ages after the end of the thirteenth century, the present study does not extend beyond this period. Indeed, neither the rediscovery of Aristotle's logical texts as an "Organon" in the fifth century, addressed elsewhere in this volume, nor the history of vernacular translations of logical texts, insufficiently documented so far by existing studies, has been discussed.

We have seen that the study of the legacy of ancient Greek logic in the Middle Ages generally means an examination of texts that were translated into Latin, on the one hand, and into Syriac and Arabic, on the other hand, but the two contexts are to be distinguished. While this method is fully justified for European schools and universities, where knowledge of languages was not a common skill, the multilingual context in Syriac schools and then in Damascus and Baghdad, where many philosophers were non-Arabic, means that influences can go beyond texts translated into Syriac and Arabic, not only for authors who had knowledge of Greek but also for those who could have been indirectly in touch with Greek texts in their intellectual circles.

A major methodological choice here has been to take as "ancient logical legacy" the set of texts that were considered as "logical" texts stemming from Antiquity by medieval logicians themselves, as well as those that were taught as part of "logic" in Antiquity and transmitted in one way or another to the Middle Ages. This explains why Augustine has not been included here, despite his fundamental role in medieval noetic and semantic reflections; the same could be said, to a lesser degree, of the Greek Fathers for their theories on the signification of names, unity, trinity, difference, universals, etc.[14] By contrast, Cicero's rhetorical and dialectical writings have been listed,

---

[14] See, for instance, Ayers 1979 for Tertullian and Augustinus; Zachhuber 1999, Cross 2002, and Erismann 2011 for universals in Greek patristic.

since rhetoric was often considered as part of logic in ancient and medieval contexts, or at least as a connected discipline, together with grammar, in the medieval *Trivium*. Strong relationships between medicine and logic, long recognised in Galenic studies, have only been hinted at. What was considered as the core of logic in ancient and medieval higher education systems has been privileged, i.e. logic as the art of rational discourse based upon argumentation in its varieties. As a consequence, many 'non-logical' texts that have heavily contributed to topics that were then also considered as part of logic, such as methodology of science, epistemology, psychology, noetic, philosophy of language, semantics, theory of truth, etc., have nonetheless not been considered. All these aspects of the history of logic, marginal as they may appear, have nourished recent research and are to be considered a necessary complement for any deeper understanding of the legacy of ancient logic in the Middle Ages, but for reasons of space could not be treated in the present contribution.

2   Arabic Logic up to Avicenna

Ahmad Hasnawi and Wilfrid Hodges

In this chapter we discuss, first, how the Arabic logicians up to the end of the tenth century took over Greek material and added to it material of their own and how they reshaped the subject of logic in the process. We have included references to the young Averroes, although he wrote in the twelfth century, inasmuch as he belongs in the tradition of al-Fārābī (d. 950). After this we turn to the formal innovations of Avicenna's in the early eleventh century. Many of the questions that we discuss are treated also in Street (2004).

2.1 THE GREEK LOGICAL HERITAGE

Arabic logic as a branch of philosophy was heir to ancient Greek logic, and it belonged essentially to the Peripatetic tradition. Arabic grammar, Islamic jurisprudence and Islamic disputative theology (*kalām*) developed independent methods of reasoning and inevitably there was some interaction between these methods and those of logic as a philosophical discipline. This interaction ranged from conflict to absorption. The Greek Peripatetic logic was embodied in Aristotle's logical texts, which later became known as the *Organon*, together with the commentaries on them by Roman Empire scholars of various philosophical persuasions. These commentaries were the product of an activity which had run for eight centuries when the Arab philosophers became aware of it.

The Arabic *Organon* was in fact the extended *Organon* first contemplated in Late Antiquity, which began with Porphyry's *Isagoge* as an introduction and went on to include Aristotle's *Rhetoric* and *Poetics*. But what was only programmatic in Late Antiquity became a reality for the Arabic logicians. They conceived the *Organon* as embodying a system of logic. The formal heart of the system lay in its third book, the *Prior Analytics*, which aims to give the general

theory of reasoning or of the syllogism (*qiyās*). The first two treatises, i.e. *Categories* (although its place here was challenged, in particular by Avicenna) and *On Interpretation*, are preparatory to the
formal part. The remaining volumes adapt the theory of reasoning to different fields of human activity: to scientific activity, but
also to social fields of communication. Logic as providing a method
for science was the object of Aristotle's *Posterior Analytics*, while
logic as providing a tool in order to systematise various fields of social communication was the object of the rest of the books of the
Organon. Thus *Topics* give the rules of dialectical games, in which
two people reason starting from commonly accepted premises, while
Sophistical Refutations give rules for escaping being trapped by fallacies; *Rhetoric* provides the rules for producing persuasive arguments
destined for a popular audience and finally *Poetics* give the rules for
constructing discourses inducing imaginations useful for actions. It
should be noted here that there is an axiological ambivalence at the
core of this system: on the one hand, it considers the five syllogistic
arts on an equal footing; but on the other hand, it introduces a difference in status between demonstrative syllogism, which is the superior kind of syllogism, and other kinds of syllogisms. (See Black
1990 on the inclusion of *Rhetoric* and *Poetics*.)

The reception in Arabic of the Greek *Organon* is reflected
in a unique document: the Arabic manuscript Parisinus ar. 2346,
which contains what may be called a school edition of the Baghdad
Organon. Carried out mainly by the Nestorian scholar, al-Ḥasan ibn
Suwār (died after 1017), but also, at least in the case of *Rhetoric*, by
another Christian scholar Abū 'Alī b. al-Samḥ (d. 1027), this edition registers the chronological layers of the Arabic reception of
Aristotle's *Organon*. It contains a layer of ancient translations, such
as the anonymous translation of *Rhetoric*, that of *Prior Analytics*,
though the latter was revised by Ḥunayn b. Isḥāq (d. 873), and one
of the three extant versions of *Sophistical Refutations*, attributed
to Nāima al-Ḥimsī, a member of the so-called al-Kindī circle from
the early ninth century. The translation of the other treatises of

the *Organon* was the result of more recent translation activity in Baghdad: the *Categories* and *On Interpretation* were translated by Isḥāq b. Ḥunayn (d. 910); *Topics* by Abū 'Uthmān al-Dimashqī (active around 900) for books 1–7 and by Ibrāhīm b. 'Abdallāh al-Kātib (tenth century) for book 8; *Posterior Analytics* and *Poetics* by Abū Bishr Mattā (d. 940). The Parisinus includes also Porphyry's *Isagoge* in Dimashqī's translation.

The very existence of this Baghdad edition is a remarkable fact to be stressed, because it is peculiar to Aristotle's logical corpus. Nothing comparable was done with Aristotle's corpus of natural philosophy, of which only the first book, namely *Physics*, translated into Arabic by Isḥāq b. Ḥunayn, was the object of a similar edition in the Baghdad school.

In the wake of these translations and editions, Arabic became established as the main language of logic throughout the Muslim world, even in the writings of Persian and Turkic scholars. For this reason we speak of this tradition of logic as Arabic Logic.

Besides the Aristotelian *Organon*, the Arabic philosophers had access to the works of the Greek commentators. They had access to the varied aspects and stages of this exegetical tradition: to the purely Peripatetic early commentators, as represented by Alexander of Aphrodisias (second–third centuries), to the paraphrases of Themistius (d. c. 388) and also to the commentaries of the members of the late Neoplatonic school (fifth–sixth centuries). For instance we read, in the Parisinus ar. 2346, glosses on the *Categories* which reflect Simplicius' commentary on this treatise; more precisely they reflect passages from the *prooemium* of this commentary as well as specific comments from the same commentary on bits of the first chapters of the Aristotelian treatise. The scholia which accompany the Arabic translation of *On Interpretation* display, for their part, distinctive features of the late Alexandrian tradition as we know it through Ammonius' and Stephanus' commentaries on this treatise. And although the Arabic translation of Alexander's commentary on *Prior Analytics* is no longer extant, traces of it are visible in the works of al-Fārābī, Avicenna and Averroes. The same can be said about Themistius' paraphrase of *Prior Analytics*, which is lost in Greek, but of which a fragment from an Arabic version survives in Hebrew (Rosenberg and Manekin 1988). Two important pieces related also to *Prior Analytics* are still extant only in Arabic: Alexander's *On the conversion of propositions* (Badawi 1971) and Themistius' *Refutation of Maximus on the reduction of the second and third figures to the first* (Badawi 1947). Again, some of the scholia on the Arabic translation of *Posterior Analytics* in the Parisinus ar. 2346 originate from Philoponus' commentary on this Aristotelian treatise and a translation of Themistius' paraphrase of the same treatise, made from the Arabic, survives in Latin (O'Donnell 1958). We learn from *al-Fihrist* of the bibliographer Ibn al-Nadīm (1988) that Alexander's commentary on the last four books of *Topics* as well as a commentary on the first four books, due to Ammonius and about which the Greek sources are silent, were translated into Arabic. The same bibliographer reports also that Themistius' paraphrase of the central books (2–7) of this same treatise was translated into Arabic. Although this translation is now lost, many fragments of it have been recovered through Averroes' *Middle Commentary on the Topics* (Hasnawi 2007).

Within the bulk of the Greek logical learning transmitted into Arabic, special attention should be given to Galen's logical works. In his famous *Letter* on Galen's works that have been translated into Syriac and Arabic, Ḥunayn b. Isḥāq reports that he made translations of at least three logical works of Galen's: *On Demonstration*, *Introduction to Logic* and *On the Number of Syllogisms*. Ḥunayn translated each of these three works into Syriac, and then one of his pupils translated it into Arabic. Ḥunayn tells us his epic story in search of a Greek manuscript of *On Demonstration* and his recovery of a great part of its fifteen books (Bergsträsser 1925, Ar. 47–48 and 51/Ger. 38–39 and 42). Unfortunately, none of these translations has survived, except for some fragments of *On Demonstration*. This literary wreckage has also affected the Greek originals of two of these works (see, however, the reconstruction of *On Demonstration* in von Müller 1897), the third of them, namely the *Introduction to Logic*, having been recovered only in the mid-nineteenth century. It is difficult, given this situation, to have an exact idea of the influence of Galen's logical opinions on the Arabic logical tradition. One is reduced to picking out the indirect evidence. But it is all the more significant to observe a reaction against Galen's shortcomings in carrying out his avowed project of an *applied logic*; beginning with Abū Bakr al-Rāzī (d. 925), who otherwise was an admirer of Galen, this reaction continued with al-Fārābī, Avicenna and Averroes.

2.2   THE ARABIC LOGICAL WRITINGS

The logical activity in the Arabic tradition was embodied in various kinds of writing (see Gutas 1993.) The case of Avicenna's output apart, these kinds of writing were already practised in the ancient commentary literature. The first logical writing that we know of in Arabic is an *Epitome* (i.e. a summary presentation) attributed to the famous secretary and litterateur Ibn al-Muqaffa' (d. 756) or to his son. Besides this question regarding the authorship of this work, it is still difficult to settle the question whether it is a translation of a Greek or Persian work or an original composition by Ibn al-Muqaffa'. Whatever the answer to these questions may be, the important fact to be stressed is that Ibn al-Muqaffa''s *Epitome* shares some features with works from the Syriac tradition: it expounds a short *Organon*, containing in addition to the contents of Porphyry's *Isagoge*, those of *Categories*, of *On Interpretation*, and of a truncated version of *Prior Analytics* corresponding to the theory of the categorical syllogistic (Book I, chapters 1–7). It is also important to note that Ibn al-Muqaffa''s *Epitome* is a unique witness to an early stage of logical terminology; items of that old terminology surface later here or there, notably in Avicenna. We learn from Ibn al-Nadīm that al-Kindī (d. c. 870) also wrote *Epitomes* of various Aristotelian logical treatises, but none of them has survived. To recover some of al-Kindī's logical views, we must track them down in his non-logical works, and in particular in his *The Number of Aristotle's Works* (Guidi and Walzer 1940). The case of al-Fārābī's *Abridgement of Logic* is problematic: although it could in a sense be categorised as an Epitome of a long *Organon* (plus the *Isagoge*), it exhibits many innovative features which set it apart from this genre.

Another genre of logical writing was that of lemmatic commentary, in which a small unit (called lemma) of the commented text (either Porphyry's *Isagoge* or Aristotle's text) is quoted, followed by a detailed commentary. This genre is represented by al-Fārābī's commentaries on *On Interpretation* and *Prior Analytics*, the first being extant in totality, the second only as a fragment (from *ii*.11 to the end of *Prior Analytics*). The commentaries written by Abū al-Faraj b. al-Ṭayyib (d. 1043) should also be included in this strand; unfortunately, we have only his commentary on Porphyry's *Isagoge* (Gyekye 1975, 1979) and his commentary on *Categories*, which has been recently edited (Ferrari 2006). In the same strand should also be included the only long commentary composed by Averroes on an Aristotelian logical treatise, namely the one on *Posterior Analytics*. Otherwise, what Averroes wrote on Aristotle's *Organon* and on Porphyry's *Isagoge* took the form of paraphrases or middle commentaries.

Among Avicenna's voluminous writings, about 3,000 pages on logic are available in print, mostly in Arabic and partly in Persian. Nearly all of this material is in the logic sections of his encyclopaedias. The earliest is *Najāt* 'Deliverance' (Ibn Sīnā 1985, translation Ibn Sina 2011), which was written in around 1014 but published about a dozen years later. The fullest is the logic section of *Shifā'*; written in the mid-1020s, it blends Ibn Sīnā's own innovations with a commentary on the Peripatetic tradition from the *Isagoge* to *Poetics*. The volume *Qiyās* 'Syllogism' (Ibn Sīnā 1964, partial translation Shehaby 1973) presents Avicenna's own vision of both predicate and propositional logic, partly viewed from a Peripatetic perspective. Avicenna followed *Shifā'* soon afterwards with *Easterners* (Ibn Sīnā 1910), in which, as he explains, he presents his own views without making concessions to the Peripatetics; unfortunately, the logic section of the book is lost except for the first few dozen pages, and these have never been properly edited. Around 1027 Avicenna wrote the Persian *Dāneshnāmeh* 'Book of Wisdom', whose logic section (Ibn Sīnā 1952, translation Zabeeh 1971) is relatively elementary. Finally there is the terse and enigmatic *al-Ishārāt wa-al-tanbīhāt* ('Pointers and Reminders') (Ibn Sīnā 2002, translation Inati 1984) from around 1030, which Avicenna himself admitted might mislead the unwary; this work gave rise to many commentaries in later Arabic logic.

Besides the three listed genres: epitomes, literal commentaries and original presentations of the logical teaching, we should mention treatises devoted to a single topic. To this category belong Averroes' *Quaesita*. They aim to settle a controversial exegetical question, putting forward, against previous commentators – in particular Alexander and Themistius on the Greek side, al-Fārābī and Avicenna on the Arabic side – the solution Averroes thought to be at once Aristotle's and the one that conforms to the plain truth. Among these *Quaesita*, four were dedicated to the problem of mixed syllogisms (with modal premises of different kinds or with modal and non-modal premises). Some of Avicenna's minor logical writings are also answers to specific questions posed to him.

This literature both grew from and helped to create schools of logic within the Arabic tradition. As soon as Aristotle's *Organon* became available, a Peripatetic tradition was established in Baghdad, including Abū Bishr Mattā and Yaḥyā b. 'Adī (d. 974) among others (sometimes grouped together as the Baghdad Christians). Although al-Fārābī received his logical instruction in this milieu, he should be singled out as initiating a new logical tradition. This new tradition was lively in the Islamic West in Andalusia, where the treatises of his *Abridgement of Logic* were glossed by Ibn Bājja (known to the Latins as Avempace, d. 1139) and creatively imitated by the young Averroes before he turned his back on it. In the Islamic East al-Fārābī's work was assimilated by Avicenna and became one of the main stimuli to Avicenna's own innovations.

2.3 ARABIC REARRANGEMENTS OF THE MATERIAL

2.3.1 Analysis and Topic

Many authors have recognised a branch of logic devoted to heuristics: how do we search systematically for a logical resolution of a question ('p or not p?') or a proof of a particular statement that we believe to be true? Mainly on the basis of some brief remarks by Aristotle in *Prior Analytics* i.28, the Arabic logicians understood that this kind of heuristic enquiry should be called analysis (*taḥlīl*). The fourteenth-century historian Ibn Khaldūn remarked that there was a tendency in some leading logicians from the thirteenth century onwards to develop logic as a subject in its own right rather than as a source of tools for the sciences. It seems likely that he had in mind the downgrading of analysis in logicians after al-Fārābī, Avicenna and Averroes. Certainly these three scholars regarded analysis as crucially important, but one should note that they did not all understand its importance in the same way.

We begin with al-Fārābī. One conspicuous innovation in his *Abridgement of Logic* is that he brings forward *Topics* and puts them immediately after *Prior Analytics*. The reason for this is that he regards parts of *Topics* as a source of heuristic arguments. In particular the topics of accident from *Topics* 2, subjected to a selection and systematised, are conceived of as a specification of the rules given by Aristotle in *Prior Analytics* i.27–28 for constructing a syllogistic proof of a given conclusion (the so-called *pons asinorum*). Al-Fārābī regards *Topics* 4–7 as a source of rules for making definitions and *Topics* 1 and 8 as an exposition of the rules of the dialectical game.

For al-Fārābī, analysis is a method for finding, given a proposition *p*, either a proof of *p* or a proof of the negation of *p*. (The disjunction '*p* or not *p*' is the *quaesitum*, *maṭlūb* in Arabic.) The method involves decomposing *p*, or its negation, and comparing the components with a suitable matching *topos* (*mawḍi'*). In successful cases, the *topos* will provide a major premise for a proof of *p* or its negation. The name 'analysis' refers to the double process of breaking the proposition down into its components and moving backwards to the premises of a proof.

So for al-Fārābī a *topos* is a proposition schema which, when instantiated, gives the major premise of a syllogism adapted to the *quaesitum*. Averroes broadly follows al-Fārābī's account of topic, but for him a *topos* is simultaneously a proposition schema and an argument schema. For example, the following *topos* of composition gives instructions for finding a major premise for a syllogism in *Barbara*:

> Every predicate which belongs to the whole of the genus of a given subject, to its differentia, to its proprium or to an inseparable accident of that subject will belong to the whole of the subject.

Averroes gives as a concrete example of the case where the predicate sought is a genus of the subject:

> *Quaesitum*: Is the heaven in a place?
> (Syllogism constructed:)
> The heaven is a body.
> A body is in a place.
> _____
> The heaven is in a place.

The procedure is quite close to what Aristotle recommends in *Prior Analytics*, i.28. (We have summarised here the more detailed comparison of topics in al-Fārābī and Averroes given in Hasnawi 2001.)

It is worth noting that this theory of topics has implicit in it more than one classification of syllogisms. For example, different topics may yield major premises that are hypothetical or predicative. Different topics may yield demonstrative or dialectical premises, depending (to take the example of the topos given above) on whether a genus is a true genus or merely a commonly accepted one.

Avicenna was equally interested in *taḥlīl*, but from a very different point of view. For him, finding middle terms for syllogisms in *Barbara* is a problem on the border of logic, so that there is no guarantee we can solve it by algorithmic procedures. We achieve it by a range of means that include not only scrutiny of definitions, but also empirical testing, wine drinking, prayer and sleep. What the logician really needs for heuristics is a set of tools for keeping control of complex arguments (which might have up to a thousand steps, he suggests). For example, there are tools of paraphrase and representation that allow us to splice together two arguments that use different terms. Moreover, there are systematic procedures for reviewing an incomplete complex syllogistic argument to see what would be needed to complete it. He teaches his students one such procedure by a series of sixty-four example steps with hints provided. In effect he is teaching a recursive proof-search algorithm; we can verify this by reading from his text enough information to encode the procedure as an abstract state machine. This was the world's first nontrivial proof search algorithm by a margin of some 900 years. However, Avicenna shows no signs of connecting his algorithm with the algorithms pioneered by Arabic mathematicians; and unlike al-Khwārizmī, he sees no need to give a correctness proof for the algorithm (Hodges 2010).

2.3.2 *Demonstration and Definition*

For the Peripatetic tradition strictly speaking, that is in Alexander of Aphrodisias as well as in the Neoplatonic tradition (Philoponus), logic has an epistemological orientation: it is oriented towards the method of demonstration as expounded in *Posterior Analytics*. And this method itself should be followed in the exposition of science: physics, psychology and metaphysics. This view was also endorsed by Galen as a physician. It is also assumed by Arabic philosophers, and systematically so from al-Fārābī onwards.

Perhaps the ideal of demonstrative method found its way to the Arabic tradition first through the medical channel as represented by Galen. One should remember that more than a hundred of Galen's books were translated in Hunayn's school, and these included, as we saw, his logical works.

We would expect that the Galenic ideal of demonstrative science would have been welcomed by the Arabic philosophers. But no such thing happened. Galen's demonstrations were, from al-Fārābī onwards, subject to bitter criticism. This has been documented in Zimmerman (1976). To take an example, Galen thought that the following argument was demonstrative:

If we cut such a nerve, voice, or sensation, or movement, is suppressed.
So the existence of this nerve is the cause of the existence of the voice, sensation, or movement.

But in fact such an argument was, for al-Fārābī and Averroes, at best sophistical, even though it could be used in rhetorical speeches, since it amounts according to them to denying the antecedent (al-Fārābī 1986, 104,9–12; Ibn Rushd 1977, Ar. 173,11–174,3/Eng. 65–66). Also, for al-Fārābī and Averroes, Galen appears to have thought that as a physician, i.e. as a practitioner of an art the object of which was the human body as subject to health and illness, he could deal scientifically with the theory of the elements or with the theory of mixed bodies. But as Averroes put it, a physician dealing with such topics could only have access to logical argumentation, that is, to an argumentation which uses predications that may go beyond the genus of the science in question and hence will not be truly *per se*. But science should use only *per se* predications (Ibn Rushd 1989, 43,18–44,7).

Per se predications are determined in terms of a predicable-based theory. *Per se* predicates are either predicates which enter into the constitution of the subject (these are the definition, the genus and the differentia), or they are predicates into the constitution of

Table 2.1 *The first type of demonstrative composition in al-Fārābī*

A = major term; B = middle term; J = minor term;
A def. B = A is a definition of B;
A gen. B = A is a genus of B;
A diff. B = A is a differentia of B;
B < def. A = B enters in the definition of B;
A ε Pdef. A = A belongs to a part of the definition of A;
A EAcc. J = A is an essential accident of J.

A def. B	A gen. B	A diff. B	B < def. A	Gen. B < def. A
B def. J	A gen. J	B diff. J	J < def. B	Gen. J < def. B
A dcf. J	A gen. J	A diff. J	A ε Pdef. A	A EAcc. J

which the subject enters (these are either *propria* or essential accidents). Al-Fārābī, who is followed in this by Avempace and Averroes, proposed eight types of demonstrative composition, each including many types of demonstrative syllogisms which are intended to be the building blocks of the demonstrative method (al-Fārābī 1987, 33–39). See Table 2.1 for examples of the main types of syllogisms of the first type of demonstrative composition.

Whereas the list of predicates *per se* and their organisation was more or less traditional, the project of identifying the elementary demonstrative structures seems to be new and deserves to be studied in detail.

We turn to Avicenna. For him, the epistemological orientation of logic must be written into the definition of logic. More precisely, logic is a science or art through which we gain knowledge that we did not previously have, and this knowledge can take one of two forms. First, we can acquire knowledge of a concept; Avicenna calls this *taṣawwur*, 'conceptualisation'. And secondly, we can acquire knowledge of a fact by coming to accept it rationally on the basis of facts we already knew; Avicenna calls this *taṣdīq*, roughly 'assent' (though any exact translation into English would be controversial). The primary logical tools for acquiring these kinds of knowledge are

definition for *taṣawwur* and syllogism for *taṣdīq*. Avicenna empha-
sises that we can't assent to a proposition before we understand it;
so the appropriate *taṣawwur* must always precede *taṣdīq*. He also
stresses that we have some concepts by nature, and that some facts
are known to us without the need for deduction. He maintains all
these positions from *Shifā'* onwards.

The use of these two notions suggests a two-track picture of
logic: we build up concepts through definition (by genus and differentiae) and alongside that we build up factual information through
deduction (by syllogism). This two-track picture will be familiar to
anyone who knows the Western logical tradition from Pascal to early
Tarski, though there is no evidence that Avicenna had any direct influence on that tradition. Avicenna structures the logic parts of both
Easterners and *Pointers and Reminders* so that topics connected
with *taṣawwur* come first (including an integrated treatment of definition, something that was missing in the *Organon*) and then topics
connected with *taṣdīq*. In *Pointers and Reminders*, where the tran-
sition comes at the end of Nahj 2 (*Ishārāt* 67; Inati 1984, 76), this
arrangement had the effect of splitting the contents of Aristotle's
Posterior Analytics into two parts, the theory of definition and the
theory of demonstration, which go respectively with *taṣawwur* and
taṣdīq.

This arrangement in terms of *taṣawwur* and *taṣdīq* greatly
influenced the post-Avicennan logical treatises. These treatises were
also shaped by another feature of *Pointers and Reminders*, namely
that in this work Avicenna limited his discussion of the applications
of logic almost entirely to demonstration and the refutation of fallacies. In earlier works, his treatment of the five syllogistic arts (demonstration, dialectic, sophistry, rhetoric and poetics) had been much
fuller, though it does still appear in *Pointers and Reminders* at Nahj
6 Section 1 (*Ishārāt* 123ff.; Inati 1984, 118ff.) and Nahj 9 Section 1
(*Ishārāt* 165f.; Inati 1984, 148f.).

Al-Fārābī and Avicenna agreed that logic is a rule-based science, with rules that regulate correct thinking. But they differed

radically about the form of these rules. According to al-Fārābī, For everything that the science of grammar gives us about rules for expressions, the science of logic gives us an analogous thing about concepts (*Iḥṣā'* 2005, 53–5). Avicenna responded that there is a major difference. The science of grammar studies how different categories of expression can be combined to form compound expressions; but the rules of logic are blind to the categories (in the Aristotelian sense) of the components of sentences. For example, the laws of syllogisms apply to qualities in exactly the same way as they apply to substances. In his treatment of the *Categories* in the *Shifa'*, Avicenna says repeatedly that Aristotle's categories are no help to logicians and might even be a hindrance. In fact one can inspect the rules and procedures that Avicenna uses in verifying that inferences are correct – through a few hundred pages of theory and examples – and no case has been found where his rules and procedures invoke a distinction between categories, for instance, a distinction between substances and accidents.

2.4 AVICENNA'S INNOVATIONS

Abū ʿAlī b. Sīnā, known in the West as Avicenna, was born near Bukhārā in present-day Uzbekhistan in the late tenth century. He died in 1037 after a career spent in the service of local princes in various parts of present-day Iran. Due to lack of space, we have concentrated here on Avicenna's formal logic, leaving aside important contributions that he made to semantics and its relation to syntax, to logical methodology, and to understanding the place of logic among the sciences. Hodges (forthcoming) provides further information and references on this.

2.4.1 *Assertorics*

Avicenna's formal logic is built on Aristotle's assertoric (non-modal) logic and its four main forms of proposition:

(*a*) Every B is an A.

(e) No B is an A.

(i) Some B is an A.

(o) Not every B is an A.

He normally assumes that the subject term B and the predicate term A are distinct.

(The names *a, e, i, o* were not known to Avicenna.)

Avicenna explains the four proposition types in terms of their meanings. He may have been the first logician to say that if nothing satisfies the subject term B, then the affirmative sentences of the forms (a) and (i) are false while the negative sentences (e) and (o) are true; but he claims that this was assumed by all earlier logicians apart from a few hotheads (Bäck 1987; Hodges 2012; Chatti 2016).

For Avicenna a syllogism is a pair of assertoric sentences which share one term. The syllogism is productive in a given figure if there is an assertoric sentence (the conclusion) whose terms are as prescribed by the figure, and which follows from the premises in the sense that assuming the premises commits us to the conclusion. But in practice Avicenna often uses 'syllogism' as short for 'productive syllogism'. He assumes that every productive syllogism has a unique conclusion, namely the strongest possible one, and he often treats this conclusion as a part of the syllogism. Like other Arabic logicians, Avicenna normally writes the minor premise (containing the subject term of the conclusion) before the major premise (containing the predicate term of the conclusion). He distinguishes three figures in the usual way; he rejects the fourth figure as unnatural.

These definitions allow Avicenna fourteen valid syllogistic moods, i.e. forms of productive syllogisms including the conclusion. He counts the first-figure moods as perfect, i.e. self-evidently valid, and he justifies the others by reducing them to moods already proved valid, using conversion, ecthesis or contraposition (i.e. reductio ad absurdum). Invalidity and non-productivity are shown by giving terms that form counterexamples. All of this follows Aristotle's *Prior Analytics* i.4–6 with only minor variations (*Najāt* 57–64; Ahmed

2011, 45–50), (*Qiyās* ii.4), (*Dāneshnāmeh* 65–80). The main variation is that he introduces an ecthetic proof of *Baroco*, which has the effect that all the non-perfect moods can be derived without the help of contraposition.

2.4.2 Quantification over Times

Though Avicenna accepts Aristotle's assertoric logic as definitive within its own sphere, he often criticises Aristotle for thinking that language stops there. In talking to each other, and even to ourselves, we constantly mean more than we say explicitly, and we expect the unspoken meanings to be understood. In practice we have knowledge that allows us to understand the unspoken meanings in things that we read or hear. For example, we know the usages and idioms of a shared language, and we know what has been stated earlier in a conversation. In Avicenna's view, Aristotle should have been sensitive to these facts about language, because often they are relevant to the validity of inferences. Avicenna points out that many of the fallacies that Aristotle discusses in *Sophistical Refutations* depend on ignoring unspoken but assumed additions or conditions to the sentences involved; but he laments that Aristotle's examples rely too often on plain misuse of language (Ibn Sīnā 1958: 14.10). Avicenna extends similar criticisms to later Aristotelian logicians who accept Aristotle's view of logic unquestioningly.

Avicenna's own efforts to expand Aristotle's logic rest on the fact that many descriptions apply to a thing at one time but not at another time. This is obvious for descriptions like 'laughing' or 'sleeping' or 'writing'. But Avicenna points out that in the external world (as he calls it), the same goes for genera and species: a horse is only a horse while it is alive, and horses do die. So in general we should regard the terms B and A as carrying a reference to time.

Normally Avicenna reads the temporalised subject B as meaning 'thing that is a B at some time during its existence'. But he allows several distinct ways of adding time to the predicate. Some that have immediate logical applications are illustrated below:

(*a-d*) Every (sometime-)B is an A all the time it exists.

(*a-ℓ*) Every (sometime-)B is an A all the time it's a B.

(*a-m*) Every (sometime-)B is an A sometime while it's a B.

(*a-t*) Every (sometime-)B is an A sometime while it exists.

(*e-d*) Every (sometime-)B is throughout its existence not an A.

(*i-ℓ*) Some (sometime-)B is an A all the time it's a B.

(*o-t*) Some (sometime-)B is sometime in its existence not an A.

The consonants *d*, *ℓ*, *m* and *t* here are not Avicenna's any more than the vowels *a*, *e*, *i* and *o* were, but they do have the merit of coming from the Arabic names that Avicenna himself offers for these proposition forms in his *Easterners*. For example, *d* is from *ḍarūrī* 'necessary', which is his name for the forms illustrated in (*a-d*) and (*e-d*) above (*Qiyās* i.3; *Easterners* 68–70). Note that the alphabetical order *d*, *ℓ*, *m*, *t* is also the order of logical strength, with *d* as the strongest. (In some recent literature, the modalities *ℓ* and *d* are referred to as descriptional and substantial. The name 'substantial' is not Avicenna's own, and is unfortunate in view of the fact noted earlier, that Avicenna disowns any connection between distinctions of category and the rules of logic.)

Pairing off the vowels with the consonants allows us sixteen propositional forms. We will refer to these sixteen forms as the two-dimensional proposition forms, borrowing the name from Oscar Mitchell (1983) who had similar ideas in the 1880s. For Avicenna himself, the two-dimensional propositions are examples of modalised predicative propositions, and he often refers to the added condition on A as a modality.

Just as Aristotle catalogued the valid simple inferences between assertoric sentences, we can do the same for two-dimensional sentences (Hodges 2015). It is not hard, but probably Avicenna himself lacked the formal skill to do it from general principles. Nevertheless his statements about which two-dimensional inferences are valid and which are invalid are entirely correct, though he reports them in a language which confusingly combines both temporal and alethic modal expressions.

Avicenna notes that in *Barbara* you might expect to get a necessary (*d*) conclusion only from necessary premises, but in fact there are valid forms of *Barbara* where either the minor or the major premise is weaker than (*d*). For example, the following is valid:

(*a-t*)   Every sometime-*C* is a sometime-B.
(*a-d*)   Every sometime-*B* is always an *A*.
(*a-d*)   Therefore every sometime-C is always an A.

(*Najāt* 74; Ibn Sina 2011, 58)

For a weaker major premise, we need at least an (*ℓ*) proposition; Avicenna offers:

(*a-d*)   All snow is coloured white throughout its existence.
(*a-ℓ*)   Everything coloured white dissociates the eye so long as it is coloured white.
(*a-d*)   Therefore all snow dissociates the eye throughout its existence.

(*Qiyās* 129.1f.)

Avicenna insists that nobody before Avicenna himself was clear about the distinction between (*d*) and (*ℓ*).

The theory of two-dimensional sentences was a self-contained, rigorous and completely new branch of formal logic. It was perhaps the only such branch to appear – apart from extensions given by Avicenna's Islamic successors in Persia and the Ottoman empire – between the ancient Greeks and the nineteenth century. But in practice Avicenna's achievement was less revolutionary than this might suggest. Many of the new valid syllogisms of two-dimensional logic can be verified by reduction to assertoric syllogisms; and Avicenna himself never came near a full exploitation of the moods that are not reducible (Hodges 2015).

The account above leaves unexplained why Avicenna presents his two-dimensional logic under the disguise of an Aristotle-style modal logic. This question has to be described as unresolved. But there are indications that Avicenna believed that the task of a logician in modal logic is to develop an abstract logic of modalities whose laws, found by analysis of the concepts of necessary and possible, would apply to any notions expressible by these modal concepts; and that he had a scheme for using his two-dimensional logic as a tool for this task. Research in this difficult area continues.

2.4.3 *Propositional Logic*

Arabic propositional logic normally takes the form of studying conditional (*sharṭī*) sentences, which are classified as either *muttaṣil* or *munfaṣil*. We return to the translation of these terms below. There are clear signs that Avicenna's view of propositional logic developed, and that some of what we have is unfinished work. We can distinguish three layers.

In the first layer, call it PL1, *muttaṣil* sentences are explained as sentences of the form 'If (or when) p then q', and *munfaṣil* as 'Either p or q'. These forms allow several possibilities, which are classified in several ways. One classification is in terms of the inferences that they enter into. Thus 'If p then q' is sometimes understood as an implication both ways, in which case 'q' and 'If p then q' together entail 'p'. Two kinds of *munfaṣil* are distinguished according to whether 'p' together with 'Either p or q' entails 'Not q'. *Qiyās* viii.1 and viii.2 represent this layer, which is very close to the account given by al-Fārābī in his *Qiyās* (Dānish Pazhūh 1987, vol. 1, 137–140).

The second layer, PL2, is undoubtedly Avicenna's invention. The *muttaṣil* sentences are redefined in the light of two-dimensional logic. Briefly, the time quantifiers are moved to the front, so as to generate *muttaṣil* sentences of each of the forms (a), (e), (i) and (o). Thus the (a) form is now 'At every time t, if p is true at t then q is true at t', and the (o) form, which is the contradictory negation of (a), is 'There is a time when p is true and q is not true'. In *Qiyās* vi.1, Avicenna presents the logic of *muttaṣil* sentences as an exact copy of that of assertoric sentences; the corresponding syllogisms are valid, and the corresponding justifications (by conversion, etc.) hold. This must be the earliest example of any logician knowingly producing two essentially different interpretations of exactly the same logical formalism.

Since the contradictory negation of an 'If ... then' sentence is not an 'If ... then' sentence, the connection between *sharṭī* and the usual sense of 'conditional' is severed. Instead Avicenna explains that *sharṭī* sentences should now be understood as ones containing subclauses that are not asserted when the whole sentence is asserted. Also his use of *a*-conversion requires that the *muttaṣil* (*a*) sentence is understood to entail that for at least one t, p is true at t; Avicenna is explicit about this feature, which was unclear in PL1.

The move to PL3 is equally radical and appears most fully in *Qiyās* vi.3 with implications elsewhere. Avicenna attempts a generalisation of the *munfaṣil* sentences to (*a*), (*e*), (*i*) and (*o*) forms. He defines these forms by *muttaṣil* paraphrases of them. For example, the paraphrase of the (*i*) *munfaṣil* sentence is (surprisingly) 'There is a time at which p is true and q is not true', and that of the (*a*) *munfaṣil* sentence is 'At every time at which p is not true, q is true'. One notable feature of PL3, which appears, for example, in the paraphrase of (*a*) above, is the free use of negation of subclauses, both antecedent and consequent. As a result, every proposition becomes convertible. This and the symmetry of *muttaṣil* (*i*) and of *munfaṣil* (*a*) suggest to Avicenna that the whole scheme of syllogistic figures might no longer be appropriate, though he never pursues this thought in detail. Also, given the paraphrases between *munfaṣil* and *muttaṣil*, the existential assumption in *muttaṣil* (*a*) becomes implausible, and in fact Avicenna discards it. Thus, for example, he is now able to deploy a form of modus ponens, 'Always p', 'Whenever p then q', therefore 'Always q', which can be used even when p is never true; he can use this in his justification of reductio ad absurdum.

PL3 has features of great interest, but Avicenna's account of it is unfortunately riddled with inadequate analyses and some downright errors, which later Arabic logicians tried to tidy up. Unsurprisingly, he backed away from PL3 when he came to sketch propositional logic in *Pointers and Reminders*.

It seems that *muttaṣil* is traceable to the Peripatetic notion *sunekhês*, and *munfaṣil* to Peripatetic *diairetikê*. Shehaby (1973) suggests translating *muttaṣil* as 'connective' and *munfaṣil* as 'separative'. These translations are excellent representations of the Arabic but they have no logical content. A slight adjustment corrects this: read *muttaṣil* as 'meet-like' and *munfaṣil* as 'difference-like'. So far as any translations can, these translations should create the right expectations; for example, the (i) *muttaṣil*s are quantified conjunctions (i.e. meets), and the complete *munfaṣil*s of PL1 precisely express logical difference.

Avicenna was an acute observer of language, and he mentioned several further forms of proposition that might be developed into logics. For example, in the case of the (t) forms, he observed that the condition 'at some time' has various modulations that arise naturally in natural language, such as 'at several times', or 'at a known time'. He never pursued the logic of these variants of (t). But he gave names for some of them; these names sometimes reappear in later Arabic logicians, with attempts to develop a corresponding logic.

Avicenna also noted that when there is an implicit time quantification, the sentence 'Most Bs are As' can be read in several ways – is it 'most individuals' or 'most occasions' or 'most pairs of individual plus occasion'? Again he never developed a logic of 'most', though he remarked that one is needed for understanding medical reasoning (*Qiyās* 175.8–177.2).

2.5 CLOSING REMARKS

The Arabic-speaking logic of the period discussed in this chapter shows an extraordinarily wide range of aspects. It ranges from the deeply conservative (Averroes) to the radical and exploratory (Avicenna), and from the metaphysical to the practical, and to the purely formal. We might note two overall differences from the later Latin Scholastic logic. First, the Arabic logicians always gave central place to Aristotle's theory of syllogisms. And second, Arabic logic was a widely recognised strand of the general culture of the Islamic empire, rather than a part of the university curriculum.

3   Arabic Logic after Avicenna

Khaled El-Rouayheb

When the North African historian Ibn Khaldūn (d. 1406) reflected on the development of logic, he distinguished – along with a number of other fourteenth-century observers – between "the early" and "the later" logicians (Rosenthal 1958, III, 143). The former included those who took their point of departure from the classical *Organon*, such as the philosophers al-Fārābī (d. 950), Avicenna (d. 1037) and Averroes (d. 1198). The first of "the later logicians", according to Ibn Khaldūn, were the Persians Fakhr al-Dīn al-Rāzī (d. 1210) and Afḍal al-Dīn al-Khūnajī (d. 1248). These disregarded the *Categories* entirely and gave short shrift to the "matter" of the syllogism: demonstration, dialectic, sophistical fallacies, rhetoric, and poetics. Instead, they focused almost exclusively on the five predicables, definition and description, propositions and their immediate implications (such as conversion, contraposition) and the formal syllogism. By Ibn Khaldūn's time, "the later logicians" had carried the day. "Logic" (*manṭiq*) had ceased to be a discipline in which one comments upon or paraphrases or summarizes the books of the *Organon*; it had become rather a field dealing with the acquisition of concepts (*taṣawwurāt*) through definition or description and the acquisition of assents (*taṣdīqāt*) through syllogism. Ibn Khaldūn himself lamented this development, but the resulting narrower view of the scope of *manṭiq* made it much closer to the contemporary understanding of "logic" than the earlier Peripatetic conception of it as a discipline that covers all the books of the *Organon*.

The roots of the new view of the scope of "logic" can be said to go back to Avicenna himself, especially to his condensed presentation of logic in *al-Ishārāt*. But Ibn Khaldūn was not guilty simply of oversight. Avicenna had followed the books of the *Organon* in his magnum opus *al-Shifā'*: *Categories, On Interpretation, Prior*

Analytics, Posterior Analytics, Topics, Sophistical Refutations, Rhetoric, and *Poetics.* His student Bahmanyār (d. 1065) similarly divided the logic part of his philosophical summa *al-Taḥṣīl* into chapters covering *Eisagoge, Categories, On Interpretation, Prior Analytics,* and *Posterior Analytics.* The powerful influence of Avicenna's *Ishārāt* was due in large part to its widely discussed commentary by Fakhr al-Dīn al-Rāzī. In turn, its novel vision of the scope of logic was consolidated by a number of influential works written in the late twelfth and early thirteenth centuries, especially Rāzī's *al-Mulakhkhaṣ* and three works on logic by Khūnajī: the short *al-Jumal,* the handbook-sized *al-Mūjaz,* and the lengthy and incomplete summa *Kashf al-asrār.*

Rāzī and Khūnajī were in a sense "Avicennan" logicians: they took their point of departure from the works of Avicenna and accepted a number of his distinct positions in logic, such as the "combinatorial" hypothetical syllogism, the "quantification" of hypotheticals and the distinction between a *dhātī* and *waṣfī* reading of modality propositions (for these positions, see the contributions to the present volume "Arabic Logic up to Avicenna" and "The Logic of Modality"). Rāzī and Khūnajī were in fact instrumental in the westward expansion of an attenuated Avicennan logic at the expense of the more strictly Aristotelian traditions of Baghdad and Islamic Spain. Nevertheless, they approached the writings of Avicenna with the same critical and independent-minded spirit with which Avicenna had read Aristotle. They delighted in raising problems, highlighted their own contributions and novelties and showed little patience for doing logic by painstaking exegesis of earlier logicians. Their spirit is encapsulated in Khūnajī's remark: "It is not our duty to preoccupy ourselves with what people may have meant, but to verify the truth and to establish what follows in case the intention is such" (Khūnajī 2010, 279–280).

The critical interventions of Rāzī and Khūnajī were in turn modified and carried forward by later generations of like-minded logicians such as Athīr al-Dīn al-Abharī (d. 1265), Najm al-Dīn al-Kātibī (d. 1277), and Sirāj al-Dīn al-Urmawī (d. 1283). These "revisionist Avicennan" logicians (I adopt the phrase from Tony Street) authored lengthy summas of logic as well as shorter handbooks that continued to be studied in Islamic madrasas until the twentieth century: Abharī's elementary *Īsāghūjī*; Kātibī's *al-Risālah al-Shamsiyyah*; and Urmawī's *Maṭāliʿ al-anwār*. These handbooks in turn became the point of departure for later logicians. Especially in Persia and India, Avicenna's logical writings continued to be prized, copied, and quoted (Ahmed 2012), but the state of the field had changed too much in the course of the twelfth and thirteenth centuries for Avicenna's writings to constitute the state of the art for logicians writing after around 1300. The following section will take a closer look at the logic expounded in the enormously influential thirteenth-century post-Avicennan handbooks (especially Kātibī 1948). The section after that will attempt to outline the development of Arabic logic in the fourteenth and fifteenth centuries.

3.1 THE POST-AVICENNAN HANDBOOKS

The "revisionist", post-Avicennan handbooks of logic typically began by dividing knowledge into conception and assent. They then noted that not all concepts and assents are evident – some must be acquired from prior concepts and assents. Logic was then presented as a discipline dealing with the rules for the acquisition of concepts and assents from already known concepts and assents. Avicenna had presented the subject matter of logic as being "second intentions", i.e. accidents that only accrue to quiddities insofar as these quiddities are in the mind, such as a quiddity being a "genus" or a "species" or a "subject" or a "predicate" (Sabra 1980). Post-Avicennan logicians, following Khūnajī, typically asserted that the subject matter of logic is simply "known concepts and assents" insofar as they lead to further concepts and assents (El-Rouayheb 2012; Street 2015, 2.1.2 and 2.1.3). At first sight, this might not distinguish logic from other sciences, all of which seek to extrapolate from known concepts and assents. But logic, on this account, is distinct by virtue of investigating ratiocination from the known to the unknown in a general, topic-neutral manner.

The handbooks typically proceeded to deal with certain linguistic preliminaries: types of reference (by convention or by nature; by correspondence or by implication); the distinction between simple and composite expressions; and the distinction between singular and universal terms. Following Khūnajī, they presented the ways in which universal terms can be logically related: The extensions of two universal terms can be equal to each other (such as "human" and "rational"); one can be more general and the other more specific (such as "animal" and "human"); the extensions can overlap partially (such as "animal" and "white"); and they can fail to overlap at all (such as "animal" and "stone"). The relations between the extensions of their contradictories were also presented: If concept A is more general in extension than concept B, then not-A is more specific in extension than not-B. If A is equal to B, then not-A is equal in extension to not-B. If A and B do not overlap in extension, then either their negations do not overlap or they overlap partially. As will be seen below, similar relations were held to obtain between propositions.

Universal terms were then divided into the five predicables: species, genus, differentia, proprium, and general accident. Various kinds of definitions (ḥudūd) and descriptions (rusūm) involving these predicables were then presented: perfect and imperfect definition, perfect and imperfect description. Avicenna's position that real definition is well-nigh impossible was largely accepted, and post-Avicennan logicians tended to believe that the most that could be hoped for is nominal definitions of things "according to our understanding".

The handbooks subsequently proceeded to the discussion of assents and their acquisition. Propositions were introduced and distinguished from other kinds of sentences (commands, questions and performative utterances such as "I hereby divorce you"). Propositions were then divided into categorical (ḥamlī) and hypothetical (shartī), the latter being subdivided into conditionals (muttaṣilāt) and disjunctions (munfaṣilāt). Disjunctions were further divided into

(i) exhaustive (the disjuncts are not both false); (ii) exclusive (the disjuncts are not both true)[1]; and (iii) "strict" (the disjuncts are not both false and not both true). Conditionals were divided into "coincidental" (*ittifāqī*) and "implicative" (*luzūmī*). In the latter case – and for Arabic logicians much more significantly – there is a causal or conceptual relation between antecedent and consequent that underlies the truth of the conditional. In the former case, the conditional is true simply if both antecedent and consequent are true (for example, "If humans speak then donkeys bray") or, alternatively, if the consequent is true (for example, "If all the trees of the world were reeds and the seven seas ink, the words of God would not be exhausted"). Similarly, disjunctions were divided into "coincidental" and "oppositional" (*'inādī*).

The immediate implications of these hypotheticals were presented, sometimes at considerable length. De Morgan's laws, for example, were recognized at least since Khūnajī: An "exhaustive" disjunction (P or Q) implies a negative "exclusive" disjunction between the negation of the two disjuncts (Not both not-P and not-Q). And conversely an exclusive disjunction (Not both P and Q) implies an exhaustive disjunction between the negations of the two disjuncts (Not-P or not-Q). A conditional (If P then Q) implies an exclusive disjunction between the antecedent and the negation of the consequent (Not both P and not-Q) and an exhaustive disjunction between the consequent and the negation of the antecedent (Not-P or Q). Conversely, both kinds of disjunctions imply conditionals. It should be noted that these implications were thought to obtain between non-coincidentally true disjunctions and non-coincidentally true conditionals. No logician in the Arabic tradition suggested that a coincidental disjunction entails an implicative conditional or even a coincidental conditional. The idea that the falsity of the antecedent

---

[1] It may seem odd to classify this as a "disjunction", but it arguably corresponds to one recognizable use of the "Either ... or ..." construction (in both English and Arabic), *viz.* to claim that the disjuncts cannot both be true (though they may both be false).

is sufficient for the truth of a conditional seems never to have been entertained in the Arabic tradition, and the same is true of the closely related idea that anything follows from a contradiction.

More controversial was Avicenna's claim, that the following implication – reminiscent of what is now widely known as Boethius' thesis – holds:

Always: If P then Q

_____

Never: If P then not-Q

Khūnajī denied the validity of the inference on the grounds that an impossible antecedent might imply both a proposition and its negation. This, he pointed out, is clear from the case of indirect proofs in which an inconsistent set of premises implies both a proposition and its negation (El-Rouayheb 2009).

Categorical modality propositions (*muwajjahāt*) were given considerable attention in non-introductory post-Avicennan handbooks. Following Avicenna, the handbooks distinguished between *dhātī* and *waṣfī* readings of such propositions. In the *waṣfī* reading, a predicate is stated to be true of a subject with a certain modality insofar as a certain description is true of this subject. In this sense, for example, all sleepers are necessarily sleeping. In the *dhātī* reading, the predicate is claimed to be true with a certain modality of the subject as such, without consideration of non-essential descriptions. In that sense, it is not true that all sleepers are necessarily sleeping. Following Rāzī and Khūnajī, the handbooks distinguished systematically between necessity and perpetuity and between one-sided and two-sided modality, for example, between possibility and contingency. These distinctions underlie the system of thirteen or fifteen modality propositions "into which it is customary to inquire" (see the chapter in this volume – "The Logic of Modality" for an account of these propositions).

With so many types of modality propositions, it became impractical to go through each and every one when discussing modal conversions, contrapositions, and syllogisms. At least since Khūnajī, it became customary to preface the discussion of such immediate implications by systematically presenting the relative strengths of the modality propositions, thus offering a shortcut by invoking the principle that what does not follow from the "more specific" (stronger) claim does not follow from the "more general" (weaker) claim, and that if the "more general" (weaker) claim does not follow from a proposition or pair of propositions, then the "more specific" (stronger) claim does not follow either. On the basis of such principles, revisionist post-Avicennans sometimes expressed incredulity at the procedures and claims of earlier logicians. For example, Avicenna had opined that a first-figure syllogism consisting of two possibility premises is evidently productive, whereas a similar syllogism with a possibility minor and a necessity major is not evident and needs proof. "How", remarked Khūnajī, "can the implication of a conclusion by a weaker set of premises be evident and the implication of that very conclusion by a stronger set of premises be non-evident?" (Khūnajī 2010, 280.)

Having presented the mentioned modality propositions, the handbooks discussed contradiction, conversion and contraposition. The post-Avicennan handbooks typically denied that contraposition as traditionally conceived is valid. A standard proof of traditional contraposition might run as follows:

(1) Every J is B   Assumption
     To prove: Every non-B is non-J
(2) Some non-B is J   Assumption for Indirect Proof
(3) Some non-B is B   2, 1 (DARII)

But revisionist Avicennan logicians denied that "Some non-B is J" is the contradictory of "Every non-B is non-J". They insisted that the following two propositions are not equivalent:

Not: Every non-B is non-J
Some non-B is J

It was generally agreed that affirmative propositions have existential import, whereas negative propositions do not. But this means that if there are no non-Bs then the second, affirmative proposition is false whereas the first, negative proposition is true. Instead, revisionist post-Avicennan logicians redefined "contraposition" (ʿaks al-naqīḍ) to mean the following immediate inference:

> Every J is B
>
> ———————————
>
> No non-B is J

This was held to be valid in the case of categorical propositions, though not in the case of conditionals. Following Khūnajī, the thirteenth-century revisionist Avicennan logicians tended to deny the following inference:

> Always: If P then Q
>
> ———————————
>
> Never: If not-Q then P

A proof for this might run as follows:

(1)	Always: If P then Q	Assumption
	To prove: Never: If not-Q then P	
(2)	It might be: If not-Q then P	A.I.P
(3)	It might be: If not-Q then Q	2,1 Hypothetical Syllogism

Revisionist Avicennan logicians denied that (3) is absurd. In other words, they denied what has come to be known as Aristotle's thesis that no proposition implies its own negation. Khūnajī had attempted to prove that a conditional of the form "It might be: If P then not-P" is true by means of a third-figure hypothetical syllogism:

> Always: If P & not-P then P
> Always: If P & not-P then not-P
>
> ———————————
>
> It might be: If P then not-P

The corollary of this is that no proposition of the form "Never: If P then Q" is true (see El-Rouayheb 2009 for references and further discussion).

After dealing with immediate implications, the handbooks proceeded to what they explicitly stated to be the heart of the discipline of logic – the syllogism. Revisionist Avicennan handbooks, by contrast to the earlier Aristotelian tradition and Avicenna himself, recognized the fourth figure of the syllogism. One of the earliest Arabic logicians to do so was Ibn al-Sarī (d. 1153) who had devoted a treatise to the defense of the fourth figure (Sabra 1965). Perhaps more consequential for the later tradition, Rāzī and Khūnajī had endorsed the fourth figure as well (Rāzī 2003, 265–271; Khūnajī 2010, 247–248).

With respect to modal syllogisms, one feature that stands out is that the revisionist handbooks denied the productivity of first-figure syllogisms with possibility minors. This in turn is closely related to the position that the extension of the subject term of a categorical proposition only includes entities of which it is actually true. Al-Fārābī (d. 950) was understood to have had the position that the subject term includes anything of which it is possibly true – to adopt a term from medieval Latin logic, the subject term is "ampliated" to the possible. On that account, a first-figure syllogism with a possibility minor seems evidently productive:

Every J is possibly B
Every B (i.e. every possible B) is necessarily A

Every J is necessarily A

Avicenna was understood to have rejected ampliation to the possible and to have upheld the view that the subject term should be understood to include only that of which it is true in actuality (past, present, or future). On this account, a first-figure syllogism with a possibility minor arguably ceases to be evidently productive and needs a proof.

Every J is possibly B

Every B (i.e. every actual B) is necessarily A

Every actual J is necessarily A

Avicenna was usually understood by later logicians to have shown the validity of such syllogisms by supposing the possibility expressed in the minor premise to be actualized (i.e. we suppose it is true that "Every J is actually B"), then pointing out that a necessity conclusion uncontroversially follows, and then arguing that therefore the conclusion must remain true with a possibility minor since supposing a possibility actualized cannot lead to an impossibility, such as a necessity-proposition changing its truth value from false to true. As shown by Paul Thom, this strategy can be given a valid interpretation in modern modal logic S5 (Thom 2008). We assume that the mentioned premises are within the scope of a necessity operator, that necessity-propositions are true in all possible worlds, and that each possible world has access to every other possible world. Avicenna, in effect, considers the possible world in which the possibility minor is true actually, shows that in that world the necessity conclusion follows, and then infers that the necessity conclusion must also be true in the original world in which the minor is only possible.

Starting with Khūnajī, revisionist post-Avicennan logicians rejected this proof. They invoked a distinction apparently first explicitly made by Rāzī. A proposition of the form "Every J is B" can be understood in two ways: (1) Every actual J in extramental existence is B; and (2) Every actual J (if it exists) is B (if it exists). According to the first, "externalist" (khārijī) reading, the proposition "Every phoenix is a bird" is false. According to the second, "essentialist" (ḥaqīqī) reading, the proposition is true: A phoenix, were it to exist, would be a bird. On the first reading, a syllogism with a possibility minor is clearly not productive. A counterexample would be:

Every horse is possibly a featherless biped
Every featherless biped is necessarily a human

The premises are true on an "externalist" reading, but even the weakest modality proposition does not follow, *viz.* "Some horse is possibly a human".

The case of "essentialist" propositions is less clear. The major premise of the just-mentioned counterexample ("Every featherless biped is necessarily a human") is false on an "essentialist" reading, since non-human featherless bipeds are possible and, were they to exist, would not be human. Khūnajī and his followers admitted that no counterexample was forthcoming when the premises are interpreted as "essentialist" propositions. They nevertheless insisted that even in that case (i) a first-figure syllogism with a possibility minor is not evidently productive and needs a proof, and (ii) the proof they attributed to Avicenna is faulty. By supposing the possibility minor to be true as an absolute proposition ("Every J is actually B"), the extension of things that are actually B has been expanded, and there is no guarantee that in such a case the major premise remains true as a necessity-proposition.

Just as Avicenna's proof can be modeled and shown to be valid in S5, Khūnajī and his followers can be seen as in effect denying the underlying principles of S5 and assuming a weaker modal system such as T. To show this, it would be helpful to backtrack to the "externalist" and "essentialist" readings of propositions. The logical relations between these two readings were systematically worked out in the thirteenth-century handbooks and their commentaries, as follows (Kātibī 1948, 96–97):

"Every J is B":

There is partial overlap between the "externalist" and "essentialist" readings. "Every phoenix is a bird" is true on an "essentialist" reading but false on an "externalist" reading. "Every featherless biped is a human" is true on an "externalist" reading but false on an "essentialist" reading. "Every human is an animal" is true in both senses.

"Some J is B":

The "essentialist" reading is "more general". In other words, if "Some J is B" is true on an "externalist" reading, then it must be true on an "essentialist" reading as well; but not vice versa.

"No J is B":

The "externalist" reading is "more general". If "No J is B" is true on an "essentialist" reading, then it must be true on an "externalist" reading as well; but not vice versa.

"Some J is not B":

There is partial overlap between the two senses. "Some phoenix is not a bird" is false on an "essentialist" reading but true on an "externalist" reading. "Some featherless biped is not a human" is false on an "externalist" reading but true on an "essentialist" reading. "Some animal is not a human" is true on both readings.

One might capture the two senses and their mutual relations in modern notation as follows:

"Every J is B":
"Externalist": $\exists x(Jx) \;\&\; \forall x(Jx \rightarrow Bx)$
"Essentialist": $\Diamond\exists x(Jx) \;\&\; \Box\forall x (Jx \rightarrow Bx)$

"Some J is B":
"Externalist": $\exists x(Jx \;\&\; Bx)$
"Essentialist": $\Diamond\exists x(Jx \;\&\; Bx)$

"No J is B"
"Externalist": $\sim\exists x(Jx \;\&\; Bx)$
"Essentialist": $\sim\Diamond\exists x(Jx \;\&\; Bx)$

"Some J is not B"
"Externalist": $\sim\exists x(Jx) \;v\; \exists x(Jx \;\&\; \sim Bx)$
"Essentialist": $\Box\sim\exists x(Jx) \;v\; \Diamond\exists x(Jx \;\&\; \sim Bx)$

On the proposed interpretation, a first-figure syllogism with a possibility minor is plainly invalid on an "externalist" reading of the premises:

$$\forall x(Jx \rightarrow \diamond Bx)$$
$$\underline{\forall}x(Bx \rightarrow \Box Ax)$$
$$\forall x(Jx \rightarrow \diamond Ax)$$

On an "essentialist" reading of the premises, matters are more controversial:

$$\Box\,[\forall x(Jx \rightarrow \diamond Bx)]$$
$$\Box\,[\forall x(Bx \rightarrow \Box Ax)]$$
$$\Box\,[\forall x\,(Jx \rightarrow \diamond Ax)]$$

In S5, for example, the argument can be shown to be valid:

1) $\Box\,[\forall x(Jx \rightarrow \diamond Bx)]$		Premise
2) $\Box\,[\forall x(Bx \rightarrow \Box Ax)]$		Premise
3) $\diamond\,[\exists x(Jx\ \&\ \Box\!\sim\!Ax)]$		A.I.P
--pw1		
4) $\exists x(Jx\ \&\ \Box\!\sim\!Ax)$		3
5) $Ja\ \&\ \Box\!\sim\!Aa$		Existential Instantiation
6) $\diamond Ba$		5, 1
--pw2		
7) Ba		6
8) $\Box\,Aa$		7, 2
9) $\sim\!Aa$		5

In the weaker modal logic T, step 8 of the proof is illegitimate. Premise (2) is "live" in the closest possible world (pw1) but not in the further possible world (pw2). In other words, assuming Ba to be true actually (and not just possibly) may affect the truth of the formula $\forall x(Bx \rightarrow \Box Ax)$. This mirrors closely the objection of Khūnajī and his followers to Avicenna's proof.

After the modal syllogism, the post-Avicennan handbooks typically presented the "combinatorial hypothetical syllogisms". This included syllogisms in which both premises are conditionals or disjunctions, such as the wholly hypothetical syllogism. It also included syllogisms in which one premise is a conditional or disjunction and the other a categorical proposition that shares only a term with the antecedent or consequent or one of the disjuncts. An example of the latter would be (Kātibī 1948, 161):

> Always: If Every A is B then Every J is D
> Every D is H
>
> ────────────────────────────────
>
> Always: If Every A is B then Every J is H

Such syllogisms, first discussed by Avicenna and then treated at great length by Khūnajī and his followers, invite a reconsideration of the widely held view that Frege was the first logician to combine propositional and predicate logic.

The handbooks then presented the "reiterative" (*istithnā'ī*) syllogisms: modus ponens, modus tollens and disjunctive syllogism. This was followed by brief discussions of indirect proof, composite syllogisms, induction and analogy. Equally briefly, the handbooks concluded by discussing the "matter" of the syllogism, distinguishing between demonstrative, dialectical, rhetorical, poetic and sophistical syllogisms. The space allotted to "the five arts" was meager, though, especially when compared to the extensive discussions of modal and hypothetical logic. Ibn Khaldūn's remark was apposite – interest in the later books of the *Organon* had come to an end, "as if they had never been".

3.2 ARABIC LOGIC IN THE FOURTEENTH AND FIFTEENTH CENTURIES

The revisionist, post-Avicennan logicians encountered resistance, and not only from the few remaining exponents of a more traditional Aristotelian approach such as 'Abd al-Laṭīf al-Baghdādī (d. 1231).

A number of thirteenth- and early-fourteenth-century logicians –
most prominently the great Persian polymath Naṣīr al-Dīn al-Ṭūsī
(d. 1274) and his students – launched a vigorous defense of Avicenna
against the criticisms of the revisionists (see Ṭūsī 1974; El-Rouayheb
2009, 2012; Street 2012). They defended the view that the subject
matter of logic is second intentions, not simply known concepts and
assents. They defended Aristotle's thesis that no proposition is implied by its own negation and Avicenna's position that "Always: If P
then Q" entails "Never: If P then not-Q". They insisted that contraposition as traditionally understood is perfectly valid and that the
new-fangled "contraposition" of Khūnajī and his followers is of no
use "in the sciences". They defended Avicenna's position regarding
the productivity of first-figure syllogisms with possibility minors.
They even sometimes complained, like Ibn Khaldūn, of the resolutely
formal orientation of logic after Rāzī and the resultant neglect of topics treated in the later books of the *Organon*. For example, Quṭb al-
Dīn al-Shīrāzī (d. 1311), one of Ṭūsī's eminent students, condemned
"the later logicians" for wallowing in topics that are of no use in this
world or the next, such as the immediate implications of hypotheticals and the hypothetical syllogism, while neglecting demonstration,
dialectics, fallacies, rhetoric and poetics (Shīrāzī 2002, 61).

In a sense, history was repeating itself. A century earlier, a
staunchly Aristotelian logician such as Averroes had argued force-
fully that Avicenna's departures from Aristotle were wrong-headed:
that there was no need for the combinatorial hypothetical syllogism, or the quantification of conditionals, or the distinction between *waṣfī* and *dhātī* readings of modality propositions (Street
2015, 1.4.2). But the thirteenth- and early-fourteenth-century resistance by more orthodox Avicennans to the revisionists proved more
effective than Averroes' resistance to Avicenna. It ensured that the
victory of the revisionist post-Avicennan logicians was never clear-
cut, despite the fact that they authored the standard madrasa handbooks on logic. Fourteenth-century commentators and glossators
on these handbooks often discussed the main points of contention

between the revisionists and the more orthodox Avicennans. The question of the subject matter of logic, for example, continued to be debated intensively in later centuries, with some commentators coming down on the side of Khūnajī and others coming down on the side of Avicenna. The fourth figure of the syllogism and the modal logic of the revisionists came to be broadly accepted. But Avicenna's position that "Always: If P then Q" entails "Never: If P then not-Q" was also widely accepted, and Khūnajī's questioning of this principle as well as of Aristotle's thesis was mostly abandoned. Some later logicians eirenically presented both contraposition as traditionally understood and as understood by Khūnajī and his followers as simply two distinct forms of immediate implication.

In the course of the fourteenth and fifteenth centuries, the pressure to resolve earlier disputes eased as the focus of logicians shifted noticeably. Especially in the Eastern Islamic world, commentators and glossators began to show less interest in the parts of the thirteenth-century handbooks that dealt with the relative strengths of modality propositions, their conversions and contrapositions, the immediate implications of hypotheticals, and the modal and hypothetical syllogism. Instead, they increasingly took to scrutinizing issues treated in the earlier parts of the handbooks: the definition of knowledge; the division of knowledge into conception and assent; the subject matter of logic; the question of the extramental existence of universals; the apparently paradoxical nature of the principle that one must conceive of something before making a judgment about it (since the principle "Everything that is not conceived in any way cannot be the subject of a judgment" seems precisely to be a judgment about what is not conceived); the liar paradox; whether the subject of a proposition is properly the extramental particulars or the universal nature; whether a proposition has three parts (subject, predicate and propositional nexus) or four (the three mentioned plus the assertion or negation of the propositional nexus).

This shift in focus becomes abundantly clear from the commentary tradition on two widely used Eastern handbooks of (non-elementary) logic: Kātibī's *Shamsiyyah* and Urmawī's *Maṭāliʿ al-anwār*. The most widely studied commentary on Kātibī's *Shamsiyyah* was written by Quṭb al-Dīn al-Rāzī al-Taḥtānī (d. 1365). The widely studied Gloss on Quṭb al-Dīn's commentary by al-Sayyid al-Sharīf al-Jurjānī (d. 1413) exhibits the shift in focus in stark terms. Approximately three-quarters of Jurjānī's glosses discuss passages in Quṭb al-Dīn's commentary dealing with preliminary matters and conceptions, and less than 10 percent discuss the sections on the immediate implications of propositions and the formal syllogism (Jurjānī 1948). Jurjānī's Gloss in turn became the subject of numerous super-glosses by fifteenth-century scholars (Wisnovsky 2004, 163–164) – glosses that further discussed points raised in Jurjānī's glosses, thus sharing and reinforcing the emphasis on the earlier parts of Quṭb al-Dīn's commentary.

The commentary tradition on Urmawī's *Maṭāliʿ* reveals a very similar trend. Again, the most widely studied commentary on Urmawī's handbook was authored by Quṭb al-Dīn al-Rāzī al-Taḥtānī. Quṭb al-Dīn still engaged at length with the later sections of Urmawī's handbook dealing with conversion, contraposition, the immediate implications of hypotheticals, and the modal and hypothetical syllogistic. But the subsequent glossators on the commentary simply ignored those sections. The widely studied Gloss on Quṭb al-Dīn's commentary by – again – al-Sayyid al-Sharīf al-Jurjānī only covered the early sections dealing with preliminary matters, the five predicables and the acquisition of conceptions (Jurjānī 1861). Yet again, Jurjānī's Gloss elicited a glut of super-glosses in the course of the fifteenth century (Wisnovsky 2004, 165–166). By contrast, the later parts of Quṭb al-Dīn's commentary dealing with contradiction, conversion, contraposition, the immediate implications of hypotheticals, and the modal and hypothetical syllogisms appear not to have elicited any gloss in later centuries.

A slightly later handbook of logic that came to be widely studied in subsequent centuries is *Tahdhīb al-manṭiq* by the fourteenth-century scholar Saʿd al-Dīn al-Taftāzānī (d. 1390). A commentary on this handbook by the Persian scholar Jalāl al-Dīn al-Dawānī (d. 1502) was arguably one of the most influential works on logic written in Arabic in the fifteenth century, eliciting numerous glosses and super-glosses in later centuries by scholars throughout Ottoman Turkey, Safavid Persia, and Mughal India (Wisnovsky 2004, 166–167). This work too illustrates the extent to which the focus of logicians in the Eastern Islamic world had shifted since the thirteenth century. Dawānī's probing and demanding commentary is incomplete and only covers the sections of the handbook dealing with preliminary matters, the five predicables, definition, and propositions. It ends before the sections dealing with contradiction, conversion, contraposition, and syllogism (Dawānī 1887).

Alongside the shift in focus there occurred a shift in literary form. After around 1300, independent summas became rare, and the prevalent format for extended writing on logic became the commentary (sharḥ) and the gloss (ḥāshiyah). In the pioneering surveys of Arabic logic by Ibrahim Madkour and Nicholas Rescher, this shift was decried on the assumption that a commentary or gloss is invariably limited to pedantic and unoriginal explication of received views (Rescher 1964, 73–82; Madkour 1969, 240–248). In recent decades, this sweeping (and largely armchair) evaluation has been questioned, and it is now recognized that commentators and glossators, though they were expected to be charitable towards the work they were discussing, often felt free to raise objections, depart from received views, and engage in controversies with other commentators or glossators. Arabic logic in later centuries remains severely under-researched, but a few examples should suffice to show that later works should not be dismissed out of hand as mere "commentary mongering".

The first two examples derive from the far-ranging and as yet little-studied controversies between Ṣadr al-Dīn al-Dashtakī (d. 1498) and the just-mentioned Jalāl al-Dīn al-Dawānī, both active in Shiraz in Persia. (For an overview of the lives, works, and rivalry between these two scholars, see Pourjavady 2011, 4–24.) In both cases, the controversy led to unprecedentedly intense scrutiny of a number of logical problems. The first controversy concerns the relational syllogism (El-Rouayheb 2010a, 92–104). A standard handbook on philosophical theology had presented the principle that a middle term in a demonstration can both be the cause of the major term being true of the minor term and an effect of the major term. The following syllogism was given as an example:

> The world is composite
> To every composite there is a composer
>
> _____
>
> To the world there is a composer

Here, the major term "composer" is a "cause" of the middle term "composite", and the middle term is a "cause" of the major being true of the minor. The problem is that the syllogism does not obviously have a middle term since the predicate of the minor is "composite" whereas the subject of the major is "to the composite". It may be tempting to reformulate the major as: "Every composite has a composer". But thus regimented the syllogism ceases to illustrate the principle in question, since the major term is now "has a composer" which is not obviously a "cause" of the middle term "composite". The problem led Dawānī, in a Gloss on the mentioned handbook, to suggest that regimentation is unnecessary. He argued that a middle term can recur "with addition" and "with subtraction" without this impugning the syllogistic implication of the conclusion. An example of a middle term recurring "with addition" is the original problematic syllogism:

> The world is composite
> To every composite there is a composer
>
> _____
>
> To the world there is a composer

In this example, the middle term is "composite" and recurs in the second premise with the addition of the preposition "to" (li-). As an example of a middle term recurring "with subtraction", Dawānī mentioned the following:

> Zayd is the brother of ʿAmr
> ʿAmr is the leader of the town
>
> ───────────────────────────
>
> Zayd is the brother of the leader of the town

Here, "brother of ʿAmr" is the predicate of the minor premise, and "ʿAmr" alone is the subject of the major.

Dawānī's position was rejected by Ṣadr al-Dīn al-Dashtakī, who pressed the point that the necessity of the recurrence of a middle term is a proven principle of logic and that it would not do to cast doubt on this principle merely by giving examples and claiming that they are productive. He challenged Dawānī to "prove the productivity" of the adduced arguments in which the middle term recurs with addition or subtraction "in a universal manner", as opposed to just giving examples. This would seem to be a fair point, but it was also a tall order for such a "proof" would have involved the construction of a new logic that would be able to formalize and validate arguments that depend on the properties of relations. Dawānī seems to have thought that the inferences in question were self-evidently productive, and hence not in need of proof. However, he was impelled by the polemical context to say more than this. He insisted that there was no proof that the middle term cannot recur with omission or addition, and added that in such cases:

> If we – in the form of addition or subtraction – take care to omit the recurrent part [of the middle term] and transfer the judgment to the minor in the manner that it is true of the middle, then productivity certainly does not fail to follow.

Dawānī's remarks at this point echo that of standard handbook explanations of why first-figure syllogisms are productive if and only if the minor premise is affirmative and the major premise universal.

Consider the argument that was at the center of the discussion in the regimented form preferred by Dashtakī:

> The world is composite
> Every composite has a composer
>
> ———————————————
>
> The world has a composer

In Quṭb al-Dīn al-Rāzī's standard commentary on Kātibī's *Shamsiyyah*, such a first-figure syllogism is shown to be productive because (i) the minor premise is affirmative, which results in the "subsumption" of the minor term "world" under the middle-term "composite", and (ii) the major premise is universal, which means that the judgment is about *every* composite thing, and hence the judgment "transmits" to the minor that is subsumed under the middle. Dawānī obviously availed himself of this manner of showing or displaying (as opposed to strictly proving) the productivity of a first-figure syllogism, and adapted it to the case of the major premise being a relational proposition. Consider the same argument *before* the suggested regimentation:

> The world is composite
> To every composite there is a composer
>
> ———————————————
>
> To the world there is a composer

The second premise is not a straightforward subject–predicate proposition. The way in which Dawānī expressed this point is by saying that "composer" is not true of "composite" in a predication of the type "that is that", but in a predication of the type "that is possessed of that". By leaving out the middle term "composite", the major term "composer" is shown to be true in this same manner of the minor term "world".

Another controversy between Dawānī and Dashtakī concerned the liar paradox. The paradox had been known to some early Islamic theologians and had begun to attract the attention of logicians in the thirteenth century (Alwishah and Sanson 2009). The debates between

Dashtakī and Dawānī led to the most sustained examinations of this problem in the Arabic-Islamic tradition, with numerous treatises and counter-treatises written by the two rivals and their students (see the texts edited in Qaramaleki 2007; Miller 1985 is an earlier discussion of this controversy, based on a more restricted textual basis). In his Gloss on the aforementioned handbook on philosophical theology, Dashtakī had raised the issue as a problem for the received view that every proposition is either true or false (Qaramaleki 2007, 3–15). He presented and found fault with the suggested solutions of thirteenth- and fourteenth-century logicians, and then presented his own solution, which runs as follows: Truth and falsity are only applicable to statements. Only if Zayd makes a statement (*khabar*) can we say that this statement is true or false. A reiteration of the truth or falsity predicate requires a further statement, *viz.* "Zayd's statement is true (or false)". Otherwise, we would have one statement and two applications of the truth or falsity predicate, resulting in badly formed sentences such as:

Zayd's statement is true (or false) is true (or false)

as opposed to the well-formed:

"Zayd's statement is true (or false)" is true (or false)

In the case of "My statement now is false", we have one statement (the one picked out by the subject term "My statement now") and one application of the predicate "false". There are, *ex hypothesi*, no further assertions and therefore no grounds for reiterating the truth or falsity predicate and describing "My statement now is false" as either true or false.

Dawānī rejected this proposed solution (Qaramaleki 2007, 78–92). An affirmative proposition is false, or so Arabic logicians tended to believe, if the subject term is empty. But this implies that the statement "Zayd's statement is false (or true)" is false if Zayd has not made any statement. It is simply not the case that Zayd must make a statement for us to apply the truth or falsity predicate. Nor do we require another statement to reiterate these predicates. If, as

Dashtakī supposes, there is no such statement as "Zayd's statement is false" then pronouncing that non-existing statement true or false would be false. Moreover, Dawānī added, in the case of the problematic sentence "My statement now is false", the subject term is *not* empty, and the whole proposition falls under it. And if the proposition says of itself that it is false and yet on Dashtakī's account is neither false nor true, then it states something to be the case that is not the case, and hence it should surely be considered false.

Dawānī's own proposed solution to the liar paradox is that the offending sentence "My statement now is false" is not a proposition. This is because a proposition must relate an independent state of affairs. A categorical proposition signifies that a certain nexus (*nisba*) obtains between a subject and a predicate. It is precisely by virtue of this that a proposition is a candidate for truth or falsity – if the nexus in the judgment corresponds to the nexus that actually does obtain between subject and predicate then the proposition is true, otherwise it is false. The offending sentence "My statement now is false" does not relate that a certain subject–predicate nexus obtains beyond itself; rather it relates that it is itself false. This self-reference can be direct, as in the case of "My statement now is false" or it can be indirect as in the case of saying today "What I will say tomorrow is false" and then saying tomorrow "What I said yesterday is true". In either case, there is no distinction between the nexus in the judgment itself and the nexus that obtains apart from the judgment. Since such a distinction is essential to being a proposition, the offending sentence is not a proposition, even though it may superficially have propositional form. The case is analogous to performative utterances such as "I hereby sell you *x*" – here too the sentence superficially resembles a proposition but does not relate that an independent nexus obtains.

Dawānī's proposed solution is reminiscent of that advanced by Ṭūsī in the thirteenth century, *viz.* that propositions are only candidates for truth or falsity if they are not self-referential. (For Ṭūsī's account, see Alwishah and Sanson 2009, 113–123.) But Dawānī explicitly rejected that position on the ground that not all cases of self-reference are paradoxical. For example, one might truthfully say, "My statement now is a complex utterance". One might also truthfully say, "Every proposition is either true or false", even though this judgment applies to itself. In both these cases, one can still draw a distinction between the subject–predicate nexus in the mind and the subject–predicate nexus outside the mind. The paradox only arises in the case of a sentence ascribing truth or falsity to itself, since it thereby nullifies what makes a sentence a proposition.

The third, and final, example comes from the opposite end of the Islamic world. The commentary by Muḥammad ibn Yūsuf al-Sanūsī (d. 1490) from Tlemcen (in modern-day Algeria) on his own handbook *Mukhtaṣar al-manṭiq* was, along with Dawānī's commentary on *Tahdhīb al-manṭiq*, the most influential Arabic work on logic from the fifteenth century, eliciting numerous commentaries and glosses by later North African logicians (Wisnovsky 2004, 168). In North Africa, the shift away from discussing formal proofs towards discussing semantic and philosophical issues was much less noticeable than in the Eastern Islamic world. Sanūsī was still primarily interested in formal inferences, and half of his handbook is devoted to discussing contradiction, conversion, contraposition, the immediate implications of hypotheticals, and the syllogism. Of particular interest is the relatively lengthy section devoted to the immediate implications of hypotheticals, in which Sanūsī gathered principles that earlier handbooks had tended to disperse throughout the sections on hypotheticals, on conversion and contraposition, and on the hypothetical syllogism (Sanūsī 1875, 82–88). This is all the more remarkable given that Eastern logicians had largely lost interest in this topic by Sanūsī's time. The immediate implications of conditionals and disjunctions presented and proved in Sanūsī's handbook are given in Table 3.1.

3.3   ARABIC LOGIC IN LATER CENTURIES

In Islamic intellectual history, the fifteenth and sixteenth centuries did not constitute in any obvious sense a turning point or the end of an age. The tradition of Arabic logic continued well into what

Table 3.1[2] *The immediate implications of conditionals and disjunctions*

1.1	If P then (Q & R) $\Rightarrow$ If P then Q; If P then R
1.2	If (P & Q) then R $\nRightarrow$ If P then R; If Q then R
1.3.1	P & (Q & R) $\Rightarrow$ P & Q; P & R
1.3.2	(P & Q) & R $\Rightarrow$ P & R; Q & R
1.4.1	P or (Q & R) $\Rightarrow$ P or Q; P or R
1.4.2	(P & Q) or R $\Rightarrow$ P or R; Q or R
1.5.1	Not both P and (Q & R) $\nRightarrow$ Not both P and Q; Not both P and R
1.5.2	Not both (P & Q) and R $\nRightarrow$ Not both P and R; Not both Q and R
1.6.1	Not: If P then (Q & R) $\nRightarrow$ Not: If P then Q; Not: If P then R
1.6.2	Not: If (P & Q) then R $\Rightarrow$ Not: If P then R; Not: If Q then R
1.6.3.1	Not: P and (Q & R) $\nRightarrow$ Not: P and Q; Not: P and R
1.6.3.2	Not: (P & Q) and R $\nRightarrow$ Not: P and R; Not: Q and R
1.6.4.1	Not: P or (Q & R) $\nRightarrow$ Not: P or Q; Not: P or R
1.6.4.2	Not: (P & Q) or R $\nRightarrow$ Not: P or R; Not: Q or R
1.6.5.1	Both P and (Q & R) $\Rightarrow$ Both P and Q; Both P and R
1.6.5.2	Both (P & Q) and R $\Rightarrow$ Both P and R; Both Q and R
2.1	If P then Q $\Rightarrow$ Not: If P then not-Q
2.2	Not: If P then Q $\Rightarrow$ If P then not-Q
3.1	If P then Q $\Rightarrow$ Not both P and not-Q
3.2	If P then Q $\Rightarrow$ Either not-P or Q
3.3.1	Not both P and Q $\Rightarrow$ If P then not-Q; If Q then not-P
3.3.2	Either P or Q $\Rightarrow$ If not-P then Q; If not-Q then P
4	(Either P or Q) & (Not both P and Q) $\Rightarrow$ If not-P then Q; If not-Q then P; If P then not-Q; If Q then not-P

[2] I have tried to keep the symbolism minimal and self-explanatory, but just to be sure: The symbol $\Rightarrow$ stands for "entails", and the symbol $\nRightarrow$ stands for "does not entail". The capital letters P, Q, and R are propositional variables standing for arbitrary propositions (such as "Every human is an animal" or "It is sunny"), whereas the capital letters A, B, and C are term variables standing for arbitrary terms (such as "human", "animal", or "sunny"). Brackets are used to disambiguate complex sentences. A semicolon (;) is used to separate independent propositions; for example, the semicolon in (1.1) indicates that two separate propositions are entailed by what is to the left of the $\Rightarrow$. I have used the symbol & to render the extensional (or truth-functional) conjunction, i.e. a conjunction whose truth is determined entirely by the truth of its conjuncts. I use "and" for intensional (or non-truth-functional) conjunctions, as in the case of the exclusive disjunction of the "oppositional" (*ʿinādī*) type.

Table 3.1 (*cont.*)

5.1.1	If P then Q ⇒ Not: Not both P and Q
5.1.2	If P then Q ⇒ Not: Either P or Q
5.1.3	(Not both P and Q) & (Not: Either P or Q) ⇒ Not: If P then Q; Not: If Q then P
5.1.4	(Either P or Q) & (Not: Not both P and Q) ⇒ Not: If P then Q; Not: If Q then P
5.2.1	Not: If P then Q ⇏ Not both P and Q
5.2.2	Not: If P then Q ⇏ Either P or Q
5.2.3	Not: Not both P and Q ⇏ If P then Q
5.2.4	Not: Not both P and Q ⇏ Either P or Q
5.2.5	Not: Either P or Q ⇏ If P then Q
5.2.6	Not: Either P or Q ⇏ Not both P or Q
6.1.1	Not both P and Q ⇒ Either not-P or not-Q
6.1.2	Either P or Q ⇒ Not both not-P and not-Q
7.1	Always: If Some A is B then Q ⇒ Always: If Every A is B then Q
7.2	Always: If P then Every A is B ⇒ Always: If P then Some A is B
7.3.1	Sometimes not: If Every A is B then Q ⇒ Sometimes not: If Some A is B then Q
7.3.2	Sometimes not: If P then Some A is B ⇒ Sometimes not: If P then Every A is B
7.4.1	Sometimes: If Every A is B then Q ⇒ Sometimes: If Some A is B then Q
7.4.2	Sometimes: If P then Every A is B ⇒ Sometimes: If P then Some A is B
7.5.1	Never: If Some A is B then Q ⇒ Never: If Every A is B then Q
7.5.2	Never: If P then Some A is B ⇒ Never: If P then Every A is B

Europeans would call the "Early Modern" period. North African logicians of the seventeenth and eighteenth centuries, for example, continued to discuss the immediate implications of hypotheticals presented by Sanūsī. Ottoman Turkish logicians of the same centuries took up Dawānī's point about relational syllogisms, dubbing them "unfamiliar syllogisms" and dividing them into figures and moods. In Ottoman Turkey and Mughal India, new and sometimes innovative handbooks on logic were written and commented upon. In Safavid Iran, some logicians came to dismiss practically all aspects of post-Avicennan logic and sought to return to the views of "the older logicians": Avicenna himself and even Aristotle (as presented in Averroes' *Middle Commentaries*). Also in the seventeenth and eighteenth centuries, Maronite and Greek Catholic Christians from Lebanon and Syria produced sometimes lengthy Arabic works on logic showing the influence of the Latin tradition. But further discussion of these developments belongs in a different volume – perhaps a *Cambridge Companion to Early Modern Logic*.[3]

[3] I would like to thank Wilfrid Hodges, Stephen Read, and Paul Thom for helpful comments on a draft of this chapter. Responsibility for remaining shortcomings is mine alone.

4 Latin Logic up to 1200

Ian Wilks

In this chapter, we review the earliest phase of medieval logic in the Latin West, from its modest first beginnings in the eighth century to its full elaboration as a subject field in the twelfth. The manuscript evidence from this extended era is incomplete, and often in a preliminary state of scholarly consolidation; so the historical account based on these materials is necessarily limited. Indeed, the very attempt to construct hypotheses about lineage and association may prove counter-productive in some cases, especially in the period prior to the eleventh century. In the eighth and ninth centuries the approach to logic in the Latin West is largely Platonist and metaphysical in character. This subsequently gives way to a more linguistically oriented study, in which we find the onset of creative investigation into inferential relations between categorical and hypothetical statements, and (somewhat later) into sentential relations between subjects and predicates. St. Anselm in the eleventh century is an eminent contributor to this tradition, followed by Peter Abelard and other notable masters of the twelfth-century Logico-Philosophical Schools (such as Gilbert of Poitiers). This final century is shaped by the vocalist/nominalist controversies, and by the recovery of major logical works of Aristotle; it is a time of great ferment.

4.1 LATE EIGHTH- AND NINTH-CENTURY PRECURSORS

The medieval era's productive involvement in the field of logic begins with the educational reforms of the Carolingian period. Alcuin of York (c. 720–806) is the central figure in these reforms. After a period of study in York, Alcuin was invited by Charlemagne to teach at the Carolingian court in Aachen in the late eighth century. He used his formidable influence as an advocate for the arts of the Trivium: grammar, rhetoric and logic. Among his many writings, we find separate treatises on each of these subjects; among these, the one on logic – *De dialectica* – has some claim to being the point of departure for medieval work in Latin in this area.

This treatise is a brief conspectus of the field of logic as it was understood in Alcuin's time. There is not much addition to knowledge attempted here (and indeed, the text itself is largely copied from sections of Isodore's *Etymologiae*, which themselves derive from Cassiodorus' *Institutiones*[1]); the point is simply to identify the divisions of logic and indicate the content of each. The layout of this text says a great deal about the state of the field at this time. The first chapter is introductory, and the second is about the *Isagoge*; the next nine chapters then focus on the *Categories* (more specifically, on the *Categoriae decem*, an anonymous paraphrase of that text[2]). Five additional chapters – one about syllogistic theory, two about definition, and one each about topical theory and *On Interpretation* – round out the work. A notable feature of this layout is the amount of attention paid to the very metaphysically oriented material from the *Categories*, compared to the other subject areas handled in the treatise (Alcuin 1863, 954D–964C). By contrast, the most technical aspects of logical theory are covered cursorily in the single chapter on syllogistic theory; logical oppositeness between statements and syllogistic reasoning are indeed treated, for example, but with no specific mention of the Square of Opposition or the forms and figures of the categorical syllogism (Alcuin 1863, 964C–966C).

This is entirely emblematic of the earliest medieval approach to logic; there is interest in the whole range of inherited writings, but the material with strong metaphysical associations is that most likely to be subject to elaboration. This tendency is evident in a set of fragments emanating from Alcuin's circle, collectively referred to

---

[1] Lewry 1981c, 90–91; Marenbon 2000c, 607–608.

[2] The paraphrase was at this time wrongly attributed to St. Augustine; it likely derives from the school of the fourth-century Aristotelian commentator Themistius (Marenbon 2008, 5). John Scottus Eriugena is likewise chiefly familiar with *Categories* doctrine through this paraphrase.

as "The Munich Passages" (Marenbon 1981, 30–55). In places, these fragments display technical competence in logical techniques by the presence of arguments cast explicitly in syllogistic format (v, vi and xi: Marenbon 1981, 53). But anything like original development of theory occurs only when discussion turns to the categories, where one fragment discusses the inapplicability of these to the divine, and two others provide commentary on the categories of place and time (Marenbon 1981, 53).[3]

By far the era's most accomplished practitioner of logic as so conceived is John Scottus Eriugena (c. 800/815–c. 877). Born in Ireland, where he studied, he succeeded Alcuin and became a dominant figure at the Palace School of Charles the Bald in France. The metaphysical viewpoint from which Eriugena is operating posits a source of all being, understood as the divine, and expresses its causal relation to the multiplicity of created things as a kind of emanation. Created beings emanate *from* the source of all being, and at the same time are directed *back to* it as the goal or ideal towards which their natures strive. These two, oppositely directed relations are captured respectively in the images of procession and return. For Eriugena and those influenced by him, the analytic tool deemed most helpful in spelling out the image of procession is the logical idea of division: "descent from the most general to the most specific" (Eriugena 1996–2003, 2: 526B).[4] For the image of return, Eriugena employs a corresponding notion of "recollection, which is like a return back, starting from the most specific and ascending to the most general" (Eriugena 1996–2003, 2: 526B). Putting this less abstractly, the method is essentially one of classification, the point of which is to show how broader kinds diversify into narrower ones, and how the narrower ones in turn range themselves under the broader. This notion of method readily motivates a definition of the field as a whole in terms of the doctrine of the *Categories*; referring to the ten

---

[3] An edition of these "Munich Passages" is found in Marenbon 1981, 151–166.

[4] Translations are from Eriugena 1987, referenced by PL number.

genera treated in that work, Eriugena describes the function of logic as being to "break down these genera into their subdivisions from the most general to the most specific, and to collect them together again from the most specific to the most general" (Eriugena 1996–2003, 1: 463B). The ensuing elaboration of *Categories* material in the first book of the *Periphyseon* to clarify the accompanying metaphysical constructions of this work could therefore seem to someone of this time to be expressing core insights of logic. An example would be Eriugena's account of predication, in which he argues for the essential logical sameness of the subject of a statement and its predicate. To some, 'Cicero' in 'Cicero is a man' might seem to pick out a kind of substance – an individual one – fundamentally different from the one picked out by 'man'. But not so, according to Eriugena: the species man is itself an individual too, even though distributed among Cicero and other men. Individuals like Cicero and other men can themselves all be construed as "an indivisible unity in the species" (Eriugena 1996–2003, 1: 470D). So subject and predicate in 'Cicero is a man' do not differentiate as picking out an individual on the one hand and a species on the other because the very distinction between individual and species is not so straightforward. The relation of predication must be understood accordingly.[5]

Note that, as we find in the Munich Passages, some parts of Eriugena's presentation also give us arguments explicitly cast in syllogistic format, either categorical (as in 489C–D) or hypothetical (491C–492A). The tradition represented by Alcuin and Eriugena is familiar with a wide range of logical materials; but even so, its creative energies seem mainly trained on issues arising from the doctrine of division. This tendency continues after Eriugena – as witnessed, for example, in the writings of intellectual followers like Heiric of Auxerre (841–876/877) and Remigius of Auxerre (c. 841–908) (Lewry 1981c, 93; Marenbon 1981, 116–138). But it does not represent a paradigm for subsequent eras in medieval logic, which for the most part

---

[5] For Eriugenean logical theory, see Erismann 2007 and Marenbon 2008, 27–34.

develop the subject along technical, linguistic lines quite removed from these metaphysical researches.

4.2 LATE NINTH-CENTURY, TENTH-CENTURY AND EARLY ELEVENTH-CENTURY TRANSITIONS

This technical, linguistic development is slow to unfold in the decades from the ninth to the eleventh centuries. It is seen in the gradual growth of a commentary tradition on various canonical texts of logic. It is also seen in the emergence of a small number of logic treatises which attempt to gather and arrange the ancient doctrine emerging from these works, as Alcuin had done before.

None of those texts initially studied in the commentary tradition are, surprisingly, by Aristotle. The anonymous *Categoriae decem* continues to be a surrogate for the *Categories*, as does Apuleius' *Periermeneias* for *On Interpretation* and *Prior Analytics*. Other canonical texts for logicians at this time are Porphyry's *Isagoge*, Book IV from Martianus Capella's *De nuptiis Philologiae et Mercurii*, Augustine's *De dialectica*, Cicero's *Topics*, and the above-noted *De dialectica* of Alcuin (Marenbon 2000b, 78); special attention is paid to *Categoriae decem*, the *Isagoge* and the excerpt from *De nuptiis Philologiae* (Marenbon 2008, 34). Throughout this period, commentary takes the form of interlinear and marginal jottings added directly to existing manuscripts; independent, continuous commentaries in the field of logic become common only in the twelfth century. Given the fragmentary, unsystematic and anonymous character of these additions, it is difficult to chart a history of the gloss tradition they comprise. But John Marenbon does report an impression "of a gradual turning away from extrinsic theological and metaphysical concerns and an attempt to understand the letter of the text" (Marenbon 2008, 36).

This impression of greater attention to detail is further confirmed when we examine logic treatises from the late ninth century on. An early specimen is the anonymous *Dialectica* from the Abbey of St. Gall, dated to the latter half of the ninth century (De Rijk 1963,

83). It is around the same length as Alcuin's *De dialectica* and is clearly intended to serve a parallel purpose: to provide a pedagogically accessible conspectus of known theory. But there are marked differences of approach. Gone is the overwhelming emphasis on *Categories* material; the relevant section is scaled back to approximate parity with the other sections. A curious feature of Alcuin's work is the placement of material from *On Interpretation* at the very end of the treatise, like a footnote or addendum (Alcuin 1863, 972C-976A). In the anonymous *Dialectica*, it finds its canonical place, after the *Categories* and before the material on syllogisms, giving correspondingly greater emphasis to its importance as a preparatory step for that material (Anonymous 1882, lx–lxiii). This work drops the section on definition found in Alcuin's work, and gives a much fuller account of the Square of Opposition and the figures (although still not the modes) of syllogistic reasoning. As rudimentary as this discussion is, it displays a conception of logic which no longer regards material on division of genus and species as its absolute centerpiece.

There is a later treatise from the tradition of St. Gall, *De syllogismis* of Notker Labeo (c. 950–1022), a Benedictine monk who entered the Abbey of St. Gall (then an independent principality in what is now Switzerland) at an early age. His treatise exemplifies a further stage in the technical presentation of the subject by eschewing the commentary-on-multiple-works format, and attempting only a focused discussion of syllogisms, both categorical and hypothetical. Notker works through these with methodical efficiency, carefully defining and exemplifying each of the nineteen modes of categorical and seven modes of hypothetical. Already we can see in his discussion sensitivity to what will become a major issue in medieval logic: the relation between the topics and hypothetical syllogisms. Following a tradition that seems to begin with Cicero, the anonymous *Dialectica* mentioned above lists three of the modes of hypothetical syllogism – including modus ponens and modus tollens – as topics (Anonymous 1882, lxvii–lxviii; Green-Pedersen 1984, 140). The problem is that, as logical devices go, hypothetical syllogisms achieve a level of demonstrative necessity absent from the general run of topics, which present themselves rather as informal techniques of argument formation. The medieval tradition must ultimately loosen this linkage of hypothetical syllogisms with topics; Notker takes the early step of at least acknowledging a difference within the family of topics between those giving rise to necessity by being connected with hypothetical syllogisms, and all the others from the traditional list (Notker 1882, 619; Green-Pedersen 1984, 142). In another area, by contrast, he is not so forward-looking. It is some time in the medieval tradition before a full understanding is gained of how to negate an 'if ... then' statement. The presumption is inherited from Boethius that negating a conditional is a matter of negating its consequent (Martin 1991). Notker accepts this to the point of believing that 'It is not the case that if it is day it is not light' is just a doubly-negated equivalent of 'If it is day it is light' (Notker 1882, 612–613; Marenbon 2008, 40). It will not be until much later that this issue is better understood.

One of the great engines of change for logical theory at this time was the slow but continuous emergence of Boethius' translations of the *Isagoge*, *Categories* and *On Interpretation*, and his commentaries on these works. Just as influential were his treatises on the topics, categorical syllogisms and hypothetical syllogisms: *De differentiis topicis*, *De syllogismis categoricis* and *De syllogismis hypotheticis* (Lewry 1981c, 95–96; Marenbon 2008, 38–39). The influence of Boethius continued to increase from this era until well into the twelfth century and was already quite pronounced in the work of Abbo of Fleury (c. 945–1004). Abbo was born near Orléans and entered the Benedictine abbey of Fleury, later studying in Paris and at Reims. His *Syllogismorum categoricorum et hypotheticorum enodatio* is a treatise like Notker's, specifically directed to the presentation of syllogistic theory. But it is considerably more technical in quality; its pages are dominated by long, orderly lists of examples with rather limited supporting commentary. We find no less than ninety distinct examples of the Square of Opposition, each generated from the fragment 'Every man is ...'

by substituting into it different kinds of predicate: one substituted predicate involves an inseparable accident present in all and only men ('Every man is capable of laughter'), another a genus present in all but not only men ('Every man is an animal'), another an accident present in only some but not all men ('Every man is musical'), and so on (Abbo 1966, 34–35). The ninety squares then arise by applying negations in the usual way. The goal seems to be to exemplify all interesting conceptual possibilities for how the square may be instantiated; a parallel program of wide-ranging exemplification is attempted for the hypothetical syllogistic as well. Abbo draws heavily on Boethius' *De Syllogismis* (Lewry 1981c, 97) and is at pains to distinguish the formulations found in that source from alternatives in Apuleius' *Perihermeneias* – as when, for example, he includes beside a diagram of the Aristotelian Square of Opposition another diagram of the differently labelled Apuleian square (Abbo 1966, 34). Abbo's heavy debt to Boethian theory is equally evident in his treatment of hypothetical syllogisms, both for good and ill. One area which reveals independence of mind is his treatment of the relation between topics and syllogisms; as with Notker, and many medieval logicians to come, Abbo is eager to cast some light on this relation. The claim he takes up in his treatise is that all syllogisms, categorical included, ultimately have dependence upon topics as providing confirmation for premises. This is because they all potentially have premises about which doubts may be entertained, and may therefore appear in a weakened state; it is through the topics that this potential failing is addressed (Abbo 1966, 50, 64 and 86–87; Green-Pedersen 1984, 144).

4.3   LATER ELEVENTH CENTURY

We now pass to an era of greater fecundity in the formation of logical theory. Three works will serve here to represent the time: *De grammatico* of St. Anselm (1033–1109); the *Introductiones dialecticae secundum Wilgelmum*, from the school of William of Champeaux (c. 1070–1121); and *Dialectica* of Garlandus (c. 1100).

Anselm was born in Italy and became a pupil of Lanfranc at the Benedictine abbey at Bec in Normandy. His *De grammatico* is the most idiosyncratic work of any treated in this chapter. It is not in any sense a survey of logic in general, but rather a focused discussion of one specific problem connected with the Aristotelian discussion of denominatives (or "paronyms"; see *Categories* 1a12). A denominative is an adjective that is inflectively related to some name; 'brave' is the denominative arising from 'bravery,' for instance.[6] Now bravery is obviously a quality, and the word 'bravery' obviously signifies that quality – in other words, it prompts a representation of that quality in the mind of the hearer. But the related word 'brave' seems to work differently. We use it to call a person brave, and in that case we do not just mean to signify bravery, although that is part of what we do; we also use it in some way to refer to the person. So there seems to be some other aspect of meaning exhibited by a denominative that is not present in the name from which it derives. This is the central issue of *De grammatico*, and through it Anselm launches an inquiry into the semantics of naming.[7] The upshot of the inquiry is to establish that something other than the direct signification of a name often contributes to meaning; this other contributor is what he calls "appellation", which works like reference, and is, more precisely, the kind of reference something acquires in a particular context of use (Henry 1964, 69).[8] The denominative 'brave' not only signifies bravery; it also appellates the persons possessing that quality. So we can say this: both the name and the denominative directly (*per se*) signify bravery, in that both prompt a representation of bravery in the mind of the hearer. But the denominative also possesses an indirect (*per*

---

[6] I follow Peter King's (2004, 92) practice of using 'bravery'/'brave' to illustrate Anselm's argument. Henry (1964, 91–94) discusses the difficulty of translating Anselm's own preferred example, *grammaticus*.

[7] Note that Anselm formulates the problem as a metaphysical one: whether (to state the point in terms of the example before us) bravery is a substance or a quality (Henry 1964, 49). His subsequent discussion of signification and appellation makes plain the semantic implications of his response.

[8] For caveats on using the notion of reference to understand Anselm on this point, see King 2004, 93 and Marenbon 2008, 53.

aliud) signification of something else, in that it prompts a representation of brave *persons*. The effect of Anselm's analysis is to expose
this distinction, which remains a staple of medieval semantic theory
through subsequent centuries.

The above explanation gives only the barest hint of what is
achieved in *De grammatico*, which takes a winding path to its objec-
tives and canvasses many technical points along the way. Note that
Anselm, like Alcuin and Eriugena, is mainly dealing with material
from the *Categories*. But the material on denominatives that Anselm
exploits is among the least metaphysically entangled of that work. In
the background here are powerful grammatical influences stemming
from the writings of Priscian (c. 500), whose expansive *Institutiones
grammaticae* was a basis for grammatical study of the Latin language throughout the period covered by this chapter. Alcuin wrote
a commentary on it, as did Eriugena, and a heavily annotated manuscript of this work is associated with the monastic community of
St. Gall. But it is in the eleventh century that grammatical studies
really show a pervasive effect on the field of logic (De Rijk 1962–
1967, II.1.97). One view of Priscian's is particularly relevant here:
that a name not only signifies a substance, but also signifies some
quality possessed by the substance (Priscian 1961, II.53) – a view from
which Anselm's analysis of denominatives clearly derives. Aristotle's
competing claim is that what a name signifies is not twofold at all;
it appeals only to the conception generated in the mind of the hearer.
Anselm's account of the semantics of naming reflects the consolidation of new factors in the discussion, thus anticipating a new trend
to come.

Introductiones dialecticae secundum Wilgelmum is closely
associated with the influential William of Champeaux (1070–
1122), either as a personal literary product or a record of his
teaching.[9] William was the head of the school of the cathedral of

---

[9] For what is known of the historical circumstances of this text, see De Rijk 1962–
1967, II.1.145; Iwakuma 1993, 45–50; and Iwakuma 2003, 3–5.

Notre Dame in Paris, later the founder of the abbey of St. Victor, and is now famous, among other things, for heated disputes with his former pupil Peter Abelard. This treatise does not manifest the same richness of semantic theory as *De grammatico*, but it is quite forward-looking as an early template for logic treatises in coming decades. The ambition is to cover the whole range of logic in a short space (like Alcuin and the author of the anonymous St. Gall *Dialectica*), not just the part of it most relevant to syllogisms (like Abbo of Fleury). But the ambition is also to organize the presentation as thoroughly as possible after the manner employed by Aristotle in *On Interpretation*, and put on full display by Boethius in his commentaries. Without the assumptions about the centrality of metaphysical doctrine in logic, it becomes intuitive to see syllogisms as constructs out of words that themselves have a basis in physical sound. So physical sound becomes the starting point for the *Introductiones*. In the ensuing expository path, vocal sounds (*voces*) are distinguished from non-vocal, conventional vocal sounds are distinguished from non-conventional ones, and names, verbs and phrases (*orationes*) are then defined as significative, conventional, vocal sounds (Iwakuma 1993, 57–58). This Aristotelian/Boethian definitory sequence becomes a staple element of logic treatises well beyond the twelfth century, as do subsequent steps from the complete phrase (*oratio perfecta*) to the definition of a statement, and thence to the distinction between its hypothetical and categorical varieties. Other basic notions that will come to achieve importance appear in turn. The distinction between first and second imposition is canvassed – in other words, the distinction (respectively) between names that apply to things in general, and the specialized names used in logic and grammar that apply to other words (Iwakuma 1993, 64). The quantifiers are singled out for description, and indefinite cases, ambiguous between the universal and particular forms, are highlighted (Iwakuma 1993, 64). Perhaps most notably, we find the negated forms of conditionals correctly identified as involving the application of the negating sign to the sentence as a whole ('It is not the case that if Socrates is a human then he is a stone'), not simply to the consequent (Iwakuma, 1993, 65).

By this time in the eleventh century, then, many foundational semantic issues around words, phrases and statements were emerging as matters of comment and controversy. Concurrent with these changes, the earlier debates over the interrelation of topics and syllogisms continue. This particular treatise offers a distinctive view on that matter. The topics are, first of all, introduced only after the discussion of conditional statements is underway, and are put to the use of justifying such statements. Their number – surprisingly, given traditional classifications – is limited to five: "from a whole", "from a part", "from an equal", "from opposites" and "from immediates" (Iwakuma 1993, 68). The notion of using a topic as a device for *inventing* arguments is absent here; nothing counts but its role in justification, which works as follows. A conditional has both an antecedent and a consequent, and both of these have a subject and predicates. The two predicates can potentially stand to each other in any of the above five topical relations, as can the two subjects; so can the first subject and the second predicate, and vice versa. There are, accordingly, lots of potential topical relations in the offing here, and some of these can be helpfully appealed to as confirming the conditional in which they appear – and thus a set of topic-based rules for conditionals is born.[10] The next step develops these insights into a scheme of justification for hypothetical and categorical syllogisms alike. The key is that both kinds of syllogism are formulated as complex conditionals. For example, Barbara ('All A is B; All B is C; therefore All A is C') is rendered thus: "If anything is predicated of something else universally, then if something else is predicated of that predicate universally then that very same is predicated of the subject universally" (Iwakuma 1993, 70); this is clearly a conditional of the form 'P ⊃ (Q ⊃ R)'. Converting an argument form in this way

---

[10] For the various rules generated in this basis, see Iwakuma 2003, 53–55; see also Stump 1989, 117–121.

yields a validation technique: just demonstrate the truth of that conditional into which it has been converted. And the way to do this,
as just noted, is through the topical relations that exist between the
subject–predicate terms of antecedent and consequent. In the end,
on this view, the logic of syllogisms is founded in the truth of conditionals, which in turn is founded in topical theory. The relationships
between these three areas of theory are thus set forth in satisfying
simplicity.

With *Introductiones dialecticae secundum Wilgelmum*, we
have arrived at something very like a twelfth-century logic treatise.
But before turning to that era, attention should be drawn to another
text – the *Dialectica*, by a shadowy figure named Garlandus[11] – which
represents a controversial interpretative practice from the late eleventh century: "vocalism", as it has been dubbed (Iwakuma 1992a).
The actual dating of that text is still under question, and the work
may even be a product of the early twelfth century. Nonetheless, it
is very reflective of vocalism, either as a contemporary witness of
the viewpoint or a subsequent echo. Vocalism contests the notion
that logic has metaphysical content; its counter-claim is that logic
is strictly about words. So in this *Dialectica* even the material of
the *Categories* is understood as far as possible along these lines. For
example, the Aristotelian principle that substance is not susceptible
to degrees of being greater and less is interpreted as a claim about how
names of substances apply to what they name; thus, says Garlandus,
'man' does not apply any less or more to Socrates than it does to Plato
and is not applied to men or removed (*remittitur*) from them in differing degrees (Garlandus 1959, 19).

The vocalist embrace of words as the true subject matter of
logic also seems at work in Garlandus' handling of material from
On Interpretation. The relevant sections of the *Dialectica* tend to
elaborate logical theory in close connection with the empirical facts

---

[11] The text was attributed to Garlandus Compotista by its editor de Rijk, but is now
generally attributed to a certain Gerlandus of Besançon (Marenbon 2007b, 133).

of (Latin) grammar – seemingly a natural offshoot of the vocalist program, which ties logic to the real properties of words. In one passage, for example, Garlandus is at pains to catalogue the whole range of grammatical items capable of serving as subject and predicate terms – since it is not just names and verbs, respectively, that do so. Whole phrases can serve in either capacity, as can demonstratives and other words that are not "regular" (*regularis*). Verbs, in the form of participles, can even serve as subjects, and names as predicates, as in 'The reading <onc> is a man' (Garlandus 1959, 48). The sort of phrase serving as predicate here raises another problem that will become conspicuous in this era: the role of the copula. Syllogistic theory focuses in the first instance on the names appearing in subject and predicate, since it is the relations between these that govern syllogistic patterns. Elaborating the logic so construed does not require any special attention to the copula. But the grammatical tradition cannot omit this word from theoretical treatment, and Priscian notably refers to it as the "substantive" verb, since it seems to signify the very being of the subject to which it is attached (Priscian 1961, 414). Garlandus is at pains to clarify its logical status. He holds that in 'Man is an animal', 'is' is predicated, but only secondarily; it is not strictly speaking part of the predicate, even though the predicate could not function as such without it (Garlandus 1959, 46–47; Tweedale 1988, 202). Other problems of squaring logical form with grammatical reality are discussed in these pages too. The Aristotelian definition of word – which requires that it have no independently signifying part – seems at odds with many actual words (like *hircocervus*, 'goat-stag': Garlandus 1959, 68–69) that are products of compounding. By contrast, there are phrases to be found (like *dyalecticus bonus*, 'good logician': Garlandus 1959, 76) which seem more word-like by having constituents whose meanings are not fully independent of each other (in this case because the meaning of 'good' is in some manner limited by the meaning of 'logician'). These are puzzles known to the ancients and transmitted in Boethian writings; but they find new life in the hands of Garlandus and his contemporaries.

Side by side with this deepening attention to semantic issues, we find continued emphasis on the problem of relating topical and syllogistic theory into a unified theory of inference. The view that syllogistic reasoning is in some sense validated by topics is found here (Stump 1989, 82–88). All the topics are useful in this regard for hypothetical syllogisms, claims Garlandus, but only three are useful for categorical ones: "from a whole", "from a part" and "from an equal" (Garlandus 1959, 114). If we compare this list of three with the list of five cited above from the school of William of Champeaux, we will note the exclusion of two: "from opposites" and "from immediates". This exclusion is rather casually presented here; Peter Abelard's subsequent championing of it provokes one of the seminal debates of medieval logic.

4.4 TWELFTH CENTURY: PETER ABELARD

By the early twelfth century, a sophisticated commentary tradition exists for all of the Aristotelian logical works then readily available. There is increasing use of sophisms and other tendentious examples to encourage analysis and technical precision. Given that students of this subject matter have by this time increased their numbers, especially in Paris and its environs, it is indeed not surprising that the early Latin tradition of logic would now be ready to produce its first colossus.

Peter Abelard (1079–1142) was, in an early phase of his career, a student of Roscelin, to whose vocalist outlook he remains broadly sympathetic.[12] But he nonetheless offers a key refinement of it by arguing that the entities studied by logic are the physical sounds of words *taken as imbued with meaning*; they are not just the sounds themselves. He explains the point via comparison with the make-up of a statue, which is not entirely equivalent to its constituent

---

[12] For an assessment of current research on vocalism and its influence on Abelard, see Marenbon 2011. For an account of Abelard's checkered career, see Clanchy 1997; or consult Abelard's own account in his *Historia Calamitatum* (2010b).

matter, but rather to that same matter taken as imbued with shape; the word taken as imbued with meaning, the *sermo*, differs analogously from the merely physical *vox* (Abelard 1933, 522; Tweedale 1976, 147–157). When a *sermo* serves as a general term, its generality does not need to be explained by associating it with a universal like humanity or animality. Associating it with the *intellectus* of humanity or animality – in other words, with a conception or understanding of the mind – suffices. An *intellectus* can achieve a more or less complete representation of whatever kind of thing it represents, and the less complete the representation is, the more general will be the *sermo* to which it is attached (Abelard 1919, 21–22). Generality is thus explained, the semantics of general terms is insulated from the problem of universals, and an anti-metaphysical conception of logic – worlds away from the Platonizing conceptions of Alcuin and Eriugena – is further entrenched.

On this foundation rests a discussion of the semantics of words, phrases and statements, with special regard for how larger structures are composed from smaller ones (Wilks 2008, 92). Abelard continues the practice of dividing word meaning into two aspects: nomination (that is, denotation) and signification (which involves generating an *intellectus* in the mind of the hearer). But it is predominantly to the latter that he appeals through most of his analysis (Abelard 2010a, 00.11). Indefinite words such as prepositions differ from names and verbs because they have signification only when taken in conjunction with names and verbs, not by themselves (Abelard 2010a, 02.19). In contrast, verbs differ from names because they have a certain extra element of signification – a mode of signification – which confers upon them predicative force; conjoined to names they appear as signs of something's being said of something else. The fact that a verb like 'runs' has both the signification of a name *and* this extra predicative mode of signification seems to be exposed by rewriting it as 'is running', where the copula seems to mark that additional content. Whether it also maintains any sort of existential meaning is, as with Garlandus, a major concern, and Abelard himself seems to have upheld both negative and affirmative views on this matter at different times.[13]

The notion of predicative force suggests the parallel notions of interrogative force, imperative force and so on; Abelard distinguishes between these different kinds of force and the common content to which they may severally be applied (Abelard 1970, 151).[14] This content is what is said, asked, ordered by the statement; it is what Abelard calls its *dictum*. The *dictum* is something along the lines of a fact, which actually causes the statement to be true or false, and also causes its modal status and inferential relations with other statements (Abelard 2010a, 04.26). This notion of propositional content turns out to be a felicitous addition to Abelard's analytic repertoire and leads him, for example, to the key insight that the logically perspicuous placement of the negation sign in a negation is not internal to the *dictum* ('He is not running') but external to it ('It is not the case that he is running') (Abelard 2010a, 07.28).

It remains to comment on Abelard's account of inference. His most notable results in this area arise from attending to the nature of the inferential relation itself. Just as in a valid syllogism the content of the conclusion is already contained in the content of the premises, so too in the relation between antecedent and consequent of a true conditional according to Abelard (1970, 253; Martin 2004, 170). This state of containment in a valid syllogism is marked by the presence of a certain verbal, syllogistic form; the result is a complete (*perfecta*) inference (1970, 253–254). A conditional is equally able to achieve this state of containment, but typically not in a way marked by a verbal form. It therefore gives us only an incomplete (*imperfecta*) inference (Abelard 1970, 255–256), which suggests that extra means must be sought as guarantor of containment. That is what a topic does. Like William of Champeaux, Abelard is

---

[13] De Rijk 1986 treats Abelard on the copula very fully; Rosier-Catach 2003b links his views to the grammatical theory of the time.

[14] For the historical importance of Abelard's insights in this regard, see Martin 2004, 166–168.

concerned to determine the topical relationships between antecedent and consequent that will ground a true conditional. Most traditional topics will not produce such relationships. One that does, however, is the topic "from species", as expressed in this principle: "Whatever the species is predicated of, the genus is predicated of too" (Abelard 1970, 347). The principle clearly applies to a conditional like 'If it is a man it is an animal', whose terms stand in the appropriate relation. In stark contrast is the case of the topic "from opposites"; this topic is expressed in the principle that "when the one is posited, the other is removed" (Abelard 1970, 393) and, in Abelard's view, erroneously confirms the conditional 'If Socrates is a man, he is not a stone' (Abelard 1970, 395). He derives a *reductio* argument purporting to show that this conditional is in fact false, to the detriment of the topic which endorses it; but (as we shall see) a parallel *reductio* is lethally deployed against him by a rival to bring his account of the matter into disrepute.[15]

4.5   TWELFTH CENTURY: THE LOGICO-THEOLOGICAL
SCHOOLS

Logical inquiry in the twelfth century becomes increasingly dominated by the intellectual products of whole schools centered around individual masters. Cultural conditions in Paris at this time favor the formation of such groupings, which are commonly referred to as the "Parisian Schools" because of their locale, or as the "Logical-theological Schools" (Iwakuma and Ebbesen 1992) because of their characteristic subject matter: each of them elaborates a distinctive body of logical theory, but often in association with material drawn from the field of theology. These seem to have arisen in proliferating numbers, but scholarly consensus has fastened on five in particular as notable for the influence of their masters and textual products.

---

[15] For full discussion of this *reductio* argument and the principles informing it, see Martin 1987.

(i) Conspicuous among these five, of course, are Peter Abelard and his followers, known as the *Nominales* (Iwakuma 1992b).[16] The name itself is worthy of remark as being the first historical precursor of the more general label 'nominalism'. But applying that label with its current associations back to the *Nominales* is likely to produce some misunderstanding, since the theses attributed to them by their contemporaries do not always have an obvious relation to what we now call nominalism (Normore 1987).

(ii) Then we have the *Albricini*, followers of Alberic of Paris (fl. 1130s–1140s). This group seems to have some historical connection with William of Champeaux and his followers. Key texts of the *Albricini* – such as *Introductiones Montane minores* and *Introductiones Montane maiores* – are structured somewhat along the lines of *Introductiones dialecticae secundum Wilgelmum*, and the contents of these texts have much in common with what is known of William's views (Iwakuma 2003, 3–4). Also characteristic of the *Albricini* seems to be a certain disdain for the views of Peter Abelard, which may be a remnant of battles William formerly waged with him.

(iii) Another school is the *Parvipontani* (also called *Adamitae*), followers of Adam of Balsham (died 1181). The group's major literary accomplishment was Adam's *Ars disserendi* (1132), an unorthodox work which self-consciously eschews metaphysical questions and aims rather to provide a theoretical foundation for techniques of verbal dispute. To this end there is much focus on the recently recovered material from Aristotle's *Sophistical Refutations*. The scheme of organization is quite novel, the choice of technical terms an idiosyncratic departure from the norm, and the result a treatise famed in its own time for the demands it makes of its reader.

(iv) The *Melidunenses* (also called *Robertini*) are a fourth school, formed around the teaching of Robert of Melun (c. 1100–1167), an ecclesiastic of some stature who was as innovative as his rivals, but seemingly less controversial. His monumental *Ars meliduna* is truly one of

---

[16] The association of the *Nominales* with Peter Abelard was in the past a matter of controversy; a compilation of sources on this issue is found in *Vivarium* 30(1) (1992).

the mother lodes of twelfth-century logical theory. This work, like the *Ars disserendi*, attempts a structure determined less closely along the lines of Aristotelian commentary. Here Robert gathers the whole field of logic systematically under four headings – "terms", "what is signified by terms", "statements" and "what is said by statements" – and develops his views in a way more open to the integration of metaphysical doctrine than is the case among the *Nominales* or *Parvipontani*.

(v) The final school, the *Porretani*, can boast a master as famous in his own time as Abelard. Gilbert of Poitiers (1085/1090–1154) is best known through theological texts – indeed, the only ones of his still extant. But he has considerable renown as a metaphysician, and the existence of the *Porretani* suggests further achievements as a logician. His work in this last area may best be approached through the *Compendium logicae Porretanum*, a loosely organized collective text emanating from his school which exemplifies many characteristic theses from his teaching. As with Robert, he develops a logic rich in metaphysical associations.

It would be no small accomplishment to piece together full descriptions of the clashing viewpoints promoted by these groups. But glimpses of how they differ doctrinally are even now available. Foremost among these is what may be observed in their differing reactions to the problem arising from Abelard's argument against the topic "from opposites".[17] A key element of that argument is the claim that a statement never implies its own negation; since the topic "from opposites" licenses that very inference, Abelard argues, it emerges as a topic of lesser strength. But, as the above-mentioned Alberic seems to have discovered, perfectly normal and seemingly acceptable steps in logic can yield a statement implying its own negation, and he puts forward the following argument as a case in point (Anonymous 1967, 65–66; Martin 1987, 394–395):

(i)   If Socrates is a man and not an animal, Socrates is not an animal.

---

[17] This school debate has been extensively treated by Christopher Martin in Martin 1987 and subsequent papers.

(ii)   If Socrates is not an animal, Socrates is not a man.

(iii)   If Socrates is not a man, it is not the case that Socrates is a man and not an animal.

(iv)   Therefore, if Socrates is a man and not an animal, it is not the case that Socrates is a man and not an animal.

Statement (iv) gives us a conditional where the consequent negates the antecedent, contra Abelard's precept that such a conditional cannot be true. But the reasoning by which (iv) is derived seems unproblematic. (i) is true because its consequent follows from the antecedent by simplification. (ii) just contraposes the obviously true 'If Socrates is a man then Socrates is an animal'. And (iii) just contraposes the equally obvious 'If Socrates is a man and not an animal, Socrates is a man'. (iv) follows by two applications of hypothetical syllogism, so its truth seems beyond question, and if so then so much the worse for Abelard's precept.

The *Albricini, Melidunenses* and *Porretani* all attempt to save the precept by exposing a fatal flaw in the above argument. The response of the *Albricini* goes to validity; their claim is that the relationships between the predicates involved are simply not such as would sustain a proper application of hypothetical syllogism. In 'If A then B; if B then C; therefore if A then C', they argue, the predication described in A should be causally relevant to the truth of the predication described in B, which should relate likewise to the truth of the predication described in C. No such causal relations apply here, and the basis does not exist for this kind of inference to go through (Anonymous 1967, 65; Martin 1987, 396). The *Porretani* and *Melidunenses*, by contrast, question the truth of the opening premise. For the *Porretani* the issue seems similar to the one raised by the *Albricini*: a lack of relevance between predicative relations present in the antecedent and consequent of (i) (Anonymous 1983, 22; Martin 1987, 397–398). The *Melidunenses* make the point via a broader principle. Nothing follows from a falsehood, they claim, and so the consequent of (i) cannot follow from its antecedent (which contains the false claim that Socrates is not an animal) (Martin 1987,

398). All of these responses place some kind of relevance requirement on formally correct inference. By contrast, the most forward-looking view, that of the *Parvipontani*, waives this requirement and is prepared to acknowledge the soundness of the inference as it stands. This opens the way to the insight that a clearly defective conclusion might indeed follow from a clearly defective premise – or, more precisely, that from an impossibility *anything* should be able to follow, making 'Socrates is a stone' a legitimate inference from 'Socrates is a man and Socrates is not a man' (Martin 1987, 398–400).[18] In this we see an early premonition of the so-called paradoxes of implication.

This fascinating debate captures but one point of difference between the schools; the full story of their doctrinal divergences and entanglements will, when it is told, be one of great complexity. A notable part of the story will be this era's idiosyncratic use of counterexample as a recurring technique of analysis. Logicians of the time were certainly impressed by the incisive power of this technique in logical debate – witness the galvanizing effect of Alberic's argument on theories of consequence. Part of the historical background to this methodological development is the introduction of Aristotle's *Sophistical Refutations* and then, more importantly, his *Topics* into the milieu, around the 1120s and 1130s respectively (Martin 2013, 66–75). From these sources it becomes possible to acquire insight into the art and practice of dialectical disputation as conceived by Aristotle; this involves disputants formally constituted as questioner and respondent, and discourse between the two that is not just investigative but competitive. The point is for the questioner to challenge the respondent in the defense of some thesis (*positio*), and the method of choice for this is to apply counterexample sentences that expose some defect in the thesis, and put the respondent under some duress. These sentences came to be known as *instantiae*. Tactically fruitful

---

[18] See De Rijk 1962–1967, II.1, 290–291, which gives a brief excerpt from the *De naturis rerum* of Alexander Neckham, a follower of Parvipontanus.

ones were duly noted by the schools, and compilations of these are common in their writings.

The anonymous *Tractatus de locis argumentationum* exemplifies this sort of content. It is a conspectus of various inferential forms – some based on topical relations, and others based on relations of immediate inference (equipollence, conversion and sub-alternation). Sub-varieties of each are distinguished wherever possible, and the author ends up covering something in the order of 109 distinct inferential forms (by the editorial numbering). The focus of the presentation is obsessively concerned with the provision of examples of these forms and real or apparent counter-instances against them, to the point that further commentary is quite sparing. For one example – more accessible than most – consider the discussion of arguments from the equipollence (i.e. equivalence) of finite and infinite terms, the ninety-fourth of the forms discussed. I cite it in full:

> Now we must discuss the equipollence that propositions have
> from finite and infinite terms; according to this equipollence
> a rule of this kind is given: "Propositions of the same quantity
> and different quality, with terms varied according to finite and
> infinite, are equipollent". According to that rule an argument is
> made thus: 'Every man is an animal. Therefore every man is not a
> non-animal'. Counter-instance: 'Every man sees an ass. Therefore
> every man does not see a non-ass'. Or thus: 'Every man was
> white. Therefore no man was non-white'. Or: 'Every man has a
> right hand. Therefore every man does not have a non-right hand'.
> (Anonymous 1981, 56)

This completes the full treatment of the inference form, which hardly does more than provide the initial example and three possible counter-instances. The inference under review may be represented schematically as a move from 'is P' to 'is not non-P', and would seem unobjectionable. The first example ('is an animal'/'is not a non-animal') shows the inference at its uncontroversial best. But the next three all present us with defective reasoning, and if they really do instantiate the inferential form in question, then we have some evidence against the validity of the form. So do they? Of the first counter-instance, one might note that it uses a subject–object structure that seems a departure from the original: 'sees an x' as opposed to 'is an x'. One might note of the second the presence of a negative quantifier ('no'), which is again a departure from the original. The third is only loosely translated above; more literally it runs thus: 'There is a right hand of everyone. Therefore there is not a non-right hand of everyone'. Rendered thus, one sees the presence of an obliquely cased element in the predicate ('of every-one'), and so another structural difference that may be enough of a disanalogy to neutralize the example. However one assesses the strength of the counter-instances, it is clear that defending against them will necessitate some fairly intricate claims about logical structure. And that is exactly the point of these troublesome cases: their aim is to goad the mind into technical analysis. One can see how a whole catalogue of *instantiae* – let alone a small literature of such catalogues – would offer a lifetime of talking points for the career logician.

What it does not offer is an accessible point of entry into the field for the non-logician. The passage just cited unfolds very much like the other hundred or so discussions of inferential forms in *Tractatus de locis argumentationum*, in a format dominated by examples with only the most sparing provision of commentary. In his *Metalogicon*, John of Salisbury reflects on the state of logical studies in the mid-twelfth century; his bilious commentary on the matter suggests a conviction that the discipline is in a crisis of obscurant-ism. It seems likely that at least part of what John is reacting to is the growing ubiquity of the *instantiae* technique (Jacobi 1988, 242–243). But while the *instantiae* literature of this time is difficult for the outsider to approach, there is no question that it offers a massive stimulus to conceptual refinement in its own time, and that many in the characteristic ideas of the terminist tradition in the following era have started taking shape in this prior one.

As a concluding remark, it is fair to claim a comparable standing for the whole period covered in this chapter relative to its posterity. Whatever items of doctrine survive from it to feed into the subsequent tradition, there can be no doubt about its much more pervasive role in adjusting the basic paradigms of study available for the field of logic in the first place. As we have seen, there is initially the shorter-lived Platonic paradigm of the eighth and ninth centuries. Then from the ninth century on, there is the paradigm that pays attention to inferential relationships, and over time goes beyond merely cataloguing syllogistic inferences to creative study of inter-relations between categorical, hypothetical and topical reasoning. And finally, from the eleventh century on, there is the paradigm that interlaces grammatical theory with the semantic speculations of Aristotle's *On Interpretation* to engender creative study of the properties of terms. The story of these early centuries seems to be told in the shedding of the first paradigm, the early development of the second and the later addition of the third.

5 Logic in the Latin Thirteenth Century

Sara L. Uckelman and Henrik Lagerlund

5.1 INTRODUCTION

In the medieval Latin philosophical tradition, the thirteenth century is set apart from other periods as perhaps the one most dominated by the influence of Aristotle. After the rediscovery and re-translation of many Aristotelian texts in the middle of the twelfth century, Aristotle's works quickly became the foundation of teaching in the Arts faculties of the universities of Paris and Oxford in the first few decades of the thirteenth century. While the new Aristotelian material from the *Physics* and *Metaphysics* gave rise to censure and a teaching ban in Paris in the 1210–1230s, this ban did not extend to logic, which was never especially controversial and remained largely unaffected by bans (see Section 5.4). Once the early controversies surrounding Aristotle's natural philosophy were resolved, the commentary tradition that developed around his texts eventually became one of the main literary forms of philosophy in the thirteenth century. In tandem, the rise of logic as a foundational subject in the universities resulted in the introduction of logical textbooks which explored radically non-Aristotelian approaches to logic and semantics.

Boethius had already translated all of the logical works of Aristotle, except *Posterior Analytics*, into Latin in the sixth century (see the chapter "The Legacy of Ancient Logic in the Middle Ages" in this volume). Although *Categories* and *On Interpretation* had been commented on since at least the ninth century, the others were not systematically studied before 1120, and it was not until the late twelfth or early thirteenth century that commentaries on these works started to appear in the Latin West. These commentaries were influenced by Arabic commentaries, especially those by Averroes, which we'll discuss below. With the expansion of commentaries and the growing importance of Aristotle's texts for university teaching, the need for new or fresh translations soon became apparent. In the 1260s, William of Moerbeke translated Aristotle's works anew or revised Boethius' old translations. At the same time, he also translated several of the Greek commentators. Others wrote new commentaries. The most important Latin commentators from the mid-thirteenth century that are known by name are Thomas Aquinas (d. 1274), Robert Kilwardby (d. 1279), Albert the Great (d. 1280), Boethius of Dacia (d. c. 1280), Simon of Faversham (d. 1306) and Radulphus Brito (d. 1320). Many more commentaries from this time are anonymous.

The logicians of the Latin thirteenth century had a pretty good grasp of Greek logic, but they also had a good grasp of logic as it had developed in the Arabic tradition. One major source for this knowledge was the *Maqāsid al-falasifa* ("The Meaning of the Philosophers") by Abu Hamid Muhammad al-Ghazali (1058–1111), a preparatory work for his later, more widely known work *Tahafut al-falasifa* ("The Incoherence of the Philosophers"). John, Archbishop of Toledo (1151–1166), commissioned a translation of al-Ghazali's work into Latin by Dominicus Gundissalinus early in the second half of the twelfth century, not more than fifty or seventy-five years after it was written. In one of the manuscripts, the Latin title is *Liber Algazelis de summa theoricae philosophiae*, and it was printed in Venice in 1506 under the title *Logica et philosophia Algazelis arabis*.

Although the *Maqasid* was a summary of Al-Farabi's and Avicenna's philosophical thought, the Latin thirteenth century also had some knowledge of Al-Farabi's and Avicenna's logic directly. A twelfth-century translation of the beginning, namely the part on Porphyry's *Isagoge*, of Avicenna's encyclopedic work *Kitab al-Shifa* ("The Book of Healing") was in circulation, as well as a fragment of the part on *Posterior Analytics*. Small fragments of some of Al-Farabi's logical works have also been discovered in Latin and others are referred to by Albert the Great.

The commentary tradition provides us with the best accounts of Aristotle's philosophy and logic; but it is in what we will call the textbook tradition that we find the seeds of the non-Aristotelian logical developments that became so influential in the fourteenth century (see the chapter "Logic in the Latin West in the Fourteenth Century" in this volume). In this tradition we find not only the so-called *summulae*, "summaries" or comprehensive compendia intended for instruction, but also other treatises with a more specific focus, such as treatises devoted to *sophismata, insolubilia, syncate-goremata* and *obligationes* (see Section 5.3). The four most important *summulae* were William of Sherwood's *Introductiones ad Logicam* (d. 1272), Peter of Spain's *Tractatus* (or *Summulae Logicales*),[1] Roger Bacon's *Summulae dialectices* (d. 1294), and Lambert of Auxerre's *Logica* (fl. 1250).[2] Of these textbooks, Peter of Spain's *Tractatus* was the most influential. In the fourteenth century as well as later, many logicians wrote commentaries on it, and it was the most read intro-duction to logic well into the sixteenth century.

The thirteenth century is often marked out as the start of a division between the English (Oxford/Cambridge/London) tradition on the one hand and the Paris or continental tradition on the other that became entrenched by the beginning of the fourteenth century – though we must stress that neither Oxford nor Paris represent homo-geneous traditions (de Libera 1982). This division developed despite the ready movement of academics across the channel, with many of the important logicians of this century studying or teaching in both places. Many differences of doctrine in the *logica modernorum* can be traced back to which twelfth-century logic book was taken as the basis of the development of supposition theory (Ebbesen 1985), but

---

[1] The author of this book was previously assumed to be the same Petrus Hispanus who became Pope John XXI, but this has recently been disputed (d'Ors 1997; Peter of Spain 2014, 1–9).

[2] Lambert's *Logica* was edited under the attribution Lambert of Auxerre by Alessio (see Lambert of Auxerre 1971); de Libera 1982 has argued against this attribu-tion. Maloney 2009 agrees with de Libera, but revises this opinion in Lambert of Auxerre 2015, xxxix.

others were influenced by external factors such as academic condemnations of Aristotelian philosophy.

In this chapter, we first discuss the commentary tradition, beginning with Averroes (who, while being neither Latin nor thirteenth century, was profoundly influential on developments in thirteenth-century approaches to Aristotle in the west) (Section 5.2.1) and ending with Kilwardby, one of the most important people in this tradition (Section 5.2.2). In Section 5.3 we discuss important institutional and doctrinal developments outside the commentary tradition, looking at the theory of syncategorematic terms (Section 5.3.1) and the rise of speculative grammar in Paris (Section 5.3.2). Before concluding (Section 5.5), we discuss the effect on logic of the condemnations and prohibitions at Paris and Oxford in the last quarter of the century (Section 5.4).

5.2 THE COMMENTARY TRADITION

In Section 5.1 we raised the idea of the existence of divergent traditions in logic in Oxford and Paris; yet when we look at the commentary tradition, there is no such divergence to be found. If one looks at all of thirteenth-century logic, then there is one feature of logic that cuts across both Oxford and Paris, and that is the deep connection between logic and metaphysics. Although the theory of supposition (see the chapter "Supposition and Properties of Terms" in this volume) is primarily a semantic theory, it is strongly underpinned by an Aristotelian realist metaphysics in both Peter of Spain's *Tractatus* and William of Sherwood's *Introduction* (Spruyt 2012). The connection is even clearer when we look at the commentary tradition. There is an unfortunate lack of edited texts from the early Latin commentaries on Aristotle's logic.[3] Albert the Great (c. 1200–1280) wrote commentaries on all the logical works of Aristotle and his works

---

[3] There is no chronological catalogue of all the Latin commentaries on the logical works of Aristotle, but there are numerous lists of commentaries available. In Marenbon 2000a, II, 77–127, all commentaries before 1150 have been listed, and, in Marenbon 2000a, VIII, 21–49, all commentaries on *Categories* and *On*

have been critically edited, as have those of Thomas Aquinas. He only wrote commentaries on *On Interpretation* and *Posterior Analytics*, however. Perhaps the most important logician in the thirteenth-century Latin commentary tradition is Robert Kilwardby. Between 1235 and 1245, he lectured on the works of Porphyry and Aristotle in Paris, and although he was clearly influenced by Averroes he still stands out as the most original thinker on logic in the thirteenth century. Unfortunately, none of Kilwardby's commentaries on Aristotle's logical works has yet been edited. Albert the Great seems to a large extent to have copied many of Kilwardby's ideas (Ebbesen 1981c; Lagerlund 2000, chapter 2; Thom 2007); he certainly gets credit for these ideas in the later Middle Ages.

5.2.1 Averroes' Influence on the Thirteenth-Century Commentary Tradition

The strong metaphysical overtones in the commentary tradition are arguably due to the influence of Averroes, the twelfth-century Arabic philosopher born in al-Andalus (present-day Spain), who was referred to by medieval Latin authors as the Commentator (just as Aristotle was the Philosopher). While tremendously influential for the Latin tradition, especially through his commentaries on Aristotle, Averroes had little to no influence on the further development of Arabic logic, or Arabic philosophy more generally. The two main reasons for this are his relative geographical isolation from the main centers of Arabic thought (see the chapter "Arabic Logic after Avicenna" in this volume), and the fact that his analytical, rationalist approach to philosophy and theology clashed with the more orthodox approaches of some powerful figures of his time (such as the Caliph Abū Yūsuf Ya'qūb al-Manṣūr).

> *Interpretation* before Abelard are as well. In Green-Pedersen 1984, all commentaries on the *Topics* are given. In De Rijk 1962–1967 and Ebbesen 1981b, one can find a list of many of the early commentaries on *Sophistici Elenchi*. In Lohr 1974, 2010, an alphabetical list of all medieval commentaries on Aristotle's logical works can be found.

Averroes wrote three kinds of commentaries on Aristotle's works, called minor, middle and major commentaries on the basis of their length. In the 1220s and 1230s, William of Luna translated Averroes' middle commentary on Porphyry's *Isagoge* and the middle commentaries on Aristotle's *Categories, On Interpretation* and *Prior Analytics*; in addition to these, a major commentary on *Posterior Analytics* was also available in Latin. In the middle commentaries, Averroes does not go much beyond Aristotle's own text, adhering closely to the original text and deviating only on occasion. When he does deviate, it is in order to provide further explanation, to rule out misunderstandings, or to say that some argument or view is wrong; however, he often does not explain why an argument is wrong or give a counterargument. An Averroes interpreter must therefore tease his views out from the text since the text itself is not very explicit. If the commentaries are read carefully, an interpretation can be obtained, though the extent of Averroes' influence in the subsequent thirteenth-century Latin commentary tradition is still not sufficiently understood.

Nevertheless, these commentaries were important for a general understanding of Aristotle's difficult texts in the thirteenth century and played a central role throughout the rest of the Latin medieval tradition; the strong connection between logic and metaphysics emphasized in his commentaries had a clear influence on the Latin logic tradition (Lagerlund 2000, 2008). In particular, Averroes' treatment of modal syllogistics is heavily metaphysical, and his view of the modal syllogistics was influential for Latin authors in the thirteenth century (Lagerlund 2000, 32) (see also the chapter "The Logic of Modality" in this volume). Here, we look more closely at what he says about modal syllogistics in his middle commentary on *Prior Analytics*, a text which is scantly studied and which led to the more developed views in the *Quaesitum*, a short treatise on mixed syllogisms. In the *Quaesitum*, Averroes focused on modal syllogistics and developed an interpretation based on the metaphysical nature of the terms involved in the different syllogisms. It has been claimed that this short work is the final result of his inquiries into modal syllogistics (Elamrani-Jamal 1995, 74), and the *Quaesitum* has been studied in detail elsewhere (Lagerlund 2000, 32–35; Thom 2003, 81–91; Lagerlund 2008, 300–302).

In his middle commentary on *Prior Analytics*, Averroes considers Aristotle's purported counterexample (see *Prior Analytics* I 9, 30a28) to XLL Barbara (27va):

> Every animal is moving
> Every human being is necessarily an animal
> _____
> Every human is necessarily moving

The premises are (assumed to be) true, but the conclusion is false, since humans are not necessarily moving. This could be turned into a valid syllogism, Averroes argues, by appealing to a rule due to Theophrastus and Eudemus, Aristotle's followers in the Peripatetic School, who both thought the conclusion in a modal syllogism must follow the weaker of the two premises. If we apply this rule to the counterexample above, we see that we can validly infer the non-modal conclusion 'Every human is moving', since 'Every human is moving' is true given the truth of the major premise 'Every animal is moving' (27vb). Averroes rejects Theophrastus' and Eudemus' suggestion, and his own account seeks to preserve Aristotle's original idea. He introduces a distinction between the whole and the part of a syllogism. The terms and the premises, for example, make up the parts, but beyond them there is also the whole of the syllogism, which binds the parts together. Averroes seems to think that the major premise determines the outcome in some way, such that the whole syllogism is contained in it and hence the conclusion follows from it. If the major premise is necessary, the conclusion will be as well, and similarly if the major premise is assertoric, then so will be the conclusion. This is why LXL Barbara is valid but not XLL Barbara (28va–b). Similar ideas can be found in later Latin thirteenth-century commentaries on *Prior Analytics* (see Lagerlund 2000).

Averroes does not elaborate the distinction between parts and whole at all, though it seems similar to the distinction in his metaphysics between the form of the whole and the form of the part, but there is no reference to the *Metaphysics*. However, given this distinction, Averroes can return to his counterexample; he has now shown that in the combination of a mixed necessary and assertoric syllogism, the necessity premise cannot be the minor premise, but has to be the major if the conclusion is to be necessary.[4] To further stress this, he considers the following syllogism:

Every walking thing is necessarily moving
Every human is walking
_____
Every human is necessarily moving

He then notes cryptically that: "And the problem with this is, that the walking [thing] is not moving by necessity by the part that is human, but by the part that is walking" (28va). He is trying to explain why the necessity does not translate to the conclusion. Such an account focuses on the terms involved in the syllogism and suggests an explanation why the seemingly valid syllogism mentioned above is not really a counterexample. It is simply not enough to say that the conclusion follows the major premise: something has to be added about the kinds of terms involved in a modal syllogism for it to conform to Aristotle's original idea. Consider again:

Every animal is moving
Every human is necessarily an animal
_____
Every human is necessarily moving

'Moving' unqualified is simply not the right kind of term for a syllogism of this kind. We have to add something to it or we have to say that in mixed syllogisms of this kind such a term cannot be used. We have to restrict it to substance terms or something similar. This is

---

[4] Note that this only holds for first-figure syllogisms. In the other figures, it is possible to have a valid modal syllogism where the minor premise is modal and the major is assertoric.

what Averroes does in the *Quaesitum* and what Kilwardby does, following him. An alternative to this approach is advanced by Avicenna, who says that 'moving' needs to be modified by adding 'while moving', expressing a type of *per se* necessity (see Lagerlund 2009). We then get the following syllogism:

Every animal is moving while moving
Every human is necessarily an animal

Every human is necessarily moving while moving

This is now a valid syllogism. Kilwardby also suggests something similar in his commentary on *Prior Analytics* (Thom 2007, 153ff.). Although Averroes' commentary on *Prior Analytics* is not as clear and as explicit as the *Quaesitum* it certainly suggests an interpretation of Aristotle's modal syllogistics that is interesting and influential, and it adds further evidence to the claim that Averroes is largely responsible for the close connection between logic and metaphysics that dominates thirteenth-century logic.

5.2.2 Kilwardby's Commentaries

Robert Kilwardby (1215?–1279) was an English Dominican who studied and taught at Paris between 1231 and 1245, and later also taught at Oxford. His commentaries on Aristotle were not only the earliest comprehensive collection, but they were also extremely influential on the remainder of the thirteenth-century developments (Silva 2011). Kilwardby's course on *Logica Vetus* contains lectures on *Isagoge, Categories* and *On Interpretation* (Lewry 1981a; Conti 2013b). He is the first logician in the thirteenth century to address Porphyry's famous questions on the nature of universals (for more on universals, see the chapter "Logica Vetus" in this volume). Kilwardby thinks universals have an existence as forms in singulars, and have a unity based on agreement in essence. He also argues that the ideas in the mind of God are formal causes and exemplars of the universals. In human cognition, the universals (forms) are abstracted from the individuals they exist in. Universals must be in singulars, he argues, since the singulars would otherwise not make any contribution to the signification of a universal. One of the main characteristics of Kilwardby's thought is the project of unifying Aristotle's doctrines in different fields of inquiry; in particular, he interprets Aristotle's logic from the point of view of Aristotle's own metaphysics (Thom 2007), something that Aristotle himself did not do with the same level of systematicity.

Following Avicenna, Kilwardby contrasts the metaphysicians' approach to universals and the logicians'. In metaphysics, universals are studied in abstraction from language, while in logic they are studied as having a nature connected with language. Universals are names that can be predicated for the logician, but their existence is prior to language, and the signification is derived from the real form. He says that a universal is a disposition of reality, and hence it is also a disposition of a name. He expands on this relation by expanding on the relation between thought and reality. Language is a representation of thought, he argues, and accordingly he defends a realist position. This close connection between language and reality, logic and metaphysics is maintained throughout all his logical works, and can also be seen in the part of this commentary on *Logica Vetus* devoted to the *Categories*, and the connection is further expressed in his commentary on *Prior Analytics* (Lagerlund 2000, chapter 2; Thom 2007, 2013). According to Kilwardby, the logician is concerned with reality (though not in the same way as the metaphysician); thus he naturally excludes a linguistic interpretation of the categories. The ten categories or the ten kinds of utterances (*voces*) signify the ten classes of reality, so while the metaphysician studies the ten classes of reality as species of being, the logician studies them as subjects and predicates.

Kilwardby's discussion of equivocation follows in the same vein: equivocation is not primarily at the level of terms but of reality. As part of his treatment of equivocation he outlines a threefold division of signification: (1) the act and form of signification; (2) the thing signified; and (3) the comparison of the sign with what is signified.

The first division is the perfection of the word, and every word has only one perfection or form. According to the second and third divisions, an utterance might have several significations. As a meaningful utterance, a name is one in the first sense with one perfection, but it may have several meanings in the sense of what is signified and in the relation of sign to signified.

Kilwardby's whole treatment of signification and definition in terms of perfections or form and matter is strikingly metaphysical. It was influenced by Averroes and it set the trend for the thirteenth century, when logicians tended to enforce the strict connections between logic and metaphysics and natural philosophy more or less explicit in Aristotle's own works. There remained a tradition of interpreting logic in this way up to the sixteenth century; while it was often done in the name of Albert the Great, it really derives from Kilwardby (see the examples mentioned in Lagerlund 2000). This strong relationship between logic and metaphysics became a target of criticism for later fourteenth-century logicians (Biard and Rosier-Catach 2003).

We see this connection again clearly in Kilwardby's interpretation of modal syllogistics. Kilwardby's commentary *In libros Priorium Analyticorum*, written in the early part of the 1240s, was the first major commentary on *Prior Analytics* in the thirteenth century.[5] It is perhaps one of the most original and interesting *Prior Analytics* commentaries ever written (Thom 2011). The discussion of the modal syllogistics is quite remarkable in its detail and originality, and it was influential on such thirteenth-century authors as Albert the Great, Simon of Faversham and Radulphus Brito, who all follow Kilwardby in their interpretations.[6]

---

[5] The first known commentary on *Prior Analytics* in the Latin West can be found in an anonymous work. The author has been called Anonymous Aurelianensis III by Sten Ebbesen, who has studied parts of the work. He dates it to c. 1160–1180 (Ebbesen 1981a). Some preliminary comparisons between Aurelianensis III and Kilwardby have been made in Thomsen Thörnqvist 2013, but she found only small similarities between the two commentaries. The whole work is now edited in Thomsen Thörnqvist 2014.

[6] This means that all the major commentators of *Prior Analytics* in the thirteenth century followed Kilwardby (Lagerlund 2000; Thom 2003, 2013).

Commentators in the thirteenth century generally assumed that Aristotle's theory was largely correct. Kilwardby follows this, making it his project to find the interpretation that shows this. He begins by considering a purported counterexample to the accidental conversion of necessity-propositions, namely: 'Every literate is necessarily human'. According to the conversion rules accepted by Kilwardby and Aristotle this should convert to: 'Some human is necessarily literate', but the first is obviously true while the second is false.

Kilwardby gives two solutions to this purported counterexample. The first is based on a distinction between different readings of the terms involved in the propositions above; we saw something similar in Averroes' discussion of modal syllogisms above. Kilwardby explains that the subject term of a sentence can stand for the subject of the inherence (the *suppositum*), or for the qualification through which the subject is specified (*qualitas/forma*). If the term 'white' stands for the *suppositum*, it refers to a thing that is white, or to 'that which is white', but if it stands for the quality (or form), it refers to the whiteness that inheres in that which is white and not to the thing in which it inheres. Kilwardby says that in the first sentence 'literate' as the subject term stands for the *suppositum*, and this is why it is true, while in the second proposition the term is taken differently and now as the predicate term it stands for the quality or form. According to Kilwardby, the meaning of the original subject term is changed when it no longer stands for the *suppositum* (the literate being), but for some abstract quality of being literate, and it is this change that prevents the conversion. If the converted proposition is read in the following way then it is true: 'Something which is human is necessarily that which is literate'. Kilwardby, however, preferred another solution to the alleged counterexamples to the conversion rules of necessity-propositions, based on a distinction between propositions that are necessary *per se* and those that are necessary *per accidens*. He writes (I, fol. 7rb):

When it is said: 'Every literate is necessarily human', this subject is not something which can be said *per se* of this predicate, but since 'literate' is not separated from that which belongs to a human being itself, the proposition is conceded to be necessary, but when a proposition is necessary in this way it is necessary *per accidens*. Therefore, when Aristotle says that necessity propositions are convertible, he means that only the propositions that are necessary *per se* are convertible.

The idea is here that since 'human' is not predicated *per se* of its subject 'literate', the first proposition above is not a *per se* necessity-proposition and, therefore, not convertible. The proposition is a necessity-proposition, but only *per accidens*, since it is necessarily true only in the sense that being a human being and being literate are not separable. The terms 'literate' and 'human' do not have the close *per se* relation Kilwardby demands of a convertible proposition. Kilwardby implies that the relation between subject and predicate term must be of a special kind if a proposition is to be called necessary *per se*, and he thinks that propositions *per se* should be understood in the way Aristotle explains them in *Posterior Analytics* I, 4–6, where four different notions of *per se* (*kath' hauto*) predication are introduced.

He also stresses that in a *per se* necessity-proposition, the subject must be '*per se aliquod ipsius predicati*'. That is, in such a proposition, the subject has the predicate as an essential property; in other words, the subject has the predicate as a necessary property through itself and not through something else. He seems to assume that in a necessity-proposition *per se*, the subject term is not an accidental term, but an essential or a necessary term, and that the subject is essentially (*per se*) linked to the predicate, and not only through inseparability. Consequently, if the subject term is necessary and the link is necessary, it follows that the predicate term cannot be a contingent (accidental) term. It must be necessary as well. A necessary proposition in a syllogism is then understood as a proposition expressing essential properties of things located in a genus-species structure. The Aristotelian theory of necessity syllogistics is thus limited to a special class of terms, which all stand for substances. The same terminology is also used to explain the syllogistic for contingent propositions, which means that Kilwardby tried to develop a uniform and highly original interpretation.[7]

5.3 THE *LOGICA MODERNORUM* IN THE TEXTBOOK TRADITION

Though Aristotle's logic was part of the curriculum from the birth of the universities at the beginning of the century, the first *summulae*, or logical compendia designed to introduce the student to the *logica modernorum*, appear in the middle of the century. The earliest known attempt to "develop the notions of the *logica moderna* in an organised way, in the way that became characteristic of the medieval logic" (Kretzmann in William of Sherwood 1966, 20) belongs to William of Sherwood, who wrote not only *Introductiones in Logicam* but also a treatise on syncategorematic terms (discussed below). William of Sherwood was born in Nottinghamshire probably in the first decade of the thirteenth century, and he studied at either Oxford or Paris, or both, before becoming a master at the University of Paris, and his works were profoundly influential on the authors of the other three most important *summulae* of the thirteenth century: Peter of Spain, Roger Bacon and Lambert of Auxerre. As noted above, Peter of Spain's treatise was one of the most important works on logic for the coming centuries, but despite its popularity, William's *Introductiones* also continued to be read, as were Bacon's *Summulae* and Lambert's *Logica*. Although these latter two were not as influential, Bacon's in particular affected the development of logic in Oxford.

---

[7] Several contemporary scholars have developed a similar interpretation of Aristotle (van Rijen 1989; Patterson 1995; Thom 1996; Nortmann 1996; Malink 2013). Kilwardby's interpretation has been worked out in detail by Thom (2003, 2007, 2013). Working out the logic of essentialism that Kilwardby is expressing is a valuable philosophical project and attempts to work out similar logics can be found in contemporary logic.

His idiosyncratic theory of signs, which preserved a strong connection with the theory of supposition and hence logic, was influential for Oxford's not succumbing to the influence of the *Modistae* (see Section 5.3.2).

5.3.1 Oxford and the Treatment of Syncategorematic Terms

Two major aspects of the *logica modernorum* were the study of the properties of terms (*proprietates terminorum*) and an account of the function of syncategorematic terms (*syncategoremata*); these together make up what is known as "terminist" logic. The properties of terms were generally dealt with in the textbooks of logic mentioned above (see also the chapters "Supposition and Properties of Terms" and "Sophisms and Insolubles" in this volume), but syncategorematic terms were usually given a separate treatment. Treatises on syncategorematic terms presupposed the material covered in the *Summulae* and were intended to develop and extend the material in the textbooks. Robert Bacon (d. 1248), John le Page (first half of thirteenth century), Peter of Spain, William of Sherwood, Nicholas of Paris (fl. mid-thirteenth century), Henry of Ghent (c. 1217–1293), and many others wrote treatises on syncategorematic terms (Braakhuis 1981); such discussions were gradually absorbed into the *sophismata* treatises in later medieval logic (Pironet and Spruyt 2015). These treatises are of particular interest for understanding the development of the Oxford and Paris traditions in logic in the thirteenth century. Braakhuis argues that because of the advanced level of logical theorizing these treatises present, they are perhaps our best witness for the existence of "some typical English way of doing logic and semantics in the thirteenth century" (Braakhuis 1981, 131), which can be contrasted with a continental tradition based around Paris. The earliest treatises on syncategorematic terms are all found in England, rather than on the continent; the treatise which Braakhuis ascribes to Robert Bacon may even date from the first decade of the thirteenth century (Braakhuis 1981, 136). In contrast, the oldest known continental treatise on syncategorematic terms was written by John le Page between 1225 and 1235.[8]

Syncategorematic terms are those which do not have any signification of their own, but only signify in the context of a wider grammatical structure (Klima 2006; Dutilh Novaes and Spruyt 2015). No two texts on syncategorematic terms covered the same list of terms, even if the treatises themselves were similar in structure, and the differences in the lists, along with the ways in which the terms are treated, provides further evidence for distinct traditions on the island and the continent. For example, in English treatises such as Robert Bacon's and William of Sherwood's, distributive terms such as 'every' are treated as syncategorematic terms, but this is not the case in the continental works of le Page, Peter of Spain and Nicholas of Paris (Braakhuis 1981, 138). In the Parisian tradition, distributive signs were treated in *Summulae* in a specific section *De distributionibus* which is not present in any English *Summulae* (Braakhuis 1981, 139).

Here, we restrict ourselves to commenting briefly on some of the interesting developments in William of Sherwood's account of syncategorematic terms. William begins by stating that if one is to understand anything, one must understand its parts, and this principle holds for statements (*enuntiationes*) as well. His approach to language is thus intrinsically compositional. He continues by pointing out that the parts of statements can be divided into principal and secondary parts. The principal parts are the substantive terms and verbs, that is, the parts that have supposition (see the chapter "Supposition and Properties of Terms" in this volume). The secondary parts are such things as adjectival names, adverbs, conjunctions and prepositions. Some secondary parts of language are determinations of principal parts in respect of the things belonging to them, like 'white' in 'a white man', and such parts are not syncategorematic terms. Other

---

[8] Braakhuis argues convincingly that it is unlikely that earlier treatises exist, as le Page's exhibits the sort of disorganized arrangement that indicates the beginning of the development of a genre (1981, 137).

secondary parts are determinations of principal parts insofar as they are subjects or predicates, like 'every' in 'Every human being is running'. 'Every' does not signify that something belonging to 'human being' is universal, but rather that 'human being' is a universal subject. The secondary parts of this kind are syncategorematic terms.

The first syncategorematic term treated by William is the distributive term 'every' or 'all' (omnis). He divides his discussion of this term with regard to its signification and to its function. 'Every' or 'all' signifies universally either as a disposition of a thing, as in 'the world is all', in which case it is not a syncategorematic term, or as a disposition of a subject in which case it is a syncategorematic term. In 'Every human being is running', 'every' signifies that the term 'human being' is universal with respect to serving as a subject and standing in a relation to a predicate.

The function of the term 'every' or 'all' is to divide the subject with respect to the predicate. This means that the term gives the condition for attaching the predicate either (i) to at least one thing of each kind under the subject, or (ii) to each individual thing belonging to the subject. According to interpretation (i), the sentence 'Every dog is an animal' is analyzed into a conjunction of 'A collie is an animal', 'A poodle is an animal', etc. According to (ii), it is analyzed into 'Fido is an animal', and 'Spot is an animal', etc. William's discussion of 'every' or 'all' is quite detailed and goes through all cases and examples in which this term functions as a syncategorematic term. It is a marvelous example of scholastic logic as it came to be referred to negatively by later authors.

William was one of the first logicians to treat 'is' as a syncategorematic term. The first question he addresses is whether 'is' pertains to the composition of the subject and the predicate or if it pertains to the predicate. To explain this he recalls the distinction between 'signification' and 'consignification', and explains that 'is' is not really a third part of the proposition, that is, a composition, since it signifies that which is said of something other than itself and this is the predicate, but it does consignify the composition, which is the function of the copula. 'Is' is also equivocal, for sometimes it indicates actual being (*esse actuale*) and at other times conditional being (*esse habituale*), which is something with some nature, but which does not actually exist although it could. If in 'Every human being is an animal', 'is' is taken in the first way, then it is false when no humans exist. If it is taken in the second way, then it is true no matter whether there are any humans or not. In this way, William commits himself to *possibilia* or to things that could exist but do not. He himself notes that this amounts to saying that things that do not exist but could have existed have a diminished kind of being (*esse diminutum*). This is an unusual position in the thirteenth century (Knuuttila 1993) and is contrasted with the view that things which do not exist, but could have existed, nevertheless have no being of any kind at all.

5.3.2   *The* Modistae

Despite condemnations of various parts of Aristotelian philosophy in the early decades of the thirteenth century, Paris had a very strong logical tradition particularly between 1240 and 1270, when many of the most original logicians that we know by name were active there (the most important of them being Kilwardby; see Section 5.2.2). But by the 1270s, the University of Paris became dominated by the *Modistae*, and as a result, the *logica modernorum* fell out of fashion (though the commentary tradition still continued) and was pushed into the background as grammar and linguistics came to the forefront. The reduced interest in Paris in the *logica modernorum* lasted several decades, and by the beginning of the fourteenth century there was a deep divide between Paris and Oxford, where the *logica modernorum* tradition had only become stronger and stronger and reached its peak with Burley and Ockham in the early fourteenth century.

The study of grammar in the Middle Ages was influenced by the study of classical Latin grammar via the works of Priscian and Donatus. These descriptive accounts of language were often in conflict with the more prescriptive accounts provided by logic (cf. Uckelman 2012), and twelfth-century approaches to grammar focused on systematizing, glossing and harmonizing the views of the classical grammarians with the logicians; the canonical result of this approach, Peter Helias' *Summa super Priscianum* (c. 1140), strongly influenced the development of terministic logic in the first half of the thirteenth century. Indeed, while grammar and logic were always closely connected and mutually influential, thirteenth-century Paris was marked out by a growing influence of grammar on logic, which culminated in the development of speculative grammar. The earliest and most important proponents of the modistic tradition were Boethius of Dacia (first half of thirteenth century – died after 1277) and Martin of Dacia (1220–1304); later, Radulphus Brito took up Boethius of Dacia's mantle, and shortly after 1300 Thomas of Erfurt wrote *De modis significandi seu grammatica speculativa*, which became not only one of the best known treatises on the topic, but also one of the last original contributions to the field.

The basic goal was to establish grammar as a science (hence the *speculativa* appellation, i.e. 'theoretical'), by moving it from the merely linguistic realm to the realm of reality. Because the individual words and vocal expressions differ from language to language, they cannot be taken to constitute a fundamental matter of inquiry; instead, it is the general meanings (*significata generalia*) of words that are cross-linguistic with which grammar is concerned, that is, nouns, verbs, cases and tenses (Pinborg 1982). The *significata generalia* can be presented in a number of ways, or modes, of intellection, signification and being (*modi intelligendi, significandi* and *essendi*); these modes are related in such a way that some linguistic item is a particular grammatical part of speech as a result of its *modus significandi*, which follows from its *modus intelligendi*, which in turn is generated by its *modus essendi* (Mora-Márquez 2014). Because of their emphasis on these modes, speculative grammarians are also known as modist grammarians or *Modistae*. Ultimately, it was these distinctions that laid speculative grammar open to criticism, specifically the charge that "they had confused linguistic distinctions with real ones" (Pinborg 1982, 257), and by the early part of the fourteenth century, the modist approach was strongly criticized by many, including both William of Ockham and Jean Buridan.

5.4   THE CONDEMNATIONS OF 1277

In Section 5.2, we discussed an important factor driving the development of logic in the thirteenth century, namely the strong metaphysical tendencies. This can be seen as an internal factor, internal to logic or even philosophy more broadly. Logic was also constrained and influenced by external factors, and during the thirteenth century one of the strongest of these was the determination of the relationship between dialectic and the other disciplines. This determination certainly wasn't new to the thirteenth century,[9] but the combination of the birth of the universities as centers of academic authority (see Introduction) and the introduction and dissemination of the new Aristotelian texts translated or rediscovered in the middle of the twelfth century (see the chapter "The Legacy of Ancient Logic in the Middle Ages" in this volume) provided a special context for tensions between disciplines to be worked out.

We see evidence of such tensions quite early in the thirteenth century; in 1210, Archbishop Peter of Corbeil and the provincial synod of Sens made public or private lecturing on Aristotle's natural philosophy by members of the Arts Faculty at Paris an excommunicable offence, and in 1228, Pope Gregory IX extended this to forbid members of the Theology Faculty as well from engaging in Aristotelian natural philosophy. The 1210 prohibition was reaffirmed in 1215 and extended to the university of Toulouse in 1245 by Pope Innocent IV. Nevertheless, expurgated versions of Aristotle's corpus of natural philosophy penetrated the Arts curriculum at Paris and was relatively well entrenched by the middle of the century (Uckelman 2010, 210–212).

---

[9] Discussions of the relationship between philosophy and theology go all the way back to Augustine and Boethius.

These various prohibitions were explicitly directed towards Aristotelian natural philosophy, of which logic and dialectic were not a part. These remained unconstrained and a foundational part of the university education, on both sides of the channel, throughout the century. Nevertheless, during the final quarter of the century, when anti-Aristotelian sentiment was at its highest (specifically directed against the Averroism or Radical Aristotelianism of people such as Siger of Brabant and Boethius of Dacia), logical doctrines did not escape unscathed. At the beginning of March 1277, on the third anniversary of the death of Thomas Aquinas, Stephen Tempier, bishop of Paris, condemned 219 propositions and two books, proclaiming that anyone who taught, defended, upheld or even listened to any of these would face excommunication if he did not turn himself in to the authorities within seven days (Uckelman 2010, 204). Among the 219 propositions, 179 can be classified as errors in philosophy and forty as errors in theology (Mandonnet 1908–1911). Of the former, none of the propositions pertains to what could be called logic, strictly speaking; however, some of them touch upon the role of argumentation and philosophizing, such as "That there is no rationally disputable question that the philosopher ought not to dispute and determine, because reasons are derived from things" (Denifle and Chatelain 1889–1897, no. 145).

Shortly afterwards, Kilwardby, as Archbishop of Canterbury, published his own list of thirty erroneous propositions, with a prohibition against their teaching. Of the thirty propositions, nearly half concerned grammar and logic (Leff 1968, 291) and included such propositions as that contraries can be simultaneously true in some material and that a materially defective syllogism is not a syllogism (Lewry 1981b, 240–241). Other propositions relate to the analyses of tensed statements, including contingent statements about the future. Unlike Tempier, Kilwardby did not declare these propositions heretical; as a result, while the punishment for transgressing Tempier's action was excommunication, the punishments at Oxford were less significant. Masters who taught the propositions would be deprived of their chairs, while bachelors would be expelled. Five years later, in 1284, Kilwardby's successor John Pecham confirmed the prohibition and further strengthened it to a condemnation: teaching these theses became grounds for excommunication (Uckelman 2010, 208, 218).

Many people have argued that Tempier's condemnation and Kilwardby's prohibition paved the way for the birth of modern science (Duhem 1906–1913, 1913–1959; Murdoch 1991). Whether this grand claim can be substantiated when all the propositions are taken into account is out of the scope of this chapter, but with respect to the effect that these two actions had on the development of logical studies *per se*, the answer is much less grand: despite the strong strictures, the prohibitions at Oxford were within a decade mostly ignored (Lawrence 1984, 117), and in 1325, Tempier's successor as bishop of Paris, Stephen de Bourret, revoked the prohibition as far as any Thomistic thesis was concerned. Thus, while the 1270s can be seen as the culmination of the rising tensions between philosophy and theology, when these tensions finally ignited, they fizzled out quickly in the end, leaving almost no mark on the development of logic in the fourteenth century.

5.5 CONCLUSION

Logic in the thirteenth century consisted primarily of two traditions, as we have seen. One is the textbook tradition, encompassing discussions of properties of terms, syncategorematic terms, and *obligationes* (see the chapter "Obligationes" in this volume); this tradition had its source in late-twelfth-century treatises. The other is the commentary tradition on Porphyry's *Isagoge* and Aristotle's *Organon*, which draws heavily on Averroes. These traditions overlap; but while textbooks cover roughly the whole of logic as it was conceived in the thirteenth century, these works are also more elementary and not as original as the most important commentaries. It is, however, important to look to both these traditions when one aims to characterize logic during this time. If this is done, then it becomes clear that during the thirteenth century, logic was heavily underpinned by metaphysics, and as such it stands in deep contrast with logic in the following century, which could be seen as freeing logic from metaphysics.

6 Logic in the Latin West in the Fourteenth Century

Stephen Read

The main advances in logical investigations in the thirteenth century in the Latin West were concentrated at the Universities of Paris and Oxford. There were other universities and *studia generalia*, such as Cambridge, Erfurt and elsewhere, where logic was taught, and on which both Oxford and Paris depended for their students, and to which they despatched many of their masters after their studies in Arts. But the real originality in driving forward the *logica modernorum*, the real innovations in developing the theories of properties of terms, of consequence, of obligations theory and the treatment of insolubles, is found for the most part in the work of masters teaching at Paris and Oxford.

All this had changed by the end of the fourteenth century. By 1400, there were many more universities, particularly in northern Europe, starting with the German universities established at Prague, Vienna, Erfurt and Heidelberg, and in southern Europe there was a revival and extension of the study of logic in Italy and Spain. In the meantime, the Black Death, striking first from 1347 to 1349, and again in 1361 and 1369 (and repeatedly for the next 300 years or so), although reducing the population by at least one-third, had surprisingly not reduced the output of logical treatises, even if it affected their vitality. Nor had the Papal Schism (see Section 6.5) apparently affected the study of logic, but if anything served to disseminate it more broadly.

Returning to the start of the fourteenth century, all real interest in logic was arguably preserved by those working in Oxford. This is the thesis propounded by Ebbesen (1985). We are, of course, dependent for our understanding of historical developments on historical traces, in particular, what logical treatises have been preserved – and indeed, on which of those that have been preserved have been studied. Nonetheless, it does seem that interest in logic waned at Paris towards the end of the thirteenth century in the face of the rise of modism, with its fascination with grammar and the so-called "modes of signifi- cation".[1] Hitherto, univocation had united a term with a single signifi- cation throughout the different things for which it supposited: e.g. the signification of 'man' is the same though the term supposits for differ- ent classes of men in 'Some man is running' and 'Socrates was a man'. The *modistae* tried to describe the distinction purely grammatically, by reference to the different modes of signifying possessed by the term in its different uses. But this threatened to divorce meaning from truth. The doctrine was fiercely attacked in the early fourteenth century.[2] In the meantime, the study of logic had been preserved in Oxford and was re-introduced to Paris in the early years of the fourteenth century.

One figure stands out at the head of the logical traditions in both Oxford and Paris in the fourteenth century: Walter Burley. So first, we should look at Burley's career and his works on logic; then we will turn to logical developments in England through the rest of the century after him; next, survey logic in Paris during the same period; take a close look at one significant debate, that between nom- inalism and realism; and finally, consider the wider picture in Europe and the dissemination of logic towards the end of the century.

6.1 WALTER BURLEY

Burley was born in Yorkshire in England around 1375, studied at Oxford (probably at Balliol) in the late 1290s, was teaching master at Merton during the first decade of the new century, then went to Paris before 1310 to study theology, becoming doctor of theology in 1322 or soon after.[3] In 1327, with the accession of the young Edward III to the throne of England, deposing Edward II and his court, Burley

---

[1] See, e.g., Pinborg 1982 and Ebbesen 1998a, 273–278.
[2] By, e.g., Burley in Brown 1974, 254; Ockham 1974a, II-4 ch. 10.
[3] See Vittorini 2013. Burley said that on 5 August 1337 he was in his sixty-second year.

became the king's envoy to the Papal court at Avignon and spent his remaining years often abroad and on diplomatic business, but also continuing to write further philosophical treatises. Around 1333, he joined the select intellectual circle of Richard de Bury, the Bishop of Durham, author of the *Philobiblon* (Bury's own neologism, meaning 'the love of books'), reportedly owner of the largest private library in England. Burley died in 1344 or soon after.

Burley's early writings are definitive of our knowledge of logic as it stood at the turn of the fourteenth century. In 1302 alone, he composed treatises on supposition theory, consequences, insolubles and obligations. De Rijk (1985, 23) suggests they may have constituted a whole course on logic, together with shorter treatises on exceptives and exclusives.

During the same period, Burley composed commentaries and questions on several of Aristotle's logical works: *On Interpretation, Posterior Analytics* and *Sophistical Refutations*. He wrote a further commentary on *On Interpretation* (the so-called 'Middle Commentary') in 1310, shortly after arriving in Paris. In this work, he spoke explicitly of a real proposition (*propositio in re*) as the ultimate significate of written and spoken propositions (Brown 1973, 1.24), though he had mooted the idea already in his earlier *Quaestiones* of 1301 (in Brown 1974, 3.553, 249): "concerning the mental utterance, it should be realised that it is composed of things which the mind asserts to be the same or different". Boethius (1877, 37) had interpreted Aristotle's remarks in the first chapter of *On Interpretation* (16a3–4) as distinguishing four levels of meaning: "for thing, concept, sound and letter are four: the concept conceives the things, spoken sounds are signs of the concept, and letters signify the sounds". In his Middle Commentary, Burley comes to distinguish explicitly between the proposition in the mind which is composed of concepts, and the real proposition composed by the mind of the things signified by those concepts, so that propositions too are four-fold: the written proposition, composed of letters, signifying the vocal proposition, made up of sounds, in turn signifying the mental proposition, which ultimately gets its meaning by signifying the real proposition. Nonetheless, the real proposition is a human construct, made true when the objects which it asserts to be the same or different really are the same or different (Burley 1973, 1.27).[4]

Burley's most substantial work on logic belongs to the end of his stay in Paris, possibly just after receiving his doctorate in theology. A shorter, incomplete version was composed no later than 1324, replaced by a longer version a few years later in which he responded to the radical nominalist claims in William Ockham's *Summa Logicae*, which we will consider shortly. Burley was not at all averse to rehashing parts of earlier works of his own (or even of others), as were his contemporaries, if not quite so blatantly. The shorter version of his new logic of the 1320s, *On the Essence of the Art of Logic*,[5] opens with material repeating arguments from his treatise on *Consequences* of 1302. The original plan of the shorter treatise is set out at the start, being conceived in four parts, of which not even the first was completed. That first part was to have three subparts (Burley 2000, 3): "first, general rules of inference will be established. The second will deal with the nature of syncategorematic words. The third will discuss certain matters concerning the supposition of terms". Only the first two subparts were completed, however. Nor were any of the other three parts, on sophistries (i.e. fallacies), on obligations and on demonstration.

Having abandoned this treatise, Burley started afresh, completing a work consisting of two treatises, the first on properties of terms (*viz.* supposition, appellation and copulation), the second and much longer treatise on compound propositions: general rules of inference, enthymemes and hypothetical syllogisms; inferences involving other compound propositions, *viz.* conjunctions, disjunctions, causal propositions (of the form '*p* because *q*'), temporal propositions (e.g. '*p* when *q*'), exclusives, exceptives and reduplicatives (e.g. 'Being

---

[4] See the chapter 'Propositions: Their Meaning and Truth' for a somewhat different interpretation of Burley's theory of the real proposition.

[5] Burley 1955, 2000. For the translation of the title, see Spade and Menn 2003.

qua being is the subject of metaphysics'} and concluding with a discussion of sophisms about 'begins' and 'ceases'.[6] Whether Burley conceived the treatise as covering more is unclear. The plan for the shorter treatise reads like an update of the 1302 *Logic* (and as noted, it contains parts of that earlier work, and covers similar ground). The longer treatise omits much of that earlier work, namely, discussion of insolubles and obligations. It is also the work in which Burley confronted Ockham's logic for the first time, though its structure is very different from that of Ockham's logical treatise.

In the period after the longer treatise, when acting as "king's clerk", Burley continued at the very least to revise and update his many texts. The main work on logic from this period is the 1337 *Expositio super artem veterem*, a discussion of the "old logic", that is, a literal commentary on Porphyry's *Isagoge* ('On Universals'), and Aristotle's *Categories* and *On Interpretation*. We will come back to Burley's late work in Section 6.4.

6.2 ENGLAND

Burley's logic laid the basis for most of the logical developments in England, at least in the first half of the century. Despite their temperamental differences, much of Ockham's logic was drawn from Burley's.

Ockham's logic is itself not particularly radical. What was radical was his semantics, and the metaphysics which it underpinned (see, e.g., Read 2007). Ockham was born in about 1287 in Ockham in Surrey, and joined the Franciscan Order at an early age, spending much of the next twenty years or so at the Franciscan house in London. He was in Oxford in 1317–1319, when he gave the lectures on Peter Lombard's *Sentences* that all bachelors of theology were required to do, but whether he spent much or any other time in Oxford is unclear. He was in London in the early 1320s, disputing with fellow Franciscans Walter Chatton and Adam Wodeham, and it

---

[6] See Spade's 'Introduction' to Burley 2000, x–xvii.

was there that he composed his discussions of Aristotle's *Categories*, *On Interpretation* and *Sophistical Refutations*, and his mighty *Summa Logicae*, with its reductionist and iconoclastic metaphysics, in 1323. He travelled to the Papal court in Avignon in 1324, though whether that was simply to lecture at the Franciscan studium or whether he had already been called to answer charges of heresy in his theological views is a matter of dispute (see Knysh 1986). In any event, such charges came to a head in 1327–1328, and for whatever reason, he left Avignon along with Michael Cesena, the head of the Franciscan Order, in a chaotic hurry in May 1328, excommunicated by Pope John XXII and bringing his own charges of heresy against the Pope for his views on apostolic poverty. He spent his final years at the court of the Holy Roman Emperor in Munich, writing on politics and theology. There is some suggestion two logical treatises of the 1340s are authentic (see Buytaert 1964, 1965–1966). He died there in 1347 (or possibly 1348).

Burley and Ockham are often portrayed as embodying realism *versus* nominalism (see Section 6.4). Burley believed, with Aristotle, that there really are things outside the mind common to all things sharing that common nature, immanent in individuals. Ockham believed he was following Aristotle too, in holding that everything outside the mind was an individual, so those qualities must also be individuals (often nowadays termed "tropes"). Take Burley's real proposition, for example, 'The dog eats the bread'. Ockham jokes that if the subject and predicate of this proposition really were the dog and the bread (put together by the mind into the proposition), then the subject would eat the predicate; or in the real proposition, 'Robert persecutes John', the subject would persecute, slay and burn the predicate. "This is absurd", he protested (Ockham 1980, III 12, 248). Rather, he says, the subject and predicate of the mental proposition are concepts, which gain their signification not by signifying non-existent common natures but individuals. The signification of 'dog' is the class of all dogs: "the universal term 'man' signifies many things", he writes, "but since it does not signify many things which are not men, it must signify many men" (Ockham 1974a, 96; 1974b, 114).

Burley strikes back: near the start of the longer version of *De Puritate*, he argues that on Ockham's view "sounds would continually lose their significates, nor could someone move his finger without a word losing its significate, because when the finger was still the word 'still' would signify the finger, but when the finger moved the word would no longer signify the finger. That's absurd" (Burley 1955, 9; 2000, 90). 'Man' doesn't signify individual men, like Socrates and Plato, for the hearer can understand the term without being acquainted with each and every man (Burley 1955, 8; 2000, 88). Rather, common nouns signify common natures. We will explore the realist–nominalist debate further in Section 6.4.

Despite their different accounts of signification, and the fact that much of Ockham's reductionist programme is articulated through his theory of supposition, Ockham took over a great deal of that supposition theory from Burley's 1302 treatise. Burley's other early treatises were also very influential. The doctrine found in his treatise on obligations became known as the *responsio antiqua*, the account to which later theories were opposed (see the chapter on obligations). Much the same is true of Burley's proposed solution to the insolubles (see the chapter on 'Sophisms and Insolubles'): it is his version of the restrictivist doctrine which is criticized at length by Thomas Bradwardine, whose novel proposal became the starting point for most theories put forward later.

The 1320s ushered in a golden age in the intellectual life of Oxford, centred around the so-called Oxford (or Merton) Calculators. The five leading figures were Bradwardine, Richard Kilvington, William Heytesbury, John Dumbleton and Richard Swineshead. Their main focus was mathematical physics, and their work in this area marks the first real advance in the subject since Aristotle, to some extent anticipating the scientific revolution of the seventeenth century (see, e.g., Sylla 1982). But the first four also made significant contributions to logic. Bradwardine's ideas about insolubles, false because they each signify their own truth as well as their own falsehood (and so are implicitly contradictory), have just been mentioned. Bradwardine composed his treatise on insolubles as a young regent master at Oxford. His style reveals his mathematical bent of mind: he expounds his theory by two definitions, six postulates and three theorems, each proved with care and in detail. He showed the same "geometrical precision" (Fleming 1964, 72) in his mathematical works, which inaugurated the two decades of work by the Calculators, and in his theological masterpiece, *De Causa Dei*, a blast against the Pelagians (such as Ockham), who believed one could earn one's way into heaven by good works, reaffirming Augustine's doctrine (later revived by Calvin) that salvation is entirely due to God's grace. Bradwardine's character often reveals itself, as when at the start of the sixth chapter of the *Insolubles*, having argued against other views, he embarks on his own solution with the words, "Having rid ourselves of false and mistaken opinions ...". He had previously closed his attacks with such phrases as "the aforesaid view is completely annihilated" (*penitus adnullata*) and "the view of the nullifiers (*cassantes*) is sufficiently nullified (*cassata*)" (Bradwardine 2010, 4.2.8 and 5.6). Bradwardine, too, joined the Bishop of Durham's circle, became confessor to Edward III, and was briefly Archbishop of Canterbury before succumbing to the Black Death in 1349.

Dumbleton also died in 1349, but the other Calculators survived (two out of five is close to the national death toll of one in three), though Kilvington died in 1361 when there was a second wave of the pestilence. Another significant figure at Oxford, though not a Calculator, was Roger Swyneshed. He challenged Bradwardine's account of insolubles, but is perhaps more famous for his challenge to Burley's rules for obligations. Robert Fland (or Eland: see Read forthcoming), an author of treatises on obligations, insolubles and consequences whose identity is unknown, writing at Oxford some time between 1335 and 1370, described Swyneshed's revised rules for obligations as a "*nova responsio*" (Spade 1980a, 42). Swyneshed seems to have liked to frame his theses in arresting ways, announcing, for

example, that in an obligational disputation one could deny a conjunction both of whose conjuncts one had granted, where the explanation was rather more mundane, namely, that by his rules responses
were determined only by the *obligatum*, not by previous responses
(e.g. those where the conjuncts had been granted) (Spade 1977, 257).
A similar liking for jest is displayed in his treatise on insolubles,
where he claims, for example, that two contradictories can both
be false – e.g. the liar sentence, *L*, *viz.* '*L* is false', and its (apparent)
contradictory, '*L* is not false' (Spade 1979, 189).

Another Mertonian from the 1340s and 1350s whose logical
writings had significant impact was Richard Billingham, with his
Speculum Puerorum, often known by its *incipit*, '*Terminus est in
quem*', a treatise on the "proofs of propositions" (*probationes propositionum*). This sparked a genre of treatises on the truth and falsehood
of propositions, by which terms and propositions might be expounded
to exhibit their truth conditions. For example, 'Every man runs' is
expounded or "proved" as 'A man runs and nothing is a man unless it
runs', thus showing the existential import of universal affirmatives.
Again, 'A man runs' is expounded as 'This runs and this is a man',
from which 'A man runs' follows by an expository syllogism. Indeed,
the expository syllogism is at the heart of the resolution of terms.
Billingham's first rule says that "a consequence is valid from an inferior to a superior without distribution or any word with the force
of negation", which he says is the basis of the expository syllogism
in the third figure (and so of every affirmative syllogism), and the second rule that "a consequence holds from an inferior to its superior
with an 'existence postulate' (*constantia*) regarding the subject and a
word with the force of negation placed after the inferior and superior",
which he says is the basis of the negative expository syllogism and so
of every negative syllogism (Billingham 1982, §§9 and 15).

Two issues are being raised in the "proof" of a proposition. Recall
that '*probation*' means "testing", as did the English word 'proof' in
earlier times (cf. the proverb "the proof of the pudding is in the eat-
ing"). These issues are, first, what is the significance of the (spoken)

proposition; secondly, what makes it true? We've seen that Burley presented the real proposition as answer to the first question, and the real identity of the objects composed by the mind as what made it true (and so derivatively, the mental, spoken and written propositions). A third question is an epistemological one: what is the object of knowledge? It is often thought that a single thing will answer all three questions, and there is a vast gulf between those who, like Burley, think that there is something (the *propositio in re*, or the complexly signifiable, which we will discuss shortly, or a state of affairs) in the world having propositional complexity and those, like Ockham, or Walter Chatton (and as we will see, John Buridan) or Richard Ferrybridge, who vehemently rejected such entities.

Billingham's work is a link to the second half of the century in Oxford. This period is still less well researched than the first half, but what is known about it suggests that it was largely a period of consolidation rather than one of significantly new ideas. For example, large parts of Ralph Strode's *Insolubles* (composed in the 1360s) repeat the texts of Bradwardine, Swyneshed and Heytesbury, translated into the third person (see Bradwardine 2010, Appendix B). Ferrybridge was at Oxford in the 1350s and 1360s, as was Richard Brinkley, a Franciscan whose *Summa Logicae* was written at Oxford in the 1360s (see Gál and Wood 1980). Although an elementary work, it is a diatribe against the nominalists. Probably the most original logician working in Oxford in the second half of the century was John Wyclif, strongly influenced by Burley and his realism. Two of his logical treatises (a simple logic textbook, *De Logica*, and a much more substantial and deeper work, *Logicae Continuatio*) were edited in the nineteenth century, but the editions have many errors and new editions are urgently needed. Born in Yorkshire around 1325, Wyclif was teaching master at Balliol by 1360, receiving his DTh in 1372/3. His views on the Eucharist led to charges of heresy in the late 1370s, while his logical works date from the 1360s. A further logical treatise, arguably by Wyclif himself, is entitled *Summa Insolubilium*, though some manuscripts attribute it to Wyclif's follower John Tarteys, writing at Oxford at the turn of the fifteenth century. Wyclif's view on insolubles (for it is also found in the *Logicae Continuatio*) distinguished three notions of truth: truth as being, as being as a proposition precisely signifies, and as being as it precisely signifies provided this primary significate (for Wyclif, a logical being or being of reason – neither a substance nor an accident) is not dependent on the proposition itself (see Wyclif 1986, xxxi). Talk of primary signification *versus* consequential signification (*ex consequente*) recalls Bradwardine's claim that a proposition signifies the consequences of anything it signifies (Bradwardine 2010, 6.3 and 7.2.5). Wyclif's idea is that a liar sentence is false in the third sense but true in the second. But, as Spade and Wilson observe (Wyclif 1986, xxxiii), distinguishing these senses of 'true' risks a revenge paradox with the sentence 'This sentence is not true in the second sense', for if it is true (as Wyclif says) then its primary significate does not exist, and so it is (also) false (in the second sense). Nonetheless, Wyclif's ideas were taken up by Robert Alyngton, fellow of Queen's College in the 1380s, and Tarteys (fellow of Balliol around 1400) among others.

Henry Hopton was also in Oxford in the 1360s. In a short work *On the Truth and Falsehood of Propositions*, Hopton considers what propositions signify and what makes them true. He rejects Chatton's view that it is just the significate of the subject, Crathorn's claim that it is some *modus rei*, a way things are, and Ockham's theory that it is the mental proposition itself.[7] Nothing is needed to make it true, he says: "what the proposition signifies ... is neither an *aliquid* nor an *aliqualiter*" (cited in Ashworth and Spade 1992, 53). Rather, "for it to be true it suffices and is required that it precisely signifies as it is assertively and directly" (Maierù 1993, 113).

De Rijk observes that Johannes Venator (*aka* John Huntman) contrasts "signifying precisely" with "signifying assertively" (De Rijk 1982a, 176; cf. Maierù 1993, 114). Huntman was at Oriel College from 1373 to 1387, and denounced in 1382 for sympathizing with the heretical views of Wyclif. His *Logica* consists of four treatises, in

---

[7] See Ashworth and Spade 1992, 51–53; Maierù 1993, 111–112.

chapter 4 of the first of which he asks us to consider the proposition 'You are not': "it signifies you are, and it signifies that you are not. But from this it does not follow that it is impossible, because it does not signify assertively that you are and you are not" (De Rijk 1999, I 216). In the third treatise (chapter 2), he spells out the truth and false-hood of propositions at length.

6.3 PARIS

We have little evidence of logical activity at Paris in the first quarter of the fourteenth century, apart from the presence of Burley. The earliest indigenous treatise on logic, as one might call it, is Gerard Odo's *Logica*, composed at Paris, probably in the 1320s. Born in the south of France, Odo replaced Michael of Cesena as Minister General of the Franciscans in 1329 after the latter's excommunica-tion. He died of the plague in 1349. The *Logica* is in three books, 'On Syllogisms', 'On Supposition' and 'On Two Universal Principles of Knowledge' (*De duobus communissimis principiis scientiarum*), namely, the Laws of Excluded Middle and of Non-Contradiction (*"de quolibet esse vel non esse"* and *"de nullo simul esse et non esse"*). In one manuscript of the work, excerpts from Odo's *Sentences* com-mentary have been inserted, that following the first book being on the nature of contradictory opposition. Odo maintains that contra-diction is the strongest form of opposition (*"maxima oppositio"*), cit-ing Aristotle's *Metaphysics* X 4 (1055b1–2) in support. The annex is in fact a riposte to Burley, who had claimed in a treatise probably written in Paris shortly beforehand, that contradiction was in fact the weakest form of opposition. The crux of Burley's argument was that the contradictory opposite is entailed by any opposite, and so, being included in any opposite, is the weakest of the opposites (De Rijk 1996, 184). Odo tried to confute Burley by his own arguments, for one can infer greater opposition from less (Odo 1997, 208). But here they are arguing past one another, since Burley proves that the impossible entails anything whatever by the topic 'from the less', but concedes that "from the impossible there need not follow just anything whatever, for from the less impossible the more impossible does not follow".[8]

Odo's aim in Book 3 is not so much to prove the laws of Excluded Middle and Non-Contradiction, for he says that, being principles, they are indemonstrable; rather, the aim is to explore their range of validity, and to show that they satisfy the conditions for being principles of reasoning: namely, universal consensus and indispensability for disputation. In the course of the discussion (1997, 382–383), he considers the liar paradox in the form 'I say something false' (ego dico falsum), and also in the jazzed-up version, 'The miser says he will give you a talent if the first thing you say to him is true', to which you reply, 'You ought not to give me a talent'. He rejects any restrictivist suggestion that self-reference is impossible or unacceptable, and argues that the liar sentence has multiple meanings and is implicitly contradictory (and so false) for it both affirms the unity of the predicate with the subject (being affirmative) and denies it (since the predicate is 'false') (Odo 1997, 395–398).

This solution can be seen as an interesting precursor of the solution offered by the first major home-grown logician at Paris in the fourteenth century – indeed, arguably the greatest logician of the century, John Buridan. Unlike almost every other fourteenth-century philosopher of note, Buridan remained resolutely a teaching master in the Arts Faculty at Paris through a forty-year career there. Born in Picardy in the 1290s, he was rector (in charge of all teaching for a three-month period) from 1327/8. He died in 1360 or thereabouts. His writings are exclusively commentaries on Aristotle and works on logic. The former include Questions on all the books of the Organon, the latter a Treatise on Consequences from the late 1330s or early 1340s, and a massive Summulae de Dialectica, composed in nine books and variously revised over a twenty-year period. It is ostensibly a commentary on the Tractatus of Peter of Spain from a hundred years earlier, though in places, e.g. the fourth book, on supposition

---

[8] In the shorter treatise: Burley 1955, 248; 2000, 61–62.

theory, Buridan substitutes his own text on which to comment. The final book, the *Sophismata*, sometimes appearing separately, is a self-contained introduction to logic via a succession of sophisms.

In his longer treatise *On the Essence of the Art of Logic*, Burley wrote: "Formal consequence is of two kinds: one kind holds by reason of the form of the whole structure ... another kind ... holds by reason of the form of the incomplex terms, e.g., a consequence from an inferior to a superior affirmatively is formal, but holds by reason of the terms" (Burley 1955, 86; 2000, 173). Consequence holding by reason of the form of the terms is a distinctively English notion, often expressed by saying it holds if the consequent is "understood in" the antecedent.[9] In contrast, the structural account is typical of Buridan and others writing at Paris. Buridan wrote: "Consequence is called 'formal' if it is valid in all terms retaining a similar form" (Buridan 1976, 2015, I 4). An inference from inferior to superior, such as 'A man is running, so an animal is running', is for him a material consequence, for it is not valid in all terms. Nonetheless, the latter inference is valid, he says, for the consequent has more causes of truth than the antecedent (Buridan 1976, 2015, I 8, conclusion 8). That does not mean that the consequent is true whenever the antecedent is, for Buridan's nominalism decrees that the consequent does not exist and so cannot be true if it is not uttered. Rather, he says, things cannot be as the antecedent signifies unless they are also as the consequent signifies (Buridan 2001; *Sophismata*, chapter 8, 955). Take the consequence, 'Every proposition is affirmative, therefore, no proposition is negative'. This is valid, since things cannot be as the antecedent signifies without being as the consequent signifies. But the antecedent can be true without the consequent being true – indeed, if the antecedent is true the consequent does not even exist.

Yet even this criterion, in terms of signification, is not quite right, Buridan argues. Others, appearing to follow Aristotle, he says,

---

[9] See, e.g., Ashworth and Spade 1992, 39, citing Billingham, Strode, Hopton, Fland (or Eland) and Lavenham.

claim that truth consists in the existence of the significate of the proposition.[10] But Buridan rejects this interpretation:

> if we can explain everything by positing fewer, we should not, in the natural order of things, posit many, because it is pointless to do with many what can be done with fewer. Now everything can be easily explained without positing such *complexe significabilia* [see below], which are not substances, or accidents, or subsistent per se, or inherent in any other thing. Therefore, they should not be posited.[11]

All that corresponds to a proposition are the significates of its terms. But they are the same whether the proposition is affirmative or negative. So truth cannot be defined simply in terms of the signification of a proposition. Rather, a particular affirmative is true if subject and predicate supposit for the same, a negative if they don't, and so on for all the various kinds of proposition (Buridan 2001; *Sophismata* chapter 2 conclusion, 14, 858–859).

There are two obscure figures who seem to have worked at the University of Paris in the 1320s, 1330s or 1340s. We know the name of one of them: Thomas Maulfelt, but we know nothing else about him; we do not even know the other's name. He is often referred to as 'Pseudo-Scotus', since the treatise of his which we know, *Questions on the Prior Analytics*, was printed in the seventeenth-century edition of the works of Duns Scotus, but is definitely not by Scotus. Nor is it by the author of the *Questions on the Posterior Analytics* also included in that edition, also not by Scotus and attributed in one manuscript to John of Cornwall. Scotus died in 1308 and John of Cornwall in 1316. The *Questions on the Posterior Analytics* might plausibly be written before 1316, but the *Questions on the Prior Analytics* refers to the doctrine of the complexly signifiable

---

[10] Buridan, *Questiones in Metaphysicen* Book 6 question 10, cited in Klima 2009, 219.

[11] Buridan, *Questiones in Metaphysicen* Book 5 question 7, cited in Zupko 2003, 128.

(*complexe significabile*), first mooted by Adam Wodeham in his *Sentences* lectures at Oxford in 1331.[12] It was introduced to Paris either in the works of Gregory of Rimini in the early 1340s, or possibly in those of Nicholas of Autrecourt, whose works were condemned in 1340 and burned in 1346, when he confessed: "I once said in the rue de Fouarre [the location of the Arts schools in Paris] that ... what is complexly signifiable by the proposition 'God and a creature are distinct' is nothing. False and scandalous" (cited in Tachau 1988, 354). Pseudo-Scotus considers the view "that [the *dici de omni*] is a complexly signifiable, because this proposition, '[the predicate] is said universally of the subject' signifies more than these two terms 'predicate' and 'subject'. Therefore, in addition to the significates of those terms some other significate corresponds to the said proposition, none other than what is complexly signifiable by the proposition".[13] He rejects the account on the grounds that such complexly signifiables would transcend God's power, and would lead to an infinite regress (cited in Tachau 1988, 284 a–b).

Another indication of date and place comes from the fact that Pseudo-Scotus appears to refer to Buridan's *Questions on the Posterior Analytics* (probably composed in the late 1320s or 1330s; see Lagerlund 2000, chapter 6), and that in his *Treatise on Consequences* Buridan himself rejects a suggestion made by Pseudo-Scotus for the analysis of propositions of the form 'Every S can be P'.[14]

Maulfelt is an enigma. Many treatises on logic attributed to him are preserved in libraries in Eastern Europe. They identify Maulfelt as English; Lorenz claims that he summarized logical doctrines at Paris in the 1320s and 1330s, but by 1339 had left, possibly for Erfurt and/

---

[12] Wodeham mostly uses the phrase 'significabile per complexum'. For a case where he speaks of 'complexe significabile', see Tachau 1987, 181 n. 39.

[13] Pseudo-Scotus 1639, q. 8, 283 b: "Tertio arguitur, quod sit significabile complexe; quia ista propositio, *Dici universaliter de subiecto*, plus significat quam isti duo termini, *predicatum*, et *subiectum*; igitur praeter significata illorum terminorum correspondet aliquod aliud significatum dictae propositioni, et non aliud quam significabile complexe per propositionem".

[14] See my 'Introduction' to Buridan 2015, 4–5.

or Louvain. Van der Helm casts a sceptical eye on Lorenz's claims; the conclusion must be that we simply do not know.[15] Maulfelt's textbooks had a significant influence on spreading these logical doctrines throughout Europe in the fifteenth century. His most iconoclastic doctrine is found in his commentary on Aristotle's *Categories*: where others had reduced Aristotle's ten categories to three, and Ockham to two, Maulfelt reduced them to just one, namely, quality, denying the existence, or need for, substance, at least on rational grounds (though he concedes its admission may be founded on authority).[16] Another distinctive doctrine of Maulfelt's is the identification of a fourth mode of descent, conjunct descent, as permissible for terms with merely confused supposition (see Read 1991a, 76). For example, from 'Socrates differs from every man' one can descend to 'Socrates differs from this man and from that man and so on', since, he says, the occurrence of 'not' removes the distributive power of 'every'. Since 'man' has merely confused supposition, says Maulfelt, we must define such supposition as allowing disjunct or conjunct descent.

If Maulfelt was at Paris, he will have been a member of the English Nation. However, he may have been called '*anglicus*' simply because he was a member of that Nation, which also included Saxons, the most famous of whom, at least among logicians, was Albert of Saxony, born in Rickmansdorf around 1316, who arrived in Paris in 1351. Author of many commentaries on Aristotle, his logical works include *A Really Useful Logic* (*Perutilis Logica*), a collection of *Sophismata* and a set of *Twenty-Five Questions on Logic*. Charged with founding the University of Vienna in 1365 (see Section 6.5), he left straightaway to become bishop of Halberstadt, and died in 1390. In his *Perutilis Logica*, he disagreed with Maulfelt about the mode of supposition of 'man' in the above example: for one can licitly descend disjunctively on 'man'; however, he seems to have revised this judgement in his later *Sophismata* (Read 1990, 79–82; Fitzgerald 2015).

---

[15] See Lorenz 1996; van der Helm 2014, chapter 2.
[16] See Andrews 2008 and van der Helm 2014.

'Socrates differs from every man' means Socrates is not every man, and so Socrates is not this man or Socrates is not that man and so on. Conversely, if Socrates is not this man, then Socrates is not every man. So 'man' satisfies the criterion for determinate supposition, and conjunct descent is not needed.

Thomas of Cleves, writing in Paris in the early 1370s, would not agree. His treatise on logic has not survived, but there are later references to his doctrines. He left Paris in 1376 to teach at St Stephens school in Vienna (the foundation of the University having failed after Albert's departure), was present at its refounding in 1383, taught later in Heidelberg, and died in 1412. He is credited with claiming not only a fourth mode of descent, but in fact a fourth mode of common personal supposition corresponding to it, e.g. in 'All the apostles of God are twelve', from which one descends to 'Simon Peter and Matthew and John and so on are twelve' (see Read 1991b, 55–56). Another example, of 'man' in 'Every animal differs from every man', is attributed to Thomas' student, Paul of Gelria, who remained at Paris until 1382, when he joined Thomas at Vienna, via a year's teaching in Prague (see Read 1991b, 54).

Thomas was a student of William Buser (Bos and Read 2000, 15), the author of an influential treatise on obligations (Pozzi 1990), as also was Marsilius of Inghen, all members of the English Nation at Paris. Marsilius wrote several treatises on logic, some of which have been edited (Marsilius of Inghen 1983). He remained at Paris before leaving for Heidelberg, serving as its first rector in 1386, and dying there in 1396.

Although Thomas' works on logic have not survived, treatises of his and Paul's on *Concepts* have, both written in Paris (though Paul's seems to have been revised after his visit to Prague) (Bos and Read 2000, 21). A much more famous philosopher and theologian, Peter of Ailly, also wrote such a treatise, paired with another on *Insolubles*, composed in Paris in 1372, at much the same time as Thomas' (see Spade 1980a). Ailly came from the village of the same name in Picardy, so he was, like Buridan, a member of the Picardian

Nation. He was later heavily involved in negotiating an end to the
Papal Schism, rising to the rank of Cardinal and dying in 1420. His
work on insolubles derives ultimately from Bradwardine, via adaptations by Gregory of Rimini and Marsilius of Inghen, and was itself
influential in the fifteenth and sixteenth centuries (see Spade 1980a,
6). Indeed, possibly because of Ailly's eminence, Parisian logicians
largely followed the *via Buridani* (see the chapter on 'The Post-
Medieval Period').

6.4   REALISM AND NOMINALISM

The challenge of Ockham's nominalism was countered in England by
Burley in his later writings (see Conti 2013a, 'Introduction') and by
Wyclif, so that Oxford philosophy became predominantly realist in
the second half of the century. In contrast, although Paris also rejected
Ockhamist philosophy, it was won over by Buridan's nominalism, so
that it became something of a hotbed of nominalism after 1350.

At the heart of the dispute between Burley and Ockham, as
discussed in Section 6.2, lay the metaphysics of the categories – how
many kinds of things are there? Aristotle appeared to have said there
were ten such broad categories – but perhaps he just meant ten kinds
of predication, not of things. Burley and Ockham agree that this is
far too many: in his earlier writings, Burley expressed a modest realism, claiming that there are three such kinds (substance, quality and
quantity), the other seven being mere aspects (*respectus*) of those
three: "The first mode of being belongs to the three absolute categories, namely, substance, quality and quantity; but the mode of being
in relation to something else belongs to the other seven categories".[17]
Ockham wanted to reduce the number even further, to two, by rejecting quantity as real (and denying that the other eight had any reality
at all, even as aspects).

Fabrizio Amerini contrasts what he describes as Ockham's
horizontal reduction of the categories to two with a vertical

---

[17] Burley, *Tractatus super librum Predicamentorum*, cited in Dutilh Novaes 2013,
66 n. 64.

elimination of genus, species and differentiae in favour of the individual (Amerini 2005a, 189). This eliminativist reduction took place in two stages: first, Ockham demoted universals to the status of mere *ficta*, fictive entities having only "objective being", that is, existing only as objects of thought, having no real existence, in particular, not falling under any of the categories. Subsequently, he eliminated the object of thought as universal completely in his *actus* (or *intellectus*) theory, so that abstractive thought had no single object, but rather embraced the things which fall under the name. It is in this way that the theory deserves the title 'nominalism', albeit universals are mental names having subjective (i.e. categorial) being in the mind. This is far from the nominalism of the twelfth century, whereby universals were dismissed as mere *flatus vocis*, a breath of air (see, e.g., Biard 2010, 667).

Although in his later writings Burley was reacting to Ockham, Ockham himself was reacting to the early Burley and to Duns Scotus' defence of moderate realism. Scotus was a fellow Franciscan who had studied in Oxford at the end of the thirteenth century, before heading for Paris in 1302, where he taught until 1307, and finally at the Franciscan studium in Cologne, where he died in 1308 in his early forties. His realism about universals was based on the claim that though not really distinct from the individual, they were formally distinct from it. In this way, he sought to explain how individual and universal can be partly the same yet partly different. Nonetheless, regarding the horizontal distinction, he held that elements of all ten categories are really distinct.

Ockham viewed Scotus' doctrine as incoherent. If the universal is really identical with the individual then it has contradictory properties in different individuals. For example, the universal is universal and common to many; the individual is not. So if universal and individual are identical, the universal is both common and not common to many, and similarly for the individual (Ockham 1974b, chapter 16, 82–83). He inferred that individual and universal have to be distinct; and if the universal has to belong to the categories, it has to subsist in something, and that place is in the mind. Hence "the universal is an intention of the soul capable of being predicated of many" (Ockham 1974, chapter 15, 81).

The later Burley could not fault Ockham's argument against moderate realism. "If the one is predicated of something of which the other is not predicated, they are not the same, but different; and if something is predicated of the one which is not predicated of the other, they are not the same".[18] His response was to embrace an extreme realism in which universals are really distinct from their subjects. Where Ockham sought to explain every linguistic distinction in terms of a simpler ontology, Burley maintained an isomorphism between language and the world.[19] Just as there is a *propositio in re* corresponding to written, spoken and mental propositions, distinct from the objects which compose it as the terms are distinct from the linguistic proposition, so too there is a real universal corresponding to each predicate distinct from the objects to which it is common and of which it can be truly and commonly predicated.

Ockham's arguments were challenged elsewhere, for example, by Francis of Prato, a Dominican who arrived at the convent of Santa Caterina in Pisa in 1332, shortly after Ockham's departure from Pisa, where he had gone after fleeing Avignon (Amerini 2005b, 8). Francis, in his *Logica* of 1344–1345, probably written in Perugia (Amerini 2005b, 25), invoked Aquinas and the Thomist Hervaeus Natalis in affirming real universals but, unlike Scotus, denying their real unity. They are united and identical only in the mind. This blocks Ockham's argument appealing to their real identity, as proposed by Scotus and Burley. Moreover, Ockham's theory (whereby in a mental proposition, a concept is predicated of a concept) is impossible, for an individual (*res singularis*) cannot be predicated universally of anything, though it can be universal by representation, by causality (natural likeness) and by signification.[20]

[18] Burley, *Expositio super Praedicamenta Aristotelis*, cited in Conti 1990, 131.
[19] Conti 1990, 128; cf. Biard 2010, 671.
[20] Amerini 2005b, Part I tract 4 article 1, 309.

Similar moderate realist doctrines were held in Oxford by Wyclif and his followers, such as John Sharpe (fellow of Queen's College in the 1390s). See Sharpe (1990), which also contains relevant excerpts from the works of Alyngton, Milverley, Tarteys, Whelpdale and Paul of Venice.

Ockham's, and Ockhamist, nominalism were specifically condemned at Paris in 1339 and 1340, rejecting such attempts to distinguish a literal sense of language and its nominalist interpretation (Kaluza 1998, 438). But Paris had its own nominalist, Buridan, whose doctrines were enthusiastically taken up by his successors.

Buridan's nominalism is not dissimilar to Ockham's, so it is surprising that it proved so acceptable and indeed, attractive in Paris where Ockham's did not.[21] Perhaps the reason is that Buridan was careful to restrict his metaphysical observations to strictly logical ones. For example, commenting on an apparent counterexample to expository syllogism, with true premises and heretical conclusion: 'God is the Father, God is the Son, so the Son is the Father', he writes: "whether ... syllogisms in divine terms are formally valid and what that form is, I leave to the theologians ... because it is not for me, an Arts man, to determine [such matters]" (Buridan 1976, 2015, III-1 4, first conclusion).

6.5   THE DISSEMINATION OF LOGIC

We have seen that, although most advances in logic in the early fourteenth century were made in Oxford and Paris, work was being done elsewhere – e.g. Ockham's writing his *Summa Logicae* in London, and Francis of Prato's contesting Ockham's nominalism in Italy. Moreover, the logic from Oxford and Paris was carried all over Europe by scholars travelling south to Avignon (the Papal residence from 1309) and elsewhere. With the rise of the universities in the latter half of the century, logic became even more widely disseminated.

---

[21] For a discussion of Buridan's nominalism, see Klima's 'Introduction' to Buridan 2001, liii–lxii.

The Charles University was established in Prague in 1348, and Albert of Saxony studied there before becoming a teaching master at Paris in 1351 (see Biard 2015, §1). But mostly the movement was the other way. As we noted, Paul of Gelria left Paris for Prague in 1382; Thomas of Cleves went from Paris to Vienna and thence to the University of Heidelberg, when it was founded in 1391. John of Holland, from Amsterdam, studied in Oxford, then taught at Prague from 1366. He authored treatises on supposition, fallacies, obligations, insolubles, consequences and a collection of sophisms.

Two external factors played a particular role in this dissemination. One was the start of the Hundred Years War between England and France. This led to a gradual reduction, and in the end almost complete absence of English students at the so-called English Nation at Paris, which had always included Saxons, Scandinavians and Germans, but by the end of the century was known as the Anglo-German or even German Nation. Coupled to the so-called "Avignon captivity" of the Pope, and from 1378 the existence of two popes during the Papal Schism, one in Avignon and one in Rome, this led to a divorce between Oxford and Paris, Italian students and masters coming to Oxford (and vice versa), Germans to Paris and back.

Not all Italian masters came to Oxford (or Paris). We saw that Francis of Prato learned his Ockham in Italy. Another major Italian logician was Peter of Mantua, in the next generation (Francis died in 1345, Peter in 1399). Peter studied in Padua and taught in Bologna. Although he never came to England, his *Logica* is clearly heavily influenced by English logicians, Burley, Heytesbury, Billingham and Wyclif in particular, as well as by the Parisians, Buridan, Marsilius and Albert (see Strobino 2009). Further evidence of the presence of logic beyond Oxford and Paris is shown by Vincent Ferrer's *Treatise on Supposition* (Ferrer 1977), composed in his early twenties in Lerida in 1372.

The most famous of the Italian masters who did visit Oxford is Paul of Venice, who was there from 1390 to 1393, so that his massive *Logica Magna*, composed in the mid-1390s, is one of our

best witnesses to the development of logic at Oxford in the fourteenth century. For example, in his final treatise of Part II (as yet
unedited), on insolubles, Paul enumerates fifteen different solutions (and adds an unnumbered sixteenth, due to Peter of Mantua),
of which those of Kilvington, Scotus, Dumbleton, Bradwardine,
Albert of Saxony, Heytesbury, Peter of Ailly and Walter Sexgrave
have been identified. The fifteenth is Paul's own, an elaboration of
Swyneshed's.

Finally, John Dorp, born near Leiden in the Low Countries,
concluded the century in Paris by composing around 1393 a *Really
Useful Compendium of all of John Buridan's Logic* (Dorp 1965/1499),
revising Buridan's *Summulae de Dialectica* and replacing Buridan's
commentary with his own, which became highly popular throughout
Europe in the fifteenth century.

7 The Post-Medieval Period

E. Jennifer Ashworth

Making a clear division between the medieval and the post-medieval periods is impossible, especially if the end of the fourteenth century is taken as a cut-off point. The next century and a half certainly embraced big and important changes in the study of logic, but the new humanist developments were contemporary with continued work in the areas thought of as specifically medieval, such as supposition theory, and indeed there was a flowering of medieval logic in early-sixteenth-century Paris with the work of such men as John Mair (or Major). However, by the mid-sixteenth century, specifically medieval developments had largely died out, leaving behind only fragments of supposition theory and some simplified work on consequences. Aristotle's logic continued to be centrally important throughout the period, but the approach to it came to be very different from that of the Middle Ages. The Greek text of *Organon* was widely available by the end of the fifteenth century, and could be studied by senior students and teachers, but the main undergraduate teaching came to be done largely through elementary textbooks that summarized Aristotelian logic in simpler language and without the lengthy doctrinal discussions and illustrative sophismata that had characterized many medieval commentaries.[1]

This chapter has two main parts. The first part discusses the effects that historical events and movements had on educational systems and the logical studies thought to be suitable for undergraduates. The Western reception of the printing press in the middle of the fifteenth century was perhaps the most important event, for it accentuated the impact of the other events and movements. Suddenly it

---

[1] For more detailed information about the post-medieval period and more extensive bibliographies, see Ashworth 1974, 1985, 1988 and 2008.

became possible to produce books cheaply, in relatively large numbers, and without the differences between one copy and another that
often make work with manuscripts so difficult. By the end of the
fifteenth century, many university towns had presses able to print
the textbooks needed by the faculty of Arts, and teachers could disseminate their own works. Moreover, publishers, especially in Italy,
were able to print the works required for serious scholarship, such as
Aristotle's Organon in Greek and the newly discovered Greek commentaries on Aristotle, while in the sixteenth century, the writings
of the Protestant reformers and their Roman Catholic opponents
could be widely circulated.

The second main part looks at some specific doctrines, including supposition theory and consequences, in order to show that
medieval doctrines were developed in interesting ways before they
were finally abandoned, and to highlight some of the important
changes that took place.

7.1   THE GREAT SCHISM AND RIVAL SCHOOLS IN THE
FIFTEENTH CENTURY

During the Great Schism, which lasted from 1378 to 1417, there
were two, and at one time three, rival popes. Individual rulers across
Europe exploited this unhappy situation both during and after the
schism by expanding their own political powers, and, among other
things, by founding new universities in the cities they controlled.
The number of universities that existed in 1378 had more than dou-
bled by the end of the fifteenth century, and even the most northern regions of Europe now had their own institutions. All of them
had their own teachers of logic, with an interest in developing their
own textbooks. The production of commentaries on Aristotle greatly
increased, as did the copying and circulation of works by earlier logicians such as Buridan who remained on the official curricula of the
universities.

A related effect of the Great Schism, which is closely related to
the foundation of new universities, was the increased movement of

students and teachers across Europe.[2] For instance, in Scotland the University of St Andrews, which received its charter in 1412, began because Scottish students, who could not go to English universities because of wars with England, could now not go to Paris because the Scots and the French supported rival popes. That problem was later overcome, and in early-sixteenth-century Paris, there were many Scottish students and teachers, including John Mair. Just as Scottish students were affected by the Great Schism, so too were German and Italian students. In the last two decades of the fourteenth century, Oxford received a large influx of German and Italian students who had left Paris, again because of differences over which pope should be supported. Later the Germans returned to the newly founded German universities, taking English books and learning with them, and the Italians returned to Italian studia and universities. Many of the surviving manuscripts of the fourteenth-century English logicians were copied by Italians and are found in Italian libraries. Others were taken to Spain from Italy, and influenced the logic teaching at Spanish universities.

Paul of Venice (c. 1369–1429) is the most prominent of the Italians who had studied at Oxford, having spent three years there, from 1390 to 1393. His works include commentaries on Aristotle's logic, the massive *Logica Magna*, which contains much material taken from English logicians among others, and the very successful *Logica parva* which is closely related to the loose collection of texts then in use at Oxford and Cambridge, and printed a number of times in the early sixteenth century (see Ashworth 1979). Tract 1 gave a very brief presentation of the material of the summulae, dealing with terms, nouns, verbs, propositions, equipollence, conversion, hypothetical propositions, predicables, categories and syllogisms, but not with topics and fallacies. Tract 2 dealt with the material of the *parva*

---

[2] These movements were possible because Latin remained the standard language of instruction well into the seventeenth century and, in some places, even into the eighteenth century.

logicalia,[3] tracts 3, 5, and 6 dealt with consequences, obligations and insolubles. Tract 4 was devoted to the proof of terms; and the last two tracts took up objections to the summulae and to the consequences. About eighty manuscripts of the *Logica parva* survive, and, so far as we know, in 1472 it became the first logic text to be printed.[4] Many more printed editions were to follow, with the last one appearing in 1614.

During the fifteenth and early sixteenth centuries, Paul's *Logica parva* was also the subject of a number of commentaries by Italian scholars (Perreiah 2002, xx–xxii). Italian commentaries on other works show the continued influence of English logicians throughout the fifteenth century, and various encyclopaedic publications in Italy provide apt examples of this. For instance, in 1493 Bonetus Locatellus in Venice published a volume containing Strode's *Consequentiae* and *Obligationes* and Ferrybridge's *Consequentiae*, along with commentaries by Alessandro Sermoneta (d. 1486), Gaetano da Thiene (1387–1475), and Paul of Pergula (d. 1451) on Strode's *Consequentiae*, and by Gaetano da Thiene on Ferrybridge.

Curiously, neither Oxford nor Cambridge in the fifteenth and early sixteenth centuries seem to have paid any scholarly attention to fourteenth-century English logicians, and no new works appeared after about 1410. Apart from the various editions of the loose collections of much earlier works known as *Logica Oxoniensis* and *Logica Cantabrigiensis*, the only significant English publication was *Logica* published in Oxford by Theoderic Rood in 1483. This contained some earlier English texts, but it also contained much of Paul of Venice's *Logica Parva*, as well as long extracts from Buridan's *Summulae*, and material on velocity from Albert of Saxony's *Proportiones*, all carefully integrated and unacknowledged.

Fourteenth-century English logicians such as Richard Billingham and Heytesbury were also read outside Italy, but such

---

[3] The *parva logicalia* (little logicals) included supposition, ampliation and so on, but might also include exponibles and syncategoremata.
[4] For an incomplete printing history of logic texts from 1472 to 1800, see Risse 1965.

authors as Buridan, Albert of Saxony and Marsilius of Inghen were probably more widely used, especially in Germany and Eastern Europe. However, universities in these areas underwent a number of changes linked to the Council of Constance (1414–1418) which had brought the Great Schism to an end. The Council had taken a firm stand against what the church considered to be heresy, condemning the theology of John Wyclif and burning two of his followers at the stake, and this hardening of theological attitudes was a contributing factor to a new self-consciousness about schools of thought. In turn, this gave rise to what German scholars have dubbed the *Wegestreit*, or conflict between the viae or ways (see Gilbert 1974 and Hoenen 2003). The most obvious division was between the way of the realists (by the fifteenth century often called the *antiqui*: the old thinkers) and the way of the nominalists (by then often called the *moderni*: the new thinkers),[5] but the realist schools were themselves divisible into Thomists, or followers of Aquinas, Albertists, or followers of Albert the Great, and Scotists, or followers of John Duns Scotus. At the University of Cologne, the main division was between Thomists and Albertists, but other divisions were possible. For instance, in the early sixteenth century, the Spaniard Juan de Celaya (c. 1490–1558) who taught at Paris, published commentaries on Aristotle's logic 'with questions in accordance with the triple way of St Thomas, the realists, and the nominalists', where by 'realists' he clearly meant the Scotists.[6] In other contexts, 'realists' were identified with Wyclif and his followers, and were immediately taken to be tainted with heresy. Thus, when Louis XI of France forbade the teaching of nominalism at the University of Paris in 1474 (a ban that was lifted in 1481, but whose removal only took full effect in 1482), the nominalists defended themselves on the grounds that

---

[5] On the use of the terms *antiqui* and *moderni* in the fifteenth century, see Gilbert 1974.

[6] For titles and publication details, see Farge 1980, 76–77. This work contains a great deal of useful information about publications of logic texts, since theologians usually began by doing some undergraduate teaching in logic.

their doctrines did not lead to heresy, unlike those of the realists (see Kaluza 1995).

Realists tended to retaliate by linking nominalism with Ockham, who had also been condemned by the Roman Catholic Church, but we have to bear in mind that in the later fourteenth and fifteenth centuries, Ockham was considered less important than John Buridan and his followers, including Marsilius of Inghen. Ockham continued to be read, but it was Buridan and Marsilius who provided the textbooks that were actually used by the universities, and that appeared on their curricula. Indeed, the condemnation of Ockhamists by the University of Paris in 1340 had probably strengthened Buridanism (Kaluza 1995, 294, n. 2), and Buridan's works spread across Europe (Markowski 1984). The introduction of printing changed the situation slightly, for while Buridan's works on sophismata and consequences were printed a few times, his *Summulae* appeared in the version produced by John Dorp, which replaced Buridan's own commentary on the rewritten text of Peter of Spain by that of Dorp, and this version was not reprinted after 1510. It is interesting to note that the 1510 edition, like that of 1504, has annotations by John Mair (Farge 1980, 308). On the other hand, Ockham's *Summa logicae* was printed as late as 1591 (Venice) and 1675 (Oxford). Nevertheless, neither Ockham nor Buridan ever achieved the popularity of Peter of Spain, whose *Tractatus*, along with commentaries on it, was steadily reprinted throughout the sixteenth century and well into the seventeenth century.

Both Peter of Spain and Aristotle himself were generally taken to be outside the conflict between realists and nominalists, at least in the sense that both sides could regard them as authorities. Accordingly, given the central role of these authors, one might wonder how much impact the various forms of *Wegestreit* would have on the content of logic texts, except in discussions of universals or of theories of signification. However, there was certainly a difference in attitude. In their 1474 manifesto, the Parisian nominalists accused the realists of neglecting the properties of terms, including supposition, ampliation and restriction, even though these were essential to the assessment of truth, and of failing to recognize that obligations and insolubles provide a solid foundation for assessing arguments.[7] The nominalist insistence on the properties of terms and on the criticism of language as a precondition for philosophical analysis sets them apart from the realists, but also from the humanists, whose own approach to language had more to do with vocabulary and style.

The *Wegestreit* had an effect both on the presentation of the medieval additions to Aristotle and on the types of Aristotelian commentary that were produced. The University of Cologne provides a useful test case (see Braakhuis 1989 and Kneepkens 2003). Throughout the fifteenth century, nominalist views were considered, and both the *parva logicalia* and the three treatises 'of the moderns', namely obligations, insolubles and consequences, remained on the curriculum, but after about 1420, realism tended to predominate. Teaching was done by the bursae, which were schools outside the main faculty structure, and among these the bursa montana was strongly Thomist while the bursa laurentiana was Albertist. The masters of the bursa montana, one of whom was Lambertus de Monte, were particularly productive in the last decades of the century and published commentaries on *Logica Vetus* and *Logica Nova* 'in accordance with the way of the Thomists' or 'following the teaching of St Thomas Aquinas'[8] as well as commentaries on Peter of Spain, especially his *parva logicalia*, and the three tracts of the moderns.[9] These tracts seem to be early-fifteenth-century works, but their authorship is not certain. In their introduction to the *parva logicalia*, the masters remarked that many distinguished men think that the *parva logicalia* are not necessary, claiming that they are wrong about this. They went on to speak

---

[7] For an edition of this passage of the text, see Ehrle 1925, 322–323.

[8] Both formulations appear in the titles given in various editions.

[9] The commentaries are usually attributed to Lambertus de Monte, but in fact they seem to be a collaborative effort. All references are to the second part of [Lambertus de Monte] 1490, which is foliated separately from the first part containing the commentary on Peter of Spain's *Tractatus*.

about the three tracts of the moderns, saying that both the insolubilia and the obligationes were curious rather than necessary, and they warned students that the consequentiae contained many errors of the *moderni* (De Monte 1490, f. ii^{r-v}). Nonetheless, they obviously felt obliged to follow the curriculum by teaching these works.

Another series of works frequently published in Cologne and used at the university there, among many other places, was written by the Parisian author John Versor (died after 1482).[10] In his commentaries on Aristotle's logic, whether he used Aquinas or Albert seemed to depend on what each had written,[11] and he aligned himself with neither school. These commentaries enjoyed only a few printed editions, but his commentary on Peter of Spain had a runaway success, being printed as late as 1639 in Venice.[12] In the mid-fifteenth century, Versor's influence had reached as far as Prague and Cracow, and probably played a role in Cracow in the replacement of Buridan's nominalism by more realist views from the 1440s on. Buridanism had waned much earlier in Prague, after the exit of German students to the newly founded University of Leipzig in 1409 (Markowski 1984, 152–154).

The University of Paris itself, where Versor had been Rector in 1458, had a number of productive logicians in the nominalist tradition such as George of Brussels and Thomas Bricot (d. 1516) in the last decades of the fifteenth century, but it also had logicians in other traditions, such as the Scotists Pierre Tartaret and Johannes de Magistris.[13] The titles of the latter's commentaries on Aristotle and Peter of Spain, published several times between 1487 and 1490, said that they 'follow the mind of the Subtle Doctor Scotus'. In the first three decades of the sixteenth century, there was a burst of

[10] For Versor's life and works, see Rutten 2005.
[11] Aquinas only commented on *On Interpretation* and *Posterior Analytics*.
[12] However, Risse 1965 lists no library for this. The latest edition I have seen is Cologne, 1622, in the University Library, Cambridge.
[13] This Johannes de Magistris is probably Johannes de Caulaincourt, but a number of other Parisian masters had very similar names, such as 'Johannes Magistri' and 'Jean le Maistre'; see Bakker 2007, 195–199.

activity, largely involving logicians from Spain and Scotland. The leading Scotsman and the author of many logical works was John Mair (1469–1550), who received his MA in 1494, and subsequently taught logic at the College of Montaigu while pursuing his theological studies (see Farge 1980, 304–311 and Broadie 1985). His courses were apparently very popular, and the college became the centre of nominalism in Paris. In 1517 he left Paris to teach in Scotland, and although he did return for some years, his main production of logical works had ceased, and their publication also soon came to an end. Leading Spanish logicians, many of whom were associated with Mair, included Gaspar Lax (1487–1560), Juan de Celaya, and Fernando de Enzinas (d. 1523). Those who moved back to Spain were instrumental in introducing Parisian nominalism to the universities there, where it flourished until at least 1540. Another outstanding Spaniard was the Dominican Domingo de Soto (1494–1560). He only spent about three years in Paris, taking his MA in 1517 and subsequently teaching there while studying theology, but his *Summulae,* first published in 1529, was extremely important for the transmission of Parisian logic to later Spanish and Portuguese authors. The second edition of 1539–1540 was heavily revised along more humanist lines, and subsequent editions followed the second edition closely.

7.2   HUMANISM AND THE NEW GREEK TEXTS

So far we have considered only logic in the medieval tradition, but despite the popularity of English logic in fifteenth-century Italy, and of nominalism in early-sixteenth-century Paris, humanism was already influential, first in Italy, then in Paris, where the humanists Jacques Lefèvre d'Étaples (c. 1460–1536) and Josse Clichtove (1472–1543) were contemporary with the nominalists, and finally in northern Europe. One of the main inspirations for this movement arose from the gradual conquest of the Byzantine Empire by the Turks, which ended with the capture of Constantinople (now Istanbul) in 1453. Byzantine scholars had long seen the writing on the wall, and many of them fled to Italy, taking with them not only Greek manuscripts hitherto unknown to the Latin-speaking West but also the ability to teach Greek in schools and universities, as well as to private patrons. At first, humanism was a largely literary movement, characterized by an interest in classical literature and in the teaching of such subjects as poetry, rhetoric, moral philosophy and history. These interests produced an insistence on the use of classical language, and an obvious disgust when faced with the technical language and tortured formulations used in late medieval logic texts. The Italian humanist Leonardo Bruni (c. 1369–1444) attacked the barbarian British dialecticians 'whose very names make me shudder: Ferebrich [Ferrybridge], Heytesbury, Ockham and others of this kind' and the sophismata that formed an integral part of their writings.[14] In his *Dialectica* another prominent humanist, Lorenzo Valla (1407–1457), attacked fundamental notions of Aristotelian logic including predicables such as genus and species, the ten categories, and the Square of Opposition. According to him, dialectic was a part of rhetoric and all arguments should be persuasive and presented in clear language.[15]

Valla's work had only a limited circulation, whether in manuscript or printed versions, and by far the most successful of the fifteenth-century humanists was Rudolph Agricola (1443/4–1485), a Dutchman who spent a large portion of his life in Italy. In his *De inventione dialectica libri tres*, written around 1479 but not published until 1515, though it had circulated in manuscript form, Agricola made invention, which uses the topics to find the subject matter for argumentation, the central part of dialectic, and in so doing he integrated traditional parts of rhetoric including rhetorical invention and the disposition of arguments into dialectic. He then argued that the only function of rhetoric was to handle matters of style. Agricola's book was one of the most widely published dialectic texts of the sixteenth century, receiving more than forty editions, but it did not fit

---

[14] For translation and Latin text, see Jardine 1988, 177–178 and n. 23.

[15] For discussion of Valla, see Nauta 2007. There are three versions of *Dialectica*, whose full title is *Repastinatio dialecticae et philosophiae*. For Valla, Agricola, and their reception by later humanists, see Mack 1993.

easily into university curricula, because the formal logic included took the form of a few remarks about the syllogism. As a result, in the earlier part of the sixteenth century, it was often paired with the work of another fifteenth-century humanist, the short *Isagoge dialectica* by George of Trebizond (1395–1472/3), a Greek scholar who had settled in Italy in 1416. This work, written around 1440, summarized Aristotelian logic, and was steadily published throughout the first six decades of the sixteenth century. Another approach was to integrate Agricola's work into fuller textbooks, such as those by Philipp Melanchthon. All these works were marked by their use of simplified language, classical vocabulary and the use of literary allusions in place of sophismata to illustrate logical points.

Another very important aspect of humanism was the publication, philological analysis and subsequent translation of newly discovered Greek texts. In addition to the logic commentaries known in the Middle Ages, the Latin-speaking West now had access to the Greek texts of commentaries on the *Topics* and *Prior Analytics I* by Alexander of Aphrodisias, on the *Categories* and *Prior Analytics I* by Ammonius, both probably from student notes, on the *Categories* by Porphyry, and on the *Categories*, the *Prior Analytics* and the *Posterior Analytics* by John Philoponus. The wide dissemination of these commentaries was made possible by the new printing presses, and in addition the whole of Aristotle in Greek was published in 1495–1498. New Latin translations both of Aristotle's logic and of the commentaries on it then began to appear. Towards the end of the fifteenth century, there was also a wave of translations of Arabic texts, including some by Averroes. Some of these came via Hebrew intermediaries. A revival of interest in Averroes led to a wide diffusion of his works, especially in Italy, and between 1550 and 1552 the great Giunta edition of Aristotle with the commentaries of Averroes was printed.

During the late fifteenth and sixteenth centuries, changes in the availability of texts were matched by changes in the production of commentaries on Aristotle. Though Walter Burley's much earlier

commentary on *Logica Vetus* continued to be popular, one development was the publication of commentaries on the entire *Organon*,
a title for Aristotle's logic that seems to have become established
during the sixteenth century, rather than separate commentaries on
Logica Vetus and *Logica Nova*. In Paris in 1493, the nominalist George
of Brussels and the Scotist Pierre Tartaret published such commentaries, both of which were reprinted a number of times in the following decades. Shortly afterwards, in 1503, Lefèvre d'Étaples published
his paraphrases and annotations on all of Aristotle's logic. During the
sixteenth century, a number of other commentaries were produced
across Europe, including that by the Spanish Jesuit Francisco Toledo
(1532–1596), published in Rome in 1572 and regularly reprinted until
at least 1616. Another popular work was the edition of the *Organon*
(under that name) published by the Italian Protestant Giulio Pace,
or Pacius (1550–1635) in 1584. It contained the Greek text side-by-
side with a new translation designed not only to read well but also
to capture the philosophical significance of Aristotle's words. Pace
added a commentary dealing with difficult points both of theory and
of translation in the margins. However, perhaps the most widely influential commentary was that published in 1606 by the Coimbra
Jesuits, which was read across Europe.[16] It contained a new translation of the Greek text accompanied by chapter summaries and
textual commentary, and it added lengthy questions on particular
points. Marginal notes gave references to realists, nominalists and
a range of individual classical, medieval and post-medieval authors.
The 1606 edition also had the original Greek, but the 1607 edition
does not.

Commentaries on the individual books of Aristotle's logic
also continued to be published. Some of these were medieval,
including Aquinas' commentaries on *On Interpretation* and
Posterior Analytics, and Paul of Venice's commentary on *Posterior*

---

[16] The 1604 edition sometimes referred to is apparently a pirated version, based on
lecture notes sold to the publishers.

Analytics, but new commentaries appeared that made full use of the new humanist scholarship. For instance, the Italian Agostino Nifo (1469/70–1538) published commentaries on all the books of the *Organon* except the *Categories*. In these commentaries he used material from medieval writers, including Robert Kilwardby and Marsilius of Inghen, but he gave pride of place to the ancient Greek commentators, and at the end of his *Topics* commentary he spoke harshly of those who tried to explain Aristotle while ignorant both of the Greek language and of the Greek expositors. A little later Domingo de Soto published substantial commentaries on Porphyry's *Isagoge*, the *Categories* and *Posterior Analytics*. Commentaries on *Posterior Analytics* were particularly influential in Italy, where university education, especially in Padua, tended to focus on logic and natural philosophy as preparation for the study of medicine, and a significant contribution was made by the commentary on this work by Jacopo Zabarella (1533–1589), first published in Italy in 1582, and frequently republished in Germany, along with Zabarella's other works.

7.3   REFORMATION, COUNTER-REFORMATION AND THE NEW TEXTBOOKS

How far this attention to Aristotle was reflected in ordinary textbooks depended to some extent on the interaction between humanism and the religious divisions of the sixteenth century which were produced by the Protestant Reformation and the Catholic Counter-reformation, and which replaced the earlier divisions of the *Wegestreit*. While theologians used logic to support conflicting views, logic texts themselves do not usually take up theological positions, with the possible exception of the issue of whether expository syllogisms can be used in discussions of the Trinity. Nonetheless, theology and humanism combined had their effect on the production of textbooks. Although Martin Luther had attacked all aspects of human philosophizing, the Protestant insistence on the importance of bible study for all believers led to a special emphasis on education, which was exemplified

by Luther's collaborator Philipp Melanchthon (1497–1560), who became known as the teacher of Germany (*praeceptor Germaniae*).
Melanchthon insisted that the use of dialectical and rhetorical tools
was essential to the proper uncovering of the sense of scripture, and the
first of his many textbooks were on rhetoric, *De Rhetorica* of 1519, and
logic, *Compendiaria Dialectices Ratio* of 1520. He produced revised
and enlarged versions of both, and his final work on logic, *Erotemata
Dialectices*, appeared in 1547. All his works show the influence of humanism through the use of classical authors and classical examples,
as well as through his presentation of simplified Aristotelian material,
and his scorn for medieval developments. Nonetheless, his works
show a progressive elaboration and formalization of basic logical material, for he soon came to realize that the small humanist handbook
of logic was insufficient for educational purposes, at least at the university level. In particular, the *Erotemata* contains a section on consequences which does not appear in the *Compendiaria* (Melanchthon
1963, cols. 626–636), and, despite an attack on the futility of the *parva
logicalia*, which he says belong to grammar rather than logic, he also
includes some remarks on how supposition theory can usefully be
employed (Melanchthon 1963, cols. 750–751).[17]

A later humanist-inspired Protestant was the Frenchman Peter
Ramus (Pierre de la Ramée, 1515–1572), whose death during a mas-
sacre of Protestants made him a Protestant martyr, and contributed
to his popularity in Protestant institutions across Europe, and even
in New England, where Harvard University, founded in 1636, used
Ramist texts. In his earlier works he attacked Aristotle with some
vigour, and his short *Dialectique*, first published in French in 1555
but published in Latin the following year, contained a minimal
amount of what would count as Aristotelian logic. As a result, it
generally came to be used in high schools rather than universities, as
many Protestant teachers still believed that undergraduates needed

---

[17] See Meier-Oeser 2013 for more on the fate of supposition theory in the Protestant
tradition.

a solid foundation in Aristotelian logic, though certainly not in any medieval additions to it, and from the last decades of the sixteenth century onward, a number of Aristotelian textbooks were produced, especially in Germany and the Netherlands. These textbooks often had extra sections dealing with various aspects of method, including not only method as a way of ordering discourse and Ramist method but also the scientific method of Zabarella.

The Roman Catholic Counter-reformation also had an impact on education, not only in Europe but also in the new Spanish colonies in the Americas. For instance, in 1554 the Augustinian Alonso de la Vera Cruz (1507–1584) who taught at the University of Mexico, founded in 1551, published works covering the material of Peter of Spain's *Tractatus* and Aristotle's *Organon* for the use of his students there. These were later published in Spain. The Jesuit order, founded in 1540, was particularly influential, for it founded a number of educational institutions, including La Flèche where Descartes was to study. Two popular Jesuit logicians, whose works were read in Jesuit schools, were Francisco Toledo who, in addition to his commentary on Aristotle's logic, wrote an introduction to dialectic (*Introductio in dialecticam*) which received the first of eighteen editions in 1561, and the Portuguese Pedro da Fonseca (1528–1599) whose even more popular *Institutionum dialecticarum libri octo* was first published in 1564, and received fifty-three editions. Fonseca's work, like that of Toledo, focused on basic elements of Aristotle's logic, presented in clear language, but both authors also discussed some parts of specifically medieval logic, including supposition and consequences.

We now turn to some more detailed discussion of the most important changes in the medieval additions to Aristotelian logic, and their ultimate fate.

7.4   TERMS AND PROPOSITIONS

At the University of Paris there were a number of significant changes in the subjects with which individual treatises dealt. Proof of terms, the composition and division of terms, syncategoremata and sophismata, apart from a short treatise by George of Brussels, were no longer dealt with separately, though some of these topics continued to appear in more general treatises. On the other hand, at least twenty distinct treatises on the properties of terms themselves were written by Parisian authors including Mair and Fernando de Enzinas (d. 1523), and there were also a number of treatises on opposition, that is, the logical relations between different kinds of categorical propositions. Both the production and the publication of all these treatises largely ceased in the 1530s.

The most interesting developments, which related to the signification of terms, the mental correlates of syncategorematic terms and the semantics of propositions,[18] were brought together in a series of treatises on a new topic, notitiae or notions (see Ashworth 1978a and 1982). One such treatise was by the Scotsman George Lokert (d. 1547),[19] first published in 1514, and another, by Enzinas, was in print by 1521. The 1526 edition had the explanatory title 'On the composition of the mental proposition, showing the nature of syncategorematic acts, and introductory to notions'.[20] These treatises show the influence of Peter of Ailly, whose insolubilia prefaced by a work on concepts (conceptus), was published several times in Paris before 1500. In that work, Ailly discussed signification, giving as his definition: 'to signify is to represent some thing, or some things, or in some way to a cognitive power' (Spade 1980b, 16). This definition was taken up not only by Parisian nominalists but by Soto and by later authors such as Fonseca. It focuses on signification as a psychological–causal property of significant spoken terms and became part of an increased emphasis both on the spoken term as one type of sign among others[21]

---

[18] 'Propositions' in this context were occurrent declaratory sentences, whether written, spoken or mental. See the chapter on propositions.

[19] For a discussion of his works, see Broadie 1983.

[20] This posthumous edition was edited by the Scotsman Robert Wauchope. The titles of the various editions varied.

[21] See Meier-Oeser 1997. Soto's work on signs in his Summulae was both detailed and influential, and the Coimbra commentary on Aristotle's logic includes a long discussion of signs.

and on the philosophy of mind, given that mental terms were also regarded as signs.

The application of Ailly's definition also played a role in the question of whether a proposition signified some thing or some things or in some way. The idea of signifying in some way had been used in the explanation of syncategorematic terms such as 'every', and their mental correlates were said to be syncategorematic acts. Such acts were now appealed to in the explanation of how the mind can put together ordinary concepts such as those corresponding to the spoken words 'man' and 'animal' to form propositions such as 'Every man is an animal', but they also served to explain how propositions could be said to signify without the need to postulate special objects, called complex signifiables (*complexe significabilia*) to serve as their significates. Thus Enzinas argued that instead of treating the dictum of a proposition, that is the phrase 'man's being an animal' in the sentence ' "Man is an animal" signifies man's being an animal', as a name of some kind, one should regard propositions as analogous to syncategorematic terms. They signify, not some thing or some things, but in some way. As a result, the question 'What does this proposition signify?' can only be responded to by a paraphrase, such as ' "Man is an animal" signifies that man is an animal'.

7.5   THE *PARVA LOGICALIA* AND SUPPOSITION THEORY

The treatises on terms had discussed a range of possible classifications of terms including noun and verb, categorematic and syncategorematic, equivocal and analogical, but other properties of terms such as supposition, appellation, ampliation and restriction were discussed in the *parva logicalia*. As we have seen, these were also linked with the 'three tracts of the moderns' on insolubles, obligations and consequences, and both sets of treatises posed problems for those who regarded Aristotle as the logician par excellence. Terms were easily related to the *Categories*, and propositions to *On Interpretation*, but if these other topics were really important, why had Aristotle not devoted treatises to them? The Cologne Thomists were among those who took up this problem. They remarked that one could simply say that it was legitimate to go beyond Aristotle, but they preferred to say that the different parts of Aristotle's logic and his *Metaphysics* contained the basic principles which were now further developed. For instance, the principles of supposition theory are found in *On Interpretation*, those of ampliation and restriction in the *Sophistical Refutations*, those of obligations in *Prior Analytics* along with *Metaphysics IX*, those of insolubles in *Metaphysics IV*, and those of consequences in *Prior Analytics* and the *Topics* (De Monte 1490, f. i^{r-v}). Many later textbook writers were to solve the problem more simply, by suppressing most if not all of the medieval developments.

Another feature of the Cologne Thomists' discussion of the *parva logicalia* and 'the three tracts of the moderns', was their warnings about the errors into which the *moderni* (nominalists) fall, and they listed five such errors in relation to supposition (De Monte 1490, f. xxx^{r-v}). Unsurprisingly, they rejected the view that simple supposition should be replaced by material supposition, but they also accepted Peter of Spain's view that the predicate of 'Every man is an animal' should be taken as having simple supposition. The Parisian Versor adopted the same view, albeit tentatively (Versor 1586, 392B). This put them at odds with other logicians such as Soto who realized that treating the predicate as having merely confused supposition, that is, interpreted in terms of reference to individuals rather than common natures, was crucial for saving the view that suppositional ascent and descent, at least where standard categorical propositions were concerned, allows for logical equivalences between those propositions and the disjunctions or conjunctions of propositions containing singular terms into which they were analysed.

Earlier logicians, including Ockham and Buridan, had not attempted to provide a full set of such equivalences, but Albert of Saxony and Marsilius of Inghen gave a full account of descent, and by the end of the fifteenth century, corresponding rules of ascent had also become standard.[22] In early-sixteenth-century Paris, there was a good deal of discussion about what phrases would need to be added in order to guarantee the validity of the equivalences (Ashworth 1974, 214–221), and roughly speaking it was agreed that such phrases as 'and so on for all the singulars' and 'these are all the As there are' were needed. For instance, Soto exemplifies conjunctive (*copulativa*) ascent like this: 'this A is B and this A is B and so on for all the singular terms (where "this A" counts as a singular term) and these are all the As there are, therefore every A is B' and he exemplifies the corresponding descent like this: 'every A is B and these are all the As there are, therefore this A is B and this A is B, and so on for all the singulars' (Soto 1529, f. xxv[rb]).

Other rules were added to overcome two objections to the process.[23] The first objection is that the attribution of merely confused supposition to the predicate in 'Every A is B' militates against any neat analysis into disjunctions and conjunctions of singular propositions, because B can now only be analysed into the disjunct phrase 'this B or that B or the other B'. The second objection is that the attribution of distributive supposition to the predicate in 'Some A is not B' renders analysis in terms of descent and an equivalent ascent invalid. The problem is this. If we assume that there are two men (Socrates and Plato) and two Greeks (Socrates and Plato once more) and we take the false proposition 'Some men are not Greek' we can apparently descend from B to obtain 'Some man is not Socrates and some man is not Plato', and then descend from A to obtain '(Either Socrates is not Socrates or Socrates is not Plato) and (either Plato is not Socrates or Plato is not Plato)'. That is, we get a truth from a falsehood, while the corresponding ascent yields a falsehood from a truth, which renders it invalid. It seems, then, that one cannot claim

---

[22] For details see Ashworth 2013a. Logicians admitted that if we are dealing with simple supposition, or with merely confused supposition in the context of collective terms or such special signs as 'promise', we will not obtain this desirable result.

[23] The objections have been most fully formulated by twentieth-century writers, but they were known to post-medieval logicians.

any equivalence between propositions and their descended forms, any more than one can claim that descent is intended to provide an analysis of truth conditions.

Soto's response to such objections was simple: we must apply a rule of priority: 'in any proposition whatsoever, one should first ascend or descend from the term with determinate supposition, and then from the term with distributive supposition, and then disjunctively from the term which did supposit confusedly in relation to the distribution, for when the distribution has been taken away, it supposits purely determinately' (Soto 1529, f. xxx^{vb}). This rule solves the problem of 'Some A is not B' by ensuring the validity of the desired equivalence through the requirement that the descent from A must precede that from B, and it solves the problem of 'Every A is B' by means of another kind of double descent. That is, from 'Every A is B' one first moves to 'A$_1$ is B or A$_2$ is B or so for all the singulars'. We now have a sequence of singular propositions whose predicates have determinate supposition instead of the original merely confused supposition, and so for any number i we can descend correctly to 'A$_i$ is B$_1$ or A$_i$ is B$_2$ or so for all the singulars'. As a result, any standard proposition can be reduced to logically equivalent conjunctions and/or disjunctions, either immediately or after some antecedent reduction. Soto's rules were touched on briefly by Toledo in his introductory textbook (Toledo 1985, 30A), but otherwise later discussions of supposition theory tended to ignore the problems of suppositional ascent and descent altogether, and reduced the theory to its bare bones.

Another development that seems to have begun in the early fifteenth century was the use of letters of the alphabet as special signs, not only to allow different interpretations of standard categorical propositions but also to handle sentences of non-standard form such as 'Of every man some donkey is running' and all the variations of this (see Ashworth 1978b).[24] Especially in their discussions

---

[24] For early uses of 'a' to produce merely confused supposition, see Ashworth 2013a, 386, n. 4.

of opposition, logicians wanted to explain how to provide contradictories and contraries for such sentences which preserved the relevant
truth conditions, and which allowed their analysis and evaluation by
means of suppositional descent. The letters 'a' and 'b', which acted
rather like modern quantifiers, were used to do this. For instance, if
one writes 'a. man is not an animal', this, unlike the falsehood 'Some
man is not an animal', turns out to be true because if each of several
men is identical to a different animal, it is true to say of each animal
that one or more men is not identical to that animal. Similarly, if
one writes 'Every man is b. animal' this, unlike 'Every man is <an>
animal', signifies by virtue of the special sign that every man is identical to one and the same animal, and hence is false. Soto explained
that the subsequent letters of the alphabet could used to indicate
cases of mixed supposition, in which the type of supposition changed
during the stages of suppositional descent (Soto 1529, f. xlviii[rb]). The
humanist Juan Luis Vives (1493–1540), who had himself studied under
the nominalists at the College of Montaigu, found this procedure particularly repellent. In his diatribe *Against the Pseudodialecticians* he
wrote: 'a, b, c, d can make those suppositions confused, determinate,
and a mixture of both. Indeed you can add more commixtions than
any quack pharmacist ever made – e, f, g, h, i, j, k – so that some of
these men already have recourse to letters down as far as the tenth
letter of the second alphabet, dreaming up and combining wonderful
kinds of suppositions' (Guerlac 1979, 61). Soto came to agree, for in
the second edition of his *Summulae* he described the use of these
letters to deal with oppositions as barbarous, and spoke of them as
figments of the *moderni*, which were never thought of by the *antiqui*
(Soto 1539–1540, f. xxxix[ra–rb]).

7.6 THE THREE TRACTS OF THE MODERNS

We shall not dwell on the first two of these tracts, the insolubilia
and the obligations, for they were soon to disappear. Some interesting discussion of insolubles is found in Bricot and Mair, who both

wrote treatises on the topic in which they developed Swyneshed's theory in different ways.[25] Bricot's view was discussed by Soto in his *Summulae*, but in the revised edition, Soto said that the *moderni* had spent too much time on this topic, and that he would go over the material quickly because it was of little utility (Soto 1539–1540, f. xcii^rb). So far as obligations are concerned, Bricot wrote a lengthy treatise in which he discussed the views of Burley and others, while Mair and Soto both wrote treatises in which they followed Marsilius of Inghen.[26] However, in his second edition, Soto remarked in his introduction to the tract that obligations were a game for boys, and at the end, in the very last words of the revised *Summulae*, he said that to pursue them could only produce nausea.

Unlike other topics that show the continuation of specifically medieval developments, only a handful of separate treatises on consequences was produced in the post-medieval period. These included an unfinished treatise by John Mair that was completed by the Spaniard Antonio Coronel (d. c. 1521) and first published around 1503.[27] However, discussion of consequences was frequently included in longer treatises, and the topic was still discussed, albeit briefly, in later textbooks by such authors as Toledo and Fonseca.

An important focus of discussion for authors in the fifteenth and early sixteenth centuries was the relationship between definitions of validity, formality, and the status of the rules EIQ (from the impossible anything follows) and its corollary, NEQ (the necessary follows from everything).[28] One approach was first to adopt the modal or truth criterion whereby a consequence was valid if and only if it was impossible to have a true antecedent together with a false consequent, or alternatively for the conjunction of the

---

[25] For discussion and bibliography, see Hanke 2014.

[26] For details of the works by Bricot, Mair and Soto see Ashworth 1994. The work by Marsilius was published in Paris but attributed to Peter of Ailly.

[27] The work is reprinted in Mair 1519. There is a copy of the early edition, printed by Denis Roce in Paris, in the University Library, Cambridge.

[28] EIQ: *Ex impossibili sequitur quodlibet*; NEQ: *Necessarium sequitur ex quolibet*.

antecedent and the negation of the consequent to be inconsistent,[29] and to supplement this with the criterion of substitution whereby a valid (bona) consequence was formally valid if and only if all its substitution instances were valid. Given these definitions, an instance of EIQ would be formally valid when the antecedent was an explicit contradiction, and materially valid when this was not the case. Other fourteenth-century logicians preferred to use a criterion for formal validity which guaranteed a relationship between the antecedent and the consequent through the requirement that the consequent be understood in the antecedent. This led to the claim that instances of EIQ and NEQ were only materially valid. Both Paul of Venice and his follower, Paul of Pergula were influenced by their predecessors, but approached the issue somewhat differently. For formal validity they required that it be impossible both in reality and in imagination or conception for the negation of the consequent to be consistent with the antecedent.[30] A materially valid consequence was then one in which, contrary to reality, one could imagine or conceive that the negation of the consequent was consistent with the antecedent without an obvious contradiction. On this account, instances of EIQ and NEQ were materially valid unless there was a further rule that formally validated them, as with 'A man is an ass, therefore a man is an animal' (Paul of Pergula 1961, 88; Paul of Venice 2002, 53). However, in his *Logica Magna*, Paul of Venice went further. He examined the case of impossible antecedents that were either contradictions or implied a contradiction, and in this case, he allowed instances of EIQ to be provable and hence formally valid (Paul of Venice 1990, 94–98).

The standard argument, going back to the twelfth century, used by Paul to support the formal validity of instances of EIQ whose antecedent is an explicit contradiction took the form:

---

[29] This latter version of the criterion is found in Paul of Venice 2002, 52 and in Paul of Pergula 1961, 87. Mair 1519, f. lxxx[ra], preferred Buridan's formulation in terms of signification rather than truth: see Buridan 2014, 67.

[30] Paul of Venice 2002, 52 and in Paul of Pergula 1961, 87–88. Paul of Venice refers to the imagination, Paul of Pergula to what can be conceived.

If P and not P then P,

if P then (P or Q),

if (P or Q) and not P then Q,

therefore, 'if P and not P then Q' by the rule 'from first to last'.

This argument was examined and explicitly rejected by Cologne Thomists on the grounds, taken from Peter of Spain's treatise on syncategoremata,[31] that the contradiction is assumed for the purposes of disputation, and one part cannot be used to cancel the other part, as it is in the move from '(P or Q) and not P' to Q (De Monte 1490, f. cxxxiiii^v–cxxxv^r). Paul of Venice in his *Logica Magna* had hinted at another possible form of attack, later used by Domingo de Soto (Soto 1539–1540, f. liii<i>^{va}), which denied that the rule from 'first to last' could be used to justify 'If P and not P then Q' (Paul of Venice 1990, 163–164). The rule as normally presented requires that each antecedent of an intermediate step should be the exact consequent of the previous step, but to obtain the conjunction '(P or Q) and not P' from 'P and not P' by a rule of conjunction introduction will require intermediate steps that do not obey this pattern.

Given that an impossible proposition may still imply another proposition when there is an appropriate relationship between the antecedent and the consequent, it was still possible for those who rejected the rule EIQ to accept that an impossible proposition can imply different types of proposition, namely, necessary, contingent and impossible propositions (De Monte 1490, f. xxxv^v). This generic approach to EIQ and its companion NEQ is what appears in sixteenth-century discussions of consequences. Thus Fonseca first explains NEQ by saying that 'the necessary follows from everything, that is, it can follow from the necessary and the contingent and the impossible', and he then gives a similar explanation of EIQ (Fonseca

---

[31] Peter of Spain's *Syncategoremata* was often printed (without commentary) in editions of Lambertus de Monte's and Versor's commentaries on Peter of Spain.

1964, 342–344). His examples make it plain that he does not accept the earlier version of these rules.

In their accounts of the criteria for validity, Paul of Venice and Paul of Pergula had added a further distinction, that between consequences formally valid *de forma*, which are those such that all consequences similar in form are valid, and consequences formally valid *de materia*, which are such that not all consequences similar in form are valid (Paul of Venice 2002, 53–54; Paul of Pergula 1961, 88–89). One might suppose that similarity in form has to do with the substitution criterion as accepted by Buridan and others, but this is not the case, for both Pauls claimed that formal similarity included exhibiting a similar type of argument involving terms rather than propositional structure. For instance, 'A man runs, therefore an animal runs' is formally valid *de forma*, because similar arguments from the inferior term to the superior term, such as 'whiteness is seen, therefore colour is seen', are also valid. This implicit reference to the role of topical rules was taken up by later logicians, though without the distinction between 'formally valid' and 'formally valid *de forma*'. Thus Mair explained the view that instances of EIQ and NEQ are only materially valid by referring to the argument that these instances involve no intrinsic locus or topic and that one can imagine the opposite of the consequent to be consistent with the antecedent (Mair 1519, f. lxxx^va–vb). This view, he said, is held in Oxford and Cambridge, but is not so common in Paris. Soto provides another example of the appeal to topical rules, for he claimed that a consequence is formally valid if and only if each consequence with the same form, including dependence on the same topical rule, is valid (Soto 1539–1540, f. lxxvii^ra).

7.7   CONCLUSION

While such authors as Soto still showed a good knowledge of the specifically medieval contributions to logic, and while slightly later authors such as Fonseca still retained some remnants of them, by the seventeenth century, interest in them had largely been lost. Medieval works were still printed, and in 1675 Obadiah Walker even sponsored a new edition of Ockham's *Summa logicae,* but it had little if any impact. It was not until the twentieth century that new editions of medieval manuscripts combined with new developments in formal logic alerted historians of logic to interesting parallels between medieval and contemporary logical systems, and much work remains to be done.

PART II Themes

8   Logica Vetus

Margaret Cameron

Logica Vetus (or Old Logic, hereafter *LV*) is the set of logical works
that had been in circulation in the Latin West before the wave of new
translations of Aristotle's remaining logical treatises, called *Logica
Nova* (or New Logic, *LN*), became available.[1] These treatises cover
fundamental philosophical issues, including the division of everything into categories, the nature of the relationship between language,
thought and reality, the structure of linguistic terms and sentences,
the character of definitions, the status of universals, modal reasoning, and the nature of truth, to name just the big topics. *LV* is sometimes thought of as Boethian logic, since all but one of the texts were
made available by the hand of the fifth-century Boethius (c. 480–525/
6). Boethius aimed to translate from Greek to Latin all the works of
Plato and Aristotle and to provide detailed commentaries on them,
although only Aristotle's *Categories* and *On Interpretation*, as well
as an introduction to the *Categories*, called *Isagoge*, written by the
third-century Neoplatonist Porphyry (c. 234–c. 305), were transmitted
to the Latin West. Medieval scholars also inherited from Boethius
lengthy commentaries written to explain every line of the original
material and, since Boethius' habit was to refer to other ancient commentators' critical arguments and interpretations when giving his
own, these commentaries preserved a rich heritage of the late ancient
reception of Aristotelian logic. In addition to *Isagoge*, *Categories* and
On Interpretation, the *LV* included a twelfth-century treatise written
to supplement *Categories*, known as *Book of Six Principles* (*Liber
de sex principiis*, hereafter *LSP*). While other Boethian treatises were

---

[1] The *LN* includes *Prior* and *Posterior Analytics*, *Topics* and *Sophistical Refutations*.
For the dates of translations, see Dod 1982. All these logical works were continuously available to the medieval Arabic tradition, and so this distinction does not
apply to them. See Madkour 1969; Black 1990.

included in this set in the twelfth century, they gradually fell out of circulation when the *LN* became available.[2]

The texts of *LV* played a major role in university instruction. Taking note of how they were studied provides insight into the ways they were interpreted. Accordingly the first section of this chapter will outline the ways this material was used by masters and students. Given that philosophers often engaged in metalogical reflections about the subject matter of logic itself, a brief review of the principal shifts in the characterizations of logic during this period will follow. Our focus will be on the four core *LV* texts – *Isagoge*, *Categories*, *LSP* and *On Interpretation* – with a focus primarily on their reception in the thirteenth and early fourteenth centuries (although these texts were continuously read as curriculum texts in universities until the sixteenth century). A core question will be how medieval logicians understood these treatises as belonging to the discipline of logic.

WAYS *LOGICA VETUS* MATERIAL WAS STUDIED

LV texts formed the foundation of logical instruction, and were the first treatises of philosophy that a student encountered. For the most part, *LV* texts were studied by being commented upon. Commentaries began to be produced in the schools in and around Paris in the early twelfth century, and by the time university instruction had begun, they were a staple method for studying the ancient, authoritative philosophical treatises. Commentaries in each of the periods displayed distinctive features. In this section, we look at the commentary genres organized roughly chronologically from the early- to mid-thirteenth to early fourteenth centuries, and will conclude with brief comments about the extent of the influence of the *LV* outside of the commentary tradition.

Thirteenth-century literal commentaries were written by Arts masters and were part of the course of lectures on *LV*. These have

---

[2] See Wilkes in this volume.

been described as very boring (Ebbesen 2003), and this is sometimes true, but they teach us a lot about the intellectual milieu and, especially, the training in logic that was required for students. They generally begin with a discussion of: the position of the text within the *LV* series; the subject matter of the work; and the division of the text. A brief passage, or even just a line of text (called a *lemma*), is followed by comments; brief objections are raised and popular interpretive problems discussed; and there are frequent appeals to the authority of Boethius. At the end of either each chapter or the work as a whole, there is a series of questions (*quaestiones*), doubts (*dubia*) or notes (*notabilia*), which served to reinforce good studying practice for students, since they direct students' attention to necessary and sufficient conditions, to the adequacy of definitions, and to the demand for cogency across Aristotle's writings. The literal commentaries are likely to be products of *reportationes*, so-called fair copies made either by masters themselves or by students on the basis of lectures.[3]

The context of their use was to prepare students to take their examinations at the university. What were the requirements for the logic course? According to the Statute of 1215 at the University of Paris, both *LV* and *LN* were to be studied in the ordinary (i.e. a deep reading done in the morning), not cursive (i.e. a rapid, cursory), style (Denifle and Chatelain 1889, I, §20, 78; see Weijers 1994). Later statutes required both ordinary and cursive readings, and the specific length of time for the study of each text was explicitly given (for example, they were to have been taught by the time of the feast of Annunciation of the Sacred Virgin, and so on) (Denifle and Chatelain 1889, I, §246, 277–279). There were guides for preparing for the examinations, some of which closely correspond to the literal commentaries and help us see what issues were of interest during this period (Lafleur 1997).

---

[3] Dating these commentaries has been hard work for scholars. Throughout I am mainly dependent on the work of Lewry 1978 and Peter of Auvergne 1988.

At the end of the thirteenth century, question commentaries rose in popularity. These commentaries contained *only* questions and answers, without literal exposition of the commented text but certainly presuming knowledge of it. By this time a greater literacy in Aristotelian ideas could be assumed, and philosophers displayed increased confidence to direct their lectures according to their own interests. Question commentaries come in different styles, some closely reflecting the content of the text, some only loosely connected to its subject matter. Most of the thirteenth-century question commentaries produced at Paris were written by Modistics, otherwise known as speculative grammarians (Pinborg 1967; Rosier-Catach 1983).

Commentaries continued to be a popular means to study the *LV* into the fourteenth century, although for historians of logic they have perhaps been overshadowed by developments in supposition theory, the theory of consequences, and other products of the *logica modernorum* for which authors during this period are more famed.[4]

Although in this chapter the focus will be on the *LV* commentary tradition, it is important to recognize that the philosophical material contained in those texts was subject to intense study in venues other than commentaries directly addressing them. For example, lengthy discussions of *LV* issues were taken up in analyses of other philosophical works (such as commentaries on other Aristotelian works, as well as *Quodlibeta*) as well as in theological contexts (for example, in commentaries on Peter Lombard's *Sentences*). As the foundational treatises of a student's education, *LV* texts served as basic tools for intellectual engagement, providing basic vocabulary for any study in the Aristotelian tradition. They introduced such

---

[4] Study of *LV* continued into the fifteenth century, but there have been few studies on the subject. The general tendency during this century seems to have been to provide an exegesis of *LV* according to the views of one or other thirteenth- or fourteenth-century master: there were Albertists, Thomists, Scotists, Ockhamists, Buridanists and so on, although there is indication that the lines of school identification, and the motivations for the return to thirteenth-century masters, were not as simple or straightforward as had been previously considered (Kaluza 1988).

fundamental concepts as substance, accident, subject, predicate, species, genus and so on, all of which are requisite for tackling any of Aristotle's other works, not to mention the many commentaries by ancient Greek and Arabic philosophers that were used in the service of their interpretation beginning in the early to mid-thirteenth century. In addition, any master's interpretation of key issues contained in *LV* treatises often carried crucial implications for theology and religious belief. Although, officially, logic masters were prohibited from discussing theological topics in logic courses, it was not unusual for masters' positions on such themes to be censured and condemned because of their tacit theological implications, an historical fact which helped to shape the trajectory of logical development.

8.1   SHIFTING CHARACTERIZATIONS OF LOGIC

There were three major currents in the development of thirteenth- to early-fourteenth-century logic: logic as (1) a linguistic science, (2) an intentional (psychological) science concerned with logical objects of thought and (3) a discipline focused solely on linguistic and mental terms. It is important to note that none of these currents was precisely demarcated, and there is ample evidence of overlap. In this section, we will review these shifting characterizations of logic, since they entailed different interpretations of *LV* texts.

Commentators often seized the opportunity to engage in metalogical reflection on logic as a discipline. This meant providing an explicit account of the subject matter of logic, a question that had been asked since Antiquity but was given new focus in the thirteenth century under the influence of Aristotle's *Posterior Analytics*. In that treatise, Aristotle outlines the criteria for qualifying as *scientia* (roughly, as scientific knowledge): it requires a unified subject matter, so accordingly the logical subject needed to be univocal. It also required identifying the necessary properties of the subject (as entailed by the definition), as well as a determination of the subject matter's causes (formal, material, efficient and final). Philosophers set out not only to define the subject matter of logic, but also to establish how each logical treatise itself met the criteria for being *scientia*. This approach dominated logic in the thirteenth century, but was abandoned by proponents of the terminist tradition in the fourteenth century.

Logic as Linguistic Science: During the early to mid-thirteenth century, logic was broadly characterized as linguistic science (*scientia sermocinalis*), closely connected to the preceding study of grammar. The principle used to justify the sequence of the books of logic (both the *vetus* and *nova*) was their contribution to the study of the syllogism: *Categories* treats incomplex expressions (e.g. 'human', 'runs'), *On Interpretation* complex expressions (e.g. 'a human runs'), *Prior Analytics* sets out syllogisms themselves, which are compounds of propositions, and the other *LN* treatises – *Posterior Analytics*, *Topics* and *Sophistical Refutations* – handle types of syllogisms. The placement of the *LV* texts *Isagoge* and *LSP* had to be justified on their own, since they much less obviously pertain to the subject matter of the syllogism. During this period, although practitioners characterized logic as a linguistic science, there was a tendency to treat the discipline of logic as concerned with either language, cognitions or extramental reality, or all three together, since they thought that the ways we speak and think do track reality itself.

Logic of Second Intentions: While late-thirteenth-century logical masters continued – indeed, increased – their commitment to logic as *scientia*, a new characterization comes to supplant logic as linguistic science. Introduced by Albert the Great (c. 1200–1280, writing c. 1245), intentionalist logic was derived from the newly available writings of the Islamic philosopher Avicenna, for whom logic is the science of second intentions.[5] These are to be distinguished from first intentions, which are our concepts of extramental reality (for example, 'Jane', 'runs'). Second intentions were variously characterized

---

[5] Avicenna, *The Healing* I, 2: The subject matter of logic is the secondary intelligible concepts, which depend on the primary intelligible concepts with respect to the manner by which one arrives through them at the unknown from the known (trans. Hasse 2014).

as concepts that follow upon either how we understand extramental reality, how we compare objects in extramental reality with one another, or from the intellect reflecting upon its own operations, as well as a number of other formulations (see Pini 2002). In every case, second intentions are logical objects of cognition. Until John Duns Scotus (1265/6–1308, writing c. 1290s), however, it was usually held that these cognitions had as their object extramental reality insofar as it is understood. After Scotus, logicians began to exhibit an increasing irrealism about logic and its subject matter.

Although still broadly organized around the study of the syllogism, the intentionalist logicians explain the sequencing of the logical treatises anew according to the three operations of the intellect:

(i) First operation of simple apprehension: apprehension of extramental individuals, the subject matter of *Categories* (as well as *Isagoge* and *LSP*, considered adminiculative for studying *Categories*).

(ii) Second operation of composition and division of concrete first intentions: composition and division of concepts derived from simple apprehension into propositions, the subject matter of *On Interpretation*.

(iii) Third operation of comparison or discursion: comparing one composite (i.e. one proposition) to another, or the inferences from cause to effect and from antecedent to consequent, the subject matter of the treatises on syllogisms.

Terminist Logic: There was a further current in the conception of logic in this period according to which logic is the study of terms; hence, this development was known as terminist logic, or modern logic (*logici moderni*).[6] The branches of terminist logic are covered elsewhere in this volume, so here we will emphasize rather its main differences from the other traditions. First, terminist logicians have no interest in justifying the subject of logic as *scientia*. In his prologue to the commentaries on the *LV*, William of Ockham (c. 1287–1347)

---

[6] Terminist logic has its roots in the twelfth century and developed alongside the other characterizations of logic. Generally scholars recognize its heyday as being the fourteenth century.

makes this point repeatedly, indicating that neither the subject of logic as a whole, nor any of its treatises, admit a unified subject matter (Ockham 1978; *Prooemium* 6, 84–87, 112). He abandons the earlier practice of identifying the causes of logic in terms of Aristotle's four-fold causal theory by noting that, since logic deals with simple, non-composite things, i.e. linguistic and mental terms, it has only an efficient cause (i.e. the author of the text) and a final cause (i.e. cultivating cognitive habits). Terminism gave its practitioners remarkable flexibility by moving away from the Aristotelian scientific paradigm. Finally, with regard to the usefulness of logic, the terminist tradition ushers in a new, hermeneutic focus that emphasizes the importance of developing more sophisticated tools, such as the doctrine of supposition, theory of consequences and so on, to interpret authoritative texts and engage in critical debate.

8.2   ISAGOGE

The first treatise in the course of logic was Porphyry's *Isagoge*. It was written as an introduction to *Categories*, although in its very first paragraph it is clear that it is also meant as an introduction to Aristotle's logic more broadly. Porphyry sets out what philosophers have said about what genus and difference are, as well as species, property, and accident ... since reflection on these things is useful for giving definitions, and in general for matters pertaining to division and demonstration (Porphyry 1966, 5.3–6). Genus, species, difference (*differentia*), property and accident became known to medieval authors as the five predicables, or universals, since the words for these things are what are put into predicative statements, for example, 'Socrates is human', 'Cats are mammals'. According to Porphyry, being predicated of several things is common to all of them. Before proceeding to describe each of the predicables, however, Porphyry announced that he would not investigate the status of the predicables, since, [s]uch business is profound, and requires another, greater investigation (Porphyry 1966, 5.14–15). These more profound inquiries were pursued with zeal by Porphyry's readers, becoming the logical touchstone for what became one of the most hotly contested issues in the Middle Ages, namely, the problem of the status of universals: are universals linguistic expressions, mental objects or acts of thought, or are they aspects of reality? The difficulty is presented in Boethius' characterization of universals as whatever can be present in several things as a whole and at the same time (Boethius 1906, 162ff.), and in Aristotle's as what is naturally able to be predicated of many (Aristotle 1984, *On Interpretation* 7 17a39). The problem was especially acute for medieval authors who subscribed to Aristotle's theory of cognition, according to which our understanding of reality is generated on the basis of our sense experiences, but we have sense experience only of particular, or individual, items in reality, not of universals.

For the mid-thirteenth-century philosophers eager to render its doctrine into a *scientia*, they needed to establish how the five predicables or universals can be a univocal subject matter capable of being defined. The logicians who considered logic to be a linguistic science took their status as predicables as their unifying feature. That is, the subject matter is words signifying universals in reality that can be predicated of many. It is the universal insofar as it falls under discourse, as one proponent explained (Anglicus 2005, §41, 280). These early to mid-century thinkers promoted a fairly unsophisticated explanation for how universals are essentially the same, whether they are located in extramental reality or in the mind. As Robertus Anglicus (writing c. 1245) explains:

> Note that the universal and the singular are one and the same according to essence (*essentia*), although they are not one and the same according to existence (*esse*). For example, this form [i.e. predicable, universal] 'human', according to which it is multiplied in this [individual] and that [individual] is a universal; it is, however, abstracted from this [individual] and that [individual] and from its conditions here and now. However, this form, in essence, according to what it is in and considering its conditions here and now, is a particular. (Anglicus 2005, §32, 276)

Since on this account, the universal that is in extramental reality as its form, and the universal that is abstracted from this and exists in the mind, are *essentially the same*, there can be a science of universals.

The turn to characterizing logic as an intentional science permitted greater sophistication in answering the question about the *Isagoge* as *scientia*. Following Thomas Aquinas (1225–1274), many philosophers identified a close, if not for some an isomorphic, relationship between modes of being (*modi essendi*), modes of predicating (*modi praedicandi*) and modes of signifying (*modi significandi*) (Aquinas 1995, lect. 9, 238 n. 890). Modes of predicating are dependent upon and derived from modes of reality, that is, from the ways things are in reality. For intentionalist logicians, modes of predicating are called intentions, which are logical objects of thought. They began to introduce finer distinctions: first, between first and second intentions; and second, between abstract and concrete intentions.[7] According to one schema given by Radulphus Brito (c. 1270–1320, writing c. 1290s), primary intentions are cognitions of individual items in extramental reality:

(i) An *abstract primary intention* is the mental product of multiple sense impressions of the individual thing having been collected in the imagination from which the cognition of the thing is abstracted.

(ii) This is distinguished from the *concrete primary intention*, which is a cognition of the extramental individual thing according to its mode of being (not according to the way it is being cognized).

Secondary intentions are separate orders of cognitive operation, but are dependent upon primary ones for their operation.

(iii) A *secondary abstract intention* designates the mode, or way, in which some extramental item, which is known to be common to different things, is cognized in comparison with something else. For example, comparison between the secondary intention of the shared feature

---

[7] There is considerable variability amongst intentionalist logicians about the details of their theories. See de Libera 1996; Pini 2002.

felinity with the cognizer's primary intention of an actual cat currently present to him.

(iv) Finally, the *concrete secondary intention* is the species, or universal, itself in reality – e.g. felinity itself, not in comparison with anything else but insofar as it is common to others and predicable of many (from Brito 1499 – writing c. 1290; see Pini 2002).

The close parallelism between modes of being and modes of predicating meant that, for Radulphus Brito, intentions have to do with reality *as it is understood*. This complex mental architecture, refined over many years, was meant to explain how the universal, that is, the common nature or species of, e.g. felinity, which exists in reality but cannot be sensed by us, can also be in the understanding. Accordingly, it can be the subject of logic as a science of second intentions.

But the tone of moderate realism that dominated the thirteenth century was disrupted first by Scotus, who, while building on the intentionalist doctrines of his predecessors and peers, urged a rupture between modes of being and modes of predicating. For Scotus, genus and species and the other predicates in Porphyry's *Isagoge* are not intentions, or concepts, that are produced by extramental reality, but are generated by the mind's own operations, e.g. by reflecting on its own concepts and operations. Secondary intentions such as genus and species are caused when the mind reflects on what it understands about its primary intentions – e.g. when after having had the primary intention of a white thing, the mind reflects on the mode of understanding that primary intention and comes to see its mode *as universal*, that is, that the whiteness in that thing is capable of being in many things and is predicable of many (Duns Scotus 1999). Scotus' shift from other intentionalists such as Radulphus Brito may seem subtle but it is crucially different: for Scotus, universals are purely mental products. However, the universal in the mind can be denominated, by which Scotus meant that a concrete adjective (e.g. 'cat') can be derived from the concept and used, as a word of primary intention, in predications (e.g. 'Bugsy is a cat').

Nominalist philosophers in the terminist tradition in the early fourteenth century radically overturned the paradigm of moderate realism that had prevailed in the thirteenth century. For Ockham, logic had nothing whatsoever to do with extramental reality, but only with mental and linguistic terms. According to Ockham's terminist logic,

> All those who treat of logic try to show that arguments are
> composed of propositions and propositions of terms. Thus, a term
> is simply a component part of a proposition. When he defines the
> notion of a term in the first book of the *Prior Analytics*, Aristotle
> says, I call that a term into which a proposition is resolved
> (i.e., the predicate or that of which it is predicated), when it is
> asserted or denied that something is or is not the case. (Ockham
> 1974a, I, 1)

Ockham's metaphysical nominalism held that only individuals, that is, particular, not universal, things exist in reality. How, then, could he account for the subject matter of *Isagoge*, which is a treatise about five universals? According to Ockham, universals are mental words. Using the terminists' doctrine of supposition, Ockham is able to explain away the appearance of real universality:

> it must be held that genera and species are not substances
> outside of the mind but exist in the intellect alone, because
> they are nothing but certain intentions or concepts
> formed by the intellect, expressing the essences of things and
> signifying them. (Ockham 1978, 14, 130–134; trans.
> Kluge 1973)

Ockham retains the language of intentions that express and signify (i.e. give rise to a concept of) things' essences. But talk of essences here should not be misunderstood, since Ockham applied the doctrine of supposition to indicate precisely what is expressed and signified:

they are certain terms that are predicable of things, but not as
standing for themselves, because when a genus is predicated
of a species, the genus [term] and species [term] do not stand
for themselves because they do not have *simple supposition*.
Instead, they have *personal supposition* and thus stand for
their significates, which are singular things. (Ockham 1978, 14,
135–139)

Supposition is a device used by terminist logicians to specify that to
which terms, or words, used in complex contexts such as declarative
sentences refer. Terms with *simple supposition* stand for the concept,
whereas terms with *personal supposition* stand for the individual(s)
signified by the term. Thus,

these genera [terms] and species [terms] are predicated of
things: the very things which they signify. For instance, in
'Socrates is an animal', the word 'animal' does not stand for itself
but for a thing, in this case for Socrates himself. (Ockham 1978,
14, 139–141)

'Animal' is a species term, but here it is a term of first intention
in the sense that it signifies individual animals in extramental
reality. In this case, the term 'animal' supposits for Socrates himself
(Ockham 1978, 22, 50–71). What about the terms of the five predicables themselves? According to Ockham, in the sentence, 'Human is a
species', the term 'species' is a term of second intention. In this case,
the term 'species' has *simple*, not personal, supposition, since there
is nothing in extramental reality to which 'species' refers. Rather, it
supposits for the mental term 'species'. In this sense, Ockham was
able to classify the five predicables as names of second intentions,
suppositing not for items in extramental reality but for signs in the
human mind.[8]

---

[8] This is not the end of the story of the controversies over universals, and even in
their own day nominalism was sharply challenged. See Conti 2013a.

8.3 CATEGORIES

Categories served as an entry point for the study of Aristotelian logic proper, and for Aristotle's philosophy more generally. It appears, like *On Interpretation*, to be missing its introduction, leaving readers without Aristotle's own statement about the purpose of the book. This left its readers with three main options: is *Categories* about linguistic expressions, concepts or reality? From its earliest interpretation in the ancient world, commentators divided the book into three sections.

(i) *Ante-praedicamenta* contain definitions of univocity, equivocity and paronymy. Aristotle states, Of things that are said, some involve combination while others are said without combination (Aristotle 1984, *Categories* 1a17–18) (e.g. 'human', 'runs'), and not things said with combination (e.g. 'A human runs'). Aristotle then gives the extremely influential division of beings according to two criteria: *being said-of* and being *present in*.[9] The result is a division of beings into essential universals, accidental particulars, accidental universals and non-accidental particulars.

(ii) The *praedicamenta* are Aristotle's ten categories – substance, quantity, relatives, quality, where, when, being-in-a-position, having, doing and being affected – only the first four of which receive sustained examination. According to Aristotle, further discussion of the remaining categories would be superfluous given their obviousness.

(iii) *Post-praedicamenta* discuss opposition, priority, the more-and-less, and coincidence, which were considered helpful to understand the preceding section.

How did medieval authors consider *Categories* to be a *logical* treatise? According to mid-thirteenth-century philosophers who took logic to be a science of language, this *scientia* is not of the ten categories, but of the incomplex sayable (John Pagus 2012, I, q, 1 (13.1–2) – writing c. 1231–1235). The 'incomplex sayable' to which

---

[9] Aristotle explains that being present-in is 'what is in something, not as a part, and cannot exist separately from what it is in' (Aristotle 1984, *Categories* 1a24–25). He does not define being said-of.

these authors refer is derived from Aristotle's text (quoted above): Of things that are *said*, that is, what is sayable, some involve combination while others are said *without combination*, that is, what is incomplex. These incomplex sayables are capable of being ordered, by which is meant that they can be ordered as genera, species and individuals (*ordinabile in genere*) according to the doctrine of the categories. Thus the doctrine of the categories can be *scientia* since it has a unified subject matter, incomplex significant sayables. Note, however, that with regard to their being ordered into genera, the categories are not univocally, but only analogically related.[10] This is also put in terms of being attributable to one thing: For all [of them] are attributed to substance, and so evidently there can be one *scientia* of them (Peter of Auvergne 1988, 2.2, 361 – writing c. 1245). 'Attribution to one thing' is an allusion to a doctrine borrowed from the Islamic commentator Averroes (1126–1198), upon which Latin commentators argued that the unity of *scientia* can be derived, not from univocal subjects that are capable of being defined, but from *analogical* subjects, that is, subjects who are, by being ordered to one thing, related to one another. In this case, each of the nine accidents is analogously related to the category of substance, in the sense that they all bear some non-reducible, but nevertheless similar relation to substance, i.e. they are its accidents.

The intentionalist logicians considered *Categories* to belong to logic insofar as they are studied as logical concepts, not insofar as they are either words or items in extramental reality. But they gave a lot of thought to the question of how the categories are a logical subject, since they are studied both in *Categories* and in Aristotle's *Metaphysics*. For example, Radulphus Brito devoted six prolegomenic, metalogical questions totalling more than 5,000 words to discuss the subject matter of the *Categories*:

---

[10] See Robert Kilwardby in Hansen 2012, I, Proem (writing 1237–1245), transcribed in 73n61. On the doctrine of analogy, see Ashworth 2013b.

(i) whether *Categories* can be *scientia*;

(ii) whether the science of *Categories* belongs to logic;

(iii) whether, regarding the subject matter of this book, the incomplex sayable is its subject;

(iv) whether a category is a real or a rational being;

(v) whether pure logic is able to make distinctions among the categories; and

(vi) whether a logical category and a metaphysical category are one and the same category.

There were good reasons to question the status of *Categories* as a logical treatise. For example, as Brito notes, while it is true that the logician takes secondary intentions as the subject of logic, the logician (following Avicenna) treats them adjoined to primary intentions – or, as they put the point, the logician considers *things in reality* insofar as they are denominated from (i.e. named by) second intentions. Putting the question slightly differently, secondary intentions are produced by items in extramental reality, and so does the logician also study extramental reality (Brito 1499, *In Cat.* Q2)? Moreover, Brito reports, both the logical and metaphysical categories share the same properties; for example, logical substance and metaphysical substance both receive contraries, are not in a subject, and do not have a contrary, and so on. But things that share the same properties would belong to the same *scientia*.

In response, Brito admits that it is not possible to distinguish between logical and metaphysical categories, and hence they are one and the same. The secondary intentions studied by the logician are derived from the metaphysically real categories themselves. At the same time, however, they can be formally distinguished by reason, since in logic the categories are considered as modes of predicating the superior of the inferior, that is, the genera of the species, and species of individuals. In metaphysics, they are rather considered in terms of differences of real being (Brito 1499, *In Cat.* Q6).

Both this characterization of logic and correspondingly the subject matter of *Categories* were met with significant challenge and a

radical rethinking in the fourteenth century. Many factors contributed to the nominalists' reductivist, even eliminativist, reading of
the categories, including whether there can be a deduction of the categories (see Wippel 1987), the problems presented by concrete accidental terms (such as 'white', as opposed to abstract accidental terms
such as 'whiteness') (see Ebbesen 1988), and the effects of new logical
tools – especially the doctrine of supposition – developed as part of
the *logica modernorum*. Here we will focus on how Ockham charac-
terizes the logic of the categories.

First, Ockham contests the reality of the ten categories,
preserving only substance and quality. Discussion about the suf-
ficiency of the categories (e.g. why list these ten, why only these
ten, and so on) had been taking place among thirteenth-century
commentators. Some philosophers had begun to demote the metaphysical status of several of the categories (usually the latter six
or seven) to modes of being. But Ockham's reasons for admitting
only substance and quality were a consequence of his semantic
theory, specifically his introduction of a distinction between absolute and connotative terms.[11] Any significant term is absolute if
it does not signify something principally and another thing (or the
same thing) secondarily. For example, the term 'horse' or 'stone'
signifies all the things that are horses and stones, and nothing else.
These are what we call 'natural kind terms'. By contrast, a term is
connotative if it 'signifies one thing primarily and another thing
secondarily' (Ockham 1974b, §10, 69–71). For example, 'father',
which signifies not just the man who is a father but also his daughter. By this distinction, Ockham was able to show that there is
no need to posit a category of relation to explain the meaning of
'father': the individual father and his individual daughter suffice.
Applied to the interpretation of *Categories*, Ockham could demonstrate that all of the categories except substance and quality
could be eliminated.

[11] Ockham also had theological reasons; see Adams 1987.

8.4   BOOK OF SIX PRINCIPLES – *LSP*

The *LSP* was variously attributed, but its author remains unknown. Apparently written in the twelfth century, it presents the latter six categories – where, when, being-in-a-position, having, doing and being affected – affording them as much detail as Aristotle does the former four. *LSP* opens with a definition of form: form is something which falls to a composition consisting in a simple and unchanging being (Anon., *LSP* §1). After noting a number of form's characteristics, the text paraphrases the passage from *Categories* in which he sets out the division of being into what is *said of x* and what is *present in x* (Aristotle 1984, *Categories* 1a17–18, quoted above). Notably, *LSP* describes that which is said of and what is present in as *forms*. *LSP* then sets out a distinction that becomes widespread in the medieval tradition between intrinsic and extrinsic forms. Those forms that are intrinsically present in substance are the former four categories (substance, quantity, relation, quality), whereas the latter six extrinsically advene. To advene extrinsically means that substances are formed by these principles from something external to them, for example, a cup's being moved (which is the form of passion, being moved) by my hand. The remainder of the treatise is devoted to setting out the characteristics of these extrinsic forms.

In one of the earliest-known thirteenth-century commentaries on *LSP*, the question whether the treatise properly belongs to the subject of logic or natural science was raised at the start (Kilwardby 1978, 391, 13–18). More than other *LV* texts, *LSP* seemed to its readers to belong rather to natural science, since in its description of the category (or principle or form) of action, the author deals both with the motion and matter of things that act. According to the earlier commentaries written by proponents of logic as a linguistic science, however, insofar as moving, enmattered things are examined, this topic does belong to natural science, although in this context things are considered in abstraction from their motion and matter. At the same time, however, unlike *Categories*, *LSP* is more concerned with issues about the real world than with linguistic expressions (Kilwardby 1978). Still, it can be considered a science for the same reasons as these earlier commentators considered *Categories* a science: *LSP* deals with incomplex sayables that can be ordered according to their *genera*.

In subsequent commentaries by intentionalist logicians, the metalogical questions about the status of *LSP* as a logical treatise ran parallel to those given in *Categories* commentaries, and so need not be further canvassed here. Of all its features, the definition of form given in the very opening lines of *LSP* is what enjoyed the most extensive influence: form is something which falls to a composition consisting in a simple and unchanging being. 'Form' is used here in a typically twelfth-century fashion to signify both *differentiae* (i.e. substantial forms) and accidents. The forms are what the author of *LSP* calls 'principles', and he treats them as non-overlapping, non-reducible categories.

LSP's distinction between intrinsic and extrinsic forms could well have had a significant impact on how the interpretation of the doctrine of the categories evolved throughout the Middle Ages (Anon., *LSP* §§14–15). According to Albert the Great, the reason these are called principles and are extrinsic to their subjects is that, unlike intrinsic forms, they do not play any role in determining the being of the subject they are in: on this account, they are more forms, that is, remaining *outside*, than they are essences. This distinction was comfortably upheld by philosophers who argued for the reality and distinctness of each of the ten categories, that is, by the late-thirteenth-century moderate realists.[12]

---

[12] Classifying the latter six principles, and sometimes also relation, as modes (which accordingly have a lesser degree of reality than substances, quantities and qualities) reached a crisis in the work of Peter John Olivi (1248–1298), whose effort to render all of the categories as modes, and thereby to collapse the essential distinctions between the categories, generated a condemnation in 1283 because of its unwanted theological implications: To say that the predicaments are not really distinct is contrary to the Philosopher and especially dangerous in the cases of relation and quantity (*Littera septem sigillorum contra doctrinam Petri Ioannis Olivi* in Fussenegger 1954, 52; Burr 1976, 55).

For early-fourteenth-century terminist philosophers, the distinction between intrinsic and extrinsic forms was even more pronounced. As discussed above, the ultra-nominalist Ockham recognized only the categories, or forms, of substance and quality. With regard to the latter six, Ockham explains them away as being merely ways of signifying substances: 'action' and 'passion' are not themselves forms but are verbs (Ockham 1974b; *Summa* I §57; Spade 1974, 180–183). 'When' and 'where' are adverbs, and 'position' and 'having' are simply ways substances can be arranged. Another fourteenth-century nominalist, John Buridan (c. 1300–1362), directly targeted the author of *LSP*. Contending that all but substance, quantity and quality were merely ways of speaking of substance, Buridan complained,

> We should note that concerning action and passion and the four other remaining categories I do not intend to follow the doctrine of the author of [*LSP*]. For I think that he was mistaken, since he believed that no terms that pertain to diverse categories can supposit for [that is, refer to] the same thing, and so he maintained that action is one form and passion is another, and that passion would hence be an effect of action; this is totally false, and thus his doctrine made many people err. (Buridan 2001; *Summulae de Dialectica* 3.6.1, 193)

The error of the author of *LSP*, according to Buridan, consists in interpreting the six principles as non-overlapping, irreducible types of things. For Buridan, the problem is that it is difficult to see what these words mean (*significare*) and to what they refer (*supponere*). They are not candidates to be categories, since categorical terms are what are to be used in either the subject or predicate positions in sentences. But how, Buridan wonders, can the expression 'in the year of our Lord one thousand three hundred', which is supposed to be in the category of 'when', be used predicatively (Buridan 2001, 3.7.1)? In the end, Buridan is completely dismissive of the value of *LSP*: We should note that Aristotle said that these four categories are so obvious that it was sufficient to explain them by examples. The author of [*LSP*], however, made what was manifest obscure (Buridan 2001, 3.7.1).

8.5 *ON INTERPRETATION*

Aristotle's *On Interpretation* had been placed between *Categories* and *Prior Analytics*, which was the first treatise in the sequence of *Logica Nova* in the order of studying Aristotelian logic. This seemed the obvious position for it, since it explains how words are used in combination (e.g. 'A human runs') to form propositions and how propositions stand in logical relations to one another such as contrariety and contradiction, so providing the basis for the doctrine of syllogistic. Chapters 1 through 4 treat the relationship between spoken and written expressions, concepts or understandings, and reality, providing the well-known semantic triad. Aristotle then sets out the simple enunciative statement and its parts, the name (*nomen*) and verb (*verbum*). An enunciative statement is a declarative sentence capable of being used in syllogistic reasoning. Two species of simple enunciative proposition are given, affirmation and negation, and Aristotle considers what problems are raised by their being true or false. According to Aristotle, 'If every affirmation is true or false, it is necessary for everything either to be the case or not to be the case' (Aristotle 1984, *On Interpretation* 18a34–35). This contention raises serious difficulties for future contingent propositions, and raises some deep questions about the nature of actuality, possibility and necessity. Aristotle discusses these and other related issues in the remaining chapters, most famously in chapter 9, with the example of the Sea Battle (see Knuuttila 2010).

In comparison with the commentaries on the other *LV* texts, commentaries on *On Interpretation* convey scant interest in metalogical questions about the subject matter of the treatise (which they took to be the simple enunciative proposition) or its status as a logical treatise.

In the mid-thirteenth century, the strong association between the study of grammar and that of logic provoked a highly linguistic-oriented interpretation of *On Interpretation*. This is evident from the start when determining both what the treatise's subject matter is and why it is titled as it is. Students would have been taught grammar before logic, and they needed to establish how each linguistic subject was a *scientia* capable of meeting the criteria set out by Aristotle in *Posterior Analytics*. Both linguistic sciences deal with the noun and the verb, which according to *On Interpretation* are the basic parts of sentences. But the main authority for grammatical science was Priscian's *Institutiones grammaticae*, which provides a different definition of the noun – which signifies a substance with a quality[13] – than does Aristotle's treatise – a spoken sound significant by convention, without time, none of whose parts is significant in separation (Aristotle 1984, *On Interpretation* 16a19–20). For linguistic logicians, considering nouns as signifying substance with a quality is the starting point for being able to grammatically construe the sentence in grammar to determine congruity or incongruity. Considering nouns as having conventional meaning, on the other hand, is done by the logician whose ultimate concern is their contribution to the truth and falsity of sentences (Nicholas of Paris 2011, §3, *ad* Q2; see also Kilwardby 1978). Linguistic expressions are the subject of study for the logician because by being put into signifying, complex expressions such as sentences they can be evaluated for their truth or falsity. It is their ability to be true that enables this subject matter to be treated as *scientia*, since truth is incorruptible.

Nicholas of Paris exemplifies the mid-thirteenth-century attitude that it does not matter whether we say that linguistic expressions signify understandings or reality:

a vocal expression is not imposed for the purpose of signifying something unless previously the thing is grasped

---

[13] Priscian, *Instit. Gramm.* II.IV.18, 55: '*Proprium est nominis substantiam et qualitatem significare*'.

by its likeness ... Whence the vocal utterance is a sign of the
understanding immediately, and the understanding is a sign of
the external thing. And in this way, when the vocal utterance
signifies a thing through the understanding, it amounts to the
same to say 'thing' or 'understanding', since one [signifies]
through the other. (Nicholas of Paris 2011, §1, Q4)

The formal equivalency between understanding and reality is supported by the prevailing theory of knowledge acquisition at this time,
a theory given in the very first passage of one mid-thirteenth-century
commentary. According to this cognitive theory, known as the doctrine of illumination, the process of acquiring knowledge begins in
sensory apprehension, but this only provides to the faculty of imagination particulars, which must be combined with others by the
activity of the intellect. To have intellective cognition, i.e. to have
the kind of understanding that satisfies the requirements of science,
namely, universality, requires the mind's being illuminated by the
agent intellect. But what is illumined just is what is in reality, and
so as far as signifying expressions go, it does not matter whether
one says that they signify what is in the mind or what is in reality
(Nicholas of Paris 2011, §1 Prooemium).

However, as a consequence of developments in epistemology
beginning with Albert the Great and Thomas Aquinas, the landscape
of commentaries on *On Interpretation* changes dramatically. Of primary concern is the question of how to interpret what Aristotle says
about the relationship between linguistic expressions, understanding and extramental reality at the start of the treatise, depicted as
follows:

WRITTEN   SPOKEN   PASSIONS OF
EXPRESSIONS ---------> EXPRESSIONS --------> THE SOUL -------------> REALITY
     signs of   *signs of*   *likenesses of*[14]

---

[14] Aristotle 1984, On *Interpretation* 16a3–9 (modified).

The debates that occupy philosophers at this time are motivated by the effort to make sense of what Aristotle says here within the confines of the prevailing epistemological debates. According to Aquinas' version, something can be known either through the sensitive faculty or through the intellective faculty. Aquinas held that the imagination abstracts from the sense impressions an imaginative impression. However, in place of the doctrine of illumination maintained by earlier thinkers such as Nicholas of Paris, Aquinas held that the agent intellect abstracts from this impression something called the intelligible species. For Aquinas, the intelligible species is not in the first place the *object* of knowledge, but it is that *by which* the extramental thing is known (although by reflection on its own cognitive operations, the intelligible species can come to be known as a second-order object of thought) (see Spruit 1994). The intelligible species is that by which the essences of things in extramental reality are known. As Scotus puts it, the intelligible species is the intelligible similitude of the extramental thing which is in the soul as in a subject (Scotus 1891, I.2, n. 1).

This theory prompted many questions with regard to the semantic triangle presented at the start of *On Interpretation*. For example, philosophers asked what Aristotle meant by the expression 'passions of the soul'. According to Walter Burley (c. 1275–1344, writing 1310s), at least four things could be meant:

(i)   the intelligible species;
(ii) an act of knowing;
(iii) a term, or endpoint (*terminus*) of an act of knowing, that is, something formed by the intellect as an image or similitude of the extramental thing; or
(iv) the extramental thing itself insofar as it has the ability to move the intellect. (Walter Burley 1973, 42–44)

Relatedly, commentators wondered whether linguistic expressions signify extramental reality either *mediately* (i.e. by way of one of the first three construals of passions of the soul listed above) or *immediately* (i.e. by way of the fourth). Note, however, that by 'immediately' none of these philosophers thought that signification is direct, i.e. without any intervening intellectual component. This is in part because the definition of 'to signify' was 'to give rise to an understanding' of something in someone. It was also in part due to the Aristotelian lesson that things must first be understood in order that they signify.[15]

The logic of the terminists shifted the debate again. As we saw in the case of Ockham's treatment of the problem of universals, terminists drew on the resources of the doctrine of supposition, eliminated the epistemic theory of intelligible species, and argued that the signification of spoken and written expressions is subordinated to a universal mental language (see Panaccio 2004). Being subordinated means that spoken and written expressions, which are conventional signs, fall under natural, mental signs, such that 'to signify' is for the mental term to bear a natural relationship to individual extramental things as its sign (Ockham 1974a, I, 1).

8.6   CONCLUSION

In this chapter, we have narrowly focused on the question of how medieval interpreters from the mid-thirteenth to early fourteenth centuries considered four of the treatises of the *LV* to belong to the discipline of logic and how they construed the subject matter of each treatise accordingly. We have seen how the shifting conceptions of the subject of logic as a whole had important theoretical implications for identifying and characterizing each treatise's subject matter. Very few of the commentaries on *LV* from this period have been translated into modern languages. Indeed, only recently have commentaries from the thirteenth-century linguistic and intentionalist traditions even been edited. Only once more of this material becomes available can a fuller history of the complicated period of the study of the *LV* be given.

---

[15] For example, Aquinas 1962, 78: Names signify things only through the mediation of the intellect.

9 Supposition and Properties of Terms

Christoph Kann

9.1 INTRODUCTION

In the late twelfth and early thirteenth centuries, the writings of Aristotle became central to the logic curriculum (see Chapters 4 and 5). However, in a number of new developments, some topics with which Aristotle had not been concerned now began to make an appearance, and went on to become crucial within the tradition. These innovations were not regarded as an alternative to the Aristotelian logic, but rather supplemented it under the heading "logic of the moderns" (*logica moderna* or *logica modernorum*) (De Rijk 1962–1967). Probably the most prominent among the new topics were the doctrines of the so-called properties of terms (*proprietates terminorum*), which are generally considered the basis for later medieval semantic theorising and adjacent issues.

Terms (*termini*) in the technical sense presupposed here (and pointing to the "terminist" tradition) are descriptive words which function as subject or predicate in a proposition. The basic idea of the "properties" (or terministic) approach is that an analysis of the semantics of (compound) linguistic expressions should proceed by analysing the semantic properties of the terms occurring in it. In handbooks of logic from the later Middle Ages, the treatment of the properties started with signification (*significatio*), the capacity of terms to function as signs; supposition (*suppositio*), the property of terms functioning as subject or predicate in propositions, was its centrepiece, but the framework also covered related properties like copulation, appellation, ampliation, restriction, and distribution.

In the earlier stages of development, supposition had been one among the other properties with equal standing. From the works of

Anselm of Canterbury, Peter Abelard and other less-well-known or anonymous authors, supposition theory began to emerge in the (late) twelfth century, and was then further developed through the thirteenth and fourteenth centuries. Though clearly dependent on grammarian traditions (Ashworth 2010, 152ff.) and closely connected with the theory of fallacies in its early stages, later on the framework developed in response to a variety of sometimes divergent needs in clarifying truth conditions, investigating the validity of inference forms, and making ontological commitments explicit. It is thus important to keep in mind that both across the centuries and in terms of different applications, the doctrines of the properties of terms form a rather heterogeneous collection in terms of function and application, as well as in terms of details of the machinery (Read 2015).

9.2 SIGNIFICATION

The medieval treatises on the properties of terms rest upon the initial distinction between signification and supposition. The theory of signification deals with the capacity of descriptive terms to function as signs, i.e. their pre-propositional and context-independent property of being meaningful prior to their particular occurrences or uses (Spade 1982a, 188–192; Meier-Oeser 1995; Ebbesen 1998b, 390–402). The theory of supposition is concerned with the semantics of propositions in relation to the different modes of use of the terms involved in their functions as subject and predicate (Spade 1982a, 192–196; Parsons 2008; Dutilh Novaes 2010a). The fact that supposition is acquired by a term when it occurs in a particular propositional context gives rise to a "contextual approach" (De Rijk 1962–1967 vol. II–1, 113–117, 123–125). But since a term can have personal supposition only in virtue of signifying its *supposita*, supposition as well as the other context-dependent properties ultimately depends on the term's signification.

The properties approach thus deals primarily with descriptive terms functioning as subject or predicate in a proposition, i.e. with signifying or categorematic words (*categoremata*) in contrast to merely consignifying or syncategorematic words (*syncategore-mata*). The latter contribute to or constrain the signifying components of a proposition and perform some logical function(s) within it by negating, conjoining, disjoining, quantifying, etc. (e.g. negations, connectives, and quantifiers) (Kretzmann 1982; Klima 2006; Dutilh Novaes and Spruyt 2015). Signification as the term's being meaningful on its own, i.e. irrespective of any propositional context, belongs to categorematic words by virtue of their ability to serve as language signs. Supposition, in contrast, is acquired by an already meaningful term when it functions as subject or predicate of a proposition. Supposition theory was used to describe what a categorematic term in its function as subject or predicate of a proposition means in a particular context including consignifying or syncategorematic words and thus integrates formal and non-formal features of language (Kann 2006). Among other things, it could serve to diagnose fallacies – the analysis and avoidance of fallacies is one of the main issues of medieval logic. Moreover, when medieval logicians claimed a proposition to be *de virtute sermonis* or literally false, they maintained that the theory of supposition enables us to analyse the proposition's true meaning, which may be covered up by misleading grammatical features.

The core set of ideas and doctrines from which medieval philosophers developed their theories of signification came mainly from Aristotle's reflections on the relationships between (spoken or written) names, concepts, and things (the so-called "semantic triangle") (*On Interpretation* 1–3, 16a3–b21), from Boethius' commentary *On Interpretation*, and from Augustine's doctrine of sign and signification. Augustine divides the sign into two main classes, natural signs (*signa naturalia*) and given or conventional signs (*signa data*). The preeminent role among all sorts of given signs that Augustine attributes to words results from the fact that everything that is indicated by nonverbal signs can be put into words but not *vice versa* (*De doctrina christiana* II 7). Augustine's ideas on signs, as well as Aristotle's account of the relationship between linguistic and extra-linguistic items, remained fundamental to the entire tradition of the properties approach.

With regard to signs and their signifying function, there was a lively debate over the principal signification of uttered words. The question was whether a spoken word like 'human' signifies the individual objects concerned, or incorporeal natures in the Platonic sense, or mental entities like concepts (*conceptus, intellectus*), representations (*imaginationes*), or affections of the soul (*passiones animae*). According to the two main conflicting positions, words uttered either name extramental things by signifying concepts (or universals) understood as likenesses abstracted from these things, or, as Augustine had held, signify things by means of concepts. The question of whether words uttered exclusively or primarily signify concepts or things remained a constant issue for centuries and inspired subtle reflections and solutions.

Abelard, e.g., in his *Logica Ingredientibus*, employs a distinction between signification of concepts (*significatio intellectuum*) and signification of the thing (*significatio rei*), the latter more properly called nomination (*nominatio*) or appellation (*appellatio*) (De Rijk 1962–1967 vol. II, 192–197). In the thirteenth century, a crucial issue under debate was the significative functions of concepts and of utterances. Lambert of Lagny – otherwise known as Lambert d'Auxerre (Maloney 2009) – for instance, referring to Aristotle, *On Interpretation* 1, 16a3–5, explained that utterances are signs of states in the soul or of concepts, which are signs of things; whence, by transitivity, utterances are themselves signs of things (Lambert of Auxerre 1971, 205). Thus, an utterance was regarded as a sign of a sign, namely a sign of a concept directly (being a sign itself), but a sign of the thing indirectly. According to William of Ockham, however, who identified the mental act or the concept with the universal, 'human' signifies all individuals falling under that term by virtue of its subordination to the concept (Adams 1987, 73–75; Panaccio 2004). A general term, as Ockham states in his *Summa Logicae* I, 33, signifies all those individuals of which it can be truly predicated.

9.3 SUPPOSITION AND ITS MODES

Supposition theory deals with the semantic interpretation of propositions due to the different modes of use of their subject and predicate
terms. The underlying idea is that a term, while retaining its signification, does not always stand for the same kind or range of objects in
different propositional contexts. As there are propositions that "must
be distinguished" with regard to their different senses (*propositiones
distinguendae*), i.e. which allow for different readings, supposition
theory was used to clarify what a categorematic term, i.e. the subject
or the predicate of a proposition, stands for, depending on its particular propositional embedding (including syncategorematic words).
Since the theory could help to diagnose fallacies, to explain inferential relations or to analyse a proposition's meaning, it was closely
linked with or integrated into treatises on consequences and *sophismata* or *insolubilia*. The supposition of a term, at least when taken
significatively, was defined by, e.g., William of Ockham, *Summa
Logicae* I, 63, as a term's standing for something else in a proposition in such a way that the term is truly predicated of that thing (or
of a pronoun pointing to the thing). On the basis of definitions such
as this one, some authors constructed a supposition-based theory of
truth conditions for categorical sentences.

Treatises often start with a division of proper and improper
supposition in order to distinguish the genuine uses of a term from,
e.g. its metaphorical use as the less relevant branch. The theory of
proper supposition was used for two remarkably different purposes.
On the one hand it served as a tool for semantic distinctions and on
the other hand it constituted a kind of theory of quantificational
analysis.

Some authors distinguished accidental (personal) supposition
(*suppositio accidentalis*) from natural supposition (*suppositio naturalis*) – allowing a term to stand for all instances including past, present and future (resembling the idea of signification) (De Rijk 1971;
1982b, 168–170). Other authors, in contrast, insisted on supposition

as unanimously context-dependent and propositional. This debate was linked to or interwoven with the doctrines of ampliation and restriction (cf. Section 9.3.3). In the thirteenth century, the Parisian logician John Page (Johannes Pagus), as did John Buridan in the fourteenth, tended to ascribe natural supposition to terms in universal necessary truths as a crucial type of scientific propositions – with the result that ampliation became irrelevant in this area, while in non-scientific propositions supposition was regarded as restricted in various ways (Ashworth 2010, 155). In contrast to this Parisian tendency to consider the supposition of terms in scientific propositions as a matter of its own, English logicians in the thirteenth century regarded supposition in general as context-dependent, and they proposed that ampliation was relevant in all instances in which a proposition goes beyond the range of present existing things, e.g. in modal contexts.

9.3.1 *Personal, Material, and Simple Supposition*

The semantic distinctions provided by supposition theory run basically as follows: If we take, e.g., the proposition 'Human is an animal', the term 'human' stands or supposits for (*supponit pro*) its significates, as when it is taken for individual human beings like Socrates, Plato, etc. In this case, 'human' has personal supposition (*suppositio personalis*). In contrast, in the proposition 'Human is a noun', the term 'human' – provided that the proposition is true – does not stand for what it usually signifies, namely humans, but for the word 'human' itself, and has thus material supposition (*suppositio materialis*). William of Sherwood gives a more detailed explanation, according to which supposition is called material when a word supposits either for the very utterance itself or for the word itself, composed of the utterance and the signification (William of Sherwood 1995, 136). A third case of supposition is represented by the proposition 'Human is a species', where the word 'human' stands neither for its significates nor for the word itself, but for the universal, the form or the concept expressed by it, and then it has simple supposition (*suppositio simplex*) (Parsons 2008, 192–202). The last of these was a highly controversial issue – for the very reason of the disputed status of the universals, forms, or concepts themselves.

But what causes or determines the kind of supposition of a term in a given proposition? According to the prevailing view, the mode of supposition of the subject term is (on the semantic level outlined here) largely determined by the predicate term. For example, in 'Human is an animal', the predicate 'animal' causes personal supposition for the subject 'human'. In contrast, predicates like 'is a noun' or 'is a monosyllable' cause material supposition for an adjoining subject, while the predicate 'is a species' causes the subject to have simple supposition, due to a general principle stated, e.g., by William of Sherwood: subjects are of such characters as their predicates may have permitted (William of Sherwood 1995, 144).

The division into personal, material, and simple supposition represents the three basic types of proper supposition or the genuine uses of a term. Nevertheless, authors like Walter Burley do not start with this threefold distinction, but rather with the twofold distinction of *suppositio materialis* and *suppositio formalis*, and divide the latter into *suppositio personalis* and *suppositio simplex* in a second step. The idea underlying this approach is to separate material supposition as a non-significative use of a term from two significative uses under the heading of formal supposition, namely one for concrete significates in the sense of, e.g., single human beings and the other for a general form or universal nature.

While simple supposition, as described e.g. by William of Sherwood and Walter Burley, occurs when a general term supposits for the universal or the form signified by it, William of Ockham and others, due to their nominalistic inclinations, denied that terms signified universals (Dutilh Novaes 2013). Rejecting the assumption of universals as autonomous units, and explaining them in the sense of mental acts or words of an inner language, Ockham considered simple supposition as the non-significative use of a term for an intention of the soul. While his realist counterpart Walter Burley, appealing to the authority of Aristotle's *Categories*, claimed in *De Puritate Artis Logicae* I, 1, 3 that, e.g., the general term 'human' signifies a second substance, namely human as a species, Ockham held in his *Summa Logicae* I, 64 that a term like 'human' signifies nothing but its individual instances. For him, a mental, spoken, or written term can supposit for a concept of the mind and thereby have simple supposition. Just as a term having material supposition sometimes supposits for itself and sometimes for something else, a mental term suppositing simply stands sometimes for itself, as in 'Human is a species', and sometimes, as Ockham explains in his *Summa Logicae* I, 68, for some other intention of the soul which it does not, nevertheless, signify, as in a mental proposition like 'That human is an animal is true'. Whereas John Buridan, viewing universals as terms of a mental language, proposed that terms suppositing for them are standing for a kind of linguistic item and should therefore be included under material supposition (Buridan 1957, 202), Albert of Saxony withdraws from completely eliminating it, but reintroduces it on the level of conventional (i.e. spoken or written) language (Albert of Saxony 2010, 248). On the level of mental language, however, Albert restricts supposition to its personal and material modes, and hence takes a position between Ockham and Buridan (Berger 1991; Dutilh Novaes 2008b, 449–452; Panaccio 2013).

Finally, it was Buridan's student and follower Marsilius of Inghen who applied the distinctions traditionally pertaining only to personal supposition also to its material counterpart. In his model, discrete supposition as well as the three modes of common supposition (see section 9.3.2) were subdivided into a personal and a material branch (Marsilius of Inghen 1983, 55–59). For example, *suppositio confusa et distributiva materialis* applies to propositions like 'Every human is a noun'. Marsilius of Inghen's enriched version of material supposition became quite influential and was adopted by, e.g., Paul of Venice (Dutilh Novaes 2008b, 457–461).

Though material supposition shows affinities with twentieth-century quotation devices, it cannot be identified entirely with the modern notion of the mention of a word in contrast to its use. The idea of mentioning a word, nowadays usually indicated by quotation marks, is closely connected to the assumption that by quotation marks a new term ('human') with quotation marks is generated in order to refer to the original term (human) without quotation marks. While the modern approach is based on the distinction of two different language signs, one of which is introduced to refer to the other, the medieval theory of supposition is based on the quite different idea of assuming different modes of use (*acceptio sive usus*) of one and the same term, one of these modes being the material use (Kann 1993; 2006, 112). In the later medieval tradition it became commonplace to introduce a sign of the material use of a term (*nota* or *signum materialitatis*), which meant prefixing a phrase like 'this term' (*iste terminus*) or the particle '*ly*' (taken from the French definite article) to a materially suppositing term.

9.3.2   The Modes of Personal Supposition

Personal supposition is firstly divided by most authors into discrete and common supposition. Discrete supposition occurs when a singular term, i.e. a proper name or a common term preceded by a demonstrative pronoun, is used in a proposition for just one particular thing, such as the terms 'Socrates' or 'this human' standing for an individual person, e.g. in a proposition like 'Socrates is a human' or 'This human is an animal'. Common supposition, in contrast, occurs when a general term is used for more than one particular thing, such as the term 'human' in a proposition like 'Some human is running' or 'All humans are running'.

Regarding propositions whose general terms stand in common supposition or are used significatively for a term's *supposita*, the theory of supposition provided a tool for distinctions nowadays treated by quantification theory (Weidemann 1979; Dutilh Novaes 2010b). In this respect, basically three modes of common supposition were distinguished, (1) determinate, (2) confused and distributive, and (3) purely (or merely) confused supposition (Parsons 2008, 222ff.).

The distinction between these three types of common supposition can be easily illustrated by the four categorical forms distinguished in the traditional Square of Opposition: (A) All As are B, (E) No As are B, (I) Some As are B, (O) Some As are not B. The subject of (I)- and (O)-propositions as well as the predicate of (I)-propositions have determinate supposition; the subject and the predicate of (E)-, the subject of (A)-, and the predicate of (O)-propositions have confused and distributive supposition; and the predicate of (A)-propositions has merely confused supposition. While these distinctions were widely endorsed, the logical characterisation of the types of common supposition varied. Sherwood explains that determinate supposition means a term's suppositing not for many, but rather for one – but for no particular one, which would constitute discrete supposition; for authors like Ockham and Burley, a term in determinate supposition stands for all the things of which it can be truly predicated, and although the term is taken to supposit for all instances, the proposition is true if it is true of at least one determinate instance. Sherwood describes confused supposition by explaining that it occurs when a term supposits for many, and Peter of Spain characterises it as the acceptance of a general term for many instances by means of a universal sign, while confused and distributive supposition occurs when the term supposits for all instances.

Many medieval authors, especially in the fourteenth century, supplemented and illustrated their analysis of general propositions as focused on the three types of common supposition by means of the doctrine of descent (*descensus*) and ascent (*ascensus*) as follows (Spade 1988):

(1) A term stands in determinate supposition (*suppositio determinata*) when it is conjoined with the existential quantifier 'some' (*aliquis*) as in the particular affirmative proposition 'Some human is running'. Here the term 'human' stands or supposits for its individual *supposita* or its "inferiors" (i.e. the things falling under it), in such a way that one can descend to or infer a disjunctive set of singular propositions. The subject terms of these propositions name all of the individuals for

which the general term stands, and the respective predicate terms are identical with that of the particular proposition. Therefore, assuming that the only humans are Socrates, Plato, and Cicero, it follows that, if some human is running, one can descend validly to or infer the disjunction 'Socrates is running, or Plato is running, or Cicero is running', and conversely can ascend validly from any singular to the particular proposition.

(2) When a term in a universal affirmative proposition is combined with a universal quantifier, e.g. 'human' in the proposition 'Every human is running', it has confused and distributive supposition (*suppositio confusa et distributiva*). This kind of common supposition given by the universal quantifier to the term immediately following it means: the term stands for all its individual instances in such a way that the descent to singulars yields a conjunction of propositions. Thus from our example 'Every human is running' we may descend to or infer the conjunction 'Socrates is running, and Plato is running, and Cicero is running'.

(3) A third type of common supposition is merely confused supposition (*suppositio confusa tantum*), the main example being that of the predicate term of a universal affirmative proposition where the term stands for all its individual *supposita*. The reduction to singulars, however, is effected in this case not by a disjunction or conjunction of singular propositions, but rather by a proposition with a disjunctive predicate. So, if we take the supposition of 'running' in 'Every human is running', we may descend to or infer 'Every human is this runner or that runner or that other runner', and conversely, from the proposition 'Every human is this runner' we could (independently of its truth) ascend to or infer 'Every human is running'. In contrast, it neither follows that every human is this runner, or every human is that runner, etc., nor *a fortiori* that every human is this runner, and every human is that runner, etc.

If descent under a term is valid, supposition is called mobile (*mobilis*), otherwise immobile (*immobilis*). Thus, type (2) of common supposition, i.e. confused and distributive supposition, is mobile if one is entitled to carry out the descent to singulars, as in 'Every human is running'. Otherwise, confused and distributive supposition is immobile, as, e.g., in the proposition 'Every human except Socrates is running'.

Due to the phrase 'except Socrates', the descent in this case is possible only in a deficient or restricted manner, caused by the exclusion of Socrates.

A subtle discussion arose in the fourteenth century on whether the three types of common personal supposition were the only types, or whether a fourth type, combined with another mode of descent, namely, with a conjunctive predicate, should be recognised. This mode was introduced and discussed in connection with *descensus copulatim*, e.g. by the Parisian master Thomas of Cleves (Read 1991a; Dutilh Novaes 2008b, 452–457). While some authors adhered to the traditional scheme of three types, others introduced a distinction of two modes of merely confused supposition or distinguished a fourth subtype, namely collective supposition (*suppositio collectiva*), as in 'Every human is hauling a boat', given that they are cooperating or doing it together (Read 1991b). Cooperation becomes transparent here by descent to a conjoint subject, for instance, in 'This human and that human and that other human etc. are all hauling a boat'. Another standard example for collective supposition was 'All the apostles of God are twelve', where descent, namely with a conjunctive subject, 'Peter and John and Judas etc. are twelve', was permissible.

The main point about the third type of common supposition, i.e. merely confused supposition, lies in the fact that it implies recognition of problems of multiple quantification, i.e. quantifying predicate terms, and of the extension of the scope of one quantifier to include another. These discussions expanded the investigation of propositions of the basic subject–predicate pattern to more complex instances like (to take an example from the later tradition) 'Some donkey of every human is running', which had to be distinguished from 'Every donkey of some human is running'. The aim was to demonstrate that different readings of a *sophisma* sentence may yield different truth values due to the order of the terms and quantifiers involved. To a large extent it was a matter of adopting peculiar instances of word order and scope, which are not present in classical Latin. Medieval logicians realised that quantifying syncategorematic words like *'omnis'*, *'nullus'*, and *'aliquis'* are not just adjectival deter-miners of only the term following them, but are simultaneously affecting the supposition of both terms combined in a proposition. For example, the case was considered in which every human is look-ing at himself, but at no other human. Here from the true proposition 'Every human is looking at a human' we cannot infer the proposition 'There is a human that every human is looking at', although the con-verse implication would be valid: from the proposition 'There is a human that every human is looking at' we can infer 'Every human is looking at a human'. Thus, logicians like William of Sherwood analysed under the head of merely confused supposition the case in which an existential quantifier falls within the scope of a preceding universal quantifier (William of Sherwood 1995, 150–152).

9.3.3 Ampliation and Restriction of Supposition

The treatment of personal supposition also includes treatment of a variety of problems concerning ampliation and restriction, i.e. accounts of how the range of supposition of a term can be affected by tense or by modal features or by intentional verbs (such as 'know' or 'promise'). The idea is that by the occurrence of those features and verbs the set of *supposita* of a term can become larger (by *amplia-tio*) or smaller (by *restrictio*) (Parsons 2008, 202–215). In contrast to the neutral situation of the subject of a present-tense proposition like 'Every human is running', in which the subject term 'human' is taken to stand for all presently existing humans, the addition of an adjective like 'white' to 'human' narrows or restricts the set of *sup-posita* to white ones. Replacing 'runs' by the future-tense phrase 'will run' extends or ampliates the range of the subject term by introdu-cing an additional set of *supposita*, namely humans who are yet to be. Similarly, 'A white thing was black' means that a thing which is now white or was white in the past was black at some time before now. Issues pertaining to ampliation were treated in analysing and solving *sophismata* like 'An old man will be a boy'. At first glance false, the proposition was said to be true in the case of referring to someone not yet born – he will be an old man at some time, and will be a boy before that (Albert of Saxony 2010, 372).

Whereas Peter of Spain (1972, 194) notes that only general terms, and exclusively those having personal supposition, can be ampliated or restricted, Lambert of Auxerre (1971, 226–229) gives a tentative classification of different word features and phrases which can produce ampliation or restriction. Restriction is "natural" (*naturalis*) when 'animal' is restricted by 'rational' in order to supposit only for human beings. In contrast, restriction is "use-governed" (*usualis*) as in the proposition 'The king is coming', in which we refer to the particular king of the country we actually have in mind and therefore narrow 'king' to supposit just for that person. Ampliation and restriction can be caused by the signification of the words involved, as in the case mentioned of 'rational animal' or in the phrase 'Socrates' donkey', where the supposition of 'donkey' is restricted by the possessive to supposit only for Socrates' donkey(s). Moreover, ampliation and restriction can be caused by consignification, i.e. by a certain feature of a word such as the gender of an adjective or the tense of a verb. For instance, in '*homo alba*' (a white human being), the feminine ending of '*alba*' restricts '*homo*' to supposit only for (white) women.

In analogy with the past and future tenses, which ampliate a subject to include past and future *supposita*, modal terms ampliate the subject to possible *supposita*. Since according to Albert of Saxony 'A human must be an animal' can be analysed into 'It is not possible that a human not be an animal', the word 'must' is said to ampliate for possible *supposita*. Likewise, in 'A human can run', the supposition of 'human' is ampliated to possibly existing humans. The same holds for propositions containing verbs like 'believe' or 'understand' and, as Albert of Saxony notes, for verbal nouns ending in '*bilis, -e*', e.g. 'credible' (*credibilis, -e*), 'audible' (*audibilis, -e*), or 'capable of laughter' (*risibilis, -e*) (Albert of Saxony 2010, 376ff.). Even the term '*supponere*' itself, as Albert acknowledges, seems to ampliate: in the case of a proposition like 'This term supposits for something', what is referred to by 'something' need not actually exist; rather, it might be past, future, possible, or merely intelligible, due to the ampliating effect of 'supposits' (Albert of Saxony 2010, 380).

Moreover, in the proposition 'I promise you a horse', the ampliating force of promising extends or ampliates the use or acceptance of 'horse' to non-existing instances. Propositions involving verbs like 'promise' were investigated with regard to the types of inferences they could figure in, and such investigations displayed a variety of more or less subtle solutions (Klima 2009, 198–200). William Heytesbury, for example, took it that 'horse' stood in purely confused supposition, while Paul of Venice qualified this claim by stating that the supposition was immobile. Buridan appealed to his later version of appellation, according to which the property of a predicate is to appellate its form (or its concept). Ockham analysed the proposition in his *Summa Logicae* I, 72 by eliminating the crucial word 'promise' and replacing the proposition by a more complex transcription like 'You will have one horse by means of my gift'. This analysis reveals similarities to a type of solution occurring in treatises on the "proofs of terms" (*probationes terminorum*; see Introduction to this volume), which, in contrast to specifying the use of the term 'horse', focused on the analysis of the word 'promise' in the sense of giving a particular claim to an object.

With respect to ampliation and restriction, William of Ockham has a special status among terminist logicians in that he refrains from using these ramifications of supposition theory or at least not speaking of them. The reason seems to be that he disagrees with the truth condition(s) usually accepted for propositions like 'A white thing was black'. Instead of meaning that either what is white was black or what was white was black, the proposition is ambiguous according to Ockham, i.e. "it must be distinguished" (*est distinguenda*) with regard to its different senses (William of Ockham 1974a, 269), namely, 'What is white was black' and 'What was black was white', with their potentially different truth values. Moreover, Ockham abstains from talk of ampliation in his treatment of modal propositions, since they turn out to be ambiguous in a similar manner: a proposition like 'A

SUPPOSITION AND PROPERTIES OF TERMS 235

white thing can be black' does not signify that either what is white or what can be white can be black, as the ampliative account would demand. Rather, it is ambiguous – in one sense potentially true and in the other self-contradictory – as Ockham explains in his *Summa logicae* II, 10.

9.3.4 Supposition of Relatives

When dealing with relations between words in the same proposition such as 'human' and 'who' in 'A human who is white is running', most authors speak of the supposition of relatives, i.e. anaphoric words or pronouns (in contrast to absolutes or absolute terms). Lambert of Auxerre (1971, 205), however, explicitly refers to relation as a property of terms, and the relation in question here is that between anaphoric words and their antecedents: A *relativum* is a word which refers to and therefore recalls something posited earlier, as, for example, the word 'who' in the proposition 'Socrates who is running is debating'.

Most treatises, pointing explicitly to the grammarians' use of the term, offer a kind of standard taxonomy of relatives: in a first step, authors like Peter of Spain (1972, 185), Lambert of Auxerre (1971, 235) and William of Ockham (1974a, 233) distinguish between relatives of substance and relatives of accident. Relatives of substance are 'who' (*qui*), 'that' (*ille*), 'someone else' (*alius*), etc., while relatives of accident are 'of what kind' (*qualis*) and 'of that (or such a) kind' (*talis*), 'of what size' (*quantum*) and 'of that (or such a) size' (*tantum*), etc. Relatives of substance are again distinguished into those of identity such as 'who' (*qui*) and 'that' (*ille*) and those of diversity such as 'the other' (*alter*) and 'the remaining' (*reliquus*). Among relatives of (substance and of) identity which are generally said to refer to their antecedent and to supposit for the same are reciprocal ones such as 'his' (*sui*), 'himself' (*sibi, se*), or 'by himself' (*a se*) and others that are non-reciprocal such as 'who' (*qui*), 'that' (*ille*), and 'same' (*idem*). Relatives of (substance and of) diversity are 'someone else' (*alius*), 'the remaining' (*reliquus*), etc., and relatives of this kind are said to refer back to their antecedent but to supposit for something different, as in 'Socrates is running, and someone else is debating'.

Concerning relatives of identity referring to common terms as their antecedent, authors widely agree that those relatives have the same supposition, but nevertheless can usually not replace the antecedent. When the antecedent of a relative is a common term standing in personal supposition, we can never, by substituting the antecedent for the relative, generate a proposition convertible with or equivalent to the original proposition. Ockham, *Summa Logicae* I, 76 gives 'A human is running, and he is debating' and 'A human is running, and a human is debating' as an example of propositions not convertible or equivalent in this way. In contrast, when the antecedent is singular, i.e. a term in discrete supposition, we actually obtain a pair of equivalents, as in, e.g., 'Socrates is running, and he is debating' and 'Socrates is running, and Socrates is debating'.

A subtler example of a common term functioning as an antecedent is 'Every human sees himself'. Here we can wonder why the reciprocal relative 'himself', though having the same supposition as the antecedent '(every) human', cannot be replaced *salva veritate* by that antecedent. According to Lambert of Auxerre (1971, 242ff.), reciprocal relatives (of identity) can replace their antecedent unless it is taken universally, as in our example, in which the reciprocal pronoun supposits for the same as its antecedent, but in a different manner, namely discretely. The reason can be found in Ockham (*Summa Logicae* I, 76): in 'Every human sees himself', the relative 'himself' supposits, as he explains, for every individual human, which gives it mobile confused and distributive supposition, but it does so singularly, so that the descent is not possible without altering both extremes simultaneously. Thus, from 'Every human sees himself' we may not infer 'Therefore every human sees Socrates'; rather, we can only descend to Socrates with respect to Socrates, so as to infer 'Therefore Socrates sees Socrates'. Whereas any relative in a categorical proposition has confused and distributive supposition due to the addition of a universal quantifier to its antecedent, a relative has merely confused supposition if in a preceding categorical the universal quantifier mediately precedes its antecedent, as the relative 'him' in the hypothetical, namely conjunctive, proposition 'Every human is an animal, and every donkey sees him'. In a proposition like 'A human sees himself', the relative 'himself' supposits determinately and yet singularly, and we could infer 'Therefore, Socrates sees Socrates, or Plato sees Plato' (and so on, for all the relevant particulars). The corresponding ascent would operate as follows: 'Socrates sees Socrates; therefore a human sees himself'. Examples like 'Human is a species, and it is predicable of many', 'Human is disyllabic, and it can be spoken or written' reveal that the supposition of relatives is not restricted to personal supposition but rather can be involved in cases of simple and material supposition alike.

9.4 APPELLATION AND ITS SHIFTS

Appellation has a complex and varied history. Whereas in an earlier phase, namely, with Anselm and Abelard, the notion of *appellatio* had been used approximately as an equivalent to that of *nominatio*, by the thirteenth century it meant the present extension of a term, i.e. its present-tense use or acceptance for a *suppositum* or for *supposita* actually existing. Another shift took place when, at the turn of the fourteenth century, appellation came to replace copulation as the relation of the predicate to its inferiors. Walter Burley, for instance, understands appellation as a property of the predicate, and thus as a counterpart of supposition as a property of the subject. When authors like Burley say that the predicate appellates its form (Burley 1955, 48) – a common thread running through the *appellatio* tradition – they apparently mean that the predicate be truly predicable at some time of a *suppositum* or of *supposita* of the subject.

We have to consider ampliation and restriction in order to distinguish appellation as a property of the predicate from properties of the subject. On the standard account, the proposition 'A white thing was black' is true only if the present-tense phrase 'is black' has at some time been truly predicable of the *supposita* of the subject, i.e. of what is or was white. The proposition 'A white thing is black', however, which is self-contradictory, will never have been true. Accordingly, the subject does not always appellate its form, and Albert of Saxony, among others, considered conversion puzzles caused by such cases. For instance, the proposition 'Socrates approaching you know' can be true, while 'You know Socrates approaching' may be false – namely if you know Socrates, but you do not recognise him approaching. Explanation might appeal to the fact of the predicate appellating its form, since 'You know Socrates approaching' requires that the predicate 'know Socrates approaching' be true of you, and so the proposition is false. In contrast, the proposition 'Socrates approaching you know' requires only that 'Him you know' be true in case of referring to Socrates, and it is true.

Buridan's treatment of the proposition 'You know the one approaching' also shows that the doctrine of appellation can be used to diagnose fallacies or analyse *sophismata*. While Scott (1966, 42–49) in his discussion of the proposition mentioned claims that Buridan's concept of appellation is novel and Spade (1980b, 109, n. 188) follows this view, Read (2015, 10) points out that Buridan's notion of appellation clearly coincides with Burley's and Albert's in that "appellating its form" requires true predication by means of demonstration. Read admits that Buridan explicitly restricts appellation to appellative terms, i.e. terms connoting something different from what they supposit for, and they appellate that which they connote as pertaining to what they supposit for; e.g. the term 'white' connotes whiteness and supposits for something white. What appears novel in Buridan, according to Read, is the extension of the doctrine of appellation to intentional verbs, which, as Buridan as well as Albert of Saxony claims, enforce the predicate terms that follow them to appellate their *rationes*, i.e. the concepts by which they signify their predicative function. In the proposition 'You know Socrates approaching', the phrase 'Socrates approaching' appellates the *ratio* or concept signifying what is meant by it, and the proposition's truth value depends on your being aware of the identity of the person who is referred to. In the proposition 'approaching Socrates you know', however, the phrase 'approaching Socrates' appellates its *ratio* or concept only under disjunction of the *rationes* of other potential substituents; thus, for 'Him you know' to be true it is sufficient that 'him' refers to Socrates under some concept or other (Klima 2009, 188ff.).

9.5 HISTORICAL OVERVIEW

As mentioned at the beginning of this chapter, the properties approach began to take shape in the twelfth century, but in this period we can at best speak of proto-theories of properties of terms; fully fledged formulations came about only in the thirteenth century. A primary distinction in the twelfth century was that between signification or univocation and appellation (De Rijk 1982b, 164–166). Already in Anselm's *De grammatico* we encounter the distinction between signifying as such (*significare per se*) and signifying relatively (*significare per aliud*), also known as appellating or naming (*appellare*). With signifying as such, an abstract form is signified, whereas in signifying relatively, a concrete thing was signified or appellated. The question of how different uses of a common name can be unified in view of the many things referred to by that name constitutes one of the most discussed problems in the philosophy of language at the time.

In the twelfth century, 'supposition' meant something different from what it came to mean at later stages. Initially, in a mainly grammatical usage dating back at least to the ancient grammarian Priscian, supposition referred to the placing of a name as subject of a proposition. The relation of this subject term to the thing named by it was called its appellation, i.e. the property of a univocal appellative name to signify a manifold of things. This appellation of the subject term was far from fixed, but rather could be ampliated or restricted by the predicate assigned to it; e.g. 'conceivable' (*opinabilis*) is a predicate that ampliates the appellation of a name such as 'human' (*homo*) to cover an extended range of humans who might have existed or might exist in the future. In the thirteenth century, appellation came to mean a property of terms standing for existing things, or the present exact usage of a term, with the result that whatever is appellated is simply something existing. Supposition gradually replaced appellation and attained central importance in the properties tradition, while appellation in the meaning outlined here underwent its own transformation. Emphasising the literal meaning of *'supponere'* as "acting as a subject", several authors from at least William of Sherwood in the 1230s up to Vincent Ferrer in the 1370s restricted supposition to subject terms and spoke of copulation as the corresponding property of predicate (i.e. adjectival or verbal) terms. However, for most of the later authors, supposition was a property of both subject and predicate.

William of Sherwood attributes supposition only to substantive names and pronouns, whereas adjectives, verbs, and participles – i.e. those terms which are attributed to something by means of the copula 'is' (*est*) or other words derived from 'to be' (*esse*) – are in his approach said to have copulation, and some of the divisions of supposition, namely those of common personal supposition, are repeated for or applied to copulation (William of Sherwood 1995, 152ff.). Peter of Spain and Lambert of Auxerre abstain from hinting at copulation as a property of predicate terms (Lambert of Auxerre 1971, 207ff.; Peter of Spain 1972, 80), and Walter Burley's treatise *De Copulatione* actually discusses the different uses of the copula *'est'* (Burley 1955, 54–59). But due to the common function of subject and predicate terms to pick out varying classes of objects while remaining a univocal word, most authors consequently extended the notion of supposition to subject and predicate terms alike. At the same time, talk of univocation as a context-independent property – i.e. a property independent of the term's occurrence in a proposition – was superseded or replaced by talk of signification.

From the beginning of the thirteenth to the middle of the fourteenth century, the development of medieval logic in general and of the terminist approach in particular took place mostly in Oxford and Paris. Modern research has focused on divergences between them, namely a British and a continental tradition (de Libera 1982; Dutilh

Novaes 2008b, 435–448). One interesting aspect is that each of these two traditions identified different lists of key properties of terms to be investigated by the theory. William of Sherwood, representing the Oxford tradition in the thirteenth century, identified four properties, namely signification, supposition, copulation, and appellation (William of Sherwood 1995, 132). Lambert of Auxerre, like Peter of Spain representing the Parisian tradition, identified five properties (apart from an introductory paragraph on signification), namely supposition, appellation, restriction, distribution, and relation (Lambert of Auxerre 1971, 205–245; Peter of Spain 1972, 79–88, 185–232). Treating ampliation as a correlative to restriction, Lambert matches the sections of Peter of Spain's *Tractatus*, the most popular textbook of the relevant tradition: *De suppositionibus* (On Suppositions), *De relativis* (On Anaphora), *De ampliationibus* (On Ampliations), *De appellationibus* (On Appellations), *De restrictionibus* (On Restrictions), and *De distributionibus* (On Distributions). Further properties like equivocation and univocation (that is, whether the term was equivocal or univocal in its signification), adjectivation and substantivation and so on should be added if we want to encompass the full range of properties of terms which were important in the prehistory and the initial stages of the doctrine in the twelfth century but were afterwards no longer treated as distinct items. Other properties were abandoned from the fourteenth century onwards, so that the most important instances representing the core of the properties approach were signification, supposition, ampliation, and restriction, supplemented by the supposition of relative pronouns or anaphora.

Another shift of the properties approach occurred in the early fourteenth century when, at the instigation of Roger Bacon and William of Ockham, signification came to be understood entirely extensionally by some authors. Occasioned by Ockham's well-known criticism of real universals, a common name (like 'human' or 'white') was taken to signify the individual instances (like all human beings or all white things) of which it can be truly predicated instead of signifying any universal nature or form (like humanity or whiteness) which the individuals share. From this nominalistic perspective, the earlier distinction of natural supposition (*suppositio naturalis*) (Peter of Spain 1972, 81) or habitual supposition (*suppositio secundum habitum*) (William of Sherwood 1995, 134) – a term's essential or genuine extension – on the one hand and accidental supposition (*suppositio accidentalis*) – a term's usage in a particular proposition – on the other tended to vanish (De Rijk 1971). While for Peter of Spain a common term signifies a form and supposits naturally for a class of objects, and the term supposits accidentally on the occasion of its actual use for a group or subclass of those objects, Ockham holds that the term signifies the class of objects and that the form or universal was no more than an intellectual figment (*fictum*) or, as he puts it later, the mental act of understanding (*actus intelligendi*), i.e. of conceiving of the individual instances themselves (William of Ockham 1974a, 42, 53).

From the beginning of the fourteenth century, signification and supposition were dominant among the properties of terms. Regarding the occurrence of terms in propositions, signification, as a basic and context-independent property, appears as a preliminary issue, while supposition, as the main context-dependent property, became the predominant subject (Read 2015). Ampliation and restriction were less properties in their own right than functions or modifications of supposition (or of appellation in its earlier meaning). Copulation as the specific property of predicate terms was dropped or subsumed under supposition. Appellation received an entirely new meaning which can be roughly described as the property of a predicate to appellate (or invoke) its form (or its concept). *Relatio* in the special meaning of supposition of anaphoric words as related to their antecedents was subject to considerable discussion in that later period. *Distributio*, which had been a distinct property in its own right, e.g. in Peter of Spain, came to be considered instead as a mode of supposition, namely, *suppositio confusa et distributiva*; treatises *De confusionibus* revealed similar items and questions as had the earlier chapters *De distributionibus* occurring in, e.g., Peter of Spain. Authors like Albert of Saxony finally raised the question of whether the traditional definition of supposition was suitable at all. The idea behind this discussion was that supposition, traditionally explained as the act of acceptance or usage of a term (*acceptio seu usus termini*), might more adequately be explained as a property of the user (*utentis vel ponentis*) of the term (Albert of Saxony 2002, 198ff.).

Whereas the properties approach continuously dominated the Oxford tradition of logic and semantics, the Parisian tradition in the later thirteenth and early fourteenth century was more marked by the "modist" (*modistae*) tradition for a brief period (de Libera 1982, 183; Dutilh Novaes 2008b, 443; see also Chapter 5). The properties approach itself was still undergoing significant modifications in the fourteenth and fifteenth centuries, though mostly in the sense of generating interesting ramifications rather than truly novel developments. It continued to receive attention until the sixteenth and seventeenth centuries, and can in fact be found in modern logic books well into the twentieth century.

9.6   CONCLUDING REMARKS

In conclusion, one must emphasise that the properties of terms in general were investigated as occurring in and related to vernacular discourse. There was no fixed system overall, but rather an open-ended set of rules governing the different accounts and their ramifications in order to handle a wide range of instances of the contextual approach to semantics. At the same time, the framework included a number of regimentations differing considerably from ordinary discourse or classical Latin (e.g. pertaining to conventions of word order and scope). Yet the properties of terms were not investigated on a merely theoretical level, but provided a framework for practical distinctions and applications. The fact that supposition theory is primarily a tool to analyse significative and non-significative uses of terms and secondarily a theory to analyse quantification resulted in the view that supposition theory is more adequately viewed as two separate theories (Scott 1966, 30; Spade 1988). Within the overarching perspective of the contextual approach to semantic issues, however, there are good reasons to regard supposition theory as a unified doctrine, integrating semantic and syntactic aspects and at the same time formal and non-formal aspects of language (Kann 2006; Dutilh Novaes 2007).

The widespread assumption that supposition is akin to recent notions of reference, extension or denotation – or, alternatively, that the distinction of signification and supposition of terms showed close similarity to the modern dichotomy of meaning and reference (Moody 1967, 530) – has been challenged by many, including Dutilh Novaes, who argues that the comparison of supposition to the recent notion of reference is misleading and that the most important function of supposition theory (at least in the fourteenth century) was the generation of all possible readings of a proposition (Dutilh Novaes 2007, 2008a). Read (2015) and Parsons (2014) illuminate aspects under which medieval logic is as rich as contemporary first-order symbolic logic, though its full potential was less envisaged at that time, and medieval logicians apparently were not interested in the development of formal systems (Ashworth 2010, 146). If at all, the properties approach is much closer in spirit to the tradition of so-called "formal semantics" than to mathematical logic. Ultimately we should refrain from assuming that the properties approach matches exactly any doctrine or tool of modern logic and semantics. Rather, it developed in response to a great variety of traditions and purposes quite different from the current logical panorama. Recent investigations (Bos 2013) focus on challenging side issues of the properties approach at its zenith in the thirteenth and fourteenth centuries, on refined perspectives on its history as well as its deployment and aftermath in the fifteenth to seventeenth centuries, on reconstruction of its metaphysical, ontological, or theological implications, on its traces in Arabic philosophy, and on studies on recent logic as a tool to elucidate its special features. Medieval logic and semantics, including the properties approach and its relation to modern applied logic, remains a promising field of research (Kann et al. forthcoming).

10 Propositions: Their Meaning and Truth

Laurent Cesalli

Medieval logicians often characterized their discipline by saying that it aims at providing efficient means to distinguish truth from falsity. Thus propositions, as truth-bearers, are items logicians spent a great deal of time and energy describing and analysing. More precisely, propositions were studied "bottom-up", i.e. as complexes of terms (subject, predicate, copula), but also "top-down", i.e. as premises and conclusions in arguments (syllogisms). When studied for themselves or as such, however, propositions give rise to three main questions: (i) What is a proposition? (ii) What does a proposition signify? (iii) How is propositional truth to be accounted for? This chapter considers medieval answers to those questions. After having expounded and discussed the different opinions and arguments put forward by logicians roughly between the eleventh and the fifteenth centuries, the chapter tackles the question of the relation between some tenets of medieval semantics of the proposition and the modern notions of facts and states of affairs.[1]

10.1 WHAT IS A PROPOSITION?

Before even approaching how medieval logicians defined propositions, the very first thing to stress is the difference between the medieval and the contemporary meaning of the technical term 'proposition'. A *propositio* – that is, a proposition in the *medieval* sense of the word – is a type of sentence, i.e. a linguistic expression (a string of words, possibly a single word) singled out by its truth-evaluable character:

---

[1] On medieval theories of the proposition, see Élie 1936; Kretzmann 1970; Nuchelmans 1973; Ashworth 1978a, 1981; Perler 1992; Büttgen, Diebler and Rashed 1999; de Libera 2002; Lenz 2003; Maierù and Valente 2004; Cesalli 2007, 2012, forthcoming.

a proposition is that kind of sentence about which it makes sense to ask is it true or false? A proposition in the *contemporary* sense of the word, by contrast, is *not* a linguistic expression. Rather, it is *what is meant* by a truth-evaluable linguistic expression (or the content of the corresponding act of judging). Accordingly, in its contemporary sense, a proposition is neither a string of words, nor a mental entity, but *something abstract* with a distinctive Platonist flavour.[2] Unless otherwise specified, this chapter uses the term 'proposition' in the medieval sense. How are propositions and judgements (or acts of judging) related? A judgement is a complex mental act of composing (for affirmative judgements) and dividing (for negative ones), i.e. the so-called second operation of the intellect, distinguished from simple apprehension (= first operation) on the one hand, and argumentation (= third operation) on the other. A proposition in the *contemporary* sense of the term in relation to a judgement is its objective meaning; a *propositio* in relation to a judgement is what is immediately expressed by it: to say 'Socrates exists' immediately expresses the judgement [Socrates exists], which, in turn, has the proposition (in the contemporary sense of the term) |Socrates exists| as its objective meaning (see Table 10.1 given in Section 10.4).

Within the Aristotelian corpus, the *locus classicus* for the definition of a proposition is the beginning of *On Interpretation*. First (16a10–12), the essential link between truth and falsity (of thoughts as well as of linguistic expressions) and a certain type of complexity is stated: truth and falsity presuppose combination and separation, which is not just any kind of complexity (cf. complex names), but *predicative* complexity.[3] In other words, a proposition is either an affirmation or a negation. Secondly (16b26–27 and 17a1–3), a

---

[2] Examples of propositions in the contemporary sense are Bolzano's *Sätze an sich*, Frege's *Gedanken*, and Husserl's *Bedeutungen in specie*.

[3] Aristotle 1984 (*Prior Analytics* 24a16): "A proposition is a statement affirming or denying something of something". In the context of this part of Aristotle's *Organon*, a proposition is defined from the perspective of the subject matter of the treatise (i.e. the syllogism), to the effect that 'proposition' renders here the Greek *'protasis'* (i.e. premise of a syllogism).

proposition is identified as a certain type of sentence (*logos*): a sentence is a complex expression whose parts are significant without being themselves an affirmation or a negation (obviously, Aristotle has only atomic sentences in mind, for molecular ones do, of course, possess parts which are significant as affirmations or negations); and only a truth-evaluable sentence (*logos apophantikos*) is a proposition.[4] The standard medieval definition of a proposition is not taken directly from Aristotle, however, but from Boethius' *De topicis differentiis*: "A proposition is a discourse signifying the true or the false" (Boethius 1990, 2, 1.22).

Medieval logicians develop highly sophisticated typologies of propositions from different perspectives.[5]

(i) From an ontological perspective: some propositions exist in the mind (*in anima*), i.e. mental propositions, and others exist outside of the mind (*extra animam*), i.e. written and spoken propositions (*scripta, prolata, mentalis*).[6] As we shall see, realists such as Walter Burley and John Wyclif extend the ontological typology beyond the realm of what belongs to language, even broadly understood (i.e. comprising not only written and spoken, but also mental language).

(ii) From the point of view of complexity: a categorical proposition (*categorica*) is an atomic one (i.e. a proposition none of whose parts is itself a proposition), while a hypothetical proposition (*hypothetica*) is a molecular one.[7]

(iii) From the point of view of quality: there are affirmative and negative propositions (*affirmativa, negativa*).

[4] When Aristotle 1984 (*On Interpretation* 19b1–4) notes that it is not necessary that all propositions be either true or false, the claim is made from the special perspective of the indeterminacy of the future (some propositions in the future are *now* neither true nor false, but it is, in principle, only a question of time until the matter gets settled).

[5] For a quite exhaustive and representative example of such typologies, see Richard Brinkley, *De propositione* (= *Summa logicae* V, c. 5). The text is edited in Cesalli 2004; see also the fundamental Maierù 1972 (*s.v.*).

[6] This distinction goes back to Boethius who introduces the idea of the so-called threefold discourse (*triplex oratio*). On that topic, see Panaccio 1999, esp. 120–136.

[7] Note that the Latin 'hypothetica' is not equivalent to the English 'hypothetical' which would correspond to the Latin 'conditionalis', i.e. a complex proposition of the form 'if *p*, then *q*' (also called a *consequentia*). Thus a conjunctive proposition of the form '*p* and *q*' is an example of *propositio hypothetica*.

(iv) From the point of view of time: there are present-, past- and future-tense propositions (*de praesenti, de praeterito, de futuro*).
(v) From the point of view of modality: there are non-modal propositions (*de inesse*, i.e. merely saying something of something), and modal ones: *de modo* expressing necessity, possibility or impossibility (*de necessario, possibili, de impossibili*).
(vi) From the point of view of truth: there are true and false propositions (*vera, falsa*).
(vii) From the point of view of quantity: there are singular (this *a* is *b*), particular (some *a* is *b*), and universal propositions (every *a* is *b*) (*singularis, indefinita, universalis*).

10.2   WHAT IS SIGNIFIED BY A PROPOSITION?

Propositions are complex, truth-evaluable linguistic expressions whose parts (names and verbs) are significant (i.e. signify something[8]); therefore, propositions themselves, i.e. as linguistic higher-order units, must signify something. But do they signify just what their constitutive parts do, or is there something like a special, *propositional* significate? The full philosophical (and polemical) potential of this question only comes to light when it is raised about *mental* propositions, for written and spoken propositions can be said to have such a special significate (which, directly or indirectly, would be the mental proposition). So the precise question to be tackled here is this: do mental propositions have special significates (i.e. significates which are not reducible to those of their constitutive parts)?

Peter Abelard, in the early twelfth century, already notices that unlike their parts, propositions do not *name* anything, but rather *say* something. From that, he concludes that spoken and written propositions, besides signifying concepts (*intellectus*) in the sense of giving rise to them (*intellectus generare*) – a semantic feature they share with their constituents, by the way – must signify something else, a

[8] I take the English 'to signify' to render the Latin '*significare*'. 'To mean' would be a possible alternative, but that term is too strongly linked to contemporary theories of meaning which only partially coincide with what medievals understood under '*significatio*' (see Cameron 2012).

dictum propositionis, which is neither a concept nor a thing. One of the reasons given by Abelard for the claim that a dictum cannot be a thing or a concept is derived from the semantics of necessary conditional propositions such as 'if it is a rose, it is a flower'. The truth of such a conditional depends on what the antecedent and the consequent mean; but the truth of the conditional at stake does not depend on the existence of contingent items such as things (e.g. roses) or concepts (e.g. concepts of roses); therefore, what propositions mean cannot be concepts or things.[9] On such a view, then, propositions *do* have special significates. As for the legitimate question pertaining to the *nature* of such special significates (*quid est significatum propositionis?*) the different answers propounded delimit the range of *realist positions* (or of "propositional realism") in the field of propositional semantics.[10]

At the other end of the spectrum, one finds nominalist views, according to which propositions *need not* have special significates. Typically, the claim is that propositional semantics is reducible to the semantics of terms: a proposition does not signify anything over and above what its terms signify. Such a position is advocated, for example, by William of Ockham (1974a, II, 2), John Buridan (*Sophismata* I, 5) and Richard Feribrigge (1978, II, 6). Another, later form of nominalism is found in Peter of Ailly's so-called "adverbial theory of signification",[11] according to which one can surely talk of the total significate of a proposition, but one should not take it ontologically seriously: an expression such as *'omnem hominem esse animal'* ('that every man is an animal'), i.e. the nominalized form of *'omnis homo est animal'* ('every man is an animal') does not supposit (i.e. stand) for anything (*Conceptus et insolubilia*, ed. 1500, fol. 17va; see Spade 1980b, 49).

---

[9] For a clear overview of Abelard's semantics of propositions, see Marenbon 1997, 202–209.

[10] On the notion of propositional realism, see Cesalli 2007, 13–15 and 419–423.

[11] The term is due to Spade 2007, 180–184. On Peter of Ailly's theory, see also Biard 1989a, 266–275, as well as Pérez-Ilzarbe 1999, 203–214.

Realist and nominalist positions are developed and discussed within different doctrinal contexts, first among which are semantics proper (mostly in commentaries on Aristotle's *On Interpretation*) and the theory of the object of knowledge (typically in the prologues of commentaries on Peter Lombard's *Sentences*).[12]

10.2.1 Semantics Proper

Abelard's theory of the *dictum propositionis* as the special, non-conceptual significate of propositions reminds one of the *lekton* (expressible) of the Stoics.[13] Indeed, there are good reasons to believe that the Latin *dictum* as well as its synonym *enuntiabile* have their roots in Hellenistic thought. In 1159, for example, John of Salisbury writes in his *Metalogicon* (II, 4) that whereas grammar is concerned with words as such, dialectics (i.e. logic) studies the meanings of linguistic expressions (*sensus* or *dicta* in Latin, the latter being presented as a translation from the Greek *lekton*). At the turn of the thirteenth century, one finds passages confirming Abelard's intuition that propositional significates must be something *sui generis*. Thus, the anonymous author of the *Ars Burana* writes that a true proposition signifies the true (*verum*) and a false one, the false (*falsum*), and that in both cases, what is signified is an *enuntiabile*, i.e. something which "cannot be seen, heard or sensed, but only grasped by the intellect" so that it possesses "a proper kind of being" (De Rijk 1962–1967, II, 208).[14]

---

[12] The Lombard's four books of *Sentences* (written in 1155–1157) became the most important standard theological textbook for medieval theologians. Commenting on the *Sentences* was a compulsory step on the way to the degree of *magister theologiae*. Other, relevant fields that have to (and can only) be mentioned here are the theological debates about the objects of faith (what exactly does the believer believe when she says I believe that Christ was born, lived, and died on the cross?), and the objects of God's knowledge (what are the correlates of epistemic attitudes of a subject such that he cannot change, and thus, cannot begin or cease to know something?). On that topic, see Cesalli 2007, 47–54.

[13] On the Stoics' logic in general and the *lekton* in particular, see Mates 1961 and Frede 1974.

[14] See also the similar passage and discussion in the (equally anonymous) *Ars Meliduna* (De Rijk 1962–1967, II, 357–360).

In the thirteenth century, Thomas Aquinas developed his famous theory of the inner word (*verbum interius*) as a mental entity distinct not only from mental acts, but also from the intelligible species produced at the end of the process of abstraction in the passive intellect by the active one. The inner word is not only a necessary condition for the production of the outer one, but also what the latter *signifies* (*De veritate*, q. 4, a. 1). And this holds for simple expressions such as names and verbs, as well as for complex ones such as propositions (*Quodlibet* V, q. 5, a. 2; see Rode forthcoming). In other words, Aquinas' *propositional* inner word is, besides Abelard's *dictum* and the *enuntiabile* of the *Ars Burana*, a third example of a positive answer to the question of the existence of a special propositional significate. What distinguishes Aquinas' from his predecessors' positions is that the inner word is existentially dependent on the activity of the intellect (it is a product of the intellect's acts), whereas the *dictum* and *enuntiabile*, as something lying beyond contingency (for the *dictum*) or possessing a proper mode of being (for the *enuntiabile*), cannot be dependent on the activity of the mind. In short, then, Abelard and the *Ars Burana* and *Ars Meliduna* conceive of the propositional significate as something like abstract meanings (akin to Bernard Bolzano's *Sätze an sich* and their later avatars), whereas Aquinas' *verbum interius* is more like the immanent object of psychic phenomena once adopted (and eventually rejected) by much later authors such as Franz Brentano and Anton Marty.[15]

A similar kind of mind dependency is found in John Duns Scotus' semantics of propositions.[16] Regarding the significates of names, there is a debate about what position is held by the *Doctor subtilis* (Perler 1993; Pini 1999 and 2001). There seems indeed to be a tension between the solution advocated at the end of the

---

[15] On Bolzano's *Sätze an sich*, see Textor 1996. For an overview of logical realism in the Austro-German tradition, see Morscher 1972 and 1990.
[16] On Scotus' theory of the propositions, see Bos 1987; Marmo 1989.

thirteenth century in his *Questiones* on Aristotle's *On Interpretation* and his later *Ordinatio*. According to the *Questiones*, names signify things as understood (*res ut intelliguntur*) as opposed to intelligible *species* (mental, intelligible similitudes of things) and things full stop (*res ut existent*, Duns Scotus 2004b, q. 2, no. 39). According to the *Ordinatio*, Scotus says that what is signified by a name, properly speaking, is not a concept (*conceptus*) but a thing (*res*, Duns Scotus 1963, d. 27, q. 1–3, no. 83). The tension between the two solutions might be an apparent one, however, for it is compatible to hold that the significate of a name is a thing as understood (and not as it exists) *and* that it is a thing (and not a concept), namely: in taking both the 'thing as understood' of the *Quaestiones* and the 'thing' of the *Ordinatio* as meaning 'the content of a *species* or *conceptus*'.[17] That Scotus takes the significate of a name to be distinct from a thing full stop is also clear from his claim that the signification of a name is indifferent to the existence or non-existence of the thing signified (Duns Scotus 2004a, q. 2, nos. 7–8).

When it comes to the semantics of propositions proper, Scotus holds the following: when a composed or complex sign (like a proposition) signifies something which is itself a sign (as in the case of a spoken proposition, which immediately signifies a mental one), the composition at stake is ultimately *not* a composition of signs (here: words or concepts), but of ultimate significates (here things, that is, the concept's significates). As a consequence, what is signified by a spoken proposition is not a composition of concepts but of things. Moreover, and in accordance with his semantics of names, Scotus makes clear that the composition of things at stake is not a composition of things *ut existunt*, but *ut intelliguntur*. In other words, Scotus conceives of the significate of propositions as the

---

[17] 'Content', here, is to be understood according to what Scotus says of the relation between a real object and the intellect: a real object affects the intellect in two ways: really (*realiter*) in causing a *species* in the mind, and intentionally (*passione intentionali*) as appearing (*relucere*) in the *species* (i.e. as the content of the latter) (Duns Scotus 1950, d. 3, pars 3, no. 386).

content of a mental proposition, a content which depends on, but is not reducible to things full stop (*ut existunt*): the composition of things as understood exists in the intellect just as what is known exists in the knowing subject (*ut cognitum in cognoscente*), and in that way, Scotus adds, "things are in the intellect, and not only *species*" (Duns Scotus 2004b, q. 2, no. 41).

Shortly after Scotus (and certainly under his influence), the young Walter Burley of 1301 developed a remarkable theory of the mental proposition as being a complex not of concepts, but of things, a position sharply criticized by William of Ockham in his *Quodlibeta septem* (III, q. 12, see Burley 1974, 248–250).[18] Later in his career (1337), Burley takes a (partly) externalist turn in claiming that the ultimate propositional significate is a *propositio in re* composed of two extramental *material* parts (its subject and predicate) and one mental *formal* part (its copula, Burley 1497, prologue, fol. c4rb). Burley's main argument runs along lines similar to the ones we saw in Scotus: what is ultimately composed in a proposition must be what is ultimately signified by its constituent parts; but what is ultimately signified by the constituent parts of a proposition are things; therefore, a proposition is ultimately composed of things (Burley 1497, prologue, fols. c3vb–c4ra).

On Burley's view then, the propositional significate is still something dependent on the activity of the mind (the copula is an act of composing or dividing), but contrary to the propositional significate as described by Aquinas and Scotus, which, in both cases, is clearly a *mental* entity, Burley's *significatum ultimum* is a hybrid entity existing partly *in* and partly *outside* of the mind.

10.2.2   The Object of Knowledge

Besides semantics proper, the problem of propositional significates is also dealt with in the framework of the epistemologically motivated

---

[18] For a recent overview on Burley's propositional semantics and literature thereon, see Cesalli 2013, 122–131. See also Lenz forthcoming.

question pertaining to the nature of the objects of knowledge (Tachau 1988; Biard 2002). When someone says "I know that man is an animal" (in Latin: *scio hominem esse animal* or, equivalently: *scio quod homo est animal*), what does the that-clause stand for, if anything? Is there a known object which 'that man is an animal' stands for in 'I know that man is an animal', just as there is a seen object that 'moon' stands for in 'I see the moon'? The relation with propositional semantics is quite obvious: what is known is also what is signified by the proposition expressing the knowledge at stake (that man is an animal is what is signified by 'man is an animal').

William of Ockham famously claims that what is known is the conclusion of a demonstration, namely, a mental proposition. This is true for the "earlier" (i.e. the pre-c. 1320) as well as for the later Ockham. What changes between the earlier and the later Ockham is the nature of the *terms* of mental propositions (i.e. the nature of concepts): singular things (= singular terms) and *ficta* (= universal terms) according to the earlier one, mental acts for both kinds of terms according to the later one.[19] According to Ockham, one has to distinguish between the object (*obiectum*) and the subject (*subiectum*) of a science: the object is the conclusion of a demonstrative syllogism, the subject is what the subject term of that conclusion stands for (Ockham 1967, prologue, q. 9, p.266). Now, the object of science cannot be a mere thing (a stone, for example) for such an object lacks the essential property of being true, and to know something is to assent to something true; but only propositions are bearers of truth; therefore only propositions can be the objects of knowledge; and since written and spoken propositions are semantically subordinated to mental ones, mental propositions will be the proper object of knowledge (Ockham 1980, III, q. 8, pp.233–234).

---

[19] For recent studies of Ockham's position (and its evolution), see Panaccio 2004; Brower-Toland 2007b. Ockham develops his earlier position in the *Ordinatio* (1317–1319), his later position from his commentary of Aristotle's *On Interpretation* (c. 1320) onwards.

Ockham's position gave rise to a lively debate. Walter Chatton, in his commentary on the *Sentences* (c. 1323) reacts against what he takes to be a strongly internalist feature in Ockham: if what is known is a mental proposition, how can we know the external world (since mental propositions clearly belong to our internal world)? Chatton's own position consists in saying that the object of knowledge is a thing (*res*), for only the formation, and not the (additional) apprehension of a mental proposition is required for an act of knowing (and if the mental proposition is not apprehended, it cannot be the object of such an act; see Chatton 1989, prologue, q. 1, a. 1, pp. 20–21 and 27).

Adam Wodeham, in his own commentary on the *Sentences* (1329–1332), criticizes the opinions of both Ockham and Chatton.[20] Against the latter, Wodeham remarks, for example, that if the object of knowledge (or, for that matter, the significate of a proposition) were a thing, then two contradictory propositions such as 'God exists' and 'God does not exist' would have exactly the same significate; but one of them must be true, and the other false, and two semantically equivalent propositions cannot have different truth values (Wodeham 1990, d. 1, q. 1, p. 184). Wodeham's argument against Ockham is complex. It aims at showing that Ockham's identification of the object of knowledge with a mental proposition (or *complexum*) follows from an incomplete analysis of an act of knowledge (i.e. of assent to a true proposition). The main lines of the argument are these:[21] an act of assent must immediately follow an act of propositional composition (for one does not assent, say, to *Socrates*, but to something like *that Socrates is wise*, for example); but according to Ockham, assent immediately follows an act of apprehension (and not of propositional composition), namely the act of apprehending a mental proposition (= the conclusion of a demonstrative syllogism); therefore, a mental proposition merely apprehended cannot be the object of knowledge. So what is it, then? Wodeham claims it is the significate of a

---

[20] On Wodeham's theory (and critique of Chatton and Ockham), see Perler 1994; Brower-Toland 2007a.

[21] Here I follow the reconstruction of Brower-Toland 2007a.

second-order proposition of the form 'the apprehended proposition is true', so that properly speaking, the object of knowledge is a "so to be in reality (as is stated by the apprehended proposition)" (*sic esse a parte rei*, Wodeham 1990, d. 1, q. 1, p. 189). Wodeham famously calls the object of knowledge a "signifiable by a mental proposition" (*significabile per complexum*) and insists that it is not any kind of entity: the question 'what is it?' (*quid est?*) raised about it is simply inappropriate (*inepta*, Wodeham 1990, d. 1, q. 1, pp. 194–195).

Wodeham's ideas are taken up by Gregory of Rimini, who comments on the *Sentences* in Paris in 1345[22]: the object of knowledge, Gregory contends, is a "signifiable complexly" (*complexe significabile*), i.e. something distinct from a thing (*res*) and from a mental proposition (*complexum*). As for the ontological status of the *complexe significabile*, Gregory is ready to say that the object of knowledge is nothing (*nihil*), but it does not follow that science does not have any object (Gregory of Rimini 1978, prologue, q. 1, pp. 9–10). The way out of this Meinong-like paradox consists in distinguishing several senses of the term '*aliquid*' (something) and, by way of consequence, of its opposite '*nihil*' (nothing): if '*aliquid*' is taken in the sense of either (i) whatever is signifiable truly or falsely, or (ii) whatever is signifiable only truly, then the *complexe significabile* is something (and thus: not nothing); by contrast, if '*aliquid*' is taken in the sense of (iii) something existing (i.e. a *res* or a *complexum*), then the *complexe significabile* is nothing (and thus: not something; Gregory of Rimini 1978, prologue, q. 1, pp. 8–9).

Summing up, one can distinguish the following main lines on the question of what propositions signify: one can say *(a)* that a proposition does not signify anything special, i.e. anything distinct from what its constituent terms signify (Ockham, Buridan). If, by contrast, one admits that a proposition *does* have a special significate (= *S*), one can *either* give an account of it in terms of items falling under

---

[22] On Gregory, see Gaskin 2003 and Bermon 2007. For Buridan's rejection of *complexe significabilia*, see Perini-Santos forthcoming.

Aristotle's ten categories, and thus claim *(b)* that *S* is a thing (Walter Chatton) or *(c)* that *S* is a hybrid entity consisting in one mental, and two extramental parts (Burley),[23] *or* give an account in terms of *sui generis* entities falling outside of the categorical frame, and claim *(d)* that *S* is a special mental entity (Aquinas, Scotus) or *(e)* that *S* is some kind of abstract entity which belongs neither to the realm of the mental, nor to that of extramental things (Abelard's *dictum*, Wodeham's and Gregory's *complexe significabile*).[24]

10.3   HOW IS PROPOSITIONAL TRUTH TO BE ACCOUNTED FOR?

Every medieval logician would agree that a proposition is true if and only if it "signifies as it is in the world" (*significat sicut est*).[25] The views come apart, however, when it comes to the question of how the '*sicut est*' is to be interpreted: are we talking about mere *truth conditions* (which is the weaker, universally accepted reading of '*sicut est*') *or* about the existence of language- and mind-independent *truthmakers* (which is the stronger, controversial reading of '*sicut est*')?

Some passages in Aristotle can be interpreted as supporting the weaker reading. For example, *Categories*, 5, 4b810, where it is said that what turns a true statement into a false one (or vice versa) is a "change in the actual thing": propositional truth is a relational property dependent on the state of the world. Depending on what Socrates does or does not do, the statement 'Socrates walks' is true or false, but the truth of 'Socrates walks' is not accounted for in terms

---

[23] Note that whereas the mental act (i.e. the copula) and the things which are the subject and predicate of Burleian *propositiones in re* indeed fall under Aristotle's categories, it is not clear that the same holds for the whole constituted by these parts.

[24] One should add here the theory of the so-called *modus rei*, contending that *S* is a mode of a thing, i.e. something which is neither a substance nor an accident, and "exists everywhere" (*est ubique*). On that theory, which is known only indirectly, see Cesalli forthcoming.

[25] An alternative, equivalent formulation reads: <*propositio*> *significat sic esse a parte rei* ("<a proposition> signifies that it is so in reality").

of a special entity which, when existing, makes the statement true (*Categories*, 12, 14b18–23 can be read along the same lines).

A clear medieval case of such a weaker reading is William of Ockham's. To the questions of what is required to account for the truth of a categorical affirmative *de inesse* (i.e. non-modal) present-tense proposition, Ockham gives a two-step answer. The first step is negative: first, it is not required that subject and predicate are really the same (*idem realiter*); second, it is not required that what the predicate stands for inheres in (*realiter insit*) what the subject stands for; third, it is not required that what the predicate stands for is really coupled (*uniatur a parte rei extra*) with what the subject stands for (Ockham 1974a, II, 2).[26] In the second step, Ockham gives his own solution: all that is required for the truth of such a proposition is that the subject and predicate stand for the same thing (Ockham 1974a, II, 2, 250). What Ockham is carefully avoiding is not the correspondence theory of truth – indeed, his theory *is* a correspondence theory – but what we would nowadays call the reification of the predicate: the truth of 'this one is an angel' ('*iste est angelus*') does not commit one to the existence of a "second thing" which would correspond to the predicate only (something like *angelitas*) and would then enter a kind of composition with the thing for which the subject stands. All that is required is the existence of just one thing, and that the two extremes of the proposition supposit for it.

Coming back to Aristotle and the two readings of the '*sicut est*', other passages suggest he acknowledges the existence of something like states of affairs (i.e. entities corresponding to statements), to the effect that there are things underlying affirmations and negations, which are not themselves affirmations or negations, but which are opposed *in the same way* as affirmation and negation are opposed

---

[26] 'To stand for' (or 'to supposit') is the central technical term of the so called medieval theory of supposition (on that topic, see Chapter 9 of the present volume). As it turns out, the three options rejected by Ockham correspond precisely to views endorsed by Burley 1972, 55–56, for the first of the rejected opinions, and Burley 1974, 3.553, 249 as well as 3.62, 250–251 for the second and third ones).

(*Categories*, 10, 12b5.15).[27] Such entities (i.e. states of affairs) are not necessarily truthmakers, however, since true as well as false sentences will have corresponding "underlying things" (e.g. 'Socrates walks' and 'Socrates does not walk'). On such a view, the states of affairs corresponding to true sentences are obtaining states of affairs, and the ones corresponding to false sentences are non-obtaining states of affairs.

In the *Metaphysics* (Aristotle 1984, 1051a34–1052a12), by contrast, one finds something like an Aristotelian theory of truthmaking (and thus, authoritative support for the stronger reading of '*sicut est*').[28] The terms 'being' and 'non-being' in the strictest sense, says Aristotle, are truth and falsity. Being with respect to the being true of a statement depends on the obtaining of a (positive or negative) state of affairs, while non-being with respect to the being false of a statement depends on the non-obtaining of a (positive or negative) state of affairs: 'Socrates walks' or 'Socrates does not walk' are true just in case the corresponding states of affairs obtain. Thus one finds in Aristotle authoritative passages for a theory of (obtaining and non-obtaining) states of affairs correlating true as well as false statements, but also for a theory of obtaining states of affairs as special correlates of true statements (for only obtaining states of affairs are said to be, while non-obtaining ones are said not to be). These are the lines along which the (crucial) distinction is made between what propositions signify and what makes them true (if they are true). The distinction is crucial because equating propositional significates with truthmakers prevents false propositions from having significates, which is unsatisfactory (if there are propositional significates, true as well as false propositions must have significates, but only true propositions, by definition, can have truthmakers).

Did the medieval proponents of propositional significates make the distinction between what a proposition signifies and what makes

---

[27] On Aristotle's theory of truth, see Crivelli 2004 and Barnes 2007.
[28] On the notion of truthmaking, see Mulligan et al. 1984 as well as Monnoyer 2007, where the paper by Mulligan et al. is republished (pp. 9–49).

it true? The answer is yes, although its justification requires a bit of reconstructing. Whereas there is nothing like a fixed (i.e. reliable) terminological criterion to pick out truthmakers in the medieval philosophical jungle,[29] the following conceptual criterion will do the job: whenever a philosopher accepts propositional significates and *either* accepts them for true propositions only, *or* accepts special correlates for true propositions only *besides* or *on the top of* their significates, then the theory at stake is a medieval theory of truthmaking.

Peter Abelard is an interesting case in that respect. As we saw above, he considers that propositions have special significates (*dicta*). A true proposition is such, Abelard says, in virtue of its signifying a true *dictum*, and reciprocally, a false proposition is such in virtue of its signifying a false *dictum* (Abelard 2010a, IV, §26).[30] An asymmetry occurs, however, in the case of true propositions, for they *alone* are correlated by what Abelard calls events (*eventus rerum*, Abelard 1956, II, ii, 11). This entails that one has to distinguish between *dicta* (i.e. propositional significates) and *eventus rerum* (truthmakers).

A similar distinction can be found in Walter Burley's theory of the proposition. Whereas *propositiones in re*, as extramental things (i.e. subject and predicate) composed by a mental act (i.e. the copula), seem to correspond to both true and false propositions – nothing prevents me from composing (truly) man and animal, and (falsely) man and ass – true propositions (and only they) enjoy entirely extramental correlates: thus, for example, the true proposition '*homo est animal*' corresponds not only to the things man (subject) and animal (predicate), but also to a *relation of identity* holding between them (i.e. the extramental correlate of its copula; Burley 1497, prologue, fol. c4va).

The theory of the *complexe significabile* developed by Adam Wodeham and Gregory of Rimini also displays such an asymmetry.

---

[29] See, however, Schmutz 2011 on the technical term '*verifactivum*' which, nonetheless, appears only in the second scholasticism of the seventeenth century.

[30] This amounts to distinguishing between primary and secondary truth-bearers: *dicta* are primary truth-bearers, while the complex concepts (also) signified by propositions and propositions themselves are secondary truth-bearers.

As Brower-Toland has convincingly shown, Wodeham's critique of Ockham's position entails that he distinguishes between the representational content of a judgement and its referent (the latter being the *complexe significabile*).[31] When one assents to an apprehended mental sentence *p* (which, according to Ockham, is nothing but the object of knowledge) one thereby grasps *that p conforms to what is apprehended by it* (Wodeham 1990, d. 1, q. 1, a. 1, p. 188). Such a representational content is distinct from the *significabile per complexum* (which Wodeham will introduce only later as his own solution to the problem of the object of knowledge). This suggests that Wodeham takes the *significabilia per complexum* to be the referents of judgements, and thus, that they are the correlates of true judgements only. Gregory of Rimini, by contrast, explicitly says that *complexe significabilia* correspond to true *and* to false propositions, thereby implying that the objects of knowledge, as he conceives of them, cannot be truthmakers (Gregory of Rimini 1978, prologue, q. 1, a. 1, p. 10).

The last case to be considered in this short survey of medieval accounts of truthmaking is the so-called *modus rei* theory. It emerges around the middle of the fourteenth century and is known only indirectly.[32] Richard Billingham is traditionally considered to be an advocate of that position (Richard Billingham 1987a and 1987b), but there is a good reason to think that Billingham's view differs from the one found in the indirect sources mentioned: according to Billingham, a *modus rei* is an accident; but all the indirect sources insist that *modus rei* and accident should be sharply distinguished. The main claim of the theory is that true propositions (and only true ones) signify a mode of a thing (*modus rei*). Negatively, the *modus rei* is characterized as being neither a thing or something (*res, aliquid*), nor several things or some things (*res, aliqua*). Positively, the *modus rei* is said to be an "in this or that way" (*aliqualiter*) – an adverbial

---

[31] See Brower-Toland 2007a, esp. 613–616 and 622.
[32] The indirect sources are Richard Feribrigge 1978, c. 1350; Richard Brinkley 1987, c. 1350; Henry Hopton 1494, c. 1360; Johannes Venator 1999, c. 1380; Anonymous 2004, c. 1395; Paul of Venice 1978, c. 1396–1399.

phrase taken with a nominal value: '*aliqualiter*' is the name of the propositional significate, and not a qualification of the way a proposition signifies. The main line of argumentation in favour of such a view is the following: "something" (in the weakest possible sense) must account for the truth of true propositions; furthermore, propositional truth is to be accounted for in terms of a "local" correlation between the proposition at stake and its significate (the true proposition and what makes it true must exist at the same time *in the same place*)[33]; now: (i) since a true proposition is true everywhere (*ubique*) and no substance or accident is everywhere, the *modus rei* will be something distinct from whatever is a substance or an accident; and (ii) since there are negative truths (e.g. 'a chimera does not exist') and no existing thing can make such a negative existential true, the *modus rei* will be something distinct from an existing thing. As a result, *modi rerum* turn out to be *sui generis*, ubiquitous and non-existing entities (i.e. they *are*, but do not *exist*).

10.4 PROPOSITIONS AND THEIR COUNTERPARTS: A TENTATIVE SYNTHESIS

The first point made, at the very beginning of this short survey, was to distinguish the medieval meaning of 'proposition' from the contemporary one. As has become clear, medieval authors provided fine-grained analyses of propositions, their meaning and their truth, to the effect that one might wonder whether, to some extent, they did not anticipate some distinctions familiar to the modern reader. This last section attempts, on the one hand, to give a summarizing overview of the materials gathered so far, and, on the other hand, to establish a correspondence with some contemporary notions. This will be done on the basis of Table 10.1 displaying the different levels of analysis of the proposition and its semantics, from the judgement expressed by the proposition, to the thing the proposition is about:

---

[33] This is an implicit (i.e. reconstructed premise): as far as I am aware, it is nowhere stated explicitly. However, it is clearly entailed by the (canonical) "argument from ubiquity" put forward in favour of the view.

Table 10.1 *Propositions and their counterparts*

(0) JUDGEMENT	(3*) JUDGEMENT CONTENT
(1)	STATEMENT
(2)	OBJECTIVE MEANING
(3)	OBJECT OF JUDGEMENT
(4)	TRUTHMAKER
(5)	SUBJECT OF JUDGEMENT

The dotted line marks the limit between what is in the mind (*in anima*) and what is in the external world (*extra animam*). Let us take the judgement *Socrates is wise* as (0). (0) is a mental act, the judgement itself, (1) is the linguistic expression 'Socrates is wise'. (2) is a proposition (in the contemporary sense), i.e. the abstract meaning of (0) and (1). (3) is what is judged in (0), i.e. *that Socrates is wise*, and exists outside of the mind. Likewise, (3*) is what is judged in (0) and exists only in the mind. (4) is what makes truth-bearers true (if they are true). (5) is what (0) is about, namely Socrates himself. How are the different items considered in the first three sections of this chapter to be "located" in such a scheme? Here is a plausible distribution:

(0) Ockham's and Wodeham's mental proposition (*complexum*) and assent
(1) the *propositio* (i.e. the proposition in the medieval sense of the term)
(2) the proposition in the contemporary sense of the term (*à la* Bolzano, Frege, Husserl), but also: Abelard's *dicta*, the *enuntiabilia* of the *Ars Burana* and *Ars Meliduna*
(3) Burley's *propositio in re* (*cum grano salis*, however, since its copula is a mental act), Gregory of Rimini's *complexe significabilia*
(3*) Aquinas' *verbum interius*, Scotus' *compositio rerum ut intelliguntur*
(4) Abelard's *eventus rerum*, Chatton's objects of knowledge, Wodeham's *complexe significabilia*, Burley's entirely extramental counterpart of true propositions (having an extramental relation of identity corresponding to the mental copula), and, last but not least: the *modus rei*
(5) Ockham's subject (*subiectum*) of knowledge, Buridan's and Feribrigge's deflationist (or reductionist) position (there is nothing like a special, propositional significate)

To conclude, let us suggest some possible connections with the *contemporary* notions of propositions, facts and states of affairs.[34] The dividing line between propositions, on the one hand, and facts and states of affairs, on the other, is determined with respect to the questions of what is a bearer of truth and falsity: only propositions (2), but neither facts nor states of affairs are truth-bearers (of course, judgements (0) and statements (1) are truth-bearers as well, but we do not focus on them now). What distinguishes states of affairs from facts, is that the former correspond to both true *and* false judgements, propositions – such are our items (3) and (3*) – while the latter correspond to true propositions only – such is our item (4).[35] Provided the suggested association of medieval philosophical items with contemporary ones is correct, one can reasonably claim that medieval logicians, when reflecting on propositions, their meaning and their truth, anticipated the (crucial) contemporary distinctions between propositions, facts and states of affairs.[36]

---

[34] On that subject, see, besides the works of Morscher mentioned above: Mulligan 1989; Smith 1989; Armstrong 1997; Gaskin 2008; Reicher 2009.

[35] States of affairs corresponding to true propositions are said to obtain, states of affairs corresponding to false propositions are said not to obtain. Thus, another way to express the relation between states of affairs and facts consists in saying that a fact is an obtaining state of affairs.

[36] Many thanks to Parwana Emamzadah for careful reading of a preliminary version of this text.

11 Sophisms and Insolubles

Mikko Yrjönsuuri and Elizabeth Coppock

Just prior to the spread of universities across Europe in the fourteenth century, a systematic method for training the minds of young future leaders to think rationally began to crystallize through the practice of logical disputations. The oldest centres of logic in Europe were Oxford and Paris, both originating in the eleventh century, and rich traditions were built up there over the subsequent years. In fourteenth-century Oxford, before earning a Bachelor of Arts, a student was required to earn the title of *sophista generalis* (Leader 1989, 96). As such, he was allowed to participate in structured disputations involving a respondent and an opponent, and would have learned the art of considering a sentence called a *sophism* (Latin *sophisma*) against a hypothetical scenario or given set of assumptions, called a *casus* in Latin.[1] Typically, it was not trivial to decide whether the sentence was true or false, and arguments could be made on both sides. Sophisms thus presented a puzzle to be solved. In medieval texts, the discussion of a sophism follows a more or less strict outline that includes arguments both for and against the truth of the sentence under the assumption that the *casus* is true, and a resolution of the puzzle.

The etymologically related word *sophistry* has a connotation of gratuitous obfuscation not shared by *sophism*. The arguments for and against the same sentence reflect puzzlement, but the aim was not to invite trickery. Rather, skills achieved lay in the disambiguation of Latin expressions, in the exact formulations of their truth conditions, and in the recognition of inferential connections between them. In short, rather than sophistry, sophisms led to the treatment of Latin as a precise, logical language. This programme bears some similarity to that of Richard Montague, the founder of modern formal

---

[1] To avoid ambiguity and potentially misleading implications, we will use the technical term *casus* rather than 'scenario' or 'set of premises' in this chapter.

semantics, who wrote, "I reject the contention that an important theoretical difference exists between formal and natural languages" (Montague 1974).

Examples of sophisms, with accompanying discussion, can be found both in independent collections of sophisms and within treatises on logical topics, regarding such quantificational words as 'every' or exclusives like 'only'. One much-discussed thirteenth-century sophism is 'Every phoenix exists' (Tabarroni 1993), which occurs in many different sources, including Walter Burley's *Questions on Aristotle's 'On Interpretation'* (Brown 1974, 260–262). In discussions of this example, it is assumed, in accordance with the myth, that there is only one phoenix at a time, although over time, there are many. It is then examined whether this state of affairs warrants the use of the sign of universal quantity (namely 'every') and the present tense. If 'every' must range over at least three particulars – as some authors suggest – and the present tense requires a limited time reference, the sentence is to be judged false. Authors willing to analyse the linguistic items differently, including Burley, gave different evaluations. As a result, the function of the word 'every' was spelled out with great theoretical clarity and exactness, though not with unanimity.

Among the different sophisms, one group stands out: the insoluble (*insolubile*, plural *insolubilia*). 'Insoluble' was a technical term adopted as early as the twelfth century, applying to sophisms that are particularly difficult to resolve, including paradoxes of self-reference. For example, given the *casus* that Socrates says only 'Socrates says something false', it appears impossible to give the sentence 'Socrates says something false' any truth value. No solution to the sophism appears acceptable.

The range of topics dealt with in the sophism literature is very wide, but can be divided into four broad categories. We have already alluded to two of these: those concerning the interpretation of so-called syncategorematic terms such as 'every' and 'only', and the semantic paradoxes (insolubles). Sophisms also arose in mathematical physics through the study of terms like 'begins', 'ceases', and 'infinite'. These contributed substantially to the development of mathematics and physics, and had a considerable influence on work by Early Modern natural philosophers like Galileo Galilei (Duhem 1913; Clagett 1959). Sophisms also dealt with questions relating to knowledge and belief, including when exactly a person can be said to know something, the nature of what one believes or knows, reference *de dicto* and *de re*, and the relationship between knowledge, belief, and doubt. We will address each of these four categories of sophisms below, after a brief historical overview.

11.1 FROM THE TWELFTH CENTURY TO THE SIXTEENTH CENTURY

The practice of constructing sophisms arose from certain twelfth-century trends in learning. As analysis of language and logic gained a central role in education, authors began constructing artificial examples rather than considering existing quotations from classical sources. These gained increasing complexity, allowing for very delicate differentiation of meaning (Dronke 1992, 240–241). The practice of constructing artificial examples is also found in modern-day linguistics, where discussions often centre around constructed example sentences, sometimes in connection with artificial hypothetical scenarios, although it is not common nowadays to argue both for and against the truth of the example sentence with respect to the scenario, as in the presentation of a sophism.

The original dominant use of sophisms was educational, and so collections of sophisms started to circulate as teaching aids that were not tied to any particular theoretical approach or school. Possibly the earliest surviving collection is one from the twelfth century in a manuscript written by several hands containing, in addition to treatises on logic, a collection of some eighty sophisms (Kneepkens 1993). The section has the Latin title *Sophismata* and the sophisms contained in it appear to be presented in no particular order. Most of these sophisms have, however, a clear connection to the issues discussed in the various topical treatises in the so-called 'old logic' (see the chapter on the *Logica Vetus* in this volume) contained in the same manuscript. The collection of sophisms in the book presents examples which elucidate logical problems discussed in the main texts. Even more generally, from the end of the twelfth century until at least the end of the Middle Ages, sophisms were used in the presentation of theoretical viewpoints, applying the theses and the rules making up the core of the theory to solve the sophisms. Burley's *On Obligations* (written c. 1300), for example, gives rules concerning the respondent's duty to grant (Latin *concedo*) or deny (Latin *nego*) sentences consistently in a dynamic disputation (see the chapter "Obligationes" in this volume). The workings of these rules are illustrated through a series of sophisms containing words like 'grant' and 'deny'.

Towards the end of the thirteenth century, theoretical content within the discussions of sophisms increased, and the basic structure became more regimented. Thus, the presentation of a sophism typically consists of six parts:

(1) the sophism sentence itself;
(2) the *casus* (a hypothetical scenario or set of assumptions);
(3) the proof of (1) given (2);
(4) the disproof of (1) given (2);
(5) the reply, which determines whether (1) is true or false given (2), and explains why;
(6) depending on the direction of the reply, the author's reply to the opposing proof, i.e. to (3) or to (4).

In its outline, a sophism thus follows roughly the same structure as a standard medieval *quaestio* found, for example, in Thomas Aquinas' *Summa Theologiae*. There is, however, one significant structural difference. As the point in a standard medieval *quaestio* was to discuss what is really true, there is no hypothetical scenario, or stipulation of the supposed facts of the matter – i.e. a *casus*. In particular, the *casus* is the part that makes a sophism artificial rather than real. In most sophisms, the *casus* is an obviously hypothetical, constructed case.

The dominant type of sophism in the thirteenth century dealt with issues of logic and semantics. The fourteenth century saw new developments in the circle that is known by the name 'Oxford Calculators', so-called because of their work in mathematical physics. Among the main characters of this group were Thomas Bradwardine, Richard Kilvington, and William Heytesbury, who also worked in epistemology and on the semantic paradoxes, as will be discussed below. Richard Kilvington's *Sophismata* may be taken as a work of paradigmatic importance for this group, developing mathematical physics in genuinely new directions. At that time, sophisms seem to have been very important as a systematic part of the bachelor course.

After the work of the Oxford Calculators, the most influential author to write a collection of sophisms was John Buridan (Klima 2001a). His *Sophismata* forms the last section of his *Summulae de dialectica*, and it has to be counted as one of the most innovative collections of sophisms surviving from the Middle Ages, considering the richness of the logic developed there.

After Buridan, the currents of intellectual history brought so-called Renaissance humanism to the forefront, a movement that was not particularly friendly to the sophismatic tradition. Late-fourteenth-century sophisms did contain interesting new developments such as Albert of Saxony's sophisms related to *de se* reference discussed below. Both Kilvington's and Buridan's *Sophismata* were widely used as textbooks (Markowski 1993). But sophisms, and the peculiar Latin structures found in the literature, were one of the most explicit targets of humanist criticism. They admired the eloquent rather than logical Latin of classical authors like Cicero and Seneca.

11.2 GRAMMATICAL SOPHISMS

What modern medievalists sometimes call grammatical sophisms served to elucidate what medieval logicians called syncategorematic terms (as opposed to categorematic terms), and dealt with some of the problems that are treated in modern formal semantics. Among the syncategorematic terms are words like 'not', 'and', 'or', and 'therefore', as opposed to 'man', 'stone', 'whiteness', and 'white', which are categorematic (Buridan 2001, 232). A standard characterization of syncategorematic terms, given, for example, by the ancient grammarian Priscian, is as *consignificantia*, i.e. terms which signify something only in combination with other terms (Courtenay 2008, 32). In modern formal semantics, 'syncategorematic' is used in a similar sense, characterizing not a word but a style of analysis in which a term is given a meaning in combination with other terms, rather than in isolation.

Some authors supplemented this definition with a semantic characterization of the syncategorematic terms. John Buridan, for example, characterized a categorematic word as one that serves to pick out existing things in the world while syncategorematic words did not (Buridan 2001, 232). This way of making the distinction bears some similarity to the characterization of logical constants as those whose interpretation is constant across models (Westerståhl 1985), where models determine the extensions of predicates and relations, although the relationship between syncategoremata and logical constants is subject to debate (Dutilh Novaes and Spruyt 2015). There is a sense, then, in which grammatical sophisms dealt with the logical words of Latin.

Not all sophisms that might be called grammatical dealt with particular words. For example, as Terence Parsons discusses, medieval logicians produced innovative analyses of relative clauses in sophisms such as 'Everything that will be is' (Parsons 2014). Possession was another theme treated in this literature that can be brought under the heading of grammatical sophisms, although, like relative clauses, the issue is not connected to a particular word. Here the question concerns the interpretation of the genitive case. One popular example in this category is the sophism: 'That dog is yours; That dog is a father; So that dog is your father' from Aristotle's *Sophistical Refutations*, ch. 24, drawn from Plato's *Euthydemus*. But particular words constitute the bulk of this category, especially in the thirteenth century.

One particularly widespread collection of grammatical sophisms was written in the mid-thirteenth century by an otherwise unknown Richard known as the *magister abstractionum*. Among the
over 300 sophisms in this collection, two large groups of over sixty
sophisms concern respectively two specific kinds of syncategorematic words. One of these consists of words expressing exclusion or
exception (such as *tantum* 'only', *solus* 'alone', and *praeter* 'except'),
and the other consists of words like *omnis* 'every', which signal universal quantification of a sentence. Thus, exclusion, exception, and
universal quantification seem by this quantitative measure to be
the most important topics discussed in sophisms. There are further
groups of about thirty sophisms each, related to conditionals (words
like *si* 'if' and *nisi* 'unless'), to negations (*ne* 'not', *nullus* 'nobody',
and *nihil* 'no'), to alethic logical modalities (*necessarium* 'necessary',
impossibile 'impossible', and *possibile* 'possible') and to beginning
and ceasing (*incipit* 'begins', and *desinit* 'ceases'). Yet further syncategorematic words are considered, but not as extensively. For example,
the collection has eleven sophisms on 'in as much as' (*inquantum*)
and just three on 'or' (*vel*). The collection should not, however, be
taken to reflect the whole scene. Certain important syncategorematic
words that are found in other collections of sophisms seem to be missing from the *magister abstractionum* collection. Thus the collection
has no sophisms concerning the word 'infinite', for example. The selection and variety of topics in the *magister abstractionum* collection
also shows how linguistic, logical, and even physical analyses were
not separated in the sophismata literature (Streveler 1993).

At the turn of the fourteenth century, Walter Burley wrote distinct treatises on exclusives (*De exclusivis*) and on exceptives (*De
exceptivis*), and both topics are also discussed as chapters of his *On
the Purity of the Art of Logic* (Burley 2000). Burley proceeds through
rules, distinctions, doubts – and sophisms. The discussion on exclusives opens with an important technique often used in various kinds
of sophisms, and thus worthy of attention here. Burley says that an
exclusive proposition like

> Only Socrates runs.

can be expounded or 'unpacked' (*exponitur*) as a conjunction

> Socrates runs and nothing other than Socrates runs.

Such a technique was called exposition, and it could be applied to a wide variety of sentences. Among them, those containing the words 'begin' or 'cease' were prominent cases. Thus,

> Socrates begins to be white.

was to be analysed by the exposition

> Socrates is not white and immediately after now Socrates is white.

Burley's main focus in the treatise is on how the exclusive particle 'only' functions in relation to the structures of the standard Aristotelian predication that yields the syllogistic system. 'Only' can be attached to either the subject or to the predicate, and in each place the exposition will be somewhat different. Also, Burley considers how rules of conversion turning the predicate into the subject and vice versa work with exclusive propositions. From this, it is natural to investigate how exclusives work in structures resembling the syllogistic figures. In effect, Burley is building a logic of exclusives as an extension of the Aristotelian syllogistic system.

Comparison to contemporary theory of linguistic exclusion shows that the approach of distinguishing between the positive and the negative component in a sentence containing an exclusive expression is an accepted practice even nowadays, sometimes even explicitly connected to the medieval practice of exposition, although details of the analyses differ. There is a rich ongoing debate about how to analyse exclusives, but modern semanticists almost all agree that there is an asymmetry between the positive component and the negative component, the former commonly seen as being presupposed (Coppock and Beaver 2013). Burley and other medieval logicians, including Peter of Spain and William of Sherwood were, in contrast, what Laurence Horn calls "symmetricalists", treating the two exponents as having equal status (Horn 2011).

Burley's symmetricalism plays an important role in his treatment of the sophism 'If nothing runs then something runs', which goes, in part, as follows (Burley 2000, 223–224):

- It is proved as follows: 'If nothing runs, not only Socrates runs; and if not only Socrates runs, something other than Socrates runs; and it follows: something other than Socrates runs; therefore, something runs; therefore, from first to last: if nothing runs, something runs'.
- It is disproved as follows: The antecedent is possible; but a possible proposition never implies its contradictory; therefore, 'If nothing runs something runs' is false.
- Solution: The sophism-proposition is false, and there is a fallacy of the consequent in its proof, when it argues like this: 'Not only Socrates runs; therefore, something other than Socrates runs'. For 'Not only Socrates runs' has two causes of truth, one of which is 'Another than Socrates runs' and the other 'Socrates does not run'.

As in a modern proof, the proof explicitly mentions a rule of inference, namely "from first to last", which chains three conditionals $(p{\to}q \; \& \; q{\to}r \; \& \; r{\to}s \vdash p{\to}s)$. The rule is given by Burley in the section on conditionals as follows (Burley 2000, 155):

When many inferences occur between the first antecedent and the last consequent, if in each inference the same thing that is the consequent in the preceding conditional is the antecedent in the following conditional, then an inference 'from first to last' holds, so that the last consequent follows from the first antecedent.

To show that the proof is fallacious, Burley rejects this premise: 'If not only Socrates runs, something other than Socrates runs' but accepts this one: 'If nothing runs, not only Socrates runs'. The rejection of the first crucially depends on the assumption that 'Not only Socrates runs' can be true either because Socrates does not run or because someone other than Socrates runs (a direct consequence of the symmetricalist thesis, as Burley points out).

A modern asymmetricalist would do the opposite, accepting the first but not the second premise. According to one common analysis (originally due to Laurence Horn), the positive component of an exclusive sentence is presupposed and the negative component is part of the ordinary semantic content (Beaver and Clark 2008). In the standard Fregean theory of presupposition, this presupposition survives when the sentence is negated, and the ordinary content – the negative component, that nobody other than Socrates runs – is targeted by the negation. Hence 'Not only Socrates runs' implies 'Something other than Socrates runs' (and the first premise is valid). But 'Nothing runs' does not imply 'Not only Socrates runs' (the second premise), because 'Not only Socrates runs' presupposes that Socrates runs, and this cannot be true if nothing runs. The modern asymmetricalist thus agrees with Burley that the proof is not valid, but disagrees about why.

This is one of several phenomena dealt with in the sophism literature that are standardly treated using the concept of presupposition in modern semantics. Other cases involve quantifier domain restrictions. As mentioned above, 'Every phoenix exists' becomes puzzling under the assumption that 'every' must range over at least three objects. This kind of restriction is treated as a presupposition under standard modern accounts (Heim and Kratzer 1998). A related problem shows up in discussions concerning the sentence 'Every lunar eclipse takes place by the interposition of the earth between the sun and the moon'. Under the not-so-unusual circumstance that there is currently no eclipse of the moon, there is nothing in the domain of 'every'. John Buridan writes that the sentence is false in that case, strictly speaking, though we might get the feeling that it is true because this sentence is actually a loose way of saying 'Whenever there is a lunar eclipse, it takes place by the interposition of the moon between the sun and the earth' (Buridan 2001, 725–726). If the requirement that the domain is non-empty is a presupposition, as a typical modern semanticist would say, then the sentence is not straightforwardly false; it is common nowadays to claim that its truth value is 'undefined' in case that condition is not fulfilled. (This does not help to explain why the sentence might be felt to be true.)

11.3   SOPHISMS ON MATHEMATICAL PHYSICS

In the first quarter of the fourteenth century, as we see in Richard Kilvington's *Sophismata* (Kilvington 1990), a new kind of subject matter begins to be considered. Sophisms in natural philosophy were a flourishing oral practice at Oxford at the time (Sylla 2010), and Kilvington's work builds upon this practice.

Of Kilvington's forty-eight sophisms, forty-four deal with problems related to movement and change, both quantitative and qualitative. The central words occurring in these sophisms are 'begins' and 'ceases'. Kilvington takes the discussion to new heights as he embeds 'begins' and 'ceases' in sentences having rich structures of different tenses, in many cases combined with comparatives and superlatives expressing greater or lesser speeds, or greater or lesser intensities of whiteness (whiteness being just a placeholder for a continuously quantifiable quality). This results in elaborate discussions concerning the mathematical properties of continuous quantities, including speed.

For example, in sophism 23 we are to suppose the following *casus*. The body A (the reader might think of a slow paintbrush) is steadily moving across the body B (a plank), making B white until it reaches the endpoint C after an hour. At the half hour, a blackener D will start to move over B twice as fast as A, changing the whiteness generated by A into blackness. In this *casus*, only the part of the plank between the two moving paintbrushes will be white. Given the speeds of the two paintbrushes, they will reach the end of the plank at the same time, and thus at the end of the plank there is no space between them. The sophism to be considered is:

> A will generate whiteness up to point C, and no whiteness will be immediate to point C.

After work by Newton, Leibniz, and others in the seventeenth century, infinitesimal calculus has become part of mathematics. Thus, we can say that when the whitener A moves infinitesimally close to C, the blackener D also moves infinitesimally close to C, and the distance between A and D becomes infinitesimally small. D is nevertheless always twice as far from C as A is. Because D moves twice as fast as A, D and A will arrive at C at the same instant. Thus, the area that is whitened before it is blackened will first grow and then diminish, becoming infinitesimally small as the distance from the endpoint becomes infinitesimal. At any finite distance from C, some whiteness will be generated before it is blackened, but will there be any whiteness generated immediate to C? Does the expression 'immediate to C' refer to anything? Kilvington's solution, on which we cannot go into detail here, is based on how 'up to' and 'will generate' are to be treated in different word orders, and especially in the word order in which the sophism is actually put. He is thus providing rules of linguistic usage to aid in mathematical precision.

The crucial theme of this sophism and many others in Kilvington's collection is continuous motion, either uniform or uniformly accelerating or decelerating. Infinitesimal quantities and in some cases infinitesimal proportions also play an important role. Kilvington's younger colleagues and followers in Oxford also wrote sophisms with such themes. One work of particular importance is William Heytesbury's *Rules for Solving Sophismata*, a thematically organized guide for the student in handling various kinds of sophisms. This work is known as the first to explicate the so-called mean speed theorem, according to which, in a uniformly accelerating motion, a body moves in a given time the same distance as it would move if it moved in the same time with the mean speed of the accelerating motion (Sylla 2010). A particularly notable point here is that this result required recognition that it is possible to attribute a speed to a body at an instant despite the obvious fact that no body moves anywhere in an instant.

11.4 SOPHISMS ON KNOWLEDGE AND DOUBT

The final four of Kilvington's *Sophismata* concern the verb 'to know' as an epistemic operator. Like mathematical physics, this theme too was relatively marginal in thirteenth-century sophisms, but gained importance in the fourteenth century. Among Oxford Calculators, Heytesbury dedicated a full chapter of his *Rules on Solving Sophisms* to the problems of epistemic logic and the nature of knowledge. Furthermore, while the Parisian logician John Buridan seems not to have been interested in mathematical physics, a number of his sophisms deal with problems of knowledge ascriptions. Sophisms concerning knowledge and doubt are sometimes subsumed under a larger class dealing with so-called 'officiable' or 'functionalizable' terms (*officiabilis* in Latin, roughly translatable into modern formal semantics terminology as 'operators'), which include deontic and alethic modalities and belief-related propositional attitudes (Bos 2007).

One of the issues arising in connection with knowledge and doubt is known to modern linguists and philosophers as the distinction between *de dicto* and *de re* interpretations (Quine 1956). The sophism literature makes a similar distinction between 'composite' and 'divided' senses. This distinction plays a role in the solution to the following two sophisms of Kilvington's, which involve a demonstrative pronoun ('this'):

S45.   You know this to be everything that is this.

Casus: You see Socrates from a distance and do not know that it is Socrates.

S46.   You know this to be Socrates.

Casus: You see Socrates and Plato at the same time, and Socrates and Plato are altogether alike, and you are a little confused, so you don't know which is Socrates and which is Plato. By 'this' is indicated the one who is in the location where Socrates was before you became confused.

For S46, Kilvington puts forth the proposal that in the divided sense ('about this thing, you know it to be Socrates', a *de re* interpretation) the sophism is false, but in the compounded sense, the sophism should be doubted, because you know the sentence 'Socrates is Socrates', and you doubt whether 'This is Socrates' is the same sentence in the language of thought. It is not clear whether this constitutes a satisfactory resolution of the issue, but the discussion at least brings out important differences between demonstratives and proper names in epistemic contexts.

The distinction between composite and divided senses was an important tool in solving epistemic sophisms for Kilvington and Heytesbury, and Buridan also addresses this theme quite extensively some years later in Paris. Consider Buridan's discussion of the sophism 'You know the one approaching' (Buridan 2001, 892):

> I posit the case that you see your father approaching from afar, so that you cannot tell whether he is your father or someone else.
>
> P.1 Then [the sophism] is proved as follows: you know your father well; and your father is the one approaching; therefore, you know the one approaching.
>
> P.2 Again, you know the one who is known by you; but the one approaching is known by you; therefore, you know the one approaching.
>
> P.2.1 I prove the minor: for your father is known by you, and your father is the one approaching; therefore, etc.
>
> O.1 The opposite is argued: you do not know the person concerned when [he is such that], if asked who he is, you would truly say: 'I do not know'; but about the one approaching you will say this; therefore, etc.

The sophism sentence is argued to be true on what modern semanticists would call a *de re* reading, but false on a *de dicto* reading.[2]

---

[2] The terms *de dicto* and *de re* are medieval in origin but not commonly used at that time (Dutilh Novaes 2004).

Note that issues related to opaque contexts were not limited to discussions of knowledge. For example, in Buridan's sophism,

I owe you a horse.

part of the problem is that there is no particular horse that is owed. This case will remind the modern formal semanticist of Richard Montague's 'John seeks a unicorn' (Montague 1974), which, of course, does not entail the existence of a unicorn.

Alongside *de dicto* versus *de re*, we also find discussions of reference *de se*. John Buridan's student Albert of Saxony includes in his *Sophismata* (c. 1359) a number of sophisms where anaphoric pronouns occur in the scope of the knowledge operator (Biard 1989b). Included are two sophisms with the pronoun 'himself' (Latin *se*) used to express the kind of knowledge David Lewis called knowledge *de se* (Lewis 1979). Consider the sophism II, 34 (Albert of Saxony 1490),

Socrates can know what God cannot know.

The disproof is straightforward: God can know and indeed knows everything that is true, and Socrates cannot know anything that is not true; therefore, anything Socrates knows, God knows too. The proof of the sophism is more interesting in this case. According to the proof, Socrates can know that someone is better than he (himself), but God cannot know that someone is better than he (himself). Thus, Socrates can know something that God cannot know. As Albert explains more fully in the solution of the previous related sophism II, 33, the propositional objects considered by Socrates and God differ in what the personal pronoun 'he' (Latin *se*) refers to.

The epistemic sophism of Kilvington's that is longest and which has raised most attention among modern scholars devises a case where it appears that the respondent must admit that he both knows and doubts the same proposition. It is as follows:

S47.   You know that the king is seated.
Casus: You know that the king is seated, if he is, and you know that he is not seated, if he is not.

To solve the sophism, Kilvington engages in a discussion of the rules of responding in a sophism, apparently assuming that sophisms should be understood as obligational disputations. However, in Kilvington's view, these rules need to be modified to serve the purpose. (See the chapter "Obligationes" in this volume.)

In the chapter on knowledge and doubt in his *Rules for Solving Sophisms*, Heytesbury also considers whether one can simultaneously know and doubt the same sentence. He is thus taking up the theme of Kilvington's sophism S47, but as a substantive issue on the nature of knowledge. To some extent, his discussion also goes into the problem whether it is possible to have a second-order doubt concerning whether one knows, or whether the so-called KK-principle of Hintikka's (that knowledge entails that one knows that one knows) is true. Heytesbury defines knowledge as follows: to know is nothing other than unhesitatingly to apprehend the truth (Pasnau 1995). It can be argued that his choice not to require justification of knowledge is a conscious one (Martens 2010), but the main point that he wants to make is that knowledge is an unhesitating propositional attitude. Thus, it is different from, and contrary to, doubt.

Another of Kilvington's epistemic sophisms has features that make it arguably classifiable as an insoluble.

S48.   A is known by you.

Casus: A is one or the other of these: 'God exists' or 'Nothing granted by Socrates is known by you', and Socrates grants this and nothing else: 'A is known by you'.

In this case, we have an indirect form of self-reference: What Socrates grants is 'A is known by you', and another premise concerns your knowledge of what Socrates grants. These kinds of meta-semantic claims are characteristic of the insolubles, which we discuss in the next section.

II.5   INSOLUBLES

Among the so-called insolubles are the liar paradox ('This sentence is false'), and other sophisms containing meta-semantic terms such as 'true', 'valid', 'grant', 'deny', and 'lying', such as:

This argument is valid, so you are an ass.

(where 'this argument' refers to the argument made by the very sentence in question). This particular sophism, found in William Heytesbury's *Sophismata Asinina* (see Pironet 1993, 141), was redis-covered as Curry's paradox (Read 2001) – evidence that such soph-isms dealt with issues of deep logical significance. Heytesbury takes issue with the customary title of such sophisms, 'insolubles', claim-ing that they may not be really impossible to solve, but that providing a solution is very difficult. He writes, "although the insolubles can be solved, nevertheless they have not yet been solved" (Heytesbury 1979, 18). Unlike the other types of sophisms discussed above, insol-ubles were perhaps more often treated in separate treatises, and they were not a common topic in the thirteenth-century collections of sophisms. However, the basic structure of a sophism as it settled dur-ing the thirteenth century proves to suit the medieval way of discuss-ing the liar paradox and similar paradoxes very well.

As a genre, insolubles literature was in Heytesbury's time almost two centuries old. It seems that earlier ancient Greek, Byzantine (Gerogiorgakis 2009), and Arabic (Alwishah and Sanson 2009) treatments of the liar paradox did not have much direct in-fluence on the Latin tradition, which is considered to start with the so-called *Insolubilia Monacensia*, dated to the end of the twelfth century (Martin 2001). For a summary of the types of solutions found in the discussion up to Bradwardine, we can take the classification from his own treatise *Insolubles* (Bradwardine 2010), which dates from about the same years as Kilvington's *Sophismata*, a decade before Heytesbury's *Rules for Solving Sophisms*. As Bradwardine saw it, there were four basic types of solution differing from his.

(1) Firstly, there were restrictionists, who wanted to pose restrictions on what terms can stand for in a sentence, or for which time they can stand for the denoted things. Simply put, self-reference is to be banned in such a way that the paradoxes cannot be produced. Socrates cannot refer to his own speech act when he says 'Socrates says something false'. As Bradwardine elaborately points out, the solution appears to be *ad*

hoc, since there seems to be no natural, general way of describing what exactly is to be banned.

(2) Second, nullifiers claimed that no one can say that he is uttering a falsehood, in Bradwardine's formulation. What exactly is impossible to do is rather difficult to spell out given that a man [can] open his mouth and form the words as Bradwardine says.

(3) Third, the principle of bivalence had been denied. It had been claimed that in insolubles we find propositions that are neither true nor false. Bradwardine's straightforward counterargument is to reformulate the paradoxes through reverting to a proposition either being or not being true rather than being true or false.

(4) Fourth, one could distinguish between utterance in act (exercitus) and the thought (conceptus). This would make the actual formation of the spoken sentence as a truth-bearer different from that for which the term 'falsehood' stands for when I say 'I am uttering a falsehood'. Then the utterance in act would be true but the corresponding thought would be false. Bradwardine remarks that this solution only applies to those versions of the paradox that are based on utterances that are distinct from thoughts.

The core of Bradwardine's own solution to the paradoxes of self-reference is that a sentence that claims itself to be false entails and thus signifies not only that it is false but also that it is true. On the basis of such a signification, it is unproblematic to judge that the sentence is false because the sentence cannot be both true and false and is thus impossible (and thus false). This solution was highly influential for decades.

Bradwardine's solution concentrated on the relation between a sentence and the claim that the sentence is true. This relation is taken under scrutiny by other authors of the time. In his *Sophismata*, Richard Kilvington argues that a sentence and the claim that it is true are equivalent only under two crucial conditions (Kilvington 1990). Consider the following two sentences:

'You are in Rome' is true.

You are in Rome.

According to Kilvington, the logical relation between these sentences depends on what the sentence quoted in the first one signifies. The second does not follow from the first if 'you are in Rome' means that man is an animal. Furthermore, Kilvington points out that the first follows from the second only if the second sentence is actually formulated, spoken, or written out. That is, even if you were in Rome, 'you are in Rome' would not be true if no one makes the claim. Kilvington relies here on a generally accepted medieval understanding that the truth-bearers are actually uttered sentence tokens rather than abstract types. (See the chapter "Propositions: Their Meaning and Truth" in this volume.)

Heytesbury adopts these distinctions as the basis for his treatment of insolubles. He approaches the paradox as a problem of how the respondent should answer in a disputation. Take the *casus*,

Socrates only says 'Socrates says something false'.

The sophism to be evaluated is:

Socrates says something false.

Heytesbury tells the respondent to deny the sophism and then also deny, if asked, that the sophism signifies exactly what the words would usually signify. As the respondent is only answering by granting or denying, he cannot be forced to explain what Socrates' sentence exactly signifies in the casus. He should deny any exact formulation of what the sentence signifies, and thus leave room for the sentence having some other unspecified abnormal signification. Thus, Heytesbury argues, the respondent can remain coherent in the disputation indefinitely without having to explain why the sophism is false. Such a solution may not be a satisfactory explication of the paradox, but it does allow the respondent to conduct an actual disputation coherently.

In any case, Heytesbury's solution follows Bradwardine in locating the problem in the exact signification of the insoluble sophism. This is to some extent true of John Buridan as well. In his *Sophismata*, he renounces the view that all sentences signify their own truth, admitting that he had earlier held it. But he does not change his mind completely. He opts for saying that every sentence virtually implies rather than signifies the sentence saying that the sentence is true, and that this implication belongs to the truth conditions (Buridan 2001, 966–967). Thus, consider the following consequence:

Man is an animal; therefore, *a* is true,

where the subject term of the consequent '*a*' refers to the antecedent 'Man is an animal'. Because such a consequence is, in Buridan's view, valid for all sentences, the antecedent can be true only if things are as the consequent signifies. In this sense, the truth of any sentence is partly dependent on its own truth-claim. In the case of insolubles, this requirement clashes with other requirements imposed by the sentence, yielding falsity.

Here is how the clash comes about. Buridan asks us to consider the sentence 'no sentence is true', and the associated consequence deriving the truth-claim from the sentence itself (Buridan 2001, 967):

No sentence is true; therefore, *c* is true,

where '*c*' refers to the antecedent. In this case, the consequence is problematic. As Buridan sees it, the consequence is formally valid but the antecedent and the consequent cannot both be true. Thus, the antecedent must be false. And generally, any similar insoluble must be evaluated as false.

Buridan has a number of further examples of insolubles in his *Sophismata*, some circular in a mediated way, and even more interestingly, some practical ones. Thus, in his seventeenth sophism on insolubles, Plato promises to throw Socrates into a river if (and only if) he speaks falsely, and Socrates replies saying 'You will throw me into the river'. Plato has thus made an apparently unproblematic promise that turns out to be impossible to fulfil. It is a sign of Buridan's great influence as a logician that this sophism found its way into Cervantes' *Don Quixote*.

11.6 FINAL REMARKS

The study of sophisms contributed substantially to the development of logic during the Middle Ages. While the Aristotelian system of syllogistics remained important for logic, sophisms concentrated on topics outside Aristotelian syllogistics, as we have seen in the various examples discussed above. A number of important contributions arose out of these investigations, including, in addition to the analysis of syncategorematic terms, new ideas related to reference and propositional attitudes. The literature connected to grammatical sophisms also contains quite advanced ideas concerning the interpretation of relative clauses, as Terence Parsons argues in a new exposition of medieval logic using modern logical notation (Parsons 2014).

The proofs and disproofs of sophism sentences were literally (semi-formal) *proofs*, connecting a set of premises (the *casus*), with a conclusion (the sophism sentence), using inference rules. The inference rules specified consequence relations of a proof-theoretic nature, providing a syntactic characterization of validity, just as Aristotelian syllogisms and the sequents of modern proof theory do.[3] Among these can be counted the rules of exposition and the rule from first to last, which we saw above.[4] Crucially, all of this was happening in Latin, so the medieval authors were essentially developing a *proof system for Latin*, albeit a highly regimented form of Latin.

---

[3] It is debatable whether a rule like from inferior to superior, as in *A man is running, therefore an animal is running*, is syntactic. In *On the Essence of Logic*, Burley writes that such rules are of a special nature but nevertheless formal: "Formal consequence is of two kinds: one kind hold by reason of the form of the whole structure ... another kind ... holds by reason of the form of the incomplex terms, e.g., a consequence from an inferior to a superior affirmatively is formal, but holds by reason of the terms" (Burley 2000, 173).

[4] The rule "from first to last" allows an inference from the first antecedent to the last consequent in an arbitrarily long sequence of conditionals. It follows, as Burley points out, from repeated application of either of these more basic rules: "The second main rule is that whatever follows from a consequent follows from the antecedent. There is another rule too, almost the same as this one: Whatever is antecedent to an antecedent is antecedent to the consequent" (Burley 2000, 4).

In this endeavour, medieval authors used Latin in two ways: first, as an object of empirical study, whose properties are discoverable truths, and second, as the language for which a proof system is to be developed. The nature of the investigation was thus both linguistic and logical. Indeed, the thirteenth-century logician Robert Kilwardby writes that the study of logic can be seen in these two ways: "And thus logic is for us in one way a science of word usage (Latin 'scientia sermocinalis'), and in this way it contains grammar, rhetoric and logic strictly taken. In another way it is science of reason, and in this way it is a trivium science distinct from grammar and rhetoric" (Kilwardby 1976, 167).

Under one common style of analysis in formal semantics, originating with Montague (1974), natural language expressions are translated into expressions of a formal language, and consequence relations between sentences in natural languages derive from the consequence relations among their formal counterparts, for which consequence relations are stipulated by definition. Natural language remains an object of empirical study, and the logical properties of basic expressions remain discoverable truths.

The usual separation of natural and formal languages in formal semantics may be a natural resolution of the tension between these two roles. The convenience of having an unambiguous, regimented language when defining a proof system led fourteenth-century logicians to introduce certain modifications to their Latin. Above, we alluded to a case where Kilvington stipulated special usage conventions for up to and immediate in Latin. For another example, Burley wrote that "a negation has scope over what follows, not over what precedes" (Burley 2000, 15). This is not exactly the case in classical Latin. In modern semantics, all such creative language construction is relegated to the development of the formal representation language, and the natural language is taken as given. From a modern perspective, changing the object of study is tampering with the evidence, while changing the formal language is developing a theoretical tool.

While the modern duality between natural and formal languages may be the natural resolution of a tension, it also seems natural that thirteenth-century authors did not separate the two roles of Latin. The logical tradition at the time was not very rich, and no artificial languages had been developed. This changed over the course of the Middle Ages, thanks to the work of the scholastic tradition.

Another salient contrast between modern formal semantics and the *sophismata* literature is in the use of presupposition. Although it was not as widely used then as it is today, the notion of presupposition was not entirely foreign to medieval scholars. Buridan writes, for example, that "the question *propter quid* ['why'] presupposes a proposition to the effect that the predicate truly inheres in the subject, and what is asked for is the cause of the inherence" (Buridan 2001, 816). The Latin word *praesupponunt* 'presupposes' can be found in discussions of declarative sentences as well. Peter of Spain writes regarding the "reduplicative" expression *inquantum* 'insofar as', as in 'Man, insofar as he is an animal, is sensitive', that "such a particle presupposes [*praesupponit*] that a given predicate inheres in the subject and denotes [*denotat*] that the term to which it is attached causes that inherence" (Horn 1996, 300). Another case of presupposition in a declarative sentence is as follows (Burley 2000, 143):

> But there are certain predicates that presuppose being simply, such as predicates that denominate accidents and signify an act or a form in act, like 'white', 'black', 'hot', 'cold'. In such cases the inference does hold from 'is' as a third component to 'is' as a second component. For it follows: 'Socrates is white; therefore, Socrates is'. And it follows: 'Socrates is hot; therefore, Socrates is'.

(A predicate like 'is possible' or 'is a thinkable thing' would not have the same kind of existence presupposition.) This discussion seems to imply a notion of presupposition that is modern insofar as it licenses inferences.

However, for Burley, presupposition failure would cause falsity, or truth under negation, and was therefore much like ordinary entailment. In this respect it was very different from the modern conception of presupposition, on which presupposition failure often means that a sentence is neither true nor false. There are some examples within medieval logic where the principle of bivalence was questioned, but these are not connected to presupposition, and for the most part do not involve a truth value corresponding to nonsense. As mentioned above, one strategy for dealing with insolubles was to deny the principle of bivalence, but this seems to be the only candidate for a use of a truth value of nonsense.

Other cases where bivalence was questioned appear to have been limited to under-determination (unknowable rather than nonsense), and over-determination (true and false at the same time). One group of candidates for under-determination included future contingents like Aristotle's 'There will be a sea battle tomorrow'. Another included sophisms like Kilvington's S47 discussed above ('you know that the king is seated'). In the latter case, a respondent in a disputation was to answer 'doubt', rather than 'grant' or 'deny', which implies that the sentence is in fact either true or false, but the respondent needs more information in order to decide. These are both potential cases of unknowability (as captured by the strong Kleene interpretations of the connectives in multi-valued logic), rather than nonsense (as captured by the weak Kleene connectives). One candidate for over-determination was the possibility that two contradictory sentences might simultaneously hold at a moment of change, suggesting that a sentence might simultaneously be both true and false, rather than neither. This idea would be captured with the truth value 'both' in a multi-valued logic with truth values 'true', 'false', 'neither', and 'both' (Muskens 1995).

Common to medieval logic and modern formal semantics is that the study of natural language is an engine for the development of logic. Furthermore, while we have observed a number of differences between the medieval and modern analytical frameworks, the potential for such comparisons between them underscores the closeness in orientation of the enterprises. If a medieval logician and a modern formal semanticist were seated next to each other at a dinner party, they would not run out of things to discuss.

12 The Syllogism and Its Transformations

Paul Thom

Every medieval logic compendium, and every medieval commentary on Aristotle's *Analytics*, has something to say about the syllogism. While there is a core of standard logical syllogistic theory that is unchanging across the Middle Ages, there are also significant theoretical differences from one author to another. Some of these concern the very definition of the syllogism. Aristotle had crafted the classic definition; but at different times during the Middle Ages, and in different traditions, opinions differed on how much of the Aristotelian definition should be retained, and how the retained clauses should be interpreted. In this chapter, we examine some of the more interesting transformations that the definition of the syllogism underwent in the Arabic and Latin Middle Ages.

Conceptions of the syllogism undergo transformations over time. But the syllogism itself, as a logical structure, is also capable of certain types of transformation. One of these gives rise to what Aristotle called conversive syllogisms (Aristotle 1965, 59b1), and we will consider some medieval analyses of this type of transformation. We will also look at a related form of argument, the syllogism through the impossible. And these investigations will lead us back to the question of the nature of the syllogism.

12.1 INTRODUCTION

The Aristotelian theory of the syllogism makes use of technical terminology that was to become standard in both the Arabic and Latin traditions. A *categorical proposition* contains two *terms* – a *subject* and a *predicate*. Such a proposition states that the predicate applies to all, or to none, or to some, or to not all of the subject. Propositions of the first two of these types are *universal*, those of the last two types *particular*;

290

these two attributes give a proposition's *quantity*. Propositions of the first and third types are *affirmative*, those of the second and fourth *negative*; these attributes give a proposition's *quality*. A valid inference from two categorical propositions (the *premises*) to a third (the *conclusion*) is a *syllogism* only if its two premises share a term (the *middle term*), and each premise shares a term with the conclusion. The predicate of the conclusion is the *major term*, and its subject the *minor term*. Three different arrangements of the middle, minor and major terms were standardly recognised, and these arrangements were called the *figures* of the syllogism. In the *first figure*, the middle term is subject in one premise and predicate in the other. In the *second figure* the middle term is predicate in both premises. In the *third figure* the middle term is subject in both premises. A syllogism's *mood* is given by the quantity and quality of its premises and conclusion.

It has become standard practice to refer to the individual syllogistic moods by names devised in the Latin West in the late twelfth or early thirteenth century (see Peter of Spain 2014, 4.13). The main names are (for the first figure) Barbara, Celarent, Darii, Ferio; Cesare, Camestres, Festino, Baroco (for the second); Darapti, Felapton, Disamis, Datisi, Bocardo, Ferison (for the third). The names encode the quality and quantity of the two premises and conclusion of the named mood: 'a' indicates a universal affirmative proposition, 'e' a universal negative, 'i' a particular affirmative, 'o' a particular negative. The names also encode information about the first-figure moods to which a given mood in the other figures *reduces*: 'B' indicates that the mood reduces to Barbara (i.e. that the validity of Barbara implies the validity of the given mood), 'C' that it reduces to Celarent, 'D' that it reduces to Darii, 'F' that it reduces to Ferio. Finally, the names indicate the manner in which the named mood reduces to the first figure: 's' indicates that the terms of a proposition have to be exchanged without altering the proposition's quantity (i.e. that reduction to the first figure requires the *simple conversion* of the terms), 'p' indicates an exchange of terms while altering the quantity (i.e. that reduction to the first figure requires *partial conversion* of the terms), 'm' indicates a *permutation* of the premise-order, and 'c' indicates the use of a *conversive syllogism* (i.e. a syllogism obtained by interchanging the contradictory of the given conclusion with the contradictory of one of the given premises).

12.2 DEFINITIONS OF THE SYLLOGISM

Aristotle defined a syllogism as follows:

> A syllogism is discourse in which, several things being laid down, something other than them follows of necessity from their being so. (1965, 24b18).

A practice had started among the ancient Greek commentators of treating this definition as an authoritative text, whose clauses had to be interpreted one by one, starting with the statement of the genus to which the syllogism belongs (discourse), and proceeding to the several differentiating features which mark the syllogism off from other types of discourse. Medieval logicians in both the Arabic and the Latin traditions continued this practice.

What the two traditions have in common is a tendency, over time, towards simplifying the Aristotelian definition. We will find that these simplifications are of various types. Some seem to have a pedagogical motivation: greater simplicity is sought as a means of communicating the intended meaning in an approximate way to learners. In other cases, simplification is sought for the sake of elegance: the concept's expression may be stripped of unnecessary complications or repetitions. A third type of simplification strengthens or weakens the original concept, but with the intention of exhibiting what is seen as essential in it. A fourth type abandons the original concept in favour of one that is seen as more useful for developing logical theory.

12.2.1 Definition: The Arabic Tradition

Khaled El-Rouayheb has made a study of different versions of the definition in Arabic logic beginning with Al-Fārābī (d. 950). Fārābī counts ordinary-language arguments as syllogisms, provided that they can be expressed in the Aristotelian syllogistic language without loss of meaning (El-Rouayheb 2010a, 16). He defines a syllogism as a statement in which things more than one are posited; and if these are composed together then something else is implied by them necessarily, by themselves and not by accident. The genus statement is taken in the sense of the pair of premises; however, the premises are seen, not simply as the expression of a given content, but as directed towards a specific conclusion. In this definition there are five differentiae:

A. There are several premises.
B. The conclusion is different from the premises.
C. The premises imply the conclusion necessarily.
D. The premises imply the conclusion by themselves.
E. The implication does not hold by accident.

Point B could be understood in two different ways. It might be taken as meaning that no inference of the form

$$\frac{p \quad q}{p} \tag{1}$$

is a syllogism, no matter what proposition is put in the place of q (because in no such inference is the conclusion distinct from all the premises). Or it might be taken as meaning that no inference is a syllogism in virtue of having the above form. Taking it the first way, the inference

$$\frac{\text{Every horse neighs} \quad \text{Everything that neighs neighs}}{\text{Every horse neighs}} \tag{2}$$

is not a syllogism. Taking it the second way, (2) is not a syllogism in virtue of having the form (1); however, it is a syllogism in virtue of having the form:

$$\frac{\text{Every } A \text{ is } B \quad \text{Every } B \text{ is } C}{\text{Every } A \text{ is } C} \tag{3}$$

This is a distinction to which we shall return.

In his *al-Shifā'* (*The Cure*) Avicenna (Ibn Sīnā, d. 1037) essentially repeats al-Fārābī's definition (El-Rouayheb 2010a, 18), giving explanations of what is meant by points C–E.

Point C contrasts syllogistic inferences with inferences in which the conclusion is implied (*yalzamu*) by the premises, though not with necessity – inferences like

$$\frac{\text{No human is a horse} \quad \text{Every horse neighs}}{\text{No human neighs}} \tag{4}$$

This is a combination of a universal negative minor and a universal affirmative major in the first figure; and according to Aristotle such a combination does not produce a syllogistic conclusion. El-Rouayheb comments that in saying that the conclusion of (4) is implied but not with necessity, Avicenna would seem to be invoking a distinction between material and formal productivity (El-Rouayheb 2010a, 20). If that is right, then point C opposes syllogistic inferences to materially productive inferences. The idea of material productivity is discussed below.

Aristotle explains the single Greek phrase *toi tauta einai* ('because these things are so') in his definition: needing no further term from outside for the necessity to come about (Smith 1989, 24b20). In the Arabic tradition, this becomes two distinct points, D and E.

According to Avicenna, point D rules out inferences which rely on one or more unstated premises – inferences like

$$\frac{A \text{ is equal to } J \quad J \text{ is equal to } B}{A \text{ is equal to } B} \tag{5}$$

Both (4) and (5) can be turned into a syllogism by the addition of an extra premise. But there is a difference; in (5) the extra premise expressing the transitivity of equality is *necessarily true*, whereas in (4) the extra premise 'What horses do, humans don't' is certainly not necessarily true (and indeed, if understood as applying to *everything* that horses do, would have to be judged necessarily false according to Aristotelian theory).

The parts of a substance are such that if they are destroyed, so is a substance	The destruction of what is not a substance does not imply the destruction of a substance

The parts of a substance are substances

$$(6)$$

According to Avicenna, these premises necessitate the conclusion, and do so syllogistically, but only accidentally, since they are not stated in syllogistic form. They contain a syllogism, which becomes evident when they are restated as follows:

The parts of a substance are such that if they are destroyed, so is a substance	Everything such that if it is destroyed, a substance is destroyed, is a substance

The parts of a substance are substances (7)

In all of (4)–(6), the premises need to be changed in order for a syllogism to result. They differ in that (4)–(5) need to be *supplemented* by at least one additional premise in order for there to be a necessary inference, whereas in (6) the inference is already necessary but the premises need to be *transformed* into the language of the syllogistic theory in order for the inference to be a syllogistic one.

In Avicenna's *Najāt* (*Deliverance*), the definition of syllogism includes the same set of differentiae as in *The Cure* (Ibn Sīnā 2011, 42). But in his later *al-Ishārāt* (*Pointers and Reminders*), he adopts a simplified definition of the syllogism as a statement composed of statements which, if the propositions expressed in the statements are conceded, implies by itself another (El-Rouayheb 2010a, 21). This definition, with minor variations, was to become standard among those Arabic logicians who took their lead from Avicenna. For example, Najm al-Dīn al-Kātibī's (d. 1276/7) *Shamsiyya* defines a syllogism as a statement composed of propositions which, when conceded, imply by themselves another statement (El-Rouayheb 2010a, 80), and Afḍal al-Din al-Khūnajī's *Jumal* defines a syllogism as a statement, composed of statements, that implies another statement (El-Rouayheb 2010a, 72).

Thus, the standardised Arabic definition of the syllogism after Avicenna retains only three of the five differentiae that were present in *The Cure*'s definition. Missing are points D and E. The first of these simplifications is perhaps motivated by a desire for elegance: maybe C already implies D. But the omission of point E seems more significant. In *The Cure* Avicenna had taken it to rule out inferences that need transforming into syllogistic form; so the omission of this point perhaps signifies a narrowing of interest to the core of syllogistic theory, leaving aside the process of putting informal arguments into syllogistic form.

The resulting conception of syllogism (namely, a necessary inference from several premises to a distinct conclusion) appears to imply that (5) is a syllogism.

On the question of the definition of the syllogism, as on many other matters, Averroes (Ibn Rushd al-Ḥafīd, d. 1198) does not belong to the mainstream of the Arabic tradition. In his Middle Commentary on *Prior Analytics*, Averroes defines the syllogism as a statement that, if things more than one are posited in it, then something else different from it is implied with necessity from these posited things by themselves and not accidentally. Here we see all of points A to E. Averroes appears to be returning to Avicenna's fuller definition in *The Cure*, or to its model in Al Fārābī (El-Rouayheb 2010a, 14, 30).

Besides the Middle Commentary, Averroes composed an Epitome of *Prior Analytics*. In this work he attempts to provide a rational basis for the components in the Aristotelian definition of the syllogism. The conclusion must be other than the premises (point B), he argues, because it is the function of the syllogism to lead from the known to the unknown, and the same proposition cannot be both known and unknown. At the same time, the conclusion must follow necessarily from the premises (point C), because if it had merely to be possible in relation to the premises, then two opposite conclusions could simultaneously be yielded by the same premises (Ibn Rushd 1562, 344va, 43).

In the Middle Commentary, he pursues his general anti-Avicennian aims of returning to the texts of Aristotle and of showing that Aristotle's theorisation is better than that of all other people (Street 2015). Here he glosses the Aristotelian definition of the syllogism (Ibn Rushd 1562, 54rb, 10), appealing to what Aristotle himself says about the syllogism later in *Prior Analytics*, and he gives reasons for believing the definition to be a sound one. For example, in explaining point A, he refers to Aristotle's statement that nothing follows syllogistically from a single premise (Aristotle 1965, 34a16). Again, in explaining point C he refers to the Aristotelian distinction between necessary and non-necessary consequences in *Prior Analytics* (47a22), syllogistic consequences being necessary, but inductive or analogical inferences being non-necessary. (Avicenna had taken point C to rule out inferences whose validity was material rather than formal.) And, in explaining point E, he refers to conclusions that follow materially rather than formally (Ibn Rushd 1562, 2I), such as when a conclusion follows materially from a pair of affirmatives in the second figure if the extreme terms are convertible. (Avicenna, by contrast, had taken point E to rule out arguments like the parts of substance argument, which are not properly expressed in the regimented language of Aristotelian syllogistic.)

Concerning syllogisms from a pair of affirmatives in the second figure, presumably Averroes' idea is that we can infer a conclusion from the premises *Every B is A, Every C is A* if we assume that two of the terms are coextensive. If B and A are coextensive, then we may conclude that every C is B:

$$\frac{\text{Every } C \text{ is } A \quad \text{Every } A \text{ is } B}{\text{Every } C \text{ is } B} \quad \text{Every } B \text{ is } A \tag{8}$$

But notice that here we make no use of *Every B is A*, and the operative inference is in the first figure not the second. If C and A are coextensive, then we may conclude that every B is C:

$$\frac{\text{Every } B \text{ is } A \quad \text{Every } A \text{ is } C}{\text{Every } B \text{ is } C} \quad \text{Every } C \text{ is } A \tag{9}$$

But notice that *Every C is A* will be redundant, and again the operative inference is not in the second figure. So, what Averroes calls materially valid inferences in the second figure include redundant material, which when removed leaves us with formal inferences in the first figure, not the second.

Alternatively, we could make the free-standing propositions in (8) and (9) into premises. The resulting three-premised inferences

$$\frac{\text{Every } C \text{ is } A \quad \text{Every } A \text{ is } B \quad \text{Every } B \text{ is } A}{\text{Every } C \text{ is } B} \tag{10}$$

$$\frac{\text{Every } B \text{ is } A \quad \text{Every } A \text{ is } C \quad \text{Every } C \text{ is } A}{\text{Every } B \text{ is } C} \tag{11}$$

will then be syllogisms according to the standard Arabic definition, though they do not fall into any figure.

12.2.2 *Definition: The Latin Tradition*

In the Latin tradition, Aristotle's definition of the syllogism was transmitted through Boethius' (d. 524/5) translation of *Prior Analytics*. The last phrase in the definition ('from their being so') corresponds to point D in the Arabic definition. Lacking in Boethius is any idea of an inference that is syllogistic only accidentally, as in point E.

In his monograph on the syllogism, *De syllogismo categorico*, Boethius adds 'and granted' to 'being laid down', saying that the listener must grant what the proponent lays down, in order for what is in doubt to be shown by a syllogism. This comment appears to assume that syllogisms occur only when there is a proponent and a listener, and only when the conclusion is in doubt, i.e. Boethius seems to have a *dialectical* context in mind. By contrast, *Prior Analytics* presents a theory of the syllogism that is neutral between the dialectical and the demonstrative syllogism (Aristotle 1965, 24a22). Now, the context in which a demonstrative syllogism is put forward need not be a dialogical one. Furthermore, the conclusion of a demonstrative syllogism need not be in doubt; on the contrary, the conclusion may very well be a proposition whose truth is already accepted. Thus, the addition of 'granted' to the definition has the effect of narrowing the class of syllogisms to dialectical syllogisms.

Boethius follows the Greek commentators in providing glosses for the individual words and phrases of the definition. Some of his glosses make sense only if we assume that the premises of a syllogism have to be granted. For example, he takes 'something other than them' (point B) to distinguish genuine syllogisms from ridiculous syllogisms where the conclusion is found among the premises, arguing that it would be ridiculous to take what is in doubt as being granted.

He takes 'several things being laid down' (point A) to distinguish genuine syllogisms from ones that are not fully set out, having only one expressed premise (Boethius 2008, 70–71). Here, and in his other comments on the Aristotelian definition, it is noticeable that, rather than opposing syllogisms to non-syllogisms, Boethius opposes genuine syllogisms to other 'syllogisms' (which are presumably not quite genuine).

He takes the phrase 'from their being so' (point D) to mark off genuine syllogisms from inferences in which what is stated is less, or more, than what should be stated. His examples of these deficiencies are:

$$\frac{\text{Every human is an animal} \quad \text{Socrates is a human}}{\text{Socrates is animate}} \tag{12}$$

$$\frac{\text{Every animal is animate} \quad \text{Every human is an animal} \quad \text{The Sun is in Aries}}{\text{Every human is animate}} \tag{13}$$

$$\frac{\text{Every human is an animal} \quad \text{Virtue is good}}{\text{Every human is animate}} \tag{14}$$

None of (12)–(14) is in a syllogistic figure, but in each case the conclusion follows necessarily from the premises (assuming that it's necessary for animals to be animate). (12) and (14) stand in need of an extra premise if they are to achieve syllogistic status: in both cases the required premise is the proposition 'Every animal is animate'. (13) and (14) have to omit their last premise in order to be syllogistic. Thus, the role played by (12) is like that played by (5) in Avicenna's thought, i.e. to exemplify the idea of an inference in which a premise is missing. (13) and (14) testify to Boethius' interest in redundancy – an interest that is not conspicuous in the Arabic tradition. (13) illustrates both these deficiencies together. Peter Abelard (d. 1142) generally follows Boethius on the definition of the syllogism (Abelard 1970, 232). He says that inferences where the conclusion is the same as one or more of the premises are not properly called syllogisms or arguments, since they infer the very proposition that was granted as if it was in doubt. Here, he seems to share Boethius' focus on dialectical syllogisms. But elsewhere his use of the word 'granted' seems designed to distinguish syllogisms from conditional propositions. He says that the proposition 'If every human is an ass and no ass is a horse then no human is a horse' shares a structure with the syllogism

$$\frac{\text{No ass is a horse} \quad \text{Every human is an ass}}{\text{No human is a horse}} \qquad (15)$$

but in proposing the syllogism we grant the premises in the sense that we assume them for the sake of argument – something which we do not do in proposing the conditional proposition.

He takes the clause in the definition specifying that the conclusion arises 'from their being laid down' to mean that the entailment is *perfect* in the sense that the structure of the antecedent propositions in a way already indicates the structure of the conclusion (Abelard 1970, 233; Martin 2010, 167). This distinguishes the syllogism from structures in which what is stated is more or less than what should be stated for the necessity to come about. To illustrate this point he gives variants on examples (12)–(14).

Robert Kilwardby (d. 1279) saw the Aristotelian definition as encoding properties of the syllogism which are fully specified only later in *Prior Analytics*. This recalls the interpretive approach adopted by Averroes. But Kilwardby's treatment involves complexities not found in Averroes. His treatment is elaborate; we here summarise the main points (see Thom 2007, 41).

Two novelties are evident. First, he takes 'several things being laid down' to encode two distinct features of the syllogism. Like all other expositors, he takes point A to be part of the definition, and to be expressed in the phrase 'several things'. But he takes 'laid down' to refer to syllogistic figure and mood (Kilwardby 2016; Lectio 4,33). Categorical syllogisms that contain only common terms possess a figure and mood; but categorical syllogisms containing singular terms do not possess mood, even though they possess figure. (He doesn't accept inferences containing singular terms as properly syllogistic.) Thus, in place of point E, he adopts

E′. The premises are in a figure and in a mood.

Secondly, Kilwardby understands 'something other than them' and 'from their being so' respectively as identifying two of the fallacies discussed in *Prior Analytics* II – Begging the Question and False Cause – insofar as they are considered as faults against the syllogism as such (Kilwardby 2016; Lectio 4,39). Thus, he understands point B to imply that a syllogism does not beg the question. (For these fallacies, see Smith 1989, 204 and 209.) And in place of point D he adopts

D′. The premises do not commit the fallacy of false cause, and thus do not contain redundant material.

The great fourteenth-century Latin logicians, William Ockham (d. 1347) and John Buridan (d. 1358), adopt significant simplifications of the Aristotelian definition of the syllogism, but in different ways. Ockham accepts the view that a syllogism must be in a figure and mood: A syllogism is a locution in which a conclusion follows of necessity from two premises arranged in figure and mood (Ockham 1974a, 3.1.1.1). This redefinition accepts Kilwardby's gloss on 'laid down', but omits the requirement that the conclusion be different from the premises, and omits 'from their being so'. He defines the syllogism through points A, C and E'.

Ockham has here broadened the class of Aristotelian syllogisms so as to include Boethius' ridiculous syllogisms as syllogisms, thus also rejecting Kilwardby's idea that Begging the Question and False Cause are syllogistic fallacies whose occurrence prevents an inference from having the status of a syllogism. Inferences committing these fallacies fall squarely within Ockham's redefinition, in the form of syllogisms where the conclusion repeats one of the premises, or whose conclusion follows from a proper subset of the premises.

It comes as no surprise, then, when Ockham discusses these fallacies, that he rejects Kilwardby's view according to which they can be considered as faults belonging properly to the syllogism as such. Instead, Ockham argues that they belong to the arguer rather than the argument:

> After the fallacies in respect of which it is the *arguments* that are at fault, being formally faulty, we must speak about fallacies in respect of which it is not sophistical arguments that are at fault but in respect of which it is the *opponent* who is at fault in arguing against the respondent. Of which the first is Begging the Question, which happens when the opponent, even if he infers the conclusion which he means to, still cannot convince the respondent, because he assumes what he should be proving. (Ockham 1974a, 3.4.15)

Some of the rules that apply to Aristotle's syllogisms no longer apply under Ockham's redefinition. For instance, there are no Aristotelian syllogisms from a pair of affirmative premises in the second figure; but there are such syllogisms according to Ockham's definition, which allows for syllogisms with singular or quantified terms in predicate position (Ockham 1974a, 3.1.1.13; see Parsons 2014, 67ff.).

Buridan, in his *Questions on the Prior Analytics*, rejects Kilwardby's reading of 'laid down' as referring to syllogistic figure and mood. He defines a syllogism as a formally valid inference in which a conclusion that is distinct mentally as well as verbally from the premises follows of necessity:

> Again, you might note that, even though everyone generally says that the words 'laid down' should be glossed as meaning 'arranged in the right figure and the right mood', so as to exclude induction and many other unarranged inferences, still I believe that that exposition is unsuitable, because what a syllogism is shouldn't be explicated on the basis of its being in a good mood and in a good figure; but which are the right moods and which the useless ones should be explicated from that definition. Nor is it true that all the syllogisms about which determinations are made in this book are in these three figures, as will be seen later. And accordingly I believe that however often from some premises being posited there follows of necessity a conclusion that is not only verbally but also mentally different from those premises, and from each one of them, there is always then a good syllogism, so long as the inference is formal. (Buridan n.d., Book 1, q. 3 – my translation)

Syllogisms with more than two premises, and syllogisms from a hypothesis, are not in a figure. (For 'syllogisms from a hypothesis', see the discussion of syllogisms *per impossibile* below.) Furthermore, according to Buridan, hypothetical syllogisms such as (16) and (17) are not in a figure.

$$\frac{\text{If a man runs, an animal runs} \quad \text{A man runs}}{\text{An animal runs}} \tag{16}$$

$$\frac{\text{Every man is rational or irrational} \quad \text{No man is irrational}}{\text{Every man is rational}} \tag{17}$$

And syllogisms having a term negated in one premise and unnegated in the other, such as (18), are not in a figure.

$$\frac{\text{No non-}B \text{ is } A \quad \text{No } C \text{ is } B}{\text{No } C \text{ is } A} \qquad (18)$$

Finally, syllogisms, such as (19), in which a term occurs once in the nominative and once in an oblique grammatical case, are not in a figure.

$$\frac{\text{Socrates sees every horse} \quad \text{Brownie is a horse}}{\text{Socrates sees Brownie}} \qquad (19)$$

 This conception of the syllogism weakens Ockham's notion, dropping the latter's restriction to inferences in a figure.

 However, Buridan retains the traditional requirement that the conclusion be other than the premises. His definition comprises points A, B, C. (But we should add point D, if we take it that his requirement that the inference be a formal one implies acceptance of D.) Thus, he can retain Kilwardby's view that certain cases of Begging the Question and False Cause are faults belonging to the syllogism as such:

> The first conclusion is that the question-begging which comes about immediately errs against the syllogism if it appears to be a syllogism: because it is not a syllogism, since it does not satisfy the definition of the syllogism in respect of the clause 'it is necessary for something other to follow', so that each one of the premises ought to be other than the conclusion. (Buridan n.d., Book 2, q. 14)

This weakening of the concept of syllogism that we see in Ockham and Buridan went along with an expansion of the theory of logic to cover types of reasoning that were not directly covered by Aristotle, e.g. reasoning with grammatically oblique or negative terms. For Kilwardby, these sorts of reasoning could, and should, be resolved into standard categorical syllogisms; thus, their consideration belonged not within the theory of logic, but in the area where that theory comes into relation with pre-theoretical language. However,

Table 12.1 *Definitions of the syllogism*

	E′	D′	A	B	C	D	E
Avicenna₁							
Averroes							
Boethius							
Abelard							
Avicenna₂							
Buridan							
Kilwardby							
Ockham							

for Ockham and Buridan these are distinctive types of reasoning, re-quiring their own logical theory. The various authors' inclusion of points A to E′ are given in Table 12.1.

12.3 SYLLOGISMS *PER IMPOSSIBILE* AND CONVERSIVE SYLLOGISMS

Most medieval logicians took the definition of 'syllogism' to apply univocally to both categorical and hypothetical syllogisms such as:

$$\frac{\text{If } p \text{ then } q \quad \text{Not } q}{\text{Not } p} \tag{20}$$

Now, some of the transformations to which syllogisms are sub-ject occur only in categorical syllogisms, e.g. the process of direct reduction, whereby in certain cases the subject and predicate of a syllogistic premise can be interchanged. Other transformations are common to hypothetical and categorical syllogisms, e.g. the process of indirect reduction, whereby the contradictory of a premise can be interchanged with the contradictory of the conclusion. Clearly, such a transformation can occur regardless of whether the premises are hypothetical or categorical propositions, provided only that the notion of 'contradictory' is defined for them. This latter process is often called proof *per impossibile*.

Aristotle speaks of demonstrations *per impossibile* in two different, but related, types of case. He describes the indirect reduction of one *syllogism* to another as a proof *per impossibile* (Aristotle 1965, 28b14). And he applies the same description to a type of argumentation in which a *proposition* is proved true by showing that its opposite implies something false or impossible. He contrasts demonstrations *per impossibile* in this second sense with what he calls ostensive demonstrations, i.e. ones where the sought-after proposition is argued for *directly* by stating reasons for believing it to be true (Aristotle 1965, 62b29). In the first type of case, an inference is shown to be syllogistic by showing that it is a transformation of an already accepted syllogism; nothing is refuted, and the reasoning proceeds from what is already known. In the second type of case, a proposition is demonstrated as true indirectly, by refuting its opposite: the demonstration is effected by showing that if we suppose the opposite of the sought-after proposition, we will be led into a false or impossible consequence.

Aristotle himself recognises the difference between the two types of demonstration *per impossibile*, distinguishing between a conversive syllogism (i.e. the indirect reduction of one syllogism to another) and a syllogism *per impossibile* strictly speaking (i.e. the refutation of a proposition *per impossibile*) (Aristotle 1965, 61a22). In what follows, we follow this distinction, using the expression '*per impossibile* syllogism' for the second type of case; for the first type we use the expression 'conversive syllogism'.

Perhaps because of the ambiguity of the designation 'demonstration *per impossibile*' in Aristotle, medieval logicians devoted quite a bit of attention to the analysis of conversive and *per impossibile* syllogisms. Let us start with syllogisms *per impossibile*, and then move on to conversive syllogisms.

12.3.1 Syllogisms Per Impossibile

Logicians in both the Arabic and Latin traditions attempted to analyse the *per impossibile* syllogism as a pair of ostensive syllogisms. Here is Avicenna:

The real way to go about it – in fact, the way taken by the First Teacher [Aristotle] – is that, for example, we make *Not every J is B* the proposition to be proved. Then we say: 'if *Not every J is B* is false, then every J is B'. From one of the recombinant syllogisms that we have discussed [in *Syllogism*, vi], attaching a true premise to it, viz. *Every B is A* yields the following [connective] hypothetical: 'if *Not every J is B* is false, then every J is A'. Then we say: 'but not every J is A', since it is an impossible contradiction. We have, therefore, asserted the contradictory of the consequent, which yields the contradictory of the antecedent, viz. *Every J is B*. (Karimullah 2015, 227)

The two syllogisms are

$$\frac{\text{If } \textit{Not every J is B} \text{ is false then every J is B} \quad \text{Every B is A}}{\text{If } \textit{Not every J is B} \text{ is false then every J is A}} \qquad (21)$$

$$\frac{\text{If } \textit{Not every J is B} \text{ is false then every J is A} \quad \text{Not every J is A}}{\textit{Not every J is B} \text{ is not false}} \qquad (22)$$

Avicenna here makes use of his concept of a *recombinant* syllogism, i.e. a syllogism whose premises do not mention either the conclusion or the conclusion's contradictory (Hodges 2013, 1). These include all the standard Aristotelian categorical syllogisms. But, as Avicenna points out, recombinant syllogisms also include some conditional syllogisms (Hodges 2013, 2). In fact, the inference we call hypothetical syllogism is one such. The conclusion 'If p then r' does not appear among the premises 'If p then q' and 'If q then r', and neither does its contradictory; and yet all its propositions are conditionals. (21) is recombinant, but (22) is not.

(22) is a particular case of (20), and thus its validity is a commonplace. But what is the basis for the validity of (21)? Evidently, its validity depends in some way on that of (3). But it is not obvious how the validity of (3) implies that of (21).

Perhaps the answer is that Avicenna is assuming (23)

If $\dfrac{q_1 \quad q_2}{r}$ is a syllogism then $\dfrac{\text{If } p \text{ then } q_1 \quad q_2}{\text{If } p \text{ then } r}$ is a syllogism (23)

But to make (23) a primitive rule, to be used in explaining how syllogisms *per impossibile* work, would seem an odd procedure, since such syllogisms seem to be more easily grasped than (23).

However Avicenna's analysis of *per impossibile* syllogism is to be understood, it was not adopted by Averroes, who proposed the following analysis:

> Now concerning the syllogism of the impossible, we say that it is composed of a conditional and a categorical. And so we use it in the following way. When we wish to show the truth of some statement, we will take its contradictory and link it with a true premise whose truth is not in doubt, and they will form one of the combinations of parts in some figure which will be possible among the figures of categoricals. And so long as a conclusion of manifest falsity is concluded, we will know that the falsity does not come from the syllogistic combination (since it was a concludent combination), nor also from the true premise. So it will remain only that it will be from the contradictory of the doubtful premise. And as long as its contradictory is false, it is true. (Ibn Rushd 1562, 50F)

Averroes intends to show that the *per impossibile* syllogism can be analysed without appealing to Avicenna's notion of a recombinant syllogism: it is a pair of (ostensive) hypothetical syllogisms, the first of which has a conditionalised syllogism as its major premise. Let *Not p* be the proposition to be demonstrated. Let there be a syllogism (categorical or hypothetical) '*p, q, so r*', where *q* is true, and *r* is false. Then the reasoning can be represented as in (24)

$$\dfrac{\dfrac{\text{If } p \text{ and } q \text{ then } r \quad \text{Not } r}{\text{Either not } p \text{ or not } q \quad \quad \text{Not not } q}}{\text{Not } p}$$

(24)

Like Averroes, Kilwardby thinks that a *per impossibile* syllogism can be reduced to a pair of ostensive syllogisms. The first is a modus ponens (or, as Kilwardby says, a positing of the antecedent), whose major premise takes the form 'If X is a proof then Y is a proof'. The second syllogism does not actually occur in the reasoning, but is referred to by the first syllogism's minor premise, as shown in (25).

If 'q and r imply p; q is true; $not-r$ is false' is a proof of p then '$not-p$ and q imply $not-r$; q is true; $not-r$ is false' is a proof of p

'q and r imply p; q is true; $not-r$ is false' is a proof of p

'$not-p$ and q imply $not-r$; q is true; $not-r$ is false' is a proof of p

$$(25)$$

Here is what he says: "For from an added major proposition that is a conditional there comes about a hypothetical syllogism and it is deduced through a topical relation, *viz.* from positing the antecedent" (Kilwardby 2016; Lectio 45,176). He agrees with Aristotle that a syllogism *per impossibile* is a type of syllogism from a hypothesis (Aristotle 1965, 50a29), i.e. an argument that takes a certain indirect approach to the problem of proving a given conclusion. Instead of deriving the sought-after conclusion from premises taken to be true, one proves a proxy conclusion, on the understanding that if the proxy conclusion is proven then p will be taken to have been proven. In Kilwardby's analysis of the syllogism *per impossibile*, this understanding is expressed by his major premise, which states that you can prove a proposition by showing that the supposition of its falsity, together with an admitted truth, implies an admitted falsehood. What this understanding rests on is the principle of the conversive syllogism.

12.3.2 *Conversive Syllogisms and the Nature of the Syllogism*

In Aristotle's syllogistic, when two inferences are related as conversives, if one them is a syllogism then so is the other, i.e. rule (26) is valid.

If $\dfrac{p \quad q}{r}$ is a syllogism then $\dfrac{p \quad not\text{-}r}{not\text{-}q}$ is a syllogism

$$(26)$$

Anyone wishing to retain this feature of the syllogism while accepting a definition of the syllogism which does not preserve this feature faces a problem: there will be pairs of inferences, only one of which is a syllogism according to the definition, even though according to (26) both should be syllogistic or else neither.

Now, the standard Arabic definition of the syllogism (Avicenna$_2$ in Table 12.1) does not preserve the above feature. So anyone accepting that definition along with (26) will face a problem concerning certain inferences from a pair of mutually contradictory premises. For example, (27) is syllogistic by the definition.

$$\dfrac{\text{Every horse neighs} \quad \text{Not every horse neighs}}{\text{Not everything that neighs neighs}}$$

$$(27)$$

Its two premises necessarily imply a distinct conclusion. But, by rule (26), if (27) is a syllogism, so is (2). And yet, according to the definition (2) is not a syllogism, because its conclusion is the same as one of its premises.

It might seem that the problem can be addressed simply by distinguishing between an inference and the principle in virtue of which the inference holds. (2) and (27) hold in virtue of the principles (3) and (28).

$$\dfrac{\text{Every } A \text{ is } B \quad \text{Not every } A \text{ is } C}{\text{Not every } B \text{ is } C}$$

$$(28)$$

And both of these principles satisfy definition Avicenna$_2$. So it might seem that if the definition is understood as picking out a property of principles of inference, rather than a property of inferences, then that property will be preserved in the process of indirect reduction.

Not so. The problem reappears at the level of the most general principles of inference. For (29) and (1) are related as conversives.

$$\frac{p \quad not-p}{q} \tag{29}$$

But (29) satisfies the definition Avicenna$_2$, whereas (1) does not. But what did the Arabic logicians think about (29)? El-Rouayheb states: The principle that a necessarily false proposition implies any proposition, and that a necessarily true proposition is implied by any proposition, ... seem never to have been accepted, or even seriously entertained, by Arabic logicians (El-Rouayheb 2009, 209). If Avicenna and his successors never seriously entertained (29) even though it satisfies a definition of the syllogism which they accepted, the question arises *why* they did not think of it as a syllogism. The reason may be found in the Arabic logicians' concern with the broader question of whether there is *anything* that follows from an impossible antecedent (or whether there are any true conditionals with impossible antecedents). El-Rouayheb remarks that, in Avicenna's opinion, the answer to this latter question depends on what type of conditional we are talking about. If the conditional is supposed to hold in itself, it is false when the antecedent is impossible; but if it is merely deduced with necessity (Nabil Shehaby's translations of Avicenna in Shehaby 1973, 41), it may be true when the antecedent is impossible (El-Rouayheb 2009, 213). Given a distinction between inferences that hold in themselves and inferences that merely hold with necessity, it seems Avicenna is committed to claiming that an inference like (27) may hold with necessity, but it cannot hold in itself; and any principle governing (27), if *it* holds in itself, cannot have an impossible antecedent.

Whether or not this was Avicenna's meaning, it is clear that his commentator Naṣīr al-Dīn al-Ṭūsī (d. 1274) was of this mind. Ṭūsī allows that some things follow from an impossible antecedent, but he thinks that in such cases what follows does not follow in virtue of the antecedent's impossibility: The impossible insofar as it is impossible ... cannot be judged to imply something, but can be judged not to imply something (El-Rouayheb 2009, 217). So Ṭūsī recognised within syllogistic theory a distinction between inferences and the principles in virtue of which they hold, and saw that, while a syllogism can have mutually incompatible premises, the principle in virtue of which it holds cannot. In doing so, he anticipated an important result of Timothy Smiley's. According to Smiley, the Aristotelian syllogistic presupposes a distinction within the class of necessary inferences. Unlike some necessary inferences, a syllogistic necessitation never holds in virtue of having impossible premises or a necessary conclusion. Syllogistic necessitations hold only in virtue of principles which apply regardless of the necessity or impossibility of their premises and conclusion considered by themselves (Smiley 1973, 145).

Smiley's account employs the notion of the *antilogism* corresponding to a given syllogism, i.e. the set of premises plus the contradictory of the conclusion. A syllogism and its conversive syllogisms all have the same antilogism. Now, if we exclude syllogisms that are not most general (i.e. that involve the identification of distinct variables), then the members of any syllogism's antilogism are such that they cannot all be true together but the members of any proper subset can all be true together (Smiley 1973, 143). This is the property of the syllogism that explains why (1) and (29) are not syllogistic principles. In both of these cases, the antilogism has a proper subset whose members cannot all be true together: the members of the antilogism are p, q and $\neg p$, where p and $\neg p$ cannot be true together.

For Ṭūsī, the standard Arabic definition of the syllogism has to be understood as a definition of syllogistic principles, and the latter have to be necessitations whose antecedent is not impossible (and – we may assume – whose consequent is not necessary). Such principles are transformable as conversive syllogisms; and thus (1) and (29) are equivalent: one is syllogistic if and only if the other is syllogistic. In this instance, neither is syllogistic.

In the Latin tradition, the question of inferences from impossible premises was widely discussed in the twelfth century. The followers of Adam of Balsham (d. c. 1159), the *Parvipontani*, held that everything follows from a self-contradiction. William of Soissons (d. 1167) devised what was to become the classic proof of this theorem:

1. *p and not−p*
2. *p*
3. *p or q*
4. *not−p*
5. *q*   (30)

Other logicians at the time, followers of Robert of Melun, the *Melidunenses*, maintained on the contrary that nothing follows from a falsehood, and thus nothing follows from a contradiction (Martin 2012, 302).

In the mid-thirteenth century, Robert Kilwardby proposed a theory that in a way combined these two accounts. His theory is based on two distinctions: that between natural (or essential) and accidental inferences, and that between an inference and the principle in virtue of which it holds.

The idea of a natural inference is found in the *Syncategoremata* of William of Sherwood (died before 1272). William contrasts natural with accidental inferences, saying that in a natural inference the consequent follows from the antecedent in respect of some state of the one relative to the other and that in a non-natural inference it follows solely because of the impossibility of the antecedent or the necessity of the consequent (William of Sherwood 1941, 80).

Kilwardby, like Sherwood, holds that in a natural inference the consequent is understood in the antecedent (Kilwardby 2016; Lectio 55,78). According to him, syllogisms are natural inferences, as is the inference of a disjunction from either of its disjuncts. However, the inference of an arbitrary proposition from a contradiction is not natural but accidental (unless it happens to be governed by a principle which satisfies the definition of a natural inference, as the inference 'You are sitting and you are not sitting, so either you are sitting and you are not sitting, or evil exists' is governed by the principle that a disjunction may be inferred from one of its disjuncts).

Kilwardby applies the distinction between an inference and the principle in virtue of which it holds to inferences in which a disjunction is inferred from one or other of the disjuncts. He says that the two inferences

You are sitting, so you are sitting or you are not sitting (31)

You are not sitting, so you are sitting or you are not sitting (32)

hold in virtue of two distinct principles (Kilwardby 2016; Lectio 55,84). And we can see that there are two distinct principles here:

p, so p or q (33)

q, so p or q (34)

Evidently, Kilwardby regards these two forms as distinct, even though they both fall under the description 'arguing from one disjunct to the disjunction'.

Now, Kilwardby sides with the *Parvipontani* in accepting the theorem that everything follows from a contradiction – insofar as the theorem is applied to accidental inferences. He does not discuss the theorem's proof; but he is committed to accepting all the steps in the proof as natural inferences. For, (a) he accepts Disjunction-Introduction (step 2–3), of which Conjunction-Elimination (step 1–2 and step 1–4) is the dual; and (b) he accepts syllogistic inferences (and step 3–5 is a hypothetical syllogism). All the steps are natural inferences; but if we put all the steps together, arguing from the first to the last, we get an inference that is not natural. This is because, while each step is governed by a principle that is not specific to impossible antecedents, the principle governing the end result (*p and not p, so q*) is specific to inferences with an impossible antecedent. There is no other valid principle in virtue of which the end result holds. Moreover, it seems that no valid inference at all holds in virtue of a principle having an impossible premise; and in this sense Kilwardby sides with the *Melidunenses*. If this is right, then Kilwardby is committed to a view that is substantially the same as Ṭūsī's doctrine that, while there are syllogisms with impossible premises, no syllogism holds by virtue of the impossibility of its premises; and to this extent both logicians appear to have anticipated Smiley's account of syllogistic implication.

12.4 SUMMARY

The Aristotelian definition of the syllogism, as it was transmitted in Arabic, underwent a number of simplifications in the later writings of Avicenna, simplifications that were widely, though not universally, adopted in the Arabic tradition. In the Latin tradition, things started a little differently, with a focus on dialectical syllogisms; and the Latins took an interest in redundancy that does not seem to have been prominent among the Arabs. A tendency towards simplification is evident in both traditions. Some of these simplifications had the effect of broadening the class of syllogisms, some providing it with a more elegant definition. In both traditions, interest came to focus on syllogistic theory itself, at the expense of its application to everyday argumentation.

Both traditions were exercised about the question whether *per impossibile* reasoning could be analysed into some combination of ostensive syllogisms. Avicenna's view, highly original though it was, was not universally taken up by later logicians; many preferred to stay closer to what Aristotle had said on the matter.

Both traditions reflected on the question whether there are syllogisms from impossible premises. These reflections led a few logicians in both traditions to semantic insights that to some extent anticipate Smiley's work on the syllogism.[1]

---

[1] I would like to express my thanks to Tony Street for his generous and invaluable help with some of this material. I also thank E. J. Ashworth for her helpful suggestions.

13 Consequence

Gyula Klima

13.1 THE LIMITATIONS OF ARISTOTELIAN SYLLOGISTIC AND THE NEED FOR NON-SYLLOGISTIC CONSEQUENCES

Medieval theories of consequences are theories of logical validity, providing tools to judge the correctness of various forms of reasoning. Although Aristotelian syllogistic was regarded as the primary tool for achieving this, the limitations of syllogistic with regard to valid non-syllogistic forms of reasoning, as well as the limitations of formal deductive systems in detecting fallacious forms of reasoning in general, naturally provided the theoretical motivation for its supplementation with theories dealing with non-syllogistic, non-deductive, as well as fallacious inferences. We can easily produce deductively valid forms of inference that are clearly not syllogistic, as in propositional logic or in relational reasoning, or even other types of sound reasoning that are not strictly deductively valid, such as enthymemes, probabilistic arguments, and inductive reasoning, while we can just as easily provide examples of inferences that appear to be legitimate instances of syllogistic forms, yet are clearly fallacious (say, because of equivocation). For Aristotle himself, this sort of supplementation of his syllogistic was provided mostly in terms of the doctrine of "immediate inferences"[1] in his *On Interpretation*, various types of non-syllogistic or even non-deductive inferences in the *Topics*, and the doctrine of logical fallacies, in his *Sophistical Refutations*. Taking their cue primarily from Aristotle (but drawing on Cicero, Boethius, and others), medieval logicians worked out in systematic

[1] In this chapter, I will use this phrase broadly, to refer to medieval doctrines covering logical relations between two categorical propositions sharing both of their terms, *viz.* the doctrine of the Square of Opposition and its expansions as well as the doctrine of conversions.

detail various theories of non-syllogistic inferences, sometimes as supplementations of Aristotelian syllogistic, sometimes as merely useful devices taken to be reducible to syllogistic, and sometimes as more comprehensive theories of valid inference, containing syllogistic as a special, and important, case.

13.2   A BRIEF SURVEY OF HISTORICAL SOURCES

Accordingly, the characteristically medieval theories of non-syllogistic inferences were originally inspired by Aristotle's logical works other than his *Analytics*. Aristotle's relevant ideas were handed down to medieval thinkers by Boethius' translations of and commentaries on Porphyry's *Isagoge* and Aristotle's *Categories* and *On Interpretation*, along with Boethius' own logical works, the most relevant to the development of consequences being his *De Hypotheticis Syllogismis* and *De Topicis Differentiis*.

As Christopher Martin has convincingly argued, it was not until Abelard's "discovery of propositionality", that is, the applicability of truth-functional logical operators (in particular, propositional negation and conjunction) to propositions of any complexity, that medieval logicians found the conceptual resources to develop what we would recognize as propositional logic (Martin 2009, 2012). However, Abelard's own project, retaining certain elements of Boethius' non-truth-functional treatment of conditionals, was proven to be inconsistent by Alberic of Paris (sometime in the 1130s), leading to a great controversy in the middle of the twelfth century (see the chapter "Latin Logic up to 1200" in this volume). A number of schools, each gathered around a famous master (see the same chapter), provided a number of different solutions to the problem. Eventually, the solution of the *Parvipontani* prevailed, endorsing the claim that from an impossible proposition anything follows, *ex impossibili quodlibet* (and the complementary claim that a necessary proposition follows from anything, *necessarium ex quolibet*).

It is against this background that by the fourteenth century the literature specifically devoted to consequences crops up and flourishes, either in specific smaller works (such as Burley's, Buridan's, or Billingham's treatises on consequences) or as parts of larger works (such as Ockham's treatment of consequences in his *Summa Logicae*, or the treatment of consequences provided by Buridan in his *Summulae de Dialectica*). During the fourteenth century, two doctrinally quite clearly separable traditions developed. One of these is the Parisian tradition, represented by John Buridan, Albert of Saxony, Marsilius of Inghen, and others. The other is the English tradition, represented by Richard Billingham, Robert Fland, Ralph Strode, Richard Lavenham, and others. The main doctrinal difference in question is that whereas the Parisian tradition tied the notion of formal validity to truth-preservation under all substitutions of non-logical terms, the English tradition (in line with the earlier Parisian tradition from before the fourteenth century) required a containment principle, often described in psychological terms (requiring that the understanding of the antecedent should contain the understanding of the consequent). Several authors of the fifteenth century, such as Paul of Pergula (1961, 88–89), attempted to combine these traditions in terms of further distinctions, distinguishing between "formally formal" (*consequentia formalis de forma*) and "materially formal" (*consequentia formalis de materia*) consequences. (See the chapter "The Post-Medieval Period" in this volume.)

However, for a better understanding of these doctrinal developments, we should first clarify more precisely what these authors were talking about: what are consequences, and what are their main kinds and properties?

13.3 WHAT ARE CONSEQUENCES?

Perhaps a usefully non-committal way of characterizing consequences in general would be the following: a consequence is a propositionally complex expression, i.e. one that has parts taken without the rest would constitute a proposition, such that one of its propositional parts is designated as its consequent and the others as its antecedent, connected in such a way (by means of conjunctions like 'if' and 'therefore' and their stylistic variants) that the whole expression indicates that the antecedent warrants the consequent.

This characterization, by saying that a consequence is a propositionally complex expression without specifying what kind of expression it is, does not pre-judge the issue of whether consequences are to be regarded as complex propositions or other complex phrases, such as inferences or arguments, which we would usually take to be sets of distinct propositions. Many medieval authors would provide an explicit characterization of consequences as conditionals, and then use the term to refer to arguments. Indeed, sometimes instead of the term 'consequentia', they would use the terms 'inferentia', 'consecutio', or 'illatio' equivalently. Actually, even those authors who distinguish conditional propositions from an inference or an argument in terms of whether their propositional components are asserted or unasserted (in obvious awareness of what Peter Geach would dub "the Frege-point" in Geach 1980) would subsume both under a broader notion of consequence, as Buridan does in the following passage:

[T]here are two kinds of consequence, the first of which is a conditional proposition that asserts neither the antecedent nor the consequent (e.g., 'if a donkey flies, then it has wings') but asserts only that the latter follows from the former. Such a consequence, therefore, is not an argument, for it does not conclude to anything. The other kind of consequence is an argument, given that the antecedent is known, or is known better than the consequent, and this asserts the antecedent, and from this it assertively infers the consequent. In a conditional we use the conjunction 'if', whereas in an argument we use the conjunction 'therefore'. Furthermore, ... in a conditional the conjunction is attached to the antecedent, whether the antecedent is placed before or after the consequent, as in 'If a donkey flies, then a donkey has wings' and in 'A donkey has wings, if a donkey flies', but in an argument the conjunction is attached to the consequent, as in 'Man is risible; therefore, an animal is risible'. (Buridan 2001, 7.4.5, 575; see also Klima 2004a)

It is nevertheless generally true that the propositional components of a consequence are such that one of them is designated as the consequent and the others are designated as the antecedent, and that this designation, marked by the conjunctions 'if' or 'therefore' and their stylistic variants (such as 'provided', 'hence', etc.) signifies that the consequent *follows from* the antecedent, or in other words that the antecedent *warrants* the consequent, where the verb 'warrant' is again deliberately vague to allow for a number of more specific interpretations. This is because the warranting in question can be variously interpreted both with regard to *what* it warrants and with regard to the *strength* of the warrant it requires. Of course, the most natural candidate for *what* the warrant in question has to concern would seem to be the truth of the consequent, to be warranted by the truth of the antecedent. Accordingly, a consequence would naturally be regarded as *valid* (that is, as in fact providing this warrant, which is sometimes expressed by our authors by saying that the consequence is true [*vera*], sometimes by saying that it is good [*bona*]), if the truth of the antecedent would warrant the truth of the consequent by necessity, that is to say, if it is not possible for the antecedent to be true and the consequent not to be true (which is even today the usual definition of the validity of a deductive inference).

However, a simple argument presented by John Buridan shows that interpreting the warrant provided by the antecedent in terms of truth can lead to paradoxical results in a natural language with resources for self-reference. (Cf. Klima 2004b and Dutilh Novaes 2005, and see the chapter "Sophisms and Insolubles" in this volume.) Take the proposition 'No proposition is negative; therefore no donkey is running'. The antecedent of this consequence is a negative proposition, whence it cannot be true. But then, it is not possible for the antecedent to be true and the consequent not to be true; therefore, it would seem that the consequence is valid. However, it is certainly a possible situation in which there are no negative propositions (as was actually the case, for example, before the first human being formed the first negative proposition in the first human language), in which, however, some donkey is running, which would be precisely the scenario that would have to be excluded by the consequence in question, if it were valid. So, Buridan reformulates the requirement for the validity of a consequence in terms of the correspondence-conditions of the propositions it involves. Defining the validity of a consequence by defining what its antecedent is, he writes: "Therefore, some give a different definition [of antecedent], saying that one proposition is antecedent to another, which is such that it is impossible for things to be altogether as it signifies unless they are altogether as the other signifies when they are proposed together" (Buridan 1976, 22; 2015, 67).

This definition now guarantees that even if the antecedent automatically falsifies itself whenever it is formed, its self-falsification does not automatically validate the consequence, for it still leaves open the possibility that the situation signified by the antecedent holds without that signified by the consequent. Of course, since this revision of the definition of the validity of a consequence had to be introduced only because of the possibility of a proposition token quantifying over itself in a natural language, once one keeps this possibility in mind the definition of validity need not be totally overhauled, as Buridan himself recognized, and he used the definition based on the idea of *necessary truth-preservation* (i.e. on the idea that the truth of the antecedent is "preserved" in the truth of the consequent) without further ado concerning consequences not involving such self-referential propositions.

However, this remark immediately takes us to the other aspect of the warrant the antecedent is signified to provide for the consequent in a consequence, namely, its *strength*. For when we say the idea of the validity of a consequence requires its *necessary* truth-preservation, with the idea of *necessity* we definitely indicate that the warrant excludes the *possibility* of the truth of the antecedent without the truth of the consequent. But now further obvious questions emerge. What sort of necessity is this? What grounds this necessity? Is it absolute or relative to some conditions? And can we have valid consequences with a warrant weaker than necessity, such as *probability*?

In contemporary logic, when we talk about logical validity, we primarily mean formal, deductive validity with reference to an artificial, formal language. This notion of validity is either spelled out syntactically, in terms of *deducibility* by means of deduction rules, or semantically, in terms of all *possible interpretations* of the primitive, non-logical symbols of the language (or, equivalently, provided our language has sufficient resources to express all possible evaluations, all *possible substitutions* thereof) determining all possible evaluations of our formulae, to see whether there is a possible interpretation under which the premises are true and the conclusion is false. In fact, this is what many contemporary logicians take to constitute the *logical necessity* of a valid inference: the impossibility of the truth of the premises and the falsity of the conclusion under any possible interpretation (or substitution) of their non-logical components, as opposed to their logical components that have a fixed interpretation, constituting the logical form of the formulae or the corresponding natural language sentences in question (Tarski 1983, 409–420).

One might think that this is precisely the same idea that is indicated by Aristotle's use of schematic letters in his syllogistic. However, Aristotle never quite spelled out the idea in this way, and he certainly did not apply this notion of validity to what became treated as consequences in general in the medieval literature. Furthermore, even if some of his ancient commentators did distinguish form and matter in syllogisms in the way that tied the notion of logical validity to logical form, nevertheless, in medieval theories of consequences, this was not the primary notion of validity or of the corresponding notion of the necessity of the warrant provided by the antecedent for the consequent (Read 1994; Dutilh Novaes 2012; Thom 2012a). For Boethius, the necessity of what he called a *natural consequence* is grounded in a causal relation between what is signified by the antecedent and the consequent, but he also accepts true *accidental consequences*, the truth of which simply rests on the co-occurrence of what is signified by the antecedent and the consequent (Boethius 1969, 1.3.6). Boethius' distinction between these two types of consequences persisted until it came to be replaced by the idea of *formal* as opposed to *material* validity in the fourteenth century.

Although the latter distinction already had its anticipation in Abelard (as is the case with so many other important philosophical ideas), in his remark to the effect that only that inference is "perfect with regard to the construction of the antecedent" (*perfecta quantum ad antecedentis constructionem*) in which no substitution of the terms will be "able to abrupt the consecution" (*cessari valet consecutio*), he would still regard a consequence as equally necessary if it is based on "the nature of the terms", even if it is not perfect with regard to construction (Abelard 1956, 255).

So, the necessity of a consequence for medieval thinkers is not always the necessity *we* would recognize as logical or formal necessity (based on syntactic deducibility or semantic validity, i.e. truth-preservation under all possible interpretations/substitutions of non-logical primitives), but it can also be based on our understanding of causal, metaphysical connections of the nature of things signified by the non-logical terms involved or on the conceptual containment relations of the concepts whereby we conceive of them.

Furthermore, the necessity in question may not even be some absolute necessity, but possibly dependent on actual conditions that obtain at a given time. Indeed, William of Sherwood is willing to entertain true consequences that are not necessary whether absolutely or conditionally (William of Sherwood 1966, 34–35), and he is also satisfied with mere probability in the case of topical inferences, although he always attempts to reduce them to syllogisms with at least probably true premises, the probable truth of which rests on the probability of the topical maxim. (For further details, see Section 13.5.1.)

Others, on the other hand, such as Peter of Spain, would claim that all true conditionals are necessary and all false ones are impossible, that is, that there are no contingent conditionals (Peter of Spain 2014, 114–115 n. 17). But then again, he would also admit merely probable topical consequences.

By the fourteenth century, authors also regularly distinguished between different types of consequences based on the different strengths of the warrant provided by the antecedent, although they would make the distinction not in terms of the natural or metaphysical necessity of the consequence, but rather in terms of a consistently applied criterion separating *formal* and *material* consequences, while they would also distinguish between *simple* (*simplex*) and *as of now* (*ut nunc*) consequences, which were taken to hold at all times or just for a given time, respectively.

These two distinctions could be variously related, depending on the author. For Walter Burley, for instance, the latter distinction is the primary, and it is simple consequences that he divides into natural and accidental on the basis of whether they hold in virtue of an intrinsic or an extrinsic topic (a distinction that will be explained later), respectively. The distinction between formal and material consequences comes up for Burley only in the context of solving a problem, but not as a primary distinction of basic types of consequences *per se* (Burley 2000, 85–86). For Buridan, on the other hand, the primary distinction is that between formal and material consequences, and it is only among material consequences that he draws the distinction between *simple* and *as of now* consequences. However, as we shall see in more detail, this difference is due to their interpretation of what constitutes formal validity.

For Burley, whether a consequence is formal is based on the containment principle that allows a consequence to be formal either "by reason of the form of the whole structure" or "by reason of the form of incomplex terms", as in the case of arguing affirmatively from the inferior to the superior term, for instance, 'This is a man; therefore, this is an animal' (Burley 2000, 173). But for Buridan, the formal validity of a formal consequence is dependent solely on the form of the propositions involved, where the form of a proposition is identified as its syncategorematic structure, whereas its matter is constituted by its categorematic terms. Therefore, for Buridan, a formally valid consequence is one in which the truth of the antecedent guarantees the truth of the consequent under any substitution for its categorematic terms, whence those terms can be represented by schematic letters, leaving the formal structure of the argument immediately recognizable, pretty much in the same way as in modern formal logic.

So, let us deal first with those non-syllogistic consequences that both Buridan and the Parisian tradition following him and the English tradition would have deemed to be formal on account of their logical structural features, which would not, however, fit into any syllogistic form. Then we shall consider formal consequences that only the English tradition would have deemed formal, which the Parisian tradition would have taken to be enthymematic, but reducible to a formal consequence by the addition of some further premise. Next, we shall deal with irreducibly, but still valid material consequences and the issue of what separates the two kinds, and conclude with a systematic survey of the various criteria for validity proposed by the various authors considered here, in comparison with our modern notion of logical validity.

13.4 FORMAL CONSEQUENCES

13.4.1 Syllogisms with Oblique Terms

Standard modern histories of logic used to make the claim that Aristotelian syllogistic was incapable of handling "relational reasoning", that is, deductively valid inferences that involved propositions with relational terms. However, medieval logicians were quite aware of forms of reasoning the validity of which depends not on the connection of complete syllogistic terms, which may be of any complexity, but rather on the connection of the parts of such complex terms, which in Latin are usually in some oblique case. Hence, they treated such forms of reasoning under the heading of "syllogisms with oblique terms" (*de syllogismis ex obliquis*) (see, e.g., Parsons 2014, 5.3–5.7).

Here is just a simple example from Buridan to show how this is supposed to work. Consider the following argument: 'A donkey sees every man; every king is a man; therefore, a donkey sees every king'. Clearly, the predicate of the minor premise is only a part of the predicate of the "canonical", (subject)-copula]-{predicate}, form of the major premise (using the matching parentheses to mark out the relevant parts of the major): 'A (donkey) [is] {something seeing every man}', where the predicate term 'something seeing every man' (*videns omnem hominem*) contains 'man' (*hominem*) as a distributed term in the oblique, accusative, case (that is, within the scope of a universal quantifier), but the two premises do not share an entire complex term whether in their subject or predicate position, which a valid syllogistic form would require.

Thus, to account for the validity of this argument, Buridan distinguishes between the syllogistic terms and the terms of the propositions of the syllogism:

> in syllogisms with oblique or with complex terms, it is not necessary that the syllogistic terms, namely, the middle term and the extremities, be the same as the terms of the premises and the conclusion, namely, their subjects and predicates. This is because it is permissible to carry out a subsumption under a distributed term not only if it is placed at the beginning of a proposition, but wherever it is placed. (Buridan 2001, 5.8.2, 367)

Therefore, if the oblique term of the major is distributed, then it can be replaced in the conclusion by the oblique form of the subject of the minor, when the predicate in the minor is the nominative form of the distributed oblique term of the major. Accordingly, the syllogistic terms of this syllogism can be marked out in the following manner: {major}; [middle]; (minor); 'A {donkey} sees every [man]; every (king) is a [man]; therefore, a {donkey} sees every {king}'. Buridan treats this as an example of a syllogism resembling the syllogisms of the Aristotelian first figure. He also deals with examples resembling the other Aristotelian figures in a similar manner.

13.4.2   Syllogisms with Ampliated Terms

Again, it is easiest to handle the issue of syllogisms with ampliated terms through an example (see the chapter "Supposition and Properties of Terms" in this volume for more on ampliation). Consider the following argument: 'Nothing dead is alive, but some horse (say, Alexander's horse, Bucephalus) is dead; therefore, some horse is not alive', which appears to be a perfect substitution instance of the valid syllogistic form *Ferio*, the fourth mood of the first figure (Buridan 2001, 9.5 First sophism, 914–916). However, the premises are true, and the conclusion is false, since what is actually a horse must be alive. The solution is that despite appearances to the contrary, this is not a valid instance of *Ferio*, because the term 'dead', meaning 'something that was alive but is not' *ampliates*, that is, extends the range of supposition of the term with which it is construed to past entities, so the minor should be analysed as saying 'something that was or is a horse is dead'. But then, since in the conclusion there is no such ampliation, the inference is not valid. To cancel out the ampliative force of the term 'dead', we could instead have as the minor premise, explicitly restricting the subject's reference to present horses, 'something that is a horse is dead'. This would render the argument valid, but it would not cause a problem, since then the minor is false.

13.4.3   Consequences in Propositional Logic and Immediate Inferences

As we could see in our historical survey, in medieval logic it was some time before what we would recognize as truth-functional propositional operations, such as negation, conjunction, disjunction, or implication, came to be generally treated as such, as equally applicable to propositions of any complexity. Perhaps the most obvious

reason for this is provided by the fact that natural language negation can take virtually any scope, whence it is not just the simple
proposition-forming operation that modern logic acknowledges. But
similar observations apply to disjunction and conjunction, which
besides being propositional functions, can work as nominal operators
as well, forming nominal disjunctions and conjunctions out of nominal expressions, as the medieval theories of suppositional descents
clearly acknowledged, using the differences of nominal and propositional disjunctions and conjunctions to distinguish different modes
of supposition to make distinctions that we would represent in terms
of different quantifier-scopes.[2] Indeed, given the different possible
interpretations of nominal conjunctions, namely, distinguishing
their distributive, divisive and collective interpretations, nominal
conjunctions also served in dealing with phenomena of what *we*
would describe as plural and numerical quantification (Klima and
Sandu 1990). The case is somewhat similar with our modern notions
of material (Philonian) implication and necessary entailment, which
would be recognized only as specific cases of the variety of logical
relations that the general notion of consequence was supposed to
cover in medieval logic.

In general, dealing directly with the rich expressive resources
of a natural language, namely Latin, medieval logicians recognized
and dealt with the variety of ways in which the same expressions can
function in different contexts, not by means of a simplified artificial
language that represents only certain facets of the various functions
of our natural language expressions, but rather in terms of distinguishing the different functions of the same phrases in different contexts, and sometimes just stipulating those functions in a technical,
"regimented" Latin, for the sake of simplicity and uniformity.

This is neatly illustrated in the doctrine of so-called "immediate inferences", the doctrine of the relationships among pairs of

---

[2] For a diagrammatic summary of the relationships between suppositional descents
and quantifier scopes, see Klima 2009, 181. See also the chapter "Supposition and
Properties of Terms" in this volume.

affirmative and negative, universal and particular categorical propositions sharing both their terms, stemming from Aristotle's *On Interpretation*, usually summarized in the Square of Opposition and in "the rules of conversion".[3] Without going into much detail, I would just like to illustrate the previous general remark by a quick comparison of Abelard's treatment of the Square with what became "the standard account" and with Buridan's extension of the Square into an Octagon covering not only simple categorical propositions, but propositions with oblique terms, categorical propositions whose both terms are explicitly quantified, as well as modal propositions with two modalities.

When dealing with the propositions of Aristotle's Square, Abelard noted that one should distinguish between the negation of their verb phrase alone (verbal predicate, or copula + nominal predicate) and the negation of the entire proposition including the determiner of the noun phrase (providing the subject term). Thus, he distinguished between the contradictory, what he called "extinctive" or "destructive", negation of 'Every man runs', namely, 'Not every man runs', and the "separative" or "remotive" negation of the same, namely, 'Some man does not run'. Likewise, he also distinguished between the contradictory negation of 'Some man runs', namely, 'No man runs', and its remotive negation: 'Every man does not run' (Martin 2009, 135). The difference is that the contradictory negation destroys or extinguishes the existential import of the affirmative proposition, which the mere separative negation leaves intact. At any rate, this correctly accounts for the intuition that 'Some man does not run', as opposed to 'Not every man runs', has to entail that there are humans.

However, Abelard's distinction did not really catch on, and gave way to the stipulation that these two forms of negation are equivalent, and both express the contradictory of the corresponding universal affirmative, equally cancelling its existential import. Thus, in the

---

[3] See the chapter "The Syllogism and Its Transformations" in this volume.

"regimented" Latin of later scholasticism it became a universal rule that affirmative propositions have existential import, whereas their contradictory negations (which may be effected either by pre-positing the negative particle to the entire affirmative proposition, or by negating the verb phrase of the affirmative proposition after replacing its quantifier with the quantifier's dual) do not. This is how we get the "classic" Square of Opposition (Klima 2001b; Parsons 2015).

However, further possibilities emerge, as soon as these stipulations are in place, and in accordance with the requirements of syllogistic term logic, the verb phrase of categorical propositions is "canonically" analysed into the verbal copula and a further quantifiable noun phrase, where the affirmative copula is interpreted as expressing identity. For on this analysis, 'Every man runs' becomes 'Every man is some runner', which by way of a further stipulation can be regarded as equivalent to the "unusual" construction in which both terms precede the copula: 'Every man some runner is', which, however, has the advantage of having its quantifiers listed in the order of their decreasing scope left to right (as in "prenex normal form" in modern formal logic). Thus, a negation applied at the front can syntactically "wriggle its way through" the subsequent quantifiers, changing them into their duals, until it lands on the verb, just as it would do with the corresponding quantificational formula: $\sim(\forall x)(\exists y)(x=y)$, yielding $(\exists x)(\forall y)\sim(x=y)$, that is to say, 'Not every man some runner is' (i.e. colloquially, 'Not every man is a runner') would become 'Some man every runner is not' (i.e. colloquially, 'Some man is not any runner', 'Some man does not run').

Since the combination of the two quantifiers and negation can yield eight different types of proposition, Buridan used this "canonical form" to construct an Octagon of Opposition, listing all logical relations among the resulting propositions. Finally, having observed the analogy of the logical behaviour of dual quantifiers, quantified oblique terms and modal operators, Buridan expanded his Octagon to these further types of propositions as well. This way, he basically managed to get as close as anyone can to a formal theory of the logical relations for large classes of strictly defined propositional types (Buridan 2001, 1.5.2, 44–45; Read 2012).

But what is it exactly, one may ask, that renders such a theory strictly "formal"? Obviously, not that we use schematic letters or other symbols for the words or phrases of a natural language, although once the construction of the phrases of the natural language is strictly regulated, it becomes obvious which of those phrases can be replaced by schematic letters that then can be replaced by any natural language phrase of the same type. We know from our artificial languages that what makes a logical theory "formal" is its strict, well-defined syntax, precisely specifying the types of its primitive symbols, its rules of construction, and rules of inference (if it is a syntactic theory) or rules of interpretation (if it is a semantic theory) for the types of expression defined in the syntax. But that is exactly what Buridan's "regimentation" also achieved with regard to the several types of propositions discussed above, although, of course, not for the entirety of all possible forms of reasoning with all possible forms of propositions in Latin. Then, at least for these well-defined sets of propositions, we do have those schematic rules that allow us to regard any concrete sentence as a mere substitution instance of the schematic form for which we have effective methods for checking its logical relations with any other sentence of a similarly well-defined schematic form.

Yet it is still desirable to have a general notion of formal validity, even without having the effective syntactical or semantical methods for checking it in each and every case. After all, it is only in possession of such a general notion that we can figure out what can even count as a valid consequence, and whether its validity is due to its logical form or some other, more specific considerations. As we have seen earlier, the general intuitive criterion for the validity of a consequence in general was the repugnance or incompatibility of the negation of the consequent (conclusion) with the antecedent (premises). This intuitive idea, however, can be further articulated in a number of different ways: it can be taken to be some metaphysical, natural, causal, or conceptual impossibility, which in turn may manifest itself in the absolute or conditional impossibility of the antecedent and the negation of the consequent obtaining together either on account of the logical form of the propositions in question, under any possible substitution/interpretation of their non-logical components, or on account of some conceptual, natural, or metaphysical connection between the semantic values of those components. All this, of course, leaves us with at least two further questions: (1) what exactly is this repugnance or incompatibility that is required for the validity of a consequence, and (2) what, if anything, can be a principled basis for separating the "logical" and "non-logical" sub-components of its propositional components, which would distinguish *formal* consequences from *material* ones?

13.5 MATERIAL CONSEQUENCES

13.5.1 *Material Consequences Reducible to Formal Ones*

As we have already seen, there is, at least from our modern perspective, an intuitive way to draw the distinction between formal and material consequences, along the lines Buridan and the Parisian tradition following him did: a consequence is formal just in case it is valid on account of its form, where its form is nothing but the syncategorematic structure of its propositional components, whereas its matter is constituted by its categorematic terms, which is why those terms can be represented by schematic letters, to indicate their substitutability with any particular terms of the relevant type.

This is certainly neat and workable, as long as we have a neat and workable distinction between categorematic and syncategorematic terms, and as long as we are willing to "sacrifice" a whole lot of clearly valid inferences on the altar of extralogical connections, based on our ever-fallible knowledge of the nature of things. This is pretty much the choice Buridan and his "modern" ilk made, but also the choice nearly all of his predecessors, many of his contemporaries, and, apparently, the later "English tradition" did *not* want to make.

Take, for instance, Walter Burley. He provides the following primary division of consequences:

> One kind of consequence is simple and another 'as of now'.
> A simple consequence is one that holds for every time, so that the antecedent can never be true unless the consequent is true. An 'as of now' consequence is one that holds for a determinate time and not always, such as 'every man runs; therefore, Socrates runs'. For this consequence does not hold for every time, but only holds while Socrates is a man.[4] Simple consequence is of two kinds. One kind is natural. That happens when the antecedent *includes* the consequent. Such a consequence holds through an intrinsic topic. An accidental consequence is one that holds through an extrinsic topic. That happens when the antecedent does not include the consequent but the consequence holds through a certain extrinsic rule. For example, 'If a man is an ass, you are sitting'. This consequence is a good one, and holds through the rule 'Anything follows from the impossible'. The rule relies on the topic 'from the lesser appearance'. For the impossible appears to be less true than anything else. Therefore, if the impossible is true, it follows through the topic 'from the lesser appearance' that anything else will be true. (Burley 1955, 60–61; cf. Burley 2000, 146)

There are a number of interesting features of these divisions. The first, alluded to earlier, is that it does not contain the division of consequences into formal and material ones; that distinction comes up later in Burley's discussion, in connection with the solution of a problem. The second interesting point is that even among simple consequences, which do not require some further, extrinsic

---

[4] After Socrates dies, and so ceases to be a man, the antecedent of this consequence may be true as long as there are humans all of whom run, but the consequent is false, because then Socrates, no longer being a man, cannot run. But as long as Socrates is alive, the consequence is valid, for its antecedent cannot be true without its consequent.

conditions to hold for their validity, there is the distinction between natural and accidental consequences, a distinction based on whether they hold in virtue of an "intrinsic" or "extrinsic" topic. This is the kind of distinction that tends to puzzle modern commentators. After all, the rule that from the impossible anything follows seems to be the direct implication of the understanding of the notion of validity as the impossibility of the simultaneous truth of the antecedent with the negation of the consequent, since if the antecedent cannot be true in itself, then of course it cannot be true together with anything, let alone the negation of the consequent. However, Burley's description of the rule as being based on an extrinsic topic, validating an accidental consequence, as opposed to a natural consequence, which holds in virtue of an intrinsic topic, may suggest that the former should be somehow weaker than the latter, whereas from the point of view of our modern intuitions just the opposite seems to be the case: 'A man runs; therefore, an animal runs' is not even a formally valid consequence, whereas by Burley's lights it is a simple, natural consequence that holds by virtue of an intrinsic topic; so, one would think, it should somehow be "stronger" than 'A man is an ass; therefore, you are sitting'. So, what is going on?

Even if Burley does not quite elaborate, we can get further hints from his thirteenth-century predecessors, such as William of Sherwood, Peter of Spain and the author of the *Summa Lamberti*. A *locus* is described by these authors as "the seat of an argument" (*sedes argumenti*) or that from which an appropriate argument is elicited. Each *locus* contains several maxims, where a maxim is described as "a known general proposition containing and confirming many arguments" (*nota propositio et communis multa continens et confirmans argumenta* – William of Sherwood 1995, 78). The *loci* are commonly divided into intrinsic, extrinsic, and intermediate. Their distinction is described most succinctly by William of Sherwood in the following way:

> When there is some doubt about a proposition, we first form
> it as a question, next we find the middle and we syllogize it

affirmatively or negatively. When, therefore, an argument is elicited from an internal property of one of the terms of the question, then the locus is said to be intrinsic, when from an external property, then the locus is called extrinsic, and when from an intermediate property, then the locus is said to be intermediate. (William of Sherwood 1966, 71)

Here we should realize that the distinction between internal, intermediate, and extrinsic properties is closely related to Aristotle's doctrine of *Categories* (as is his doctrine of *Topics* in general). Accordingly, the division of *loci* into intrinsic, extrinsic, and intermediate is based on whether the middle whereby the terms of the original question are going to be joined in the conclusion is an intrinsic, extrinsic, or intermediate property of the substance of things to which the terms in the question apply. So when Burley is claiming that a consequence can be formal on account of the form of simple terms, and when such a consequence is natural that holds by virtue of an intrinsic topic, then he refers to such rules of inference that are validated "formally" for entire sets of categorematic terms, those, for instance, that are related to each other as species to genus, which is what validates, among countless others, 'This is a man; therefore, this is an animal'. So, this consequence is "formal", because it concerns not only the particular terms occurring in it (connected by a Carnapian "meaning postulate"), but any number of terms related in the same way, namely, as species and genus, respectively. Yet, this is not a formal consequence "by reason of the form of the whole structure", but "by reason of the form of incomplex terms", that is, those terms coming under the formal, second-order concepts of genus and species (which is why such concepts were often referred as "logical intentions"), applying to all sorts of simple terms related in the same way. Yet this consequence would not count as formal by Buridan's criterion, for it does not hold in all terms without any restriction, but only in those terms that would be permissible substituents in the schema: 'if x is an S; then x is a G', where S and G have to be related as species and genus. And this consequence is also simple, since it holds for all times, and natural, because the antecedent *includes* the consequent on account of the intrinsic *locus* that establishes the intensional inclusion of the predicate of the consequent in the predicate of the antecedent, and hence the intensional inclusion of the total significate of the consequent in the total significate of the antecedent. So in the end, the intrinsic topics establish the strong intensional connections of terms (whether categorematic or syncategorematic), which in turn establish the intensional inclusion-connections about certain types of propositions that can be formed with them. This is why Burley's criterion can exclude from the realm of such strong (simple, natural, formal) consequences, which *we* might even call "relevant entailments", those consequences that are instances of the rule *ex impossibili quodlibet*, which holds only in virtue of an extrinsic topic (namely, the *locus a minori*).

So, what precisely is the status of these *loci*? If we follow Burley's lead, it might seem that they are certain formal rules of inference establishing logical connections on the basis of the meanings of certain types of categorematic terms, to mark out necessarily valid consequences based on a containment criterion, which is supposed to be stronger than mere necessary truth-preservation. Alas, things are not so simple though. For there are extrinsic topics, such as the topic from contraries, that might be regarded as validating formal consequences insofar as they would validate consequences with any appropriately related terms, and yet, by Burley's criterion they would not count as natural, although they would still seem to be simple. (For example, 'Socrates is black; therefore, Socrates is not white', where the maxim validating the consequence is the following: "positing one of two contraries in a given subject, the other is removed from the same subject"; of course, along with the knowledge that 'black' and 'white' are contraries.) So, it would seem that Burley would have to accept formal, simple, yet accidental consequences as well.

In any case, it seems to be fairly certain that at least some of the topical maxims did serve as semantic rules to establish consequence relations that are stronger than mere necessary truth-preservation, establishing containment relations between various classes of propositional forms based on the formal logical relations of well-defined classes of their terms. In this sense, topics could function as defining a stronger, more restricted sense of formal validity as compared to Buridan's *syncategoremata*-based notion of formal validity, thereby providing a notion of validity closer to what is sought in modern "relevance logics". All such arguments are, therefore, formal in Burley's sense, but not necessarily in Buridan's sense.

However, they can be rendered formal even in Buridan's sense by adding a "missing" premise, which would be verified by the *locus*. This is how William of Sherwood would "reduce" topical inferences to syllogisms, and this is the practice that the *Summa Lamberti*, taking its cue from Boethius, would describe by distinguishing between two types of maxims, one that is inside the argument and one that is outside. For instance, if we say 'this is a man and every man is an animal; therefore, this is an animal', then we have just added the missing premise inside the argument that renders the argument formally valid in Buridan's sense, but the premise itself is justified in terms of the maxim "of whatever a species is predicated, its genus is also predicated", along with the knowledge that 'man' is a species of the genus 'animal'. However, by Burley's and the older tradition's lights, the maxim licenses the inference with the same strength as the added premise would, the only difference being that when we add the proposition verified by the maxim, then the strength of the warrant provided by the antecedent is *transferred* from the strength of the consequence to the strength of the antecedent.

Besides the maxims that are able to provide such a *stronger* notion of validity, several topical rules were also regarded by medieval authors as providing a *weaker* sense of validity, which would consist in a merely *probable*, rather than necessary, preservation of truth, or alternatively, if the maxim is taken to support an additional premise, then such a maxim would warrant a merely probable premise rather than a necessary one. But without the addition of the "reductive" premise, the consequence would have to be formally invalid by Buridan's criterion of formal validity.

13.5.2 Irreducibly Material Consequences (Such As Induction)

However, not all arguments are reducible to formally valid arguments in this way. This is obvious in the case of induction. As Buridan writes, "an induction is not formally valid unless by the addition of another premise it becomes a syllogism" (2001, 6.1.5, 398), namely, in the case of finite induction, where we can have a complete enumeration of all singulars. However, he continues,

> if an induction cannot be performed over all the singulars, as in the case of our concluding from the singulars that every fire is hot, then such an induction is not reduced to syllogism, nor does it prove its conclusion on account of its being a formally valid consequence, nor because it may be reduced to a formally valid consequence, but because of the intellect's natural inclination towards truth. (Buridan 2001, 6.1.5, 399)

Whatever this "natural inclination towards truth" is and how it is supposed to validate an infinite induction Buridan never tells, but it clearly takes us beyond the realm of formally valid logical consequences in such a way that we cannot tell exactly what additional premise could reduce the consequence to a formal one that is valid in every term. In fact, it is easy to see that an induction can never be logically valid in the case of accidental predicates, so it can never be valid in all terms. That is to say, 'This S is P and that S is P, ... etc.; therefore, all S are P' can be valid only if being P is essential to anything that is an S, insofar as it is an S, but if P is accidental to S, then it is always possible to have an S that is not a P, even if perhaps all previously observed S were P, which at once invalidates the consequence. Accordingly, the enumeration of singulars is not there to provide stronger corroboration with greater numbers (see the flawed logic of Russell's chicken, in Russell 2008, 44); rather, it is there to test whether the predicate is essential to the subject, which it is not a matter of logic to establish. Accordingly, induction should perhaps not even be treated as a consequence; it should rather be called scientific generalization, insofar as it is generalization over essentials, as opposed to rash generalization or prejudice, which is generalization over accidentals (cf. Klima 2005).

13.6 CONCLUSION: MEDIEVAL THEORIES OF CONSEQUENCE AND MODERN NOTIONS OF LOGICAL VALIDITY

As we have seen, medieval theories of consequence can be viewed as parts of a grand enterprise to map out the domain of logicality for natural language reasoning. The result is not what we could regard as a single, large, unified theory, defining the validity of logical consequence for all possible forms of reasoning, along with a decision procedure to sort out valid from invalid consequences. Rather, the result is a cluster of several theories covering consequences from conditional propositions of various strengths to argument forms of various strengths, ranging from what we would recognize as formal validity to mere probability. Yet this cluster of theories all relate to the focal idea that a consequence is valid just in case the denial of the consequent is in some way "repugnant" to the antecedent. This idea of "repugnancy" was spelled out in several ways with regard to different forms of consequences. Setting the standard, we find in the centre Aristotle's syllogistic, which is a complete system for a well-defined set of argument forms (along with a "decision procedure": check whether an actual argument fits into one of the valid forms). However, as the foregoing survey has shown, our medieval predecessors were well aware of the fact that there are huge numbers of valid, non-syllogistic arguments that can be just as strong in themselves, or can be reduced to arguments just as strong as syllogistic arguments or to arguments that actually *are* syllogistic arguments, or even arguments that are not as strong, although they are just as useful as syllogistic arguments are, and are to be counted within a comprehensive account of reasoning.

Actually, all these references to *natural* language reasoning are rather anachronistic from the medieval perspective: after all, the *only* kind of language medieval logicians worked with was a *natural* language (although a highly technical, "regimented" natural language), and are justified only in comparison to contemporary formal logical theories, defining logical validity for an explicitly constructed *artificial* language. So, in conclusion, let us briefly reflect on how the medieval approach to consequences compares to our contemporary enterprise.

Take the idea behind Richard Montague's project (Montague 1974): given a well-defined part of a natural language, which can be translated into a (sufficiently rich) formal (intensional) logic through automated rules of translation, we can check the validity of our natural language arguments through our formal logic without getting bogged down in "the murky business of formalization". If we look at the medieval enterprise from this perspective, it may well be regarded as an enterprise comparable to Montague's, but with one important difference. Whereas the medieval enterprise used the method of "partial regimentation", namely, regulating certain forms of natural language reasoning and working out criteria of validity *directly* for those regimented forms, indeed *various criteria* for *various kinds of validity* for several forms, Montague's uses the method of "partial formalization", where arguments formulated in the regimented part of natural language are effectively translatable into a formal language, for which we have a *universal validity checker* for a *uniformly defined notion of formal validity*.

These two different methodologies can quite naturally lead to the idea of two rather different, yet not necessarily incompatible "hypothetical projects" for a "natural logic", that is, a universal logical theory checking the validity of all possible forms of natural language reasoning:

(1) The "modern project": to "cannibalize" ever greater portions of all possible forms of natural language reasoning, expand the expressive resources of our formal language(s) for which we can have a uniform definition of validity, grounding the construction of a universal method for checking validity either in terms of deduction rules or a compositional semantics.

(2) The "medieval project": to "regulate" ever greater portions of all possible forms of natural language reasoning, regiment the syntax of our natural language as much as ordinary usage would tolerate, so as to be able to accommodate as many forms of natural language reasoning as possible, and thus to be able to separate valid from invalid consequences in accordance with a range of different criteria of validity.

What the "medieval project" could learn from the "modern project", then, is the use of a recursive definition of syntax and the corresponding semantics to account for validity relations among all possible well-formed expressions of a formal language or among all possible sentences of a similarly well-defined fragment of a natural language, allowing the construction of a universal validity-checking process for a correspondingly well-defined notion of validity. On the other hand, what the "modern project" could learn from the medieval project is the accommodation of the forms of logicality that medieval logicians recognized both in various forms of formal and material consequences, as well as in the different, but not unrelated notions of their validity. In this sense, the study of medieval logic can provide a promising "shortcut" towards a truly comprehensive theory of consequences in a contemporary "natural logic".

14 The Logic of Modality

Riccardo Strobino and Paul Thom

14.1 INTRODUCTION

The logical analysis of modalities, as initiated in Aristotle's *On Interpretation* and *Prior Analytics*, focused on the inferential relations among modal propositions, i.e. propositions concerning necessity, possibility and contingency. The Aristotelian legacy of modal logic underwent major transformations in medieval times, in both the Arabic and the Latin traditions. But these transformations took very different forms in the two traditions. The corpus of Aristotle's works was available in Arabic translation at a very early stage as a result of the translation movement that flourished under the ʿAbbāsid caliphate in eighth- to tenth-century Baghdad. Crucial works for modal logic such as Aristotle's *On Interpretation* and *Prior Analytics*, as well as texts of indirect but equally significant relevance from the physical and metaphysical corpus were known to logicians in this tradition from the very start. In the Latin tradition, a comprehensive response to Aristotle's writings on the logic of modality had to await the rediscovery in the late twelfth century of the full text of *Prior Analytics*. The early availability of the key Aristotelian texts to the Arabic world sparked an interpretive effort whose primary concerns were to understand those texts and to resolve the difficulties which they posed. The first fruits of this effort were the commentaries of al-Fārābī (d. 950), whose long commentary on *Prior Analytics* has, sadly, not survived. The commentatorial tradition in the Arabic-Islamic world reached its apogee in the works of Averroes (d. 1198). The earliest Latin commentary on *Prior Analytics*, an anonymous and incomplete work, dates from the late twelfth century. The earliest known complete Latin commentary is that of Robert Kilwardby (d. 1279), although, as we shall see below, some of his ideas about the meaning of modal sentences have precedents in the writings of Peter Abelard (d. 1142).

Long before Kilwardby's time, modal logic had received an extraordinary impulse in the Arabic-Islamic world, in the figure of Avicenna (d. 1037), who developed a new and original system that departed from Aristotle in crucial ways. Avicenna's system in effect relegated Aristotle's modal logic to a purely marginal role. The work of the post-Avicennan logicians, particularly in the twelfth- and thirteenth-century Eastern tradition, evolved in ways that are entirely independent of Aristotle and seem to be motivated exclusively by the need to go beyond Avicenna's system (Rāzī d. 1210; Khūnajī d. 1248; Kātibī d. 1276) or to defend it (Ṭūsī d. 1274).

In the Latin world, it was not until the fourteenth century that major non-Aristotelian paradigms in modal logic were developed. The two principal exponents of this new logic were William of Ockham (d. 1347) and John Buridan (died after 1358).

In this chapter, we outline the major medieval innovations in modal logic, highlighting the fine-grained understanding of temporal and alethic modalities developed by Avicenna and the post-Avicennan tradition in the Arabic-Islamic world, and the systematic development of nominalist modal logics in fourteenth-century Christendom.

14.2 THE ARABIC TRADITION

14.2.1 Avicenna

Avicenna (d. 1037) is the most influential logician in the Arabic tradition. His late work *al-Ishārāt wa-t-tanbīhāt* (*Pointers and Reminders*) became for subsequent generations the canonical text to discuss and refer to, replacing Aristotle both as a textual source and in terms of doctrine, until it was itself supplanted by Kātibī's (d. 1276) *al-Risāla al-Shamsiyya* (*Epistle for Shams al-Dīn*). Many of Avicenna's innovative contributions to the history of logic are related to modalities. Even though modal notions are central to other areas of his philosophy, especially metaphysics, we will focus here only on the logic. The context in which most of Avicenna's contributions originate is that of the sections of his logical works that correspond to Aristotle's

Prior Analytics and to a lesser extent *On Interpretation*. Central to Avicenna's modal logic are two characteristic dimensions of the analysis of categorical propositions, which will be systematised and discussed ubiquitously by his critics and followers, particularly in the thirteenth century.

(i) **Temporal and alethic modalities:** Avicenna holds the view that every categorical proposition is modalised, either implicitly (the absolute proposition) or explicitly (all other propositions). Modalities may be either temporal (e.g. at least once, always), alethic (e.g. necessarily, possibly), or a combination of both. A radical departure from Aristotle's analysis is Avicenna's understanding of the assertoric proposition, which he takes to be always qualified by an implicit temporal modality. 'Every horse is sleeping' must accordingly be read as 'Every horse is sleeping at least once'. Such a proposition he calls the absolute. On account of his reading of the absolute proposition, Avicenna rejects the traditional Square of Opposition and the standard rules of conversion for the Aristotelian assertoric e-proposition. The reason for the rejection of the traditional Square of Opposition is that the contradictory of an absolute proposition is not another absolute but rather a perpetuity proposition of opposite quality and quantity: 'Every J is at least once B' is contradicted by 'Some J is never B', not by 'Some J is at least once not B', the latter being in turn the contradictory of 'Every J is always B'. The reason for the failure of conversion of absolute e-propositions is that from the fact that B is not true at some time of every A, it does not follow that A is not true at some time of every B, as in 'No animal is always sleeping' (true) and 'No sleeping thing is always an animal' (false).

The resulting system is thus characterised by the presence of two kinds of duality: an alethic duality between necessity and one-sided possibility-propositions, and a temporal duality between one-sided absoluteness and perpetuity propositions.

(ii) **Substantial and descriptional reading:** Alongside the temporal-alethic modalisation, every categorical proposition is subject to a second fundamental dichotomy, depending on whether the predicate is taken to be true of that of which the subject is true (1) as long as the substance of the subject exists or (2) as long as the substance of the subject is described by the subject. A *locus classicus* for the distinction is (Avicenna (Ibn Sīnā) *al-Ishārāt* 1971, 264–266), and although the respective labels *dhātī* (substantial) and *waṣfī* (descriptional) for readings (1) and (2) became mainstream only at a later stage, Avicenna is the first to employ the distinction in a systematic way. The first reading may be regarded as functionally equivalent to a *de re* reading, the focus being on the relation between the predicate and the substance or essence picked out by the subject term with respect to the time of its continued existence, regardless of whether the subject is true of it only at some time, always, or necessarily. On the second reading, by contrast, the focus is on the relation between the predicate and the substance or essence picked out by the subject insofar as it is picked out by the subject, i.e. only with respect to the time at which the subject is true of it. The two readings are used to express relations of inseparability, incompatibility, separability or compatibility between (1) a substance or essence and a description (*dhātī*) or (2) between two descriptions (*waṣfī*).

By combining the two above sets of parameters, various types of propositions can be generated, and later logicians were well aware of the potential amplitude of the spectrum. In his *Asās al-iqtibās fī l-manṭiq*, Ṭūsī suggests that 217 different types can be produced (Ṭūsī 2004, 177). A more manageable list of thirteen was first isolated by Rāzī, the ultimate source of which is Avicenna himself who makes use of the following types in the substantial reading: (1) necessity, (2) perpetuity, (3) determinate temporal necessity, (4) indeterminate temporal necessity, (5) one-sided absoluteness, (6) two-sided absoluteness, (7) non-necessary absoluteness, (8) one-sided possibility, (9) two-sided possibility-propositions; and of the following types in the descriptional reading: (10) necessity and (11) perpetuity propositions.

Avicenna's analysis of modalised propositions is largely instrumental to the development of his modal syllogistic, although its impact is by no means limited to this area: the account of *dhātī*, *waṣfī* and temporal necessity is also central to his theory of demonstration and scientific knowledge (Strobino 2015). Avicenna's modal syllogistic is at variance with Aristotle's in several respects, and offers an original system which has been the object of excellent scrutiny in recent years (Street 2002, 2005a, 2015; Thom 2003, 2008, 2012b, 2016). Divergent results are a consequence, among other things, of Avicenna's use of the absolute proposition instead of the assertoric, his focus on one-sided possibility instead of two-sided possibility (contingency) propositions, his different account of conversion, according to which the absolute e-proposition fails to convert as such, and **La** and **Li** propositions do not convert to a **Li** proposition, as in Aristotle, but rather to a **M₁i** proposition (see the synoptic Table 14.1), the understanding of inferences involving possibility premises, and – closely related to the last point – the interpretation of the subject term as ampliating to whatever possibly falls under it. Avicenna's ampliationism with regard to the subject term is a general view that he shares with Buridan: in this connection, though very different, the two traditions are working roughly within the same space of "logical possibilities" (see the discussion in the section on Buridan, below, and more generally, Thom 2003, where major figures both in the Arabic and in the Latin tradition are shown to have adopted either the actualist or the ampliationist approach).

A distinctive feature of Avicenna's modal syllogistic, at the centre of a heated controversy in the post-Avicennan tradition, is the validity and self-evident character of first-figure syllogisms in LML (necessity major, possibility minor, necessity conclusion) and MMM combinations, on which all other first figure combinations (LLL, LLM, LMM, MLM) accepted by Avicenna depend (Thom 2012b).

In *al-Ishārāt*, Avicenna adopts a more systematic approach in presenting the syllogistic: he gives the valuations by figure, abandoning the Aristotelian presentation by premise pair which he himself had used in earlier works, including *al-Qiyās* (*The Syllogism*), the fifth section of the logic of the *Shifā'* (*The Healing*) and the logic of the *Najāt* (*The Deliverance*). This move enables him to present more generally his own version of the rule of the major (the modality of the conclusion is the same as the modality of the major premise) and its exceptions (Street forthcoming a).

Avicenna was also the first to work out the standard relations (conversion, contradiction, subordination) among descriptionals (Thom 2003).

Finally, Avicenna deserves credit for being among the first logicians in the Aristotelian tradition to have identified clearly the distinction between the divided and composite readings of modal propositions. In his *'Ibāra*, the fourth section of the logic of the *Shifā'* where he discusses Aristotle's *On Interpretation*, Avicenna makes use of the distinction between (1) the mode of the copula (*jihat al-rabt*) and (2) the mode of the quantifier (*jihat al-sūr*) to explain the different truth conditions of 'Every man is possibly a writer' and 'Possibly, every man is a writer'. The distinction does not crop up explicitly in modal syllogistic, but it is worth noting that the latter is developed with the implicit understanding that modalities are understood to apply to the predicate in the first sense, and not in the second (Street forthcoming a).

Two further issues that arise in connection with Avicenna's modal system are (1) the reading of the subject term and (2) his use of a problematic proof technique, which has generated some trouble to interpreters, both ancient and modern, known as "upgrading" or supposing the possible actual (three crucial proofs directly depend on it in Avicenna's system, and indirectly all proofs that are based on these). For a more elaborate discussion of both, see the chapter "Arabic Logic after Avicenna" in this volume.

14.2.2 *After Avicenna*

Post-Avicennan Arabic modal logic is still to a large extent uncharted territory: recent groundbreaking work has only started to reveal the enormous wealth of interesting and sophisticated materials it offers, and foundations are in the process of being laid in the form of critical editions, translations and studies.[1] Post-Avicennan logicians depend primarily on Avicenna's exposition of his modal logic in *al-Ishārāt* and focus on problems that are characteristic of it. Among them, the interpretation of the subject term and the evaluation of syllogisms with possibility minors are the object of special controversy. Logicians in the thirteenth century for the most part exhibit a tendency to move away from Avicenna, with the notable exception of Ṭūsī. A first wave of logicians to develop criticisms and alternative views against Avicenna includes Fakhr al-Dīn al-Rāzī (d. 1210) and Afḍal al-Dīn al-Khūnajī (d. 1248). A second group is associated with the Maragha observatory and includes its founder Naṣīr al-Dīn al-Ṭūsī (d. 1274) and Najm al-Dīn al-Qazwīnī al-Kātibī (d. 1276) (Street 2015, forthcoming b).

Rāzī's commentary on Avicenna's *Ishārāt* played an instrumental role in the process that led that text to be the main source of discussion in the thirteenth century, at least until after Kātibī. Rāzī was the first to isolate the set of propositions that became the standard focus of investigation, and to raise fundamental questions about the interpretation of the subject term. He introduced the distinction between the essentialist (*ḥaqīqī*) and the externalist (*khārijī*) readings of the subject term, which was to become one of the characteristic features of later Arabic logic (see the chapter on "Arabic Logic after Avicenna" in this volume). The distinction accounts for the truth of different types of propositions based on whether they express a relation between the essence or real nature (*ḥaqīqa*) of the subject and the predicate, regardless of whether the subject exists or not in reality, or a factual relation that depends on the subject's existence in reality. As a result, 'Every J is B' is understood to mean on the

---

[1] Two models are, in this respect, El-Rouayheb 2010b – a superb edition of Khūnajī's (d. 1248) *Kashf al-asrār ʿan ghawāmiḍ al-afkār* (*Disclosure of Secrets from the Obscurities of Thoughts*); and Street 2014 – a study with translation and commentary of the section of Khūnajī's *Kashf* devoted to conversion.

essentialist reading that everything that, were it to exist, would be J, would be, were it to exist, B; and on the externalist reading as everything that is J in reality is B in reality (*fī l-khārij*). Thus, for example, on the assumption that there exist no septagons in reality, 'Every septagon is a figure' would be true on the essentialist reading and false on the externalist reading. By contrast, on the assumption that the only existent figures are septagons, 'Every figure is a septagon' would be false on the essentialist reading (because not everything that, were it to exist, would be a figure, would be, were it to exist, a septagon), but true on the externalist reading (Rāzī 2003, 141ff.; Street 2015). Rāzī also seems to be at the root of a tendency, inspired by the concerns of Ash'arite metaphysics, to avoid an interpretation of modalities merely in terms of temporal frequency (Street 2005a, forthcoming b).[2]

Khūnajī, in his *Kashf al-asrār 'an ghawāmid al-afkār* (*Disclosure of Secrets from the Obscurities of Thoughts*), adopts a critical stance towards both Avicenna and Rāzī. In the chapter on conversion, he offers an elaborate discussion of the topic in connection with the essentialist-externalist distinction, the details of which are thoroughly examined in Street 2014. Khūnajī sees Rāzī's essentialist reading as nothing more than an ampliation to the possible. He tests the reading by allowing ampliation to certain kinds of subjects that are impossible in Aristotelian metaphysics (e.g. the-moon-which-is-not-eclipsed, the-man-which-is-not-capable-of-laughter), and develops alternative laws of conversion as a result (Street 2014). Khūnajī's analysis is also relevant for the discussion of inferences involving conjunctive terms, a further distinctive feature of later Arabic logic recently explored with regard to Abharī (d. 1265), an important figure associated with Maragha (Thom 2010), and for modal characterisations of conditional statements (El-Rouayheb 2009). Khūnajī also

---

[2] Modalities are discussed in the domain of Islamic theology (*kalām*) particularly with regard to the relation between perpetuity and necessity, possibility and actuality. Their treatment in that context, however, lies beyond the scope of this section.

seems to have inaugurated what became a common way of treating modalised propositions and their properties in terms of their relative strength rather than one by one (see below and the chapter on "Arabic Logic after Avicenna" in this volume).

Najm al-Dīn al-Qazwīnī al-Kātibī's (d. 1276) concise and influential *al-Risāla al-Shamsiyya* (*Epistle for Shams ad-Dīn*), an introductory text on logic that became a standard madrasa textbook, offers an account of modalities that can be seen as the culmination of thirteenth-century Arabic logic.[3] In *Shamsiyya* (Section 2.2.4 on modal propositions), Kātibī treats fifteen modalised propositions (listing the thirteen already explicitly identified by Rāzī, but using also two descriptionals weaker than perpetuity) that can be generated on the basis of Avicenna's analysis of temporal and alethic modalities and the distinction between substantial and descriptional reading. His first division is between six simple propositions (necessary, perpetual, general conditioned, general conventional, general absolute, general possible) and seven compound propositions (special conditioned, special conventional, special possible, non-necessary absolute, non-perpetual absolute, temporal, spread). Simple propositions consist only of one characteristic statement, alethic or temporal. Compound propositions consist of one characteristic statement, alethic or temporal, and a restriction (again, alethic or temporal). For example, 'Every human is P at least once, not necessarily' is understood as 'Every human is P at least once and every human is not always P'. The restriction can be understood either as an absolute or as a possibility-proposition of the same quantity but opposite quality. For a comprehensive list of all quality and quantity combinations, see Tables 14.1–14.3. The Arabic terminology given above is for the most part not self-explanatory. We will therefore give the original Arabic term with a label that captures the function of the propositional type

---

[3] References to the sections of Kātibī's *Shamsiyya* are given according to the table of contents and concordance in Street forthcoming c.

Table 14.1 *The canonical list of six simple propositions*

	a-proposition	e-proposition	i-proposition	o-proposition
L	Every J is necessarily B	No J is possibly B	Some J is necessarily B	Some J is not possibly B
A	Every J is always B	No J is ever B	Some J is always B	Some J is never B
L_{d1}	Every J is necessarily B as long as it is J	No J is possibly B as long as it is J	Some J is necessarily B as long as it is J	Some J is not possibly B as long as it is J
A_{d1}	Every J is always B as long as it is J	No J is ever B as long as it is J	Some J is always B as long as it is J	Some J is never B as long as it is J
X_1	Every J is at least once B	No J is always B	Some J is at least once B	Some J is not always B
M_1	Every J is possibly B	No J is necessarily B	Some J is possibly B	Some J is not necessarily B

Table 14.2 *The canonical list of seven compound propositions*

L_{d2}	Every J is necessarily B as long as it is J and no J is always B	No J is possibly B as long as it is J and every J is at least once B	Some J is necessarily B as long as it is J and it is not always B	Some J is not possibly B as long as it is J and it is at least once B
A_{d2}	Every J is always B as long as it is J and no J is always B	No J is ever B as long as it is J and every J is at least once B	Some J is always B as long as it is J and it is not always B	Some J is never B as long as it is J and it is at least once B

(*cont.*)

Table 14.2 (*cont.*)

X_2	Every J is at least once B and no J is always B	No J is always B and every J is at least once B	Some J is at least once B and it is not always B	Some J is not always B and it is at least once B
X_3	Every J is at least once B and no J is necessarily B	No J is always B and every J is possibly B	Some J is at least once B and it not necessarily B	Some J is not always B and it is possibly B
T	Every J is necessarily B at T (Det) and no J is always B	No J is possibly B at T and every J is at least once B	Some J is necessarily B at T and it is not always B	Some J is not possibly B at T and it is at least once B
I	Every J is necessarily B at T (Indet) and no J is always B	No J is possibly B (Indet) and every J is at least once B	Some J is necessarily B (Indet) and it is not always B	Some J is not possibly B (Indet) and it is at least once B
M_2	Every J is possibly B and possibly not B	No J is necessarily B or necessarily not B	Some J is possibly B and possibly not B	Some J is not necessarily B and it is possibly B

accompanied by an abbreviation (see Street 2014 for the same list in Rescher's notation).

The above types are grouped according to Kātibī's division between simple and compound propositions (with the exception of the two simple propositions X_{d1} and M_{d1} which Kātibī does not

Table 14.3 *Two additional compound propositions weaker than*
perpetuity

X_{d1}	Every J is at least once B while J	No J is always B while J	Some J is at least once B while J	Some J is not always B while J
M_{d1}	Every J is possibly B while J	No J is necessarily B while J	Some J is possibly B while J	Some J is not necessarily B while J

include in his standard list but makes use of). It may be useful, however, to look at them in terms of the modalities involved: (i) alethic,
(ii) temporal, (iii) combinations of alethic and temporal. Accordingly,
we will have the following three fundamental groups:

(i) Alethic modalities:

    L   substantial necessity (*ḍarūriyya*)

    M_1 substantial one-sided possibility (*mumkina ʿāmma*)

    M_2 substantial two-sided possibility (*mumkina khāṣṣa*)

    L_{d1} descriptional unrestricted necessity (*mashrūṭa ʿāmma*)

    M_{d1} descriptional one-sided possibility (*ḥiniyya mumkina*)

(ii) Temporal modalities:

    A   substantial perpetuity (*dāʾima*)

    X_1 substantial one-sided absoluteness (*muṭlaqa ʿāmma*)

    X_2 substantial two-sided absoluteness (*muṭlaqa khāṣṣa, wujūdiyya lā dāʾima*)

    A_{d1} descriptional unrestricted perpetuity (*ʿurfiyya ʿāmma*)

    X_{d1} descriptional one-sided absoluteness (*ḥiniyya muṭlaqa*)

(iii) Mixed alethic and temporal modalities:

    L_{d2} descriptional restricted necessity (*mashrūṭa khāṣṣa*)

    T   substantial determinate temporal necessity (*waqtiyya*)

    I   substantial indeterminate temporal necessity (*muntashira*)

    A_{d2} descriptional restricted perpetuity (*ʿurfiyya khāṣṣa*)

    X_3 substantial non-necessary absoluteness (*wujūdiyya lā ḍarūriyya*)

Table 14.4 *Basic inferential relations holding among the fifteen modalised propositions*

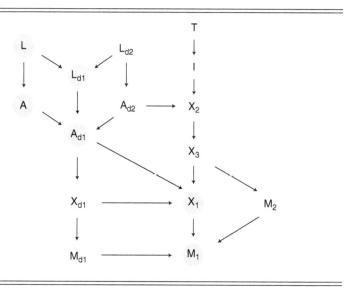

A representation of the basic inferential relations holding among the fifteen propositions is given in Table 14.4. The relations are understood to hold among propositions of the same quantity and quality (i.e. all e-, all a-, all o-, or all i-propositions).

In the section on contradiction (*Shamsiyya* 2.4.1), Kātibī first discusses the relations holding between pairs of simple propositions, when the modality is alethic or temporal, and the reading substantial or descriptional. It will be useful to develop here in full detail the consequences of Kātibī's concise statement of the duality between the four resulting modalities. Alethic substantial propositions are governed by the duality between necessity and one-sided possibility: the **L** e-proposition contradicts the M_1 i-proposition, the **L** a-proposition contradicts the M_1 o-proposition, the **L** i-proposition contradicts the M_1 e-proposition, and the **L** o-proposition contradicts the M_1 a-proposition. This set of relations, combined with standard principles of subordination (**L**a entails **L**i, **L**e entails **L**o, M_1a entails

M_1i, and M_1e entails M_1o) yields an alethic-substantial Octagon of Opposition which we find, modulo the distinction between substantials and descriptionals (unknown to the Latin tradition), in Buridan's work in the fourteenth century. However, the picture here is more complex because we also have temporal substantials, and alethic as well as temporal descriptionals. Temporal-substantial propositions are governed by the duality between one-sided absoluteness and perpetuity: the X_1 e-proposition contradicts the A i-proposition, the X_1 a-proposition contradicts the A o-proposition, the X_1 i-proposition contradicts the A e-proposition, and the X_1 o-proposition contradicts the A a-proposition. Again, this set of relations, combined with standard principles of subordination for temporals (X_1a entails X_1i, X_1e entails X_1o, Aa entails Ai, and Ae entails Ao) yields a temporal-substantial Octagon of Opposition. If we combine the two, on the basis of the principle that substantial necessity entails substantial perpetuity, substantial perpetuity entails substantial one-sided absoluteness, and substantial one-sided absoluteness entails substantial one-sided possibility (in each respective combination of quality and quantity), the above relations yield a hexadecagon of opposition of substantial propositions comprising both alethic and temporal modalities shown in Table 14.5.

The same line of reasoning can be applied to descriptionals on the basis of the corresponding duality between descriptional necessity and descriptional one-sided possibility, and that between descriptional perpetuity and descriptional one-sided absoluteness. Thus, the L_{d1} e-proposition contradicts the M_{d1} i-proposition, the L_{d1} a-proposition contradicts the M_{d1} o-proposition, the L_{d1} i-proposition contradicts the M_{d1} e-proposition, and the L_{d1} o-proposition contradicts the M_{d1} a-proposition. This set of relations, combined with similar principles of subordination for alethic descriptionals ($L_{d1}a$ entails $L_{d1}i$, $L_{d1}e$ entails $L_{d1}o$, $M_{d1}a$ entails $M_{d1}i$, and $M_{d1}e$ entails $M_{d1}o$) yields an alethic-descriptional Octagon of Opposition. The same applies to temporal descriptionals: the X_{d1} e-proposition contradicts the A_{d1} i-proposition, the X_{d1} a-proposition contradicts the A_{d1} o-proposition,

Table 14.5 *Hexadecagon of opposition for alethic and temporal simple propositions on the substantial reading*

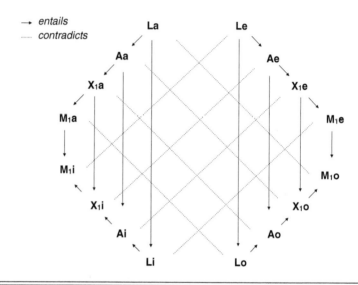

1. Substantial necessity, perpetuity, general absoluteness and general possibility: subordination and contradiction

the X_{d1} i-proposition contradicts the A_{d1} e-proposition, and the X_{d1} o-proposition contradicts the A_{d1} a-proposition. Again, this set of relations, combined with analogous principles of subordination for temporal descriptionals (X_{d1}a entails X_{d1}i, X_{d1}e entails X_{d1}o, A_{d1}a entails A_{d1}i, and A_{d1}e entails A_{d1}o) yields a temporal-descriptional Octagon of Opposition. The two descriptional octagons can also be combined on the basis of the principle that descriptional necessity entails descriptional perpetuity, descriptional perpetuity entails descriptional one-sided absoluteness, and descriptional one-sided absoluteness entails descriptional one-sided possibility (in each respective combination of quality and quantity). As a result we have another hexadecagon of opposition representing in this case relations among descriptional propositions both alethic and temporal.[4]

In the case of compound propositions the formation of contradictories depends on whether the proposition is universal (a- and e-propositions) or particular (i- and o-propositions). In the former case, the contradictories of each conjunct contradict the original proposition; for example, a L_{d2} e-proposition (which is the conjunction of a L_{d1} e-proposition and a X_1 a-proposition) is contradicted by a M_{d1} i-proposition or an A o-proposition. In the latter case, this condition is not sufficient and the requirement is "to flank a disjunctive with the contradictories of the two parts taken one by one" (Shamsiyya 2.4.1). As a result, the contradictory of a X_2 i-proposition like 'Some bodies are animals, not always' will be 'Every body is either always an animal or always not an animal'. Moreover, it is worth noting that for Kātibī (and already for Avicenna) the two-sided possibility-proposition differs from the other compound propositions in that it has a conjunctive predicate rather then being itself a conjunction of propositions.

Kātibī's exposition of conversion laws (Shamsiyya 2.4.2) makes use of the principle, which becomes standard currency after Khūnajī, that if the strongest proposition, in a given set of propositional types, fails to convert, so do all weaker propositions in the set, and conversely that if the weakest converts, so do all the stronger: "the conversion of the weak entails the conversion of the strong", which by contraposition implies that the non-conversion of the strong entails the non-conversion of the weak.

(Universal negatives) The strategy is used, for example, to argue that in seven cases universal negatives do not convert (T, I, X_2, X_3, M_1, M_2, X_1) as a result of the fact that T fails to convert. L and A convert as A; L_{d1} and A_{d1} convert as A_{d1}; L_{d2} and A_{d2} convert as A_{d1} under the condition that "[it is] non-perpetual with respect to some".

---

[4] For a presentation of the alethic-substantial octagon and its relation to the alethic-descriptional octagon, see Thom 2003, 76, where X_2 is our L_{d1} and X_3 is our M_{d1}.

(*Particular negatives*) L_{d1} and A_{d1} convert as A_{d1}; all other types do not convert, as a consequence of the fact that the strongest of them, i.e. L among simple propositions, and T among compound propositions, do not convert.

(*Universal and particular affirmatives*) All affirmatives convert as particulars. L, A, L_{d1}, A_{d1} convert as X_{d1}; L_{d2} and A_{d2} convert as X_{d2}[5]; T, I, X_1, X_2, X_3 convert as X_1.

A salient trait of Kātibī's account, which looks like a minor change, is in fact the reason why Kātibī's system is a genuine alternative to Avicenna's. Kātibī suspends judgment on the conversion of the two possibility-propositions M_1, M_2: "The status of the two possibility-propositions with respect to conversion or its failure is unknown" (*Shamsiyya* 2.4.2). The standard Avicennan proof for the respective rules depends on two assumptions, neither of which, according to Kātibī, can be verified: (1) the conversion of L e-propositions as L e-propositions, which he drops in favour of their conversion as the weaker A e-propositions, and (2) the validity of first-figure syllogisms with necessity major and possibility minors. Both (1) and (2) depend on the conversion of possibility-propositions.

Finally, Section 3.2 of *Shamsiyya* is devoted to mixes of modalised premises. The weakest modality a minor premise can have in a productive first-figure syllogism is one-sided absoluteness. As for the major, Kātibī follows the principle stated by Avicenna in *al-Ishārāt* (the modality of the conclusion is the same as that of the major premise), with four exceptions. If the major is L_{d1} or A_{d1}, the conclusion has the same modality as the minor premise (without restrictions, in case the minor has one); if the major is L_{d2} or A_{d2}, the conclusion has the same modality as the minor, with a restriction of non-necessity.

One of the distinctive features of Kātibī's approach (evident also in his treatment of the other figures, which we cannot discuss here for limits of space) is his commitment to the idea that the subject term of all propositions ampliates to what is the case at least once. For this reason, Kātibī rejects two combinations that are

---

[5] This type is introduced *ex novo* as the corresponding restricted versions X_{d1}.

characteristic of Avicenna's system, namely MMM and LML syllogisms in the first figure.

14.3   THE LATIN TRADITION

In the Latin West, we can distinguish two main approaches to modal
logic. Abelard and Kilwardby adopted an "essentialist" approach
according to which modal truths depend on the existence of subjects
having Aristotelian essences or natures. By contrast, Ockham's and
Buridan's approach requires only the existence of propositions having
modal properties.

14.3.1   Abelard

Abelard thinks that the right way to analyse a modal proposition like
'It is possible for Socrates to run' is not *de sensu* (i.e. as stating that
what is said by the embedded proposition 'Socrates runs' is possible),
but *de rebus*. He says that in a true *de rebus* necessity-proposition,
the proposition's predicate is required (*exigitur*) by the nature of its
subject. Similarly, in a true *de rebus* possibility-proposition the predicate is allowed (*patitur*) by the nature of the subject (Abelard 1970,
200). Thus, in order for a modal proposition of these types to be true,
the proposition's subject must have a nature which forms a middle
term between it and the predicate, and it is by virtue of this mediation that the proposition truly expresses a necessity or a possibility.

By way of example, Abelard says that even if Socrates is never a
bishop, so long as being a bishop is not incompatible with his nature,
the proposition 'It is possible for Socrates to be a bishop' is true. We
can see that this proposition is true by considering the fact that the
property of being a bishop is actually instantiated in other individuals of the same species as Socrates: "For, whatever is actually the case
in one, we judge to be possible in all individuals of the same species"
(Abelard 1970, 194). This is a sufficient condition for the truth of a
singular possibility-proposition. It is not stated as a necessary condition requiring that all singular possibilities be actualised, at least in
some other individual of the same species. Such a necessary condition

would amount to a limited version of the principle of plenitude – the principle that all possibilities must be actualised (Knuuttila 2015, §1). Whether or not Abelard believed in this version of the principle of plenitude, his definition of possibility does not entail it.

We can draw some corollaries from the above sufficient condition. First, any property actually possessed by an individual that has a nature, is possible for *that* individual (since the individual has the same nature as itself). The inference from actuality to possibility is valid.

A second corollary. Let P be a property actually possessed by a given individual, and thus possible for it. Then, if there is a property Q, incompatible with P, which is possible for the individual, there is a pair of possibilities simultaneously possessed by the individual, such that their joint actualisation in the individual is impossible.

Now we know, in the very example that Abelard gives, that there is a property of Socrates which is incompatible with being a bishop, namely the property of being a layman. And in general, given that any property is possible for Socrates which is not incompatible with his nature, then provided that the property in question is not required by his nature, its opposite will be compatible with his nature and so will be possible for him. These two possibilities co-exist simultaneously in the individual. So, to use the terminology of Knuuttila (2015, §1), Abelard is committed to the existence of simultaneous alternative possibilities.

Note that Abelard's *de rebus* possibilities are not possibilities of becoming, but of being. He says that a blind person can see (Abelard 1919–1933, 129–130). It is true timelessly that sight is compatible with human nature, even though it may not be possible for a blind person to become a seeing person.

14.3.2 *Kilwardby*

Robert Kilwardby's *Prior Analytics* commentary was composed during his time at the University of Paris in the 1240s. So far as modal logic is concerned, the main achievement of this work is its elaboration of a logical semantics for the necessity- and contingency-propositions that occur in Aristotle's modal syllogistic. Kilwardby's basic idea is that in order for a proposition to be necessary, it is not enough that it be true and be incapable of not being true; rather, the proposition has to state an essential and inseparable cause of the predicate's inherence or non-inherence in the subject (Kilwardby 2016; Lectio 40,162). By "an essential and inseparable cause of inherence", Kilwardby understands the *per se* predications mentioned at *Posterior Analytics* I.4, 73a35ff (Kilwardby 2016; Lectio 9,458). In the case of affirmative propositions, the necessary is that which is contained in the what-it-is, the essence, of the subject, as a part or an essential difference of that essence. In the case of negatives, it is what is excluded by the essence of the subject. In either case, necessity is grounded in the Aristotelian notion of essence.

The same is true of possibility, considered as the dual of necessity. This is the generic sense of 'possibility' (one-way possibility), which Kilwardby distinguishes from two-way possibility, the latter being subdivided into "natural" contingency and "indeterminate" contingency. A natural contingency has a dedicated cause from which its actualisation normally results provided that nothing impedes it. An indeterminate contingency is balanced equally between being so and not being so (Kilwardby 2016; Lectio 18,128 ad 32b4).

Kilwardby seems to be following an Abelard-style analysis of necessity-propositions, except that he restricts the terms of true necessity-propositions to those that pick out essences. Kilwardby's generic possibilities, like Abelard's *de rebus* possibilities, are possibilities for being, not becoming. And as with Abelard, there seems to be nothing in his account that requires acceptance of the principle of plenitude, nor anything that excludes the existence of simultaneous alternative possibilities. So, notwithstanding Simo Knuuttila's observation that "John Duns Scotus developed the conception of modality as alternativeness into a detailed theory" (Knuuttila 2015, Introduction), we see that simultaneous alternative possibilities form part of the essence-based accounts of modality given by Abelard and Kilwardby.

The situation is different for Kilwardby's "natural" possibilities. These concern becoming: going grey is a process with physiological causes which go on continuously in the human body, and normally result in the greying of the hair. But there are ways in which the process can be impeded, the most obvious of them being the early death of the subject (Kilwardby 2016; Lectio 18,534 dub.8). Since natural possibilities are normally actualised in the individuals belonging to the relevant species, there is a sense in which the principle of plenitude holds for them. The inference from actuality to possibility also holds, not in the sense that a natural possibility follows from one actual occurrence, but in the sense that it follows from what normally occurs in the species. Again, because what is naturally possible is normal in the species, there are no simultaneous alternative natural possibilities; however, because natural possibilities can be impeded, the alternative to a natural possibility must be possible in the generic sense.

Kilwardby's analysis of necessity implies that propositions like 'A grammarian is human' are not strictly speaking necessary. The predicate is indeed inseparable from the subject; but the subject, being a denominative term, does not pick out an essence; to be a grammarian is, rather, an accident of humans. Kilwardby says such propositions are necessary *per accidens* (Kilwardby 2016; Lectio 8,133).

Surprisingly, he classifies propositions like 'Everything white is coloured' as *per se* necessary, even though both subject and predicate are denominative terms (Kilwardby 2016; Lectio 15,302). The difference between the two cases is that the latter proposition can be seen as based on a species-genus predication, namely 'Whiteness is a colour', whereas the former proposition cannot.

A negative proposition like 'Nothing healthy is sick' is not *per se* necessary, because the healthy and sick do not differ by their essences, unlike health and sickness (Kilwardby 2016; Lectio 40,162).

Kilwardby's modal semantics contains one further characteristic feature. He holds that the *subjects* of affirmative necessity-propositions have to be understood differently from the subjects of negatives.

Whereas all affirmative necessity-statements are about what is under the subject, all negative necessity-statements are about what is or can be under the subject (Kilwardby 2016; Lectio 21,365). Thus, according to Kilwardby, 'All humans are necessarily animals' does not assert, of things which can be human but are not human, that they are necessarily animals; it only asserts, of those things, that they *can* be animals. On the other hand, according to him, 'No humans are possibly stones' not only says, of things which can be human but are not so, that they can be non-stones; it also asserts of those things that they cannot be stones. He does not explain why affirmative and negative necessities require different analyses in this way.

Kilwardby holds that negative, but not affirmative, necessity-propositions imply the corresponding assertorics (Kilwardby 2016; Lectio 21,532 dub.9). In the case of affirmatives, the necessity-proposition may be true, but the assertoric cannot be true, if nothing actually falls under the subject term. This commits him to holding that affirmative, but not negative, assertorics imply the corresponding possibility-propositions. If nothing actually falls under the subject terms, the negative assertoric is true, but the corresponding possibility-proposition may be false. For example, if there is no snow, 'No snow is white' is true, but the corresponding possibility-proposition 'No snow is necessarily white' is false given that 'All snow is necessarily white' is true.

Kilwardby takes non-modal predications, as they appear in modal syllogisms, to be *simpliciter* assertorics, i.e. not to be temporally restricted; and he says that in reality (*secundum rem*) they state the same thing as necessity-propositions, but differ from necessity-propositions in lacking the mode of necessity (Kilwardby forthcoming; Lectio 15,153 dub.2; Lectio 18,643 dub.11).

It follows from these stipulations that no propositions appearing in the modal syllogistic are to be read *ut nunc* (as stating something about a specific time); rather, all are to be read *habitudinally* (as statements that hold independently of the existence of individuals satisfying their terms). Kilwardby attracted a certain amount of lasting fame when, after rising to become Provincial of the Dominican order in England, then Archbishop and later Cardinal, he prohibited any teaching at Oxford that denied the habitudinal truth of the statement 'Humans are animals'.

On the basis of his account of the truth conditions of modal and assertoric propositions, Kilwardby determines which modal syllogisms are valid. For the most part, the necessity- and contingency-inferences accepted by Aristotle turn out to be valid on Kilwardby's semantics. (See Thom 2007, 177 and 239.)

But there are some difficult cases when assertoric and modal propositions are combined. For example, Barbara LXL is valid (i.e. in the first figure where the major premise expresses a necessity, the minor expresses an assertoric, and the conclusion expresses a necessity), because if all Cs are essentially B, and all Bs are essentially A, then all Cs are essentially A. But it appears that, on Kilwardby's semantics, the reasoning which shows the validity of Barbara LXL also shows the validity of Barbara XLL. Kilwardby himself thinks the two inferences differ because in Barbara LXL, the necessity-premise "appropriates" the assertoric, in the sense that it requires that the assertoric be taken *simpliciter*, whereas this is not the case for Barbara XLL. Some modern interpreters have made a similar suggestion (Crubellier 2014, 363); but, as we shall see, Kilwardby's significant medieval successors were unconvinced by his reasoning on this point.

14.3.3   Ockham

William of Ockham's *Summa Logicae* was probably written in England around 1323 (Normore 1999, 32). This classic work has been described as "a manifesto masquerading as a textbook" (King 2005, 243). It is indeed a sort of manifesto advocating a nominalist ontology that recognises only individual existents. But at the same time, the *Summa* for much of its length falls within the tradition of Aristotelian logical theory, pushing that tradition to new limits.

Unlike Kilwardby, Ockham does not ground the necessity of necessary propositions in a concept of essence. Instead, he adopts an account which is very close to the one Kilwardby explicitly rejects, namely that a necessary proposition is one which is true and cannot be false: "It should be understood that a proposition is not said to be necessary because it is always true, but because it is true if it exists, and cannot be false" (Ockham 1974a, 2.9). The qualification 'if it exists' has to be added, because Ockham holds that propositions are individual existents, namely individual utterances, inscriptions or occurrences in mental language, whose existence is contingent.

Interestingly, Ockham denies that a proposition like 'A man is an animal' is necessary. Such a proposition can be false, because it can be the case that no men exist. What *is* necessary, without any qualification, is a conditional proposition like 'If there is a man, there is an animal' (Ockham 1974a, 3.2.5).

Ockham makes extensive use of the distinction between modal propositions taken in a composite sense (where a modality attaches to a propositional *dictum*, characteristically involving an accusative and infinitive construction) and taken in a divided sense (where the modality qualifies the predicate or the copula). A composite-sense necessity-proposition is true just when the modality is true of the proposition corresponding to the expressed *dictum* (Ockham 1974a, 2.9; see Johnston 2015).

The truth conditions for a modal in the divided sense are as follows:

> It should be understood that for the truth of such propositions it is required that the predicate under its proper form belongs to those things for which the subject supposits, or to a pronoun indicating that for which the subject supposits; so that the modality expressed in such a proposition will be truly predicated of an assertoric proposition in which that same predicate is predicated of a pronoun indicating that for which the subject supposits. (Ockham 1974a, 2.10)

He gives the example of the (false) proposition 'Every truth is of necessity true'. In the divided sense, this proposition states that every proposition 'This is true' is necessary, where 'This' stands for anything for which 'truth' supposits in the original proposition. So in order for there to be true divided-sense universal necessity-propositions, there have to be true divided-sense singular necessity-propositions. But Ockham seems to have no general account of the grounding of such singular propositions.

His understanding of the *subjects* of divided-sense necessity-propositions differs from Kilwardby's. Whereas Kilwardby had taken affirmative necessity-propositions to be about what *is* under the subject term, and negatives to be about what *can be* under the subject term, Ockham understands all necessity-propositions to be about what is under the subject term. Accordingly, both affirmative and negative necessity-propositions imply the corresponding assertorics. But in the case of possibility- and contingency-propositions, he allows two readings – one where the subject stands merely for what *is* under it, the other where the subject also stands for what *can be* under it (e.g. Ockham 1974a, 3.1.34).

Ockham understands a *simpliciter* assertoric to be an assertoric proposition whose truth value does not change over time; an *ut nunc* assertoric is one whose truth value changes. (This is not the same as Kilwardby's understanding, according to which a *simpliciter* assertoric is one that expresses a necessity.)

Ockham was not the first Latin logician to formulate a semantic base from which the validity of modal syllogisms could be determined. But he was the first to give a systematic and comprehensive account of modal syllogisms based on the distinction between the composite and divided senses (Normore 1999, 33). To give an idea of his approach, he finds that Barbara LXL is valid provided that the major and the conclusion are both composite modals, or both divided modals; and Barbara XLL is invalid no matter how the premises and conclusion are read (Ockham 1974a, 3.1.31).

All this is on the assumption that nothing is specified concerning whether the assertoric premise is *ut nunc* or *simpliciter*. Ockham goes on to give some further results on the assumption that the assertoric premise is *simpliciter*.

14.3.4 Buridan

John Buridan's major logical writings include his massive *Summulae de Dialectica*, his questions on *Prior* and *Posterior Analytics*, and the treatise on consequences.

Buridan, like Ockham, was a nominalist working at (and beyond) the limits of Aristotelian logical theory. But his philosophical personality was in a way the opposite of Ockham's. Where Ockham simply excludes positions other than his own, Buridan in many instances tries, without sacrificing clarity, to find a place for mutually opposed positions within a broader perspective.

Using a single concept of necessity, Ockham says that the conditional proposition 'If there is a man, there is an animal' is necessary, but the categorical proposition 'A man is an animal' isn't. Buridan, by contrast, employs three distinct concepts of necessity. A predication is *absolutely* necessary provided that it is impossible that at some time the subject and predicate do not supposit for the same things in a proposition which has been formed; an affirmative predication is *temporally* necessary provided that its subject and predicate supposit for the same things *whenever* they supposit for anything; a predication is *conditionally* necessary provided that subject and predicate supposit for the same things *if* they supposit for anything. The proposition 'A man is an animal' is necessary temporally but not absolutely. Buridan also notes that anyone who, like Aristotle, believes in the eternity of the world and the continuity of this-worldly species, will think that 'A man is an animal' is absolutely necessary (Buridan n.d., Book 1, q. 25).

He uses this threefold typology of necessities to find a place for the opinion of "the white Cardinal" (i.e. Kilwardby, who wore the white robes of the Dominican Friars) that 'A man is an animal' is necessary (Buridan n.d., Book 1, q. 25). He also finds a way to accept the "natural" supposition which seems to be assumed in Kilwardby's opinion:

> Again, just as our intellect is able to conceive of man and animal without any distinction of time by means of the concepts whence the terms 'man' and 'animal' are imposed, so it is likely that it is able to form a complexive concept without any distinction of time. But then the mental proposition [formed with this concept] will be indifferent with respect to all present, past and future times, and so also [its] terms will supposit for everything from those times indifferently. But we do not have an utterance properly imposed to signify such a mental copula, so we can use the verb 'is' by convention [*ad placitum*] to signify such a copula by which the present time will no more be signified than is the past or the future; indeed, [it will signify] no time at all, and so there will occur a natural supposition of the terms. (Buridan 2001, 4.3.4; Klima translation)

Whereas Kilwardby had taken the subjects of affirmative necessity-propositions to be restricted to what actually falls under them but those of negatives to extend to what possibly falls under them, and Ockham had taken the subjects of all modal propositions in the first of these ways, Buridan takes the subjects of all modals in the second way (Buridan 2001, 1.8.8). However, with characteristic inclusiveness, he allows that a modal proposition can be understood as restricted to what actually falls under the subject, provided that we add the words 'which is', as in the formula 'Everything which is B is necessarily A' (Buridan n.d., Book 1, q. 33).

Buridan holds that necessity-propositions do not imply the corresponding assertorics, except in one case, namely that of the universal negative (Buridan 2015).

On Barbara LXL and Barbara XLL, Buridan's discussion takes into account this option of adding 'which is' to the subject. Barbara LXL is valid provided that this addition is made in the conclusion;

Barbara XLL and Barbara XLX are invalid but Barbara XLM is valid (Buridan 2001, 5.7.3). In his *Tractatus de consequentiis* he adds that, while first figure LX premises do not entail a universal conclusion, they do entail a particular necessity-conclusion (Buridan 2015, 124). Spencer Johnston comments that Buridan here "finds a middle way in the debate about the validity of LXL syllogisms" (Johnston 2015, 2.2). Buridan's understanding of what a *simpliciter* assertoric is differs from Ockham's; for him, as for Kilwardby, a *simpliciter* assertoric is a proposition which is necessary though not involving an express mode of necessity (Buridan 2001, 5.7.2; n.d., Book 1, q. 35).

Given the truth conditions that Buridan attributes to modal propositions, Barbara LML (i.e. where the major premise expresses a necessity, the minor a possibility, and the conclusion a necessity) will also be valid (Buridan n.d., Book 1, q. 33). This inference was not accepted either by Kilwardby or by Ockham; but it will be familiar to readers of Avicenna.[6]

---

[6] Principal author of the Arabic section is Riccardo Strobino, for the Latin section Paul Thom. The research for the Arabic section was conducted within the project 'Major Issues and Controversies of Arabic Logic and Philosophy of Language', run by Ruhr-Universität Bochum and the University of Cambridge with the financial support of the DFG and the AHRC.

15 Obligationes

Catarina Dutilh Novaes and Sara L. Uckelman

15.1 INTRODUCTION

Obligationes are a special, regimented kind of oral disputation involving two participants, known as opponent and respondent. Obligational disputations were an important topic for Latin medieval logicians in the thirteenth and especially fourteenth centuries (and beyond); indeed, most major fourteenth-century authors have written on *obligationes*. And yet, perhaps due to their highly regimented nature, modern interpreters have often described *obligationes* as 'obscure' and 'puzzling' (Stump 1982; Spade 2000). In what follows, we argue that there is nothing particularly mysterious about *obligationes* once they are placed in the broader context of an intellectual culture where disputations (of different kinds) occupied a prominent position. In effect, the inherent multi-agent character of *obligationes* must be taken seriously if one is to make sense of these theories.

In its best-known version, *positio*, opponent puts forward a first statement, the *positum*, which respondent must accept unless it is self-contradictory, thereby becoming 'obligated' towards it. (Typically, a *positum* is a false proposition.) Opponent then continues to put forward statements, the *proposita*, which respondent must concede, deny or doubt on the basis of specific rules. There were different versions of these rules, but according to the 'standard' approach, respondent ought to concede everything that follows from what he has granted so far together with the contradictories of what he has denied so far; and deny everything that is logically incompatible (inconsistent) with his previous actions and the commitments they generate. In the absence of such inferential relations with previous commitments, he should respond to a proposition on the basis of his own epistemic status towards it: concede it if he knows it to be true, deny it if he knows it to be false, and doubt those whose truth value he does not know (e.g. 'The pope is sitting right now'). So rather than tracking truth, responses were above all guided by inferential, logical relations, since these relations took precedence over the truth values of propositions.

Obligationes are essentially adversarial exchanges, as participants have opposite goals: opponent seeks to force respondent to concede something contradictory, while respondent seeks to avoid granting something contradictory. The exchange ends when respondent fails to maintain consistency, or else when opponent says 'time is up', after respondent has been able to maintain consistency long enough.

In this chapter, we begin with a systematic overview of the main sub-genres of *obligationes* and their logical properties. In the second part, we present a historical overview of the development of *obligationes*. In the third and final part, we discuss the 'point' of *obligationes*, both according to the medieval authors themselves and according to modern commentators.

15.2   KINDS OF *OBLIGATIONES*

In the thirteenth century, most authors distinguished six different species of *obligationes*: *positio, depositio, dubitatio, impositio/institutio, petitio,* and *rei veritas/sit verum*. Later authors, from the middle of the fourteenth century on, tended to reduce the six species to three: *positio, depositio,* and *impositio*. However, in terms of the types of disputation that they give rise to, it makes more sense to group *positio, depositio,* and *dubitatio* together on the one hand, and *petitio, impositio/institutio,* and *rei veritas/sit verum* on the other. Whether they identified six or only three species, *positio* is the main type, both in terms of historical development and in terms of space devoted to it in obligational treatises.

15.2.1   Positio *(and* Depositio*)*

The basic idea of a *positio* disputation is that a thesis, the *positum*, is accepted by the respondent in order to see what follows from it.

Typically, a *positum* will be a false proposition, as pointed out in the Emmeran treatise on false *positio*. This makes sense, as a true *positum* would not constitute much of a test for respondent's inferential abilities; with a true *positum*, respondent can simply respond on the basis of the truth values of the proposed propositions, and consistency will be maintained (as presumably, the actual world offers a 'model' verifying all these true propositions). True disputational skills are deployed only when assuming something one does not believe to be the case, and then being able to maintain consistency and determine what follows from it. In order to highlight the falsity of the *positum*, many authors also introduced the notion of a *casus*, i.e. an assumption external to the disputation. (Notice that '*casus*' is a juridical term – Pironet 1995.) A typical *casus* would be that Socrates is white, and the accompanying *positum* would be 'Socrates is black'.

A presentation of the 'standard' theory of *obligationes* can be found in Burley's treatise (Green 1963; Burley 1988), and this text provides the basis for the present discussion. A *positio* with a false *positum* may, but need not, start with the postulation of a *casus*. Opponent then puts forward a *positum*, which respondent must accept unless it is self-contradictory.[1] One way to think about such disputations is in terms of the *discursive commitments* that respondent undertakes when he grants, denies, or doubts the propositions subsequently put forward by opponent, the *proposita*. At each reply, a new set corresponding to the commitments of respondent up to that point is formed, and consists of the set of propositions previously granted and the contradictories of propositions previously denied. Let us refer to this set as the 'commitment set at stage *n*'.

One of the key concepts in the obligational framework is the notion of a proposition being *pertinent* to the previous commitments undertaken by respondent. A proposition proposed is pertinent at

---

[1] Thus, identifying self-contradictory, paradoxical *posita* was an important aspect in these obligational contexts, hence the connection with the *insolubilia* literature spelled out in Martin 2001. See also the discussion below on which impossible *posita* could be accepted.

stage n iff (if and only if): either it follows logically from the commitment set at stage n (*pertinens sequens*); or it is inconsistent with this set (*pertinens repugnans*).

On the basis of the notions of commitment set and pertinence, the rules of the game can be formulated as follows:

> Respondent ought to **concede** a *propositum* iff: either it is pertinent and follows from the commitment set formed so far; or it is impertinent and known to be true.
>
> Respondent ought to **deny** a *propositum* iff: either it is pertinent and inconsistent with the commitment set formed so far; or it is impertinent and known to be false.
>
> Respondent ought to **doubt** a *propositum* iff: it is impertinent and it is not known whether it is true or it is false.

The goal for respondent is to avoid granting contradictory propositions, thus destroying the consistency of his discursive commitments, while the goal for opponent is to force respondent to concede something impossible. The disputation ends when respondent grants a contradiction, or else when opponent says 'Time is up', after respondent has been able to maintain consistency for long enough.

Perhaps the best way to get a feel for what obligational disputations consist in is to take a look at an example. Table 15.1 gives one from Walter Burley's treatise (1988, 3.105, p. 403 in the English translation).

The disputation on Table 15.1 is presented, i.e. a situation in which respondent is forced by the rules of the game themselves to grant something impossible. Burley's solution is that the third proposition, 'Only this is the first proposition proposed' should be denied as inconsistent (*repugnans*) with the previously granted ones. To be sure, this is not a very convincing solution, but the sophism itself contains some of the elements that were exploited to make such disputations more difficult, such as references to previous or posterior moves in the game, and postulation of sameness of truth values. Another 'trick' was to formulate propositions containing concepts belonging to the

Table 15.1 *Example of a disputation – positio*

Proposition	Correct response
Positum: **'That you are a donkey is the same [in truth value] as the first proposition to be proposed [other than** *positum***].'**	**Admit**: it is the *positum*, and it is not self-contradictory.
'God exists.' [First proposition proposed]	**Concede**: impertinent, but true (in fact, necessary).
'Only this is the first proposition proposed.' [Indicating 'God exists']	**Concede**: impertinent, but true.
'You are a donkey.'	**Concede**: it follows from the *positum* together with a proposition correctly granted.

meta-level of obligational theories, such as 'is to be granted', 'is to be denied', etc. (For example, 'That Socrates is white must not be granted' presented as the *positum*.)

The game has a number of interesting logical and game-theoretical properties[2]:

Respondent can always 'win'. At least structurally, the rules of the game ensure that, if respondent performs adequately, he can always maintain consistency. This follows from the observation that any (non-maximal) consistent set of propositions can always be expanded with one of the elements of a pair of contradictories. In obligational terms, this means that, if the initial set is consistent (which corresponds to the requirement that the *positum* must not be self-contradictory), consistency can always be maintained by either granting or denying a given *propositum*, and the rules of the game ensure this.

But the game remains hard to play. Nevertheless, participating in an obligational disputation remains a nontrivial exercise. In practice,

---

[2] For a more extensive discussion of these properties, see Dutilh Novaes 2007, 3.3.

respondent has to update his commitment set constantly, and keep track of new inferential relations that may arise. Moreover, due to semantic intricacies of the propositions proposed – which include self-reference, reference to other propositions in the disputation (as in the example above), reference to properties of the obligational framework itself, among others – a respondent often finds himself in paradoxical situations. Many of the *sophismata* discussed in the obligational texts deal precisely with these 'difficult' cases.

The game is inherently dynamic. There are different senses in which *obligationes* can be said to be dynamic. One of them is the dependence on the order in which the *proposita* are proposed to determine the correct answer to a given proposition (in the *responsio antiqua*, that is – see below). Indeed, Burley lists this as one of the useful rules of the art: 'One must pay special attention to the order' (Burley 1988, 385). Another (related) dynamic feature is the fact that each move by respondent entails an *update* in his discursive commitments.

More generally, *positio* is simply a highly regimented account of what it means to maintain a thesis coherently in a dialogical situation: recognizing what follows from it, and accepting new commitments only insofar as they do not clash with what has been previously granted/denied (especially, but not exclusively, the initial thesis).

A *positio* disputation can also be initiated with an impossible proposition, i.e. one that is not only contingently false but necessarily so. One of the earliest known treatises on *obligationes*, the anonymous Emmeran treatise on impossible *positio* (edited in De Rijk 1974, English translation in Yrjönsuuri 2001), already spells out in quite some detail the general idea. Impossible *positio* continued to be discussed by later authors such as Ockham and Burley.

Impossible *positio* is much like false *positio*, but it requires some adaptations. For example, the logical rule according to which from the impossible anything follows cannot be enforced in the case of impossible *positio*, otherwise the whole enterprise would become trivial. So in impossible *positio*, a stricter notion of consequence is required, and the one proposed by the Emmeran treatise is based on conceptual relations of containment between consequent and ante-cedent. Moreover, discussions on impossible *positio* also point out that not any arbitrary impossibility is acceptable as a *positum*. In par-ticular, the Emmeran treatise says that an impossible *positum* that entails contradictory propositions must not be accepted.

Despite its apparent strangeness, medieval authors correctly perceived that impossible *posita* could serve as a powerful tool for logical analysis, and it is not surprising that the language of *positio impossibilis* often appears in connection with theological questions (Knuuttila 1997; Yrjönsuuri 2000).

As for *depositio*, which is sometimes presented by medieval authors as its own specific kind of *obligatio*, it is in fact structurally analogous to *positio*. In *depositio*, respondent is expected to reply as if he rejects the first proposition, the *depositum*. Given the under-lying assumptions of the framework, this is effectively equivalent to a *positio* with the contradictory of the *depositum* as the starting point, hence the structural analogy.

15.2.2 Dubitatio

In the genre *dubitatio*, opponent's primary obligation is to hold the initial proposition – the *dubitatum* – as doubtful. This means that nothing he concedes should logically imply it, and he should not deny anything that logically follows from it. The most exten-sive discussions of *dubitatio* occur in thirteenth-century texts such as *Obligationes Parisienses*, Nicholas of Paris' *Obligationes*, and the *Obligationes* attributed to William of Sherwood. *Obligationes Parisienses* is interesting because it is the only text which considers the question of whether *dubitatio* should be admitted as a legitimate distinct species of *obligatio*, given that the primary action of re-spondent is doubt, which does not fit into the bi-partite structure of disputation outlined by Aristotle (Uckelman et al. forthcoming, §3).

Of the early treatises, the clearest presentation of the rules for *dubitatio* occurs in Nicholas of Paris (Braakhuis 1998). As with *posi-tio*, which starts with false propositions, in *dubitatio* the *dubitatum* is typically a sentence whose value is known, either known to be true or known to be false. Nicholas gives seven rules for *dubitatio* (Braakhuis 1998, 72–76), many of which are structurally similar to the standard rules for *positio* and *depositio*. This results in the following obligations for the respondent:

> The respondent ought to **doubt** a *propositum* iff: it is identical to the *dubitatum*, it is logically equivalent to the *dubitatum*, it is contradictory to the *dubitatum*, or it is impertinent and its truth value is not known.
>
> The respondent ought to **concede** a *propositum* iff: it is impertinent and known to be true, or it is equivalent to something already granted.
>
> The respondent ought to **deny** a *propositum* iff: it is impertinent and known to be false, or it is equivalent to something already denied.

Nicholas' *dubitatio* has similar formal properties to *positio*. Provided that the *dubitatum* is neither a contradiction nor a tautology, it can be proved that respondent can win the disputation playing by Nicholas' rules for *dubitatio*: that is, he will never be forced either to concede or to deny the *dubitatum* (Uckelman 2011b, theorem 24).

We give an example in Table 15.2 of *dubitatio*, adapted from (Braakhuis 1998, 223–224), to give a sense of how these rules work. Because this example is intended to be one where respondent makes a mistake, Nicholas does not provide justifications for the responses.

In this example, respondent has made an error in the fourth step. He has responded correctly in the second and third rounds, since the second proposition is identical to the *dubitatum* and the third is equivalent to it, and, if his response to the fourth proposition were correct, he would have been correct in conceding the fifth, since 'black' and 'white' are exclusive, so Socrates' being white and his being black are inconsistent. However, respondent responds incorrectly to the fourth statement when he concedes that Socrates is black; for from the fact that it is doubtful whether Socrates is white

Table 15.2 *Example of a disputation – dubitatio*

Proposition	Response
1. 'Socrates is white'	Accepted: the dubitatum
2. 'Socrates is white'	Doubt
3. 'Socrates is pale/fair'	Doubt
4. 'Socrates is black'	Concede
5. 'It is false that Socrates is white'	Concede

it does not follow that Socrates is black, and further, by conceding that Socrates is black, the respondent is later forced to deny the *dubitatum*, thus violating his primary obligation.

This example may seem simple and trivial; and in fact, many modern commentators have discounted *dubitatio* as a trivial variant of *positio*, not worth further investigation in its own right (see, e.g., Spade and Yrjönsuuri 2014). In this, they follow the views of many medieval authors, such as Paul of Venice, Roger Swyneshed (not to be confused with his younger contemporary Richard Swyneshed), Richard Lavenham, John of Wesel, Richard Brinkley, and John of Holland, all of whom either reduce *dubitatio* to one of the other variants, or do not mention it at all. However, this view overlooks two of the interesting properties of *dubitatio* which set it apart from *positio*: the necessity of higher-order reasoning, and the indeterminacy of the rules.

The rules require reasoning about knowledge, not just truth. The addition of the question of knowledge, not just truth value, into the *dubitatum* requires that respondent reason at two different levels. Just as *positio* is only interesting when the *positum* is false or impossible, so *dubitatio* is only interesting when the *dubitatum* is known (whether it is true or false). Thus, in the context of a *dubitatio*, rather than simply acting as if a false proposition is not false, respondent must act as if a known proposition is not known. He must also distinguish between epistemic value and truth value. It is not the case, as some have argued (Stump 1985), that *dubitatio* involves some type of three-valued reasoning: while there is a tripartite structure to the actions of the respondent, in that some propositions must be doubted, some must be denied, and others must be conceded, these actions should not be thought of as assigning the truth values 'unassigned', 'false', and 'true' to the propositions.

The rules are nondeterministic. When a proposition is not false, there is (since medieval logic is essentially bivalent) only one option, namely, that it is true. However, when a proposition is not known, there are two options: a proposition could be not known because its negation is known, or a proposition could be not known because neither it nor its negation is known. Respondent must choose one of these options when forming his response. This is reflected in the nondeterministic nature of the rules. Burley's rules for *positio* are deterministic: for every *propositum*, if respondent has correctly responded so far, there will be a unique correct action for him to take. This is not the case for *dubitatio*. Above, we stated rules for respondent covering the cases of statements equivalent or contradictory to the *dubitatum*, and impertinent sentences. The case of pertinent (but not equivalent or contradictory) sentences was omitted. For these, Nicholas provides the following rules:

> The respondent must **not concede** a proposition iff: the proposition is antecedent to the *dubitatum*. He may, as he chooses, doubt or deny it.
>
> The respondent must **not deny** a proposition iff: the proposition is a consequence of the *dubitatum*. He may, as he chooses, doubt or concede it.

Once this feature of the rules is seen, it is clear that *dubitatio* cannot be reduced to *positio* without losing this indeterminacy (Uckelman 2011b).

15.2.3 Impositio *and* Petitio

Impositio (also called *institutio* or *appellatio*) and *petitio* can be treated together because of the way they differ from *positio, depositio,* and *dubitatio,* which is that the obligation by which respondent is bound does not concern how he is to respond to the *obligatum.* In *impositio,* respondent is obliged to redefine certain terms or phrases. For example, *Obligationes Parisienses* offers the following example of an uncertain *institutio* (uncertain because the new imposition is disjunctive): 'if the name "Marcus" is fixed to be a name of Socrates or Plato, but you would not know of which' (De Rijk 1975, 28).

At the end of the fourteenth century, Richard Lavenham provides a more complex example: 'I impose that in every false proposition in which "*a*" is put down that it signifies only a man and that in every true proposition in which "*a*" is put down that it signifies only a donkey, and that in every doubtful proposition in which "*a*" is put down that it signifies convertibly with this disjunction "man or non man"' (Spade 1978, §24, 235). Such an *impositio* should not be accepted by respondent; for consider what happens when the proposition 'Man is *a*' is put forward. If the proposition is true, then, it means 'Man is donkey', which is impossible; hence, the proposition is false. But if it is false, it means 'Man is man', which is true! Thus, if it cannot be true or false, then it must be doubtful. But if it is doubtful, then it means 'Man is man or not man', which again is true. This example shows a general characteristic of *impositiones,* namely, their connection to liar-like insolubles.

In *petitio,* opponent petitions respondent to respond in a certain way. Many authors, such as Nicholas of Paris, Marsilius of Inghen, Peter of Mantua, and Paul of Venice, argue that *petitio* can be reduced to *positio,* and few authors treat *petitio* at any length. (One exception is Walter Burley, who reduces *petitio* to *impositio* rather than to *positio.* He argues that '*petitio* is distinct from other species [of obligation], because a *petitio* posits the performance of an act that is mentioned in the statable thing [at issue], but the other species do not require this'; Burley 1988, 373–374.) There is one interesting way in which *petitio* differs from *positio*. Because the game begins with opponent's request, there is a division into relative and absolute *petitiones* which is not present in *positio*. An example of an absolute *petitio* is the following: 'I require you to concede that a man is a donkey'; an example of the second is 'I require you to concede the first thing to be proposed by me'. Such a meta-level distinction cannot be made in *positio*.

15.2.4 Sit verum

The sixth type, *sit verum* or *rei veritas*, is little discussed by later authors, most of whom treat it like *impositio* and *petitio* above, reducing it to a form of *positio*. The phrases literally mean 'let it be true' and 'the truth of things [is]', and functions similarly to the setting up of a *casus*. The most detailed discussions appear in the thirteenth-century texts. Nicholas of Paris' examples of *rei veritates* that cannot be sustained often include epistemic clauses. For examples, he says that

> it is customary to say that this cannot be sustained: 'the truth of things (*rei veritas*) is that only Socrates knows that the king is in Paris'. For if it is sustained, then a contradiction follows. For if you know that only Socrates knows that the king is in Paris, you know that Socrates knows nothing except the truth; therefore you know that the king is in Paris is true, and thus you know that the king is in France, therefore not only Socrates knows this. (Braakhuis 1998, 233)

This example shows an interesting resemblance to Fitch's and Moore's paradoxes.

Another discussion worth noting occurs in *Obligationes Parisienses*, where *rei veritas* is compared with *positio* as follows (De Rijk 1975, 28):

> And *rei veritas* differs from *positio* because in the case of *rei veritas*, then concerning anything irrelevant or not following, it

is not to be denied, but in the case of *positio*, it is to be denied. Whence given 'The truth of things is that the Antichrist exists', then to this: 'The Antichrist is white', the response should be 'prove it!', but in the case of *positio* the response to the same should be: 'It is false!'

When a disputation is prefaced by saying 'let it be true that …'. this changes the truth value of the proposition during the disputation in a way that conceding or denying a proposition does not. As a result, this type of *rei veritas* shows analogies with counterfactual reasoning (Uckelman 2015).

15.3 ORIGINS AND HISTORICAL DEVELOPMENT

It is widely acknowledged that the practice of disputation and debate occupied a prominent place in later medieval intellectual life, a trend that started as early as the eleventh century, if not earlier (Novikoff 2013). The emergence of the specific genre of disputation known as *obligationes* falls squarely within this broader trend, and as such is not exceptionally 'mysterious'. True enough, *obligationes* is a particularly regimented genre, but it is ultimately not too far removed in spirit from other kinds of disputations.

In some twelfth-century texts, we find terminology later associated with *obligationes* in discussions on disputation (Stump 1982; Martin 2001), especially the notion of *positio*, which may suggest that disputations roughly following the *obligationes* mould might have been taking place already at that point. But there seems to be no explicit reference to a genre of disputation called *obligationes*.

The (presumed) earliest texts specifically discussing *obligationes* have been tentatively dated to the first decades of the thirteenth century. These texts focus on the theory behind the practice, i.e. they are primarily directed towards the acquisition of the art of obligational disputations. In effect, we have no written record of obligational disputations as they actually took place, but we can only assume (on the basis of these texts) that they did take place.

It is also worth noticing that much of the vocabulary pertaining to *obligationes* has a distinctively juridical ring to it (Pironet 1995); '*obligatio*' itself is a legal term, famously defined in the *Institutes* of Justinian. The hypothesis that the development of *obligationes* may have been influenced by legal/juridical practices is plausible, but so far it has not been investigated in sufficient detail.

15.3.1 Ancient Precursors

A common theme in the historiography of Latin medieval logic in general is the connections between theories developed in this period and ancient sources, especially Aristotle (see Chapter 1 in this volume). In this respect, on the one hand, it makes sense to ask what could have been the ancient precursors of the genre, which may have provided the historical background for its emergence. On the other hand, we will argue that *obligationes* are a genuine medieval innovation, going beyond Aristotle.

At first sight, *obligationes* bear striking similarities with the dialectical game of questions and answers described in Aristotle's *Topics*. In these games, the participants are known as 'questioner' and 'answerer': Answerer picks an initial thesis, and then questioner tries to force answerer to concede further claims that contradict the initial thesis. *Obligationes* also involve two similar players, opponent and respondent,[3] and at least superficially the two frameworks appear to be very similar.

However, virtually none of the early texts on *obligationes* explicitly mentions the dialectical games of the *Topics*. In effect, while the framework of the *Topics* as such had been familiar to Latin medieval authors via Boethius (Stump 1989), up to the thirteenth century, medieval authors tended to focus on the material from books II to VII (Stump 1989, chapter 3; Yrjönsuuri 1993, 61). These concern the doctrine of the *loci* (roughly, argumentation schemata) more

---

[3] In the *Aristoteles Latinus* translation of *Topics* (due to Boethius in the sixth century, but only recovered in the twelfth century), 'questioner' and 'answerer' are translated as '*opponens*' and '*respondens*'.

than the issue of dialectical exchanges as such, which are discussed in books I and VIII. Presumably, it is only when Aristotle's *Topics* itself became more widely read in the thirteenth century (Dod 1982, 69) that many of these authors would have become familiar with Aristotle's own theory of dialectic.[4] By then, the development of the obligational genre was already well on its way.

Nevertheless, once the *Topics* became more widely read, some thirteenth-century authors were quick to recognize the similarities with *obligationes*. This is the case particularly with the treatise attributed to Nicholas of Paris (dated circa 1240, edited in Braakhuis 1998) and of Boethius of Dacia's questions on the *Topics* (dated to the first half of the 1270s, discussed in Yrjönsuuri 1993). In the introduction to his seminal but unpublished critical editions of the *obligationes* treatises by William of Sherwood (mid-thirteenth century) and Walter Burley (early fourteenth century), Green (1963, 25) also notes that the opening words of Burley's treatise are almost identical to the opening words of chapter VIII.4 of Aristotle's *Topics*.

But if not directly the theory of dialectic present in the *Topics*, what else, if anything, could have been the ancient sources for the historical development of *obligationes*? Early treatises refer to the idea that an impossibility be posited to see what follows from it, and attribute this idea to Aristotle. Martin (2001) claims that no such thing is to be found in Aristotle's own writings,[5] but that something similar is found in Boethius' *De Hypotheticis Syllogismis* (composed in the early sixth century), namely the idea of a proposition being agreed to not because it is thought to be true, but to see what would follow from it. These include even impossible propositions such as that a man is a stone, which presumably then gave rise to the idea of impossible *positio* (see Section 15.2.1). It is also worth noticing that in *Prior Analytics*, the concept of an argument through a

---

[4] However, note that John of Salisbury's *Metalogicon* (1159) refers extensively to Aristotle's discussions of disputation in *Topics*.

[5] However, in the *Topics* there are many passages arguably suggesting something to this effect.

hypothesis occupies a prominent position, and this too may have been an indirect source for the development of the idea of granting something so as to see what follows from it. Indeed, some later texts (e.g. John of Holland's in the fourteenth century) refer to *Prior Analytics* when discussing some aspects of *obligationes*, in particular the claim that from the possible, nothing impossible follows (*APri* 32a18–20).

Moreover, it has been convincingly argued (Martin 2001) that obligational disputations may have provided the motivation for the development of the literature on *insolubilia* (Chapter 11 of this volume). Furthermore, theories of consequence (Chapter 13 of this volume) also entertain close ties with the *obligationes* literature. Thus, three of the main topics in later Latin medieval logic appear to be closely connected.

15.3.2 Thirteenth-Century Theories

The (presumed) earliest extant treatises on *obligationes* are three anonymous and undated treatises edited by De Rijk and published in the mid-1970s: the treatise *Obligationes Parisiensis*, which is from the first half of the thirteenth century and can be tentatively dated to the first or second decade of the century (De Rijk 1975, 5); and the paired treatises *Tractatus Emmeranus de Falsi Positione* and *Tractatus Emmeranus de Impossibili Positio*, from the end of the twelfth century or the first half of the thirteenth century (De Rijk 1974, 96). None of these treatises can be dated exactly, but it is quite likely that the Emmeran treatises are the oldest. In both of these treatises, the only species of *obligatio* discussed is *positio* – giving the species a primacy which it continued to receive throughout the next two centuries.

This raises the question of what came first, the chicken or the egg? Or, in our case, *positio* or *obligatio*? As noted above, '*positio*' as a technical method is already present in some twelfth-century texts, long before the general genre of *obligationes* appeared on the scene (even if we assume that there were treatises earlier than the Emmeran ones which haven't survived). Martin (2001, 63) gives examples of how *positio* was used in the context of twelfth-century reasoning about liar-like paradoxes. Liar paradoxes do not arise in a vacuum; they can only occur in certain circumstances which are unlikely to happen accidentally. The creation of such circumstances in which a liar-like sentence can be genuinely paradoxical was achieved via the act of *positio*, hypothesis or positing. The connection between the obligational species of *positio* and this use of *positio* is clear in the Emmeran treatises, where the examples used closely resemble what Martin calls Eudemian hypotheses (Martin 2001, 65). However, the Emmeran treatises clearly go beyond this method. In the treatise on false *positio*, *positio* is described as one of the ways 'in which a respondent can be obligated in a disputation'. This dialogical aspect is missing in the earlier discussions of Eudemian hypotheses and is, of course, one of the most important aspects of *obligationes*.

We also see the conscious development of these dialogical aspects in the treatise *Obligationes Parisienses*, which likely predates the middle of the thirteenth century. This treatise reflects a more developed stage of the genre, in that it discusses the types and species of *obligatio*, identifying six (*positio, depositio, dubitetur, institutio, rei veritas*, and *petitio*), before devoting a section to each of the first three. That this text still reflects a developing stage is clear from the discussion at the start of the second section, where the author considers the question of whether 'it must be doubted' is in fact a proper obligation for a disputant; the discussion, which refers back to Aristotle's *Topics*, is instructive for understanding both the roles of the various species of *obligatio* as well as the Aristotelian roots of the genre.

Once we move past these three early treatises, into the middle and late thirteenth century, the treatises start showing a more coherent and cohesive approach to *obligationes*. The treatises generally adopt the same division of *obligationes* into six species, and the rules presented for each are clear, comprehensive, and non-overlapping. From the middle of the second half of the century, we have a number of texts with authors either explicitly ascribed or probable. These include the treatises putatively ascribed to William of Sherwood (the short *Tractatus Sorbonnensis de Petitionibus Contrariorum*, attributed to William of Sherwood, De Rijk 1976, 26, and a fuller treatment of the topic edited in Green 1963), a roughly contemporaneous treatise by Nicholas of Paris (Braakhuis 1998), a somewhat later treatise by Peter of Spain, and Walter Burley's canonical treatise (discussed in the next subsection).

What we see through the thirteenth century is the development and codification of a methodological tool which is essentially dialogical, and which can be put to use in many different contexts – be it the study of *insolubilia*, the working out of the notion of consequence, or as pedagogical exercises for students. True enough, *positio* is straightforward if one has antecedently a well-defined system of inference. But this is precisely what was being developed in the twelfth and thirteenth centuries, and the development of *obligationes* as a logical genre went in tandem with – and clearly influenced and was influenced by – the development of theories of consequence. If one doesn't already have a way of determining what follows from what, only the general constraint that an impossibility does not follow from a possibility, then *obligationes* show their utility as a method for identifying what follows from what: 'P' follows from 'Q' only if respondent's conceding 'P' after conceding 'Q' never leads to contradiction (a necessary but not sufficient condition).

15.3.3 Fourteenth-Century Theories

In the fourteenth century, *obligationes* became one of the main topics for Latin logicians. The development of the genre in this period can be summarized as follows: Walter Burley's treatise (composed in 1302) represents the standard formulation of the theory and is for the most part in line with developments in the thirteenth century. Subsequently, authors such as Richard Kilvington and Roger Swyneshed pointed out some odd properties of the standard theory;

these criticisms motivated Swyneshed in particular to introduce quite substantial modifications to the standard obligational rules in his *obligationes* treatise, written in the first half of the 1330s (Spade 1977). The two sets of rules were then referred to as *responsio antiqua* (Burley's approach) vs. *responsio nova* (Swyneshed's new approach). Swyneshed's approach seems to have garnered some adepts, but as it gave rise to its own set of problems, it eventually became entirely supplanted by the *responsio antiqua* again later in the fourteenth century. This section spells out these developments in more detail.

Before we proceed, a clarification on the content of *obligationes* treatises in general is in order. After some preliminary considerations, these treatises typically started by introducing the rules defining the correct moves in the game (generally, the rules applied only to respondent; opponent was virtually unconstrained in his moves). After that, a number of puzzles (usually referred to as *sophismata* – see Chapter 11 in this volume) were introduced so as to test the robustness and coherence of the set of rules just proposed. These puzzles were situations in which it would seem at first sight that the rules in question would lead to some incoherent result (for example, that respondent would be forced both to concede and to deny a given *propositum*). To defend his proposed rules, the author would then have to offer a solution to the puzzle by showing that his rules did offer the resources to avoid the incoherent result in question. So these *sophismata* were the main tools used to test the correctness and cogency of a given system of rules for obligational disputations; typically, the treatises have more pages discussing *sophismata* than discussing the rules as such. (See Section 15.4.1 for more on the connection between *obligationes* and *sophismata*.)

For example, Walter Burley's influential treatise spends many pages discussing puzzles that might constitute potential objections to his theory of *obligationes*, and rebuts these objections. However, later authors, in particular Kilvington in his *Sophismata*

(c. 1325) pointed out a number of other puzzling consequences of the Burley-style theory, which led Kilvington to propose some revisions of the usual rules (Stump 1982; Spade 1982b).

One of the properties of the *responsio antiqua* is that respondent may be forced to concede any falsehood whatsoever, if the *positum* is a disjunction of two (contingently) false propositions: if after the *positum* has been granted one of the two disjuncts is proposed, it should be denied as false and irrelevant (i.e. it is neither entailed by, nor incompatible with, the *positum*). But now, respondent has committed to 'P or Q' and to 'not-P', and these two commitments taken together force him to concede 'Q', i.e. the arbitrary falsehood. Similarly, if Q is proposed immediately after the *positum* instead of P, then Q will be denied and P subsequently granted, which is the exact opposite of the correct responses if P is proposed before Q. This means (as noted above) that the response a proposition should receive is also highly dependent on the *order* in which different propositions are proposed in a given disputation.

Roger Swyneshed was particularly dissatisfied with these consequences of the Burley-style theory, and proposed important modifications. The core of Swyneshed's proposed modifications is the fact that respondent's responses to impertinent *proposita* are not added to the pool of commitments on the basis of which subsequent *proposita* are to be evaluated (Dutilh Novaes 2007, 3.4). In other words, while for Burley a given *propositum* is to be evaluated on the basis of the *positum* but also the previously granted *proposita* and the contradictories of the previously denied *proposita*, for Swyneshed all *proposita* should be evaluated only on the basis of the *positum*.

In the example above, of a *positum* consisting of a disjunction of two falsehoods, both P and Q would be denied as irrelevant to the *positum* and false, regardless of the order in which they are proposed. So the 'inconvenience' of having to concede any arbitrary falsehood and the 'unwelcome' effect of order determining the responses are thereby excluded. The price to be paid, though, is that in a Swyneshed-style disputation, it may well happen that respondent will be required to concede an inconsistent set of propositions (for example, to concede a disjunction while denying both disjuncts), a possibility excluded by the *responsio antiqua*.

Swyneshed's *responsio nova* seems to have had some influence, but it was also severely criticized by later authors. Ralph Strode, in particular (writing c. 1360/70s) criticizes Swyneshed's proposed modifications (Ashworth 1993), arguing that they lead to even more absurd conclusions than the ones Swyneshed attributed to the standard theory (for example, that one could concede a disjunction while denying both disjuncts). Towards the end of the fourteenth century, the standard approach represented in Burley's treatise reigned again, in treatises by Strode, Paul of Venice (1988), and Peter of Mantua (Strobino 2009), among others. But these later authors did not simply return to the Burleian formulation of the theory: their theories offer refinements that may be seen as prompted by the challenge posed by Swyneshed's *responsio nova*. *Obligationes* remained an item on the basic logic curriculum well into the fifteenth century, even if no significant theoretical innovations seem to have been introduced in this later period.

15.4   WHAT IS THE 'POINT' OF *OBLIGATIONES*?

Modern commentators have often raised the question of the 'point' of *obligationes*; what was the *purpose* of these theories? Many have described the genre as puzzling and mysterious. However, it is clear that the genre is fully embedded in an intellectual culture where disputations of various kinds occupied a prominent role. Moreover, it is worth noticing that obligational vocabulary is widely present in texts on a range of topics, suggesting that the framework is also useful for investigation and inquiry outside purely dialogical, disputational contexts.

In what follows, we first discuss some of the rationales for *obligationes* as offered by the medieval authors themselves, and then turn to modern interpretations.

15.4.1 *According to Medieval Authors*

Spade puts *obligationes* on his list of medieval 'conspiracy theories', famously wondering 'Why don't medieval logicians ever tell us what they're doing?' (Spade 2000). As it turns out, with regard to *obligationes*, medieval authors often *did* tell us. In this section, we are interested in answering two questions: (1) What is the purpose of *obligationes* according to medieval authors? (2) How, and how well, is that purpose carried out given the rules and applications in the treatises?

As should not be surprising, earlier treatises provide more guidance concerning the purpose and use of obligational disputations. The *Tractatus Emmeranus de Falsi Positione* says the method of false position has two purposes. The first, and primary, is 'To see what follows from a statement when you assume it'. The second is the more general 'To see what happens'. This second purpose is explored in the companion treatise on impossible *positiones*; as discussed above, in impossible *positio*, an impossible proposition is put forward initially by opponent, and the author's argument for why this is not immediately problematic for respondent is that 'What we can understand we can put forward, and what we can put forward we can concede'.

Obligationes Parisienses (De Rijk 1975) offers two different purposes for the disputations, and pairs with each purpose a specific type of *obligatio*. The species of *positio* is designed for acquiring beliefs and knowledge about the consequences that hold between statements, whereas the species of *dubitatio* is designed to teach respondent the appropriate art in restricted disputations.

Nicholas of Paris' analysis is interesting for two different reasons. First, he agrees with others that *obligationes* are useful exercises, but differs from them in terms of the aim of these exercises. While many authors point towards the maintenance of consistency, Nicholas says that the aim is 'glory and victory'. (The 'victory' vocabulary is also found in Strode's treatise, composed roughly one century later in the 1360s.) As a result, Nicholas' *obligationes* can be seen as an interesting synthesis of Aristotelian dialectical and sophistical disputations – they are dialectical in the method of proceeding, but sophistical in the intended aims.[6] This rather self-centred approach to the disputations is unusual for treatises on *obligationes*, but shares some features with the treatises *De modo opponendi et respondendi*, edited by De Rijk (1980) and analysed by Pérez-Ilzarbe (2011). De Rijk dismisses the treatises in this tradition because of their overt aim of teaching the disputant how to deceive rivals (Pérez-Ilzarbe 2011, 129), but this dismissal is too quick, as being taught how to deceive also teaches one how not to be deceived – and 'avoiding traps' is one of the other explicit purposes which authors of obligational treatises offer.

In the later part of the thirteenth century and into the fourteenth century, we start to see explicit connections between obligational techniques and the solving of sophisms. Such statements can be found in the late-thirteenth-century Oxford *Tractatus Sorbonnensis* (de Rijk 1976), which cites both *falsi positio* and *petitio contrariorum* 'petition of contraries' as tools for solving sophisms. A fifteenth-century anonymous treatise, found in conjunction with a reworking of Peter of Spain's *Tractatus Syncategorematicum*, also focuses on the connection between obligational techniques and insoluble sentences. In particular, the purpose of *obligationes* is given as setting and escaping from traps, specifically that from something possible an impossibility does not follow, and that certain propositions by their signification destroy themselves. Further corroboration for this approach can be found by looking not at treatises on *obligationes* but at treatises on sophisms and insolubles, where even though obligational disputations are not defined and introduced explicitly, much of the same vocabulary – ought to concede, ought to deny, etc. – is used.

Other authors pick up on the consistency-maintenance aspect of *obligationes* as primary, such as the anonymous *De arte obligatoria*

---

[6] Notice that both *Sophistical Refutations* and the *Topics* also contain instructions on how to deceive opponent.

written in Oxford probably between 1335 and 1349 (Kreztmann and Stump 1985). The author offers three explicit purposes for his text: to test whether respondent has the art; to provide direction in exercise; and 'so that we may know what to do and how to respond when things are in fact as the false *casus* indicates'. In particular, these techniques are said to be useful for both jurists and moral philosophers.

Of course, Spade is right that not all authors provide guidance to the goal and purpose of the disputations. For example, John of Holland's (1985) *Obligationes*, written between 1369 and 1375 and a standard university text on the topic in the late fourteenth and early fifteenth centuries, does not discuss the matter at all. Nevertheless, it would be a mistake not to look at what authors who do say something actually say, and not to take these statements seriously in the determination of the function and place of *obligationes* in both medieval logic and medieval academic life.

15.4.2 Modern Interpretations

There is a certain tendency among modern scholars of medieval logic to attempt to establish the closest counterpart to a given medieval theory among modern theories or concepts. In the first instance, this may be viewed as a potentially fruitful heuristic, aiming at making the medieval theories more intelligible to modern audiences. Moreover, there seems to be another, more ideological reason for this tendency, namely the idea that such a comparison will reveal why modern readers should be interested at all in these medieval theories – i.e. insofar as they resemble modern theories and concepts, and thus speak to modern concerns. However, it has been argued (Dutilh Novaes 2007, chapter 1; Cameron 2011) that such projections may well hinder the comprehension of the medieval theories and concepts in question in that they obfuscate what is specific about them. Thus, comparisons with modern theories must be undertaken with great caution, essentially with the goal of obtaining explanatory effect, and aiming at an understanding of these theories in their own terms.

394 CATARINA DUTILH NOVAES AND SARA L. UCKELMAN

In their attempts to make sense of the 'point' of *obligationes*, modern commentators tend to focus only on *positio*, ignoring the other genres. A number of interpretations of *positio* have been proposed (Dutilh Novaes 2007, 3.2). *Positio* has been variously described as a theory of counterfactual reasoning (Spade 1982c; King 1991), as being closely connected to modern theories of belief revision (Lagerlund and Olsson 2001), as proto-axiomatic theories (Boehner 1952), and as a framework for the formulation of thought experiments (King 1991). Arguments against each of these interpretations of *positio* can be found in Dutilh Novaes (2007, 3.2) and Uckelman (2011a, 2013), but one common feature they have is the almost total disregard for the inherently dialogical, multi-agent nature of *obligationes*.

Indeed, as we've argued throughout this chapter, it is important to take the dialogical component into account when discussing *obligationes*: it is not happenstance that the framework is presented in terms of two agents, opponent and respondent, and their dialogical interactions. Now, there are numerous modern theories of dialogues, in connection with logic (in the tradition of dialogical logic), philosophy (Brandom 1994), and argumentation theory. These theories also display different levels of formalization/regimentation. We suggest that, among these modern theories, a number of them may be fruitfully compared to *obligationes*. The choice of framework for such comparisons should be made in respect of the specific aspect(s) of *obligationes* that a given analysis seeks to highlight.

Some of the explicitly multi-agent, dialogical interpretations of *obligationes* that have been proposed (not coincidentally, by the authors of the present chapter) are: *obligationes* as games of consistency maintenance (Dutilh Novaes 2007, 3.3); *obligationes* as a theory of discursive commitment management, somewhat in the spirit of Brandom's 'game of giving and asking for reasons' (Dutilh Novaes 2009, 2011); *obligationes* as formal dialogue systems (Uckelman 2013); *obligationes* as something different from dialogical logic (Uckelman 2011a).

15.5 CONCLUSION

In this chapter, we have surveyed the main features in the development of medieval theories of *obligationes*. These developments span roughly three centuries, and it is important to keep in mind the variety of approaches and concepts. Nevertheless, there is a core that remains more or less stable throughout, and we have argued that the key to understanding the obligational genre is to focus on its multi-agent, dialogical nature. In a nutshell, *obligationes* represent a highly regimented form of disputation, focusing on the phenomenon of discursive commitment transfer through inferential relations between propositions. As such, besides the obvious historical import, *obligationes* have much to offer also to modern philosophers and logicians interested in the formal, structural properties of dialogues.

Bibliography

PRIMARY SOURCES

Abbo of Fleury. 1966. *Opera inedita I. Syllogismorum categoricum et hypotheti-corum enodatio.* A. Van de Vyver (ed.). Bruges: De Tempel.

Abelard, Peter. 1919. 'Glossule super Porphyrium', in *Logica ingredientibus'.* In Abelard 1919–1933, I.

1919–1933. *Peter Abaelards Philosophische Schriften.* Bernhard Geyer (ed.). Beiträge zur Geschichte der Philosophie und Theologie des Mittelalters 21. Münster: Aschendorff.

1933. *Logica 'nostrorum petitioni sociorum'.* In Abelard 1919–1933, IV.

1956. *Dialectica.* L. M. De Rijk (ed.). Assen: Van Gorcum.

1970. *Dialectica,* second edition. L. M. de Rijk (ed.). Assen: Van Gorcum.

2010a. *Glossae super Periermeneias.* K. Jacobi and C. Strub (eds.). Corpus Christianorum Continuatio Mediaevalis 206, Turnhout: Brepols.

2010b. *Historia Calamitatum.* Whitefish, MT: Kessinger.

'Ajam, R. 1985–1986. *Al-Manṭiq 'inda al-Fārābī,* three volumes. Beirut: Dār al-Mashriq.

Albert of Saxony. 1490. *Sophismata.* Paris: George Vuolf.

2002. *Albert of Saxony's Twenty-five Disputed Questions on Logic: A Critical Edition of His Quaestiones circa Logicam.* Leiden: Brill.

2010. *Logica.* Hamburg: Meiner.

Albert the Great. 1890. *Liber I Priorum Analyticorum.* In A. Borgnet (ed.), *Opera omnia.* Paris: Vives, I.

Alcuin. 1863. *Patrologia latina* 101.

Al-Fārābī. 1960. *Commentary on Aristotle's Peri Hermeneias (De Interpretatione).* W. J. Kutsch and S. Marrow (eds.). Beirut: Imprimerie Catholique.

1971. *Kitāb al-Khaṭāba. Deux ouvrages inédits sur la Rhétorique.* I. J. Langhade (ed. and tr.). *Didascalia in Rhetoricam Aristotelis ex glosa Alpharabi(i).* II. M. Grignaschi (ed.). Beirut: Dār al-Mashriq.

1985–1986. *Kitāb al-Taḥlīl* (The Book of Analysis). In R. 'Ajam 1985–1986.

1987. *Kitāb al-Burhān wa-Kitāb Sharā'iṭ al-yaqīn ma'a Ta'ālīq Ibn Bājja 'alā al-Burhān.* M. Fakhry (ed.). Beirut: Dār al-Mashriq.

2005. *Iḥṣā' al-'ulūm.* 'U. Amīn (ed.). Paris: Dār Bibliyūn.

396

Al-Ghazali. 1965. *Tractatus de logica*. In C. Lohr (ed.), 'Logica Algazelis: Introduction and Critical Text'. *Traditio* 21: 223–290.

1969. *Logica et philosophia*. Frankfurt: Minerva.

Anglicus, Robertus. 2005. 'Scriptum super Libro Porphyrii'. In D. Piché (ed.), *Le problème des universaux à la Faculté des Arts de Paris entre 1230–1260*. Paris: Vrin, 264–333.

Anonymous. 1882. 'Dialectica'. In Paul Piper (ed.), *Die Schriften Notkers und seiner Schule*. Freiburg and Tübingen: Mohr, lvi–lxxv.

Anonymous. 1967. 'Introductiones Montane minores'. In De Rijk 1962–1967, II, 7–71.

Anonymous. 1981. 'De locis argumentationum'. In Iwakuma Yukio, 'Instantiae: A Study of Twelfth Century Technique of Argumentation with an Edition of Ms. Paris BN lat. 6674 f. 1–5'. *Cahiers de l'Institute du Moyen Âge Grec et Latin* 38: 12–60.

Anonymous. 1983. 'Compendium Logicae Porretanum'. Sten Ebbesen, Margareta Karin Fredborg and Lauge Olaf Nielsen (eds.). *Cahiers de l'Institute du Moyen-Âge Grec et Latin* 46: 1–93.

Anonymous. 2004. 'De complexe significabilibus', in *Sophistria 'Quoniam quatuor'*. In E. P. Bos (ed.), *Logica modernorum in Prague about 1400*. Leiden: Brill, §§ 85 and 86.

Aouad, Maroun. 2002. *Averroès, Commentaire moyen à la 'Rhétorique' d'Aristote Édition critique du texte arabe et traduction française*, three volumes. Union Académique Internationale, Corpus Philosophorum Medii Aevi, Averrois Opera, Series A: Averroes Arabicus, XVII. Paris: Vrin.

Aquinas, Thomas. 1962. *Aristotle: On Interpretation*. Commentary by St. Thomas and Cajetan. Jean T. Oesterle (tr.). Milwaukee, WI: Marquette University Press.

1995. *Commentary on Aristotle's Metaphysics*. John P. Rowan (tr.). South Bend, IN: Dumb Ox Books.

2000. *S. Thomae de Aquino Opera Omnia, recognovit ac instruxit Enrique Alarcón automato electronico Pompaelone ad Universitatis Studiorum Navarrensis aedes a MM A.D.* URL www.corpusthomisticum.org/iopera .html (last accessed 30 April 2016).

Aristotle. 1965. *Aristotle's Prior and Posterior Analytics: A Revised Text with Introduction and Commentary by W.D. Ross*. Oxford: Clarendon Press.

1984. *The Complete Works of Aristotle*. J. Barnes (ed.), two volumes. Princeton University Press.

Averroes: see Ibn Rushd.

Avicenna: see Ibn Sīnā.

Bacon, Roger. 1986. 'Summulae dialectices: I. De termino, II. De enuntiatione'. A. de Libera (ed.), *Archives d'histoire doctrinale et littéraire du moyen âge* 53: 139–289.

Badawi, Abd al-Rahman. 1947. *Aristu Inda l-Arab /Aristote chez les Arabes.* Cairo: La Renaissance Egyptienne.

1948–1952. *Organon Aristotelis in versione Arabica antiqua,* three volumes. Cairo: Librairie al-Nahḍa al-miṣrīya. Also published as *Manṭiq Arisṭū,* three volumes. Al-Kuwait-Beirut: Wikālat al-Maṭbū'āt-Dār al-Qalam, 1980.

1971. *Commentaires sur Aristote: Perdus en grec, et autres épîtres.* Beirut: Dar el-Mach-req.

Bahmanyār. 1970. *Al-Taḥṣīl.* M. Mutahheri (ed.). Tehran: Dānishkādeh-i Ilāhīyāt va Ma'ārif-i Islāmī.

Bergsträsser, G. 1925. *Ḥunain ibn Isḥāq über die syrischen und arabischen Galen Übersetzungen.* Leipzig: Brockhaus.

Billingham, Richard. 1982. 'Terminus est in quem sive Speculum puerorum'. In Lambertus M. De Rijk (ed.), *Some Fourteenth Century Tracts on the Probationes Terminorum.* Nijmegen: Ingenium, 45–186.

1987a. 'De significato propositionis'. In M. J. Fitzgerald (ed.), *Richard Brinkley's Theory of Sentential Reference: 'De significato propositionis' from Part V of His 'Summa logicae'.* Leiden: Brill, 143–150.

1987b. 'Utrum idem est Sortes et Sortem esse'. In M. J. Fitzgerald (ed.), *Richard Brinkley's Theory of Sentential Reference: 'De significato propositionis' from Part V of his 'Summa logicae'.* Leiden: Brill, 125–142.

2003. 'De Consequentiis'. In S. Weber (ed.), *Richard Billingham 'De Consequentiis' mit Toledo-Kommentar.* Amsterdam: Grüner, 27–78.

Boethius, A. M. S. 1877. *Commentarii in librum Aristotelis Peri Hermeneias: Editio Prima.* C. Meiser (ed.). Leipzig: Teubner.

1906. *In Isagogen Porphyrii Commentorum Editionis Secundae,* S. Brandt (ed.), Vienna/Leipzig, 135–348.

1969. *De hypotheticis syllogismis.* L. Obertello (ed.), with Italian translation. Brescia: Paideia.

1990. 'De topicis differentiis'. In D. Z. Nikitas (ed.), *Boethius' De topicis differentiis und die byzantinische Rezeption dieses Werkes.* The Academy of Athens, 1–92. The text is also printed in J. P. Migne (ed.), 1844–1855, *Patrologia Latina,* LXIV, cols. 1173B–1216D.

2008. *De syllogismo categorico.* Christina Thomsen Thörnqvist (ed.). University of Gothenburg.

Bradwardine, Thomas. 2010. *Insolubilia.* Stephen Read (ed. and tr.). Leuven: Peeters.

Brinkley, Richard. 1987. 'De significato propositionis'. In M. J. Fitzgerald (ed.), *Richard Brinkley's Theory of Sentential Reference. 'De significato propositionis' from Part V of His 'Summa logicae'.* Leiden: Brill, 34–116.

Buridan, John. 1513. *Quaestiones super decem libros Ethicorum Aristotelis ad Nicomachum*. [Paris]. Reprinted as Buridan 1968.

1957. 'Tractatus de suppositionibus'. Maria Elena Reina (ed.). *Rivista critica di storia della filosofia* 12: 175–208, 323–352.

1968. *Super decem libros Ethicorum*. Frankfurt: Minerva. Reprint of Buridan 1513.

1976. *Tractatus de Consequentiis*. H. Hubien (ed.). Louvain: Presses Universitaires.

1977. *Sophismata*. T. K. Scott (ed.). Stuttgart: Froommann Holzboog.

2001. *Summulae de Dialectica: An Annotated Translation, with a Philosophical Introduction by Gyula Klima*. G. Klima (ed.). New Haven, CT: Yale University Press.

2015. *Treatise on Consequences*. Stephen Read (tr.). New York: Fordham University Press.

n.d. *Iohannis Buridani Quaestiones in duos libros Aristotelis Priorum Analyticorum*. Herbert Hubien (ed.). Unpublished typescript. URL http://www.logicmuseum.com/wiki/Authors/Buridan/Quaestiones_in_analytica_priora (last accessed 30 April 2016).

Burley, Walter. 1497. 'Liber Praedicamentorum'. In *Expositio super Artem veterem Porphyrii et Aristotelis*. [Venice], fol. c3va–h2vb.

1955. *De Puritate Artis Logicae Tractatus Longior*. P. Boehner (ed.). Franciscan Institute Publications, Text Series No. 9. St Bonaventure, NY: Franciscan Institute.

1972. *De suppositionibus*. S. F. Brown (ed.), 'Walter Burleigh's Treatise *De suppositionibus* and Its Influence on William of Ockham'. *Franciscan Studies* 32: 15–64.

1973. 'Commentary on Aristotle's On Interpretation'. S. Brown, 'Walter Burley's Middle Commentary on Aristotle's Peri Hermeneias'. *Franciscan Studies* 33: 45–134.

1974. *Quaestiones in librum Perihermeneias*. S. F. Brown (ed), 'Walter Burley's Quaestiones in librum Perihermeneias'. *Franciscan Studies* 34: 200–295.

1980. *De consequentiis (1300)*. In N. J. Green-Pedersen (ed.), 'Walter Burley's "De Consequentiis": An Edition'. *Franciscan Studies*, 40: 102–166.

1988. 'Obligations (selections)'. In N. Kretzmann and E. Stump (eds.), *The Cambridge Translations of Medieval Philosophical Texts. Logic and the Philosophy of Language* 1. Cambridge University Press, 369–412.

Chatton, Walter. 1989. *Reportatio et Lectura super Sententias. Collatio ad librum primum et prologus*. J. C. Wey (ed.). Toronto: Pontifical Institute of Mediaeval Studies.

Dānish Pazhūh, M.-T. (ed.). 1978. *Mantiq ibn al-Muqaffa*. Tehran.

1987–1989. *Al-Manṭiqiyyāt li-al-Fārābī*, three volumes. Qum: Maktabat Āyat Allāh al-'Uẓmā al-Mar'ashī.

2000. *On the Purity of the Art of Logic: The Shorter and the Longer Treatises.* Paul Vincent Spade (tr.). New Haven, CT: Yale University Press.

Dawānī, Jalāl al-Dīn. 1887. *Sharh Tahdhīb al-manṭiq*. Istanbul: Haci Muharrem Efendi Matba'asi. [Printed with the Gloss of Mir Abu l-Fath (d. 1568) and the Tahdhīb al-manṭiq of Taftāzānī].

De Monte, Lambertus. 1490. *Copulata omnium tractatuum Petri hyspani etiam Sincategorematum et Parvorum logicalium cum textu secundum doctrinam divi Thome Aquinatis iuxta processum Magistrorum Colonie in bursa Montis regentium.* [Cologne].

Dorp, John. 1965. *Perutile Compendium Totius Logicae Joannis Buridani* [Reprint of 1499 edition]. Frankfurt: Minerva.

Duns Scotus, John. 1891. *Quaestiones super universalia, super praedicamenta, sup lib. I Perihermenias Aristotelis, In II librum Perihermenias, Secundi Opeis Perihermenias.* In L. Wadding (ed.) *Opera Omnia*, vol. 1. Paris: Vives.

1950. *Ordinatio I, dd. 1–3.* Vatican: editio Vaticana, vol. II.

1963. *Ordinatio I, dd. 26–48.* Vatican: editio Vaticana, vol. V.

1999. 'Quaestiones super Praedicamenta Aristotelis'. In R. Andrews, G. Etzkorn, G. Gal, R. Green, T. Noone and R. Wood (eds.), *Opera Philosophica.* St Bonaventure University, I, 249–566.

2004a. 'Quaestiones in duos libros Perihermeneias. In librum primum'. In R. Andrews and B. C. Bazàn (eds.), *Opera Philosophica.* St Bonaventure, NY: Franciscan Institute, II, 135–190.

2004b. 'Quaestiones in primum librum Perihermeneias'. In R. Andews and B. C. Bazàn (eds.), *Opera Philosophica.* St Bonaventure, NY: Franciscan Institute, II, 43–132.

Eriugena, John Scottus. 1987. *Periphyseon.* I. P. Sheldon-Williams (tr.), revised by John J. O'Meara. Montreal: Bellarmin.

1996–2003. *Periphyseon*, five volumes. Édouard Jeauneau (ed.). Corpus Christianorum Continuatio Medievalis 161–165. Turnhout: Brepols.

Feribrigge, Richard. 1978. 'Tractatus de veritate propositionum'. In *Paul of Venice, Logica magna, secunda pars.* F. Del Punta (ed.). Oxford University Press, 215–236.

Ferrer, Vincent. 1977. *Tractatus de Suppositionibus.* John A. Trentman (ed.). Stuttgart: Frommann-Hozlboog.

Fland, Robert. 1976. *Consequentiae.* In P. V. Spade (ed.), 'Robert Fland's Consequentiae: An Edition'. *Mediaeval Studies* 38: 54–84.

1980. *Obligationes.* In Paul Vincent Spade (ed.), 'Robert Fland's Obligationes: An Edition'. *Medieval Studies* 42: 41–60.

Fonseca, Pedro da (Petrus Fonseca). 1964. *Institutionum Dialecticarum libri octo.* Joaquim Ferreira Gomes (ed.). Universidade de Coimbra.

Garlandus. 1959. *Dialectica.* L. M. De Rijk (ed.). Assen: Van Gorcum.

Gregory of Rimini. 1978. *Lectura super primum et secundum Sententiarum.* V. Marcolino and D. Trapp (eds.). Berlin: Walter de Gruyter.

Gyekye, K. 1975. *Ibn al-Ṭayyib's Commentary on Porphyry's Eisagoge.* Beirut: Dār al-Mashriq.

——— 1979. *Arabic Logic, Ibn al-Ṭayyib's Commentary on Porphyry's Eisagoge.* Albany, NY: State University of New York Press.

Heytesbury, William. 1979. *On "Insoluble" Sentences: Chapter One of his Rules for Solving Sophisms.* Paul Vincent Spade (tr.). Toronto: Pontifical Institute of Mediaeval Studies.

Hopton, Henry. 1494. 'Omnis propositio est vera vel falsa (Pseudo-Heytesbury's De veritate et falsitate propositionis)'. In William Heytesbury, *Tractatus de sensu composito et diviso.* Venice: Bonetus Locatellus, fol. 183va–188rb.

Ibn al-Nadīm. 1988. *Kitāb al-Fihrist.* R. Tajaddud (ed.). Beirut: Dār al-Masīra.

Ibn Rushd (= Averroes). 1562. *Aristotelis omnia quae extant opera … Averrois Cordubensis in ea opera omnes, qui ad haec usque tempora pervenere, commentarii.* [Venice].

——— 1962. *Aristotelis Opera cum Averrois Commentariis.* Venice 1562–1574, reprint Frankfurt: Minerva.

——— 1977. *Averroës' Three Short Commentaries on Aristotle's 'Topics', 'Rhetoric', and 'Poetics'.* Charles Butterworth (ed. and tr.). Albany, NY: State University of New York Press.

——— 1989. *Al-Kulliyyāt fī al-ṭibb,* S. Shaybān and 'A. al-Ṭālibī (eds.), A. Sh. al-Rūbī (rev.). Cairo: al-Hay'a al-Miṣriyya al-'Āmma li-al-Kitāb.

Ibn Sīnā (= Avicenna). 1910. *Manṭiq al-mashriqiyyīn.* Cairo: al-Maktaba al-Salafiyya.

——— 1952. *Resāla-ye manṭeq-e dāneshnāme-ye 'alā'ī* (Treatise on Logic of the Book of Wisdom for 'Alā'-ad-Dawla). M. Mo'in and S. M. Meshkāt (eds.). Tehran: Anjoman-e Āthār-e Melli.

——— 1958. *Al-Shifā', al-Manṭiq VII: al-Safsaṭa.* A. F. El-Ehwany (ed.). Cairo: al-Maṭba'a al-Amīriyya.

——— 1964. *Al-Shifā', al-Manṭiq IV: al-Qiyās.* S. Zayed (ed.). Cairo: al-Hay'a al-'Āmma li-Shu'ūn al-Maṭābi' al-Amīriyya.

——— 1971, *Al-Ishārāt wa-l-tanbīhāt,* four volumes. S. Dunyā (ed.), with Ṭūsī's commentary. Cairo: Dār al-Ma'ārif.

——— 1985. *Al-Najāt min al-gharq fī baḥr al-ḍalālāt.* M. Dānishpazūh (ed.). Dāneshgāh Tehran.

2002. *Al-Ishārāt wa-al-tanbīhāt*. M. Zāre'ī. (ed.). Qom: Būstān-e Ketāb-e Qom.

2011. *Avicenna's Deliverance: Logic*. Asad Q. Ahmed (tr.) with an introduction by Tony Street. Oxford University Press.

Inati, S. C. 1984. *Ibn Sīnā Remarks and Admonitions, Part One: Logic*. Toronto: Pontifical Institute of Mediaeval Studies.

John of Holland. 1985. *Four Tracts on Logic: Suppositiones, Fallacies, Obligationes, Insolubilia*. E. P. Bos (ed.). Nijmegen: Ingenium.

John of Salisbury. 1929. *Metalogicon*. C. Webb (ed.). Oxford: Clarendon Press.

Jurjānī, al-Sayyid al-Sharīf. 1861. *Ḥāshiyah 'alā Sharḥ Maṭāli' al-anwār*. Printed as an appendix to Urmawī 1861.

1948. *Ḥāshiyah 'ala Sharḥ al-Shamsiyyah*. Printed with Kātibī 1948.

Kātibī, Najm al-Dīn. 1948. *Al-Risālah al-Shamsiyyah*. Cairo: Muṣṭafā al-Bābī al-Ḥalabī.

1988. *Al-Risāla al-Shamsiyya*. Printed in Taḥtānī 1988.

Khūnajī, Afḍal al-Dīn. 2010. *Kashf al-asrār 'an ghawāmiḍ al-afkār*. K. El-Rouayheb (ed.). Tehran: Iranian Institute of Philosophy and Berlin Institute of Islamic Studies, Free University of Berlin.

Kilvington, Richard. 1990. *The Sophismata of Richard Kilvington*. N. Kretzmann and B. Kretzmann (tr.). Cambridge University Press.

Kilwardby, Robert. 1968. *In libros Priorum Analyticorum exposition*. Printed under the name Aegidius Romanus. Frankfurt: Minerva.

1976. *De orto scientarium*. A. G. Judy (ed.). London: British Academy.

1978. 'Commentary on the Liber de Sex Principiorum'. In P. O. Lewry (ed.), *Robert Kilwardby's Writings on the Logica vetus, Studied with Regard to Their Teaching and Method*. DPhil thesis, University of Oxford, 390–407.

2016. *Notule libri Priorum: Critical Edition, Translation and Notes by Paul Thom and John Scott*. Paul Thom and John Scott (eds.). Oxford University Press.

Lambert of Lagny (Lambert of Auxerre). 1971. *Logica (Summa Lamberti)*. F. Alessio (ed.). Florence: La Nuova Italia Editrice.

1982. *Appellationes*. In A. de Libera (ed.), 'Le Tractatus de appellatione de Lambert de Lagny (Summa Lamberti VIII)'. *Archives d'histoire doctrinale et littéraire du moyen âge* 48: 227–285.

2015. *Logica or Summa Lamberti*. Thomas S. Maloney (tr.). University of Notre Dame Press.

Lavenham, Richard. 1974. *Consequentiae*. In Paul Spade (ed.), 'Five Logical Tracts by Richard Lavenham'. In J. R. O'Donnell (ed.), *Essays in Honor of Anton Charles Pegis*. University of Toronto Press, 70–124.

1978. *Obligationes*. In Paul Vincent Spade, 'Richard Lavenham's *Obligationes*: Edition and Comments'. *Rivista critica di storia della filosofia* 33: 225–242.

Mair, John. 1519. *Inclytarum artium*. [Lyon].

Marsilius of Inghen. 1983. *Treatises on the Properties of Terms: A First Critical Edition of the Suppositiones, Ampliationes, Appellationes, Restrictiones and Alienationes, with Introduction, Translation, Notes, and Appendices by Egbert P. Bos*. Dordrecht: Reidel.

Melanchthon, Phili. 1963. 'Erotemata Dialectices'. In C. Bretschneider (ed.), *Corpus Reformatorum, Philippi Melanchthonis opera, quae supersunt omnia*. New York: Johnson, XIII, 508–759.

Nicholas of Paris. 2011. 'On Aristotle's Peri Hermeneias'. In H. Hansen and A. Maria Mora Marquez (eds.), 'Nicholas of Paris on Aristotle's Perihermeneias 1–3'. *Cahiers de l'Institut du Moyen-Âge Grec et Latin* 80: 2–88.

Notker, Labeo 1882. 'De syllogismis'. In Paul Piper (ed.), *Die Schriften Notkers und seiner Schule*. Freiburg: Mohr, 596–622.

Ockham, William. 1962. *Summa Logicae Pars Secunda et tertiae Prima*. Philotheus Boehner (ed.). St Bonaventure, NY: Franciscan Institute.

    1967. *Scriptum in librum primum Sententiarum. Ordinatio. Prologus et Distinctio Prima*. G. Gál and S. F. Brown (eds.). St Bonaventure, NY, Franciscan Institute.

    1974a. *Summa Logicae*. Philotheus Boehner, Gideon Gál and Stephen Brown (eds.). St Bonaventure, NY: Franciscan Institute.

    1974b. *Ockham's Theory of Terms: Part I of the Summa Logicae*. M. J. Loux (tr.). University of Notre Dame Press.

    1978. *Venerabilis Inceptoris Guillelmi de Ockham, Expositiones in libros artis logicae prooemium et Expositio in Librum Porphyrii de Praedicabilibus*. In E. A. Moody (ed.), *Opera Philosophica II*. St Bonaventure University, 1–131.

    1980. *Quodlibeta Septem*. Joseph Wey (ed.). St Bonaventure, NY: Franciscan Institute.

O'Donnell, J. 1958. 'Themistius's Paraphrasis of the Posterior Analytics in Gerard of Cremona's Translation'. *Medieval Studies* 20: 239–315.

Odo, Gerard. 1997. *Logica* (*Opera Philosophica*, vol. I). L. M. De Rijk (ed.). Leiden: Brill.

Pagus, John. 2012. *Rationes super Praedicamenta*. In H. Hansen 2012.

Paul of Pergula. 1961. *Logica and Tractatus de Sensu Composito ed Diviso*. Sister Mary Anthony Brown (ed.). St Bonaventure, NY: Franciscan Institute.

Paul of Venice. 1978. 'De significato propositionis', section 2 of his *Logica magna, secunda pars*. Del Punta F. (ed.). Oxford University Press, 80–199.

    1988. *Logica Magna: Secunda Pars, Tractatus de Obligationibus* (= Part II, Fascicule 8). E. J. Ashworth (ed. and tr.). British Academy Classical and Medieval Logic Texts 5. Oxford University Press.

1990. *Logica Magna: Secunda Pars. Capitula de Conditionali et de Rationali.* G. E. Hughes (ed. and tr.). British Academy Classical and Medieval Logic Texts 6. Oxford University Press.

2002. *Paulus Venetus: Logica Parva.* Alan R. Perreiah (ed.). Leiden: Brill.

Peter of Ailly. 1499. *Conceptus et insolubilia.* Paris: Marchant.

Peter of Auvergne. 1988. 'Quaestiones super Praedicamentis'. In R. Andrews, *Peter of Auvergne's Commentary on Aristotle's Categories: Edition, Translation, and Analysis (Vols. I and II).* PhD dissertation, Cornell University, 359–468.

Peter of Spain. 1972. *Tractatus Called afterwards Summule Logicales.* L. M. de Rijk (ed.). Assen: Van Gorcum.

1992. *Syncategoreumata.* L. M. de Rijk (tr. and ed.). Leiden: Brill.

2014. *Summaries of Logic.* Brian Copenhaver (ed.). Oxford University Press.

Porphyry. 1966. *Porphyrii Isagoge, Translatio Boethii et Anonymi Fragmentum vulgo vocatum 'Liber Sex Principiorum'.* L. Minio-Paluello (ed.). Bruges/ Paris: Desclée de Brouwer.

Priscian. 1961. 'Institutiones grammaticae'. In H. Keil (ed.), *Grammatici latini,* II–III. Hildesheim: Olms.

Pseudo-Scotus. 1639. 'Questiones super librum primum analyticorum'. In John Duns Scotus, *Opera Omnia.* L. Wadding (ed.). Lyons: Laurence Durand, I, 273–341.

Radulphus, Brito. c. 1499. *Quaestiones super Artem Veterem,* Johannes Rubeus Vercellensis and Albertinus Vercellensis (eds.). [Venice].

Rāzī, Fakhr al-Dīn. 2003. *Manṭiq al-Mulakhkhaṣ,* A. F. Qaramaleki and A. Asgharinezhad (eds.). Tehran: ISU Press.

2005. *Sharḥ al-Ishārāt.* A. R. Najafzādeh (ed.). Tehran: Anjuman Āthār wa-Mafākhir Ferhangi.

Sanūsī, Muḥammad b. Yūsuf. 1875. *Sharḥ Mukhtaṣar al-manṭiq.* [Cairo].

Shehaby, N. 1973. *The Propositional Logic of Avicenna.* Dordrecht: Reidel.

Shīrāzī, Quṭb al-Dīn. 2002. *Sharḥ Ḥikmat al-Ishrāq.* A. Nourani and M. Mohaghegh (eds.). Montreal: Institute of Islamic Studies.

Soto, Domingo de. 1529. *Summulae.* [Burgos].

1539–1540. *Summulae (aeditio secunda).* [Salamanca].

Strode, R. 1974. 'Tractatus de consequentiis (1360)'. In W. K. Seaton, *An Edition and Translation of the Tractatus de consequentiis of Ralph Strode.* PhD Dissertation, University of California at Berkeley. Ann Arbor, MI: University Microfilms.

Swyneshed, Roger. 1977. *Obligationes.* In Paul Vincent Spade, 'Roger Swyneshed's Obligationes: Edition and Comments'. *Archives d'histoire doctrinale et littéraire du moyen âge* 44: 243–285.

1979. 'Insolubilia'. In Paul Vincent Spade, 'Roger Swyneshed's Insolubilia: Edition and Comments'. *Archives d'histoire doctrinale et littéraire du moyen âge* 46: 177–220.

Taḥtānī, Quṭb al-Dīn al-Rāzī. 1988. *Taḥrīr al-qawāʿid al-manṭiqiyya fī sharḥ al-Risāla al-Shamsiyya (1367)*. Cairo: Dār Iḥyāʾ al-kutub al-ʿarabiyya, Muṣṭafā al-Bābī al-Ḥalabī.

Toledo, Francisco de (Franciscus Toletus). 1985. *Introductio in Dialecticam Aristotelis in Opera omnia philosophica* I. Cologne, 1615–1616. Reprinted Hildesheim: Georg Olms.

Ṭūsī, Naṣīr al-Dīn. 1971. *Ḥall Mushkilāt al-Ishārāt*. Printed in Ibn Sīnā 1971.

1974. 'Taʿdīl al-miʿyār fī naqd Tanzīl al-afkār'. In M. Mohaghegh and T. Izutsu (eds.), *Collected Texts and Papers on Logic and Language*. Tehran: Anjoman-e Asar va Mafakher-e Farhangi, 137–248.

2004. *Asās al-iqtibās fī l-manṭiq*. [Cairo].

Urmawī, Sirāj al-Dīn. 1861. *Maṭāliʿ al-anwār*. Istanbul: Maṭbaʿah-i ʿAmire.

Venator, Johannes. 1999. 'De materia significati propositionis seu significabilis complexe' (Chapter 9 of Part I of his *Logica*). L. M. de Rijk (ed). Stuttgart: Frommann-Holzboog, I, 202–222.

Versor, Johannes. 1586. *Petri Hispani Summulae Logicales cum Versorii Parisiensis Clarissima Expositione. Parvorvm item Logicalivm eidem Petro Hispano ascriptum opus*. Venice.

Wodeham, Adam. 1990. *Lectura secunda in primum librum Sententiarum*. G. Gál and R. Wood (eds.). St Bonaventure, NY: The Franciscan Institute.

William of Ockham: See Ockham, William.

William of Sherwood. 1941. 'Syncategoremata'. J. R. O'Donnell (ed.). *Medieval Studies* 3, 46–93.

1966. *Introduction to Logic*. N. Kretzmann (tr.). Minneapolis, MN: University of Minnesota Press.

1968. *Treatise on Syncategorematic Words*. N. Kretzmann (tr.) Minneapolis, MN: University of Minnesota Press.

1995. *Introductiones in Logicam*. H. Brands and C. Kann (ed. and German tr.). Hamburg: Meiner.

2012. Syncategoremata, edited and translated in German by C. Kann and R. Kirchhoff. Hamburg: Meiner.

Wyclif, John. 1986. *Summa Insolubilium*. Paul Vincent Spade and Gordon Anthony Wilson (eds.). Binghamton, NY: Center for Medieval and Early Renaissance Studies.

Zabeeh, F. 1971. *Avicenna's Treatise on Logic*. The Hague: Nijhoff.

Zimmermann, F.W. 1981. *Al-Farabi's Commentary and Short Treatise on Aristotle's De interpretatione*. Oxford University Press.

SECONDARY SOURCES

Adams, M. McCord. 1987. *William Ockham*. University of Notre Dame Press.

Adamson, P. and Key, A. 2015. 'Philosophy of Language in the Medieval Arabic Tradition'. In M. Cameron and R. Stainton (eds.), *Linguistic Meaning: New Essays in the History of the Philosophy of Language*. Oxford University Press, 74–99.

Ahmed, Asad Q. 2012. 'Logic in the Khayrâbâdî School in India: A Preliminary Exploration'. In M. Cook, N. Haider, I. Rabb and A. Sayeed (eds.), *Law and Tradition in Classical Islamic Thought: Studies in Honor of Professor Hossein Modarressi*. New York: Palgrave Macmillan, 227–244.

Alwishah, A. and Sanson, D. 2009. 'The Early Arabic Liar: The Liar Paradox in the Islamic World from the Mid-Ninth to the Mid-Thirteenth Century CE'. *Vivarium* 47: 97–127.

Amerini, Fabrizio. 2005a. 'What Is Real? A Reply to Ockham's Ontological Program'. *Vivarium* 43: 187–212.

2005b. *La Logica di Francesco da Prato*. Florence: SISMEL Edizioni del Galluzzo.

Andrews, R. 1993. 'The Sophistria of Petrus Olai'. In S. Read (ed.), *Sophisms and Medieval Logic and Grammar*. Dordrecht: Kluwer, 3–30.

2008. 'Thomas Maulevelt's Denial of Substance'. In Lloyd A. Newton (ed.), *Medieval Commentaries on Aristotle's 'Categories'*. Leiden: Brill, 347–368.

Aouad, Maroun. 2003. 'La Rhétorique. Tradition syriaque et arabe (Compléments)'. In *Dictionnaire des philosophes antiques*, vol. *Supplément*. Paris: CNRS-Éditions, 219–223.

Armstrong, D. 1997. *A World of States of Affairs*. Cambridge University Press.

Ashworth, E. Jennifer. 1973. 'The Doctrine of Exponibilia in the Fifteenth and Sixteenth Centuries'. *Vivarium* 11(1):137–167.

1974. *Language and Logic in the Post-Medieval Period*. Dordrecht: Reidel.

1978a. 'Theories of the Proposition: Some Early Sixteenth Century Discussions'. *Franciscan Studies* 38: 81–121. Reprinted in Ashworth 1985, article IV.

1978b. 'Multiple Quantification and the Use of Special Quantifiers in Early Sixteenth Century Logic'. *Notre Dame Journal of Formal Logic* 19: 599–613. Reprinted in Ashworth 1985, article X.

1979. 'The "Libelli Sophistarum" and the Use of Medieval Logic Texts at Oxford and Cambridge in the Early Sixteenth Century'. *Vivarium* 17: 134–158.

1981. 'Mental Language and the Unity of the Propositions: A Semantic Problem Discussed by Early Sixteenth Century Logicians'. *Franciscan Studies* 41: 61–96.

1982. 'The Structure of Mental Language: Some Problems Discussed by Early Sixteenth Century Logicians'. *Vivarium* 20: 59–83. Reprinted in Ashworth 1985, article V.

1985. *Studies in Post-Medieval Semantics*. London: Variorum Reprints.

1988. 'Traditional Logic'. In C. B. Schmitt, Q. Skinner, E. Kessler and J. Kraye (eds.), *The Cambridge History of Renaissance Philosophy*. Cambridge University Press, 143–172.

1993. 'Ralph Strode on Inconsistency in Obligational Disputation'. In K. Jacobi (ed.), *Argumentationstheorie: Scholastische Forschungen zu den logischen und semantischen Regeln korrekten Folgerns*. Leiden: Brill, 363–386.

1994. 'Obligationes Treatises: A Catalogue of Manuscripts, Editions and Studies'. *Bulletin de philosophie médiévale* 36: 116–147.

2008. 'Developments in the Fifteenth and Sixteenth Centuries'. In D. M. Gabbay and J. Woods (eds.), *Handbook of the History of Logic*, vol. 2: *Mediaeval and Renaissance Logic*. Amsterdam: North-Holland, 609–643.

2010. 'Terminist Logic'. In R. Pasnau and Ch. van Dyke (eds.), *The Cambridge History of Medieval Philosophy*. Cambridge University Press, I, 146–158.

2013a. 'Descent and Ascent from Ockham to Domingo de Soto: An Answer to Paul Spade'. *Vivarium* 51: 385–410.

2013b. 'Medieval Theories of Analogy'. In E. N. Zalta (ed.), *The Stanford Encyclopedia of Philosophy*, Winter 2013 edition. URL http://plato.stanford.edu/archives/win2013/entries/analogy-medieval/ (last accessed 30 April 2016).

Ashworth, E. Jennifer and Spade, Paul Vincent. 1992. 'Logic in Late Medieval Oxford'. In J. I. Catto and R. Evans (eds.), *The History of the University of Oxford*. Oxford: Clarendon Press, II, 35–64.

Ayers, Robert H. 1979. *Language, Logic and Reason in the Church Fathers*. Hildesheim: Olms.

Bäck, A. 1987. 'Avicenna on Existence'. *Journal of the History of Philosophy* 25: 351–367.

1992. 'Avicenna's Conception of the Modalities'. *Vivarium* 30(2): 217–255.

Badawi, Abd al-Rahman. 1987. *La Transmission de la philosophie grecque au monde arabe*, second edition. Paris: Vrin.

Bakker, Paul J. J. M. 2007. 'Natural Philosophy and Metaphysics in Late Fifteenth-Century Paris. III: The Commentaries on Aristotle by Johannes de Caulaincourt (alias Johannes de Magistris'. *Bulletin de philosophie médiévale* 49: 195–237.

Barnes, Jonathan. 1981. 'Boethius and the Study of Logic'. In Margaret Gibson (ed.), *Boethius, His Life, Thought and Influence*. Oxford: Blackwell, 73–89.

2007. *Truth, etc.: Six Lectures on Ancient Logic*. Oxford University Press.

Beaver, D. I. and Clark, B. Z. 2008. *Sense and Sensitivity: How Focus Determines Meaning*. Malden, MA: Wiley-Blackwell.

Berger, Harald. 1991. 'Simple Supposition in William of Ockham, John Buridan, and Albert of Saxony'. In J. Biard (ed.), *Itinéraires d'Albert de Saxe. Paris – Vienne au XIVe siècle*. Études de philosophie médiévale 69. Paris: Vrin, 31–43.

Bermon, P. 2007. *L'assentiment et son objet chez Grégoire de Rimini*. Paris: Vrin.

Biard, J. 1989a. *Logique et théorie du signe au xivᵉ siècle*. Paris: Vrin.

1989b. 'Les sophismes du savoir: Albert de Saxe entre Jean Buridan et Guillaume Heytesbury'. *Vivarium* 17: 36–50.

2002. 'Les controverses sur l'objet du savoir et les *complexe significabilia* au xivᵉ siècle'. In Caroti, S. and Celeyrette, J. (eds.), *Quia inter doctores est magna dissentio. Les débats de philosophie naturelle à Paris au xivᵉ siècle*. Florence: Olschki, 1–31.

2010. 'Nominalism in the later Middle Ages'. In Pasnau 2010, II, 661–673.

2015. 'Albert of Saxony'. In E. N. Zalta (ed.), *The Stanford Encyclopedia of Philosophy*, Summer 2015 edition. URL http://plato.stanford.edu/archives/sum2015/entries/albert-saxony/ (last accessed 30 April 2016).

Biard, Joël and Rosier-Catach, Irène (eds.). 2003. *La tradition médiévale des Catégories*. Paris-Louvain: Peeters.

Biard, Joël and Zini Fosca, Mariani (eds.). 2009. *Les lieux de l'argumentation, histoire du syllogisme topique d'Aristote à Leibniz*. Turnhout: Brepols.

Black, D. L. 1990. *Logic and Aristotle's Rhetoric and Poetics in Medieval Arabic Philosophy*. Leiden: Brill.

1991. 'Aristotle's "Peri hermeneias" in Medieval Latin and Arabic Philosophy: Logic and the Linguistic Arts'. *Canadian Journal of Philosophy* 21(1): 25–83.

Bobzien, Susan. 2002. 'A Greek Parallel to Boethius' De Hypotheticis Syllogismis'. *Mnemosyne*, Fourth Series 55(3): 285–300.

2005. 'Logic: The Megarics'. In K. Algra, J. Barnes, J. Mansfeld and M. Schofield (eds.), *The Cambridge History of Hellenistic Philosophy*. Cambridge University Press, 83–92.

Boehner, Philotheus. 1952. *Medieval Logic: An Outline of Its Development from 1250 to c. 1400*. Manchester University Press.

Bos, E. P. 1987. 'The Theory of the Proposition According to John Duns Scotus' Two Commentaries on Aristotle's Perihermeneias'. In L. M. De Rijk and H. A. G. Braakhius (eds.), *Logos and Pragma: Essays on the Philosophy of Language in Honor of Professor Gabriel Nuchelmans*. Nijmegen: Ingenium, 121–140.

2007. 'Richard Billingham's Speculum Puerorum: Some Medieval Commentaries and Aristotle'. *Vivarium* 45(2): 360–373.

(ed.). 2013. *Medieval Supposition Theory Revisited*. Leiden: Brill.

Bos, Egbert and Read, Stephen. 2000. *Concepts: The Treatises of Thomas of Cleves and Paul of Gelria*. Leuven: Peeters.

Braakhuis, H. A. G. 1981. 'English Tracts on Syncategorematic Terms from Robert Bacon to Walter Burley'. In H. A. G. Braakhuis, C. H. Kneepkens and L. M. de

Rijk (eds.), *English Logic and Semantics: From the End of the Twelfth Century to the Time of Ockham and Burleigh*. Nijmegen: Ingenium, 131–165.

1989. 'School Philosophy and Philosophical Schools: The Semantic-Ontological Views in the Cologne Commentaries on Peter of Spain, and the "Wegestreit"'. *Miscellanea Mediaevalia* 20: 1–18.

1998. 'Obligations in Early Thirteenth-century Paris: The Obligationes of Nicholas of Paris (?)'. *Vivarium* 36(2): 152–231.

Brandom, Robert. 1994. *Making it Explicit*. Cambridge, MA: Harvard University Press.

Broadie, Alexander. 1983. *George Lokert: Late-Scholastic Logician*. Edinburgh University Press.

1985. *The Circle of John Mair: Logic and Logicians in Pre-Reformation Scotland*. Oxford: Clarendon Press.

Brower-Toland, S. 2007a. 'Facts vs. Things. Adam Wodeham and the Later Medieval Debate about Objects of Judgment'. *The Review of Metaphysics* 60: 597–642.

2007b. 'Ockham on Judgment, Concepts, and the Problem of Intentionality'. *Canadian Journal of Philosophy* 37: 76–110.

Brown, Stephen. 1973. 'Walter Burley's Middle Commentary on Aristotle's Perihermeneias'. *Franciscan Studies* 33: 42–134.

1974. 'Walter Burley's Quaestiones in librum Perihermeneias'. *Franciscan Studies* 34: 200–295.

Brumberg-Chaumont, J. 2013a. 'Les divisions de la logiques selon Albert le Grand'. In J. Brumberg-Chaumont 2013b, 315–416.

(ed.) 2013b. *Ad Notitiam ignoti: L'Organon dans la translato studiorum à l'époque d'Albert le Grand*. Turnhout: Brepols.

Bulthuis, N. 2014. *Walter Burley on the Metaphysics of the Proposition and Its Relation to Language and Thought*. PhD dissertation, Cornell University.

Burnett, Charles (ed.). 2003. *Glosses and Commentaries on Aristotle's Logical Texts: The Syriac, Arabic and Medieval Latin Traditions*. London: Warburg Institute.

Burr, D. 1976. 'The Persecution of Peter Olivi'. *Transactions of the American Philosophical Society* 66(5): 1–98.

Büttgen, P., Diebler, S. and Rashed, M. (eds.). 1999. *Théories de la phrase et de la proposition. De Platon à Averroès*. Paris: Editions Rue d'Ulm.

Buytaert, E. M. 1964. 'The *Tractatus Logicae Minor* of Ockham'. *Franciscan Studies* 24: 34–100.

1965–1966. 'The *Elementarium Logicae* of Ockham'. *Franciscan Studies* 25: 151–276 and 26: 66–173.

Calverley, E. E. 1933. 'Al-Abharî's îsâghûjî fî "l-mantiq"'. In *The Macdonald Presentation Volume: A Tribute to Duncan Black Macdonald*. Princeton University Press, 75–85.

Cameron, M. 2011. 'Methods and Methodologies: An Introduction'. In Margaret Cameron and John Marenbon (eds.), *Methods and Methodologies: Aristotelian Logic East and West, 500–1500*. Leiden: Brill, 1–26.

2012. 'Meaning: Foundational and Semantic Theories'. In J. Marenbon (ed.), *The Oxford Medieval Philosophy*. Oxford University Press, 342–362.

Carroll, Lewis. 1895. 'What the Tortoise Said to Achilles'. *Mind* 4: 278–280.

Cesalli, L. 2004. 'Richard Brinkley. De propositione (*Summa logicae*, V, 1–5)'. *Archives d'histoire doctrinale et littéraire du moyen âge* 71: 203–254.

2007. *Le réalisme propositionnel: Sémantique et ontologie des propositions chez Jean Duns Scot, Gauthier Burley, Richard Brinkley et Jean Wyclif*. Paris: Vrin.

2012. 'States of Affairs'. In J. Marenbon (ed.), *The Oxford Medieval Philosophy*. Oxford University Press, 421–444.

2013. 'Meaning and Truth'. In A. Conti (ed), *A Companion to Walter Burley: Late Medieval Logician and Metaphysician*. Leiden: Brill, 87–133.

Forthcoming. '*Modus rei*: An Adverbialist Theory of Truthmaking'. In L. Cesalli and J. Marenbon (eds.), *Facts and States of Affairs*. Turnhout: Brepols.

Cesalli, L. and Marenbon, J. (eds.). Forthcoming. *Facts and States of Affairs*. Turnhout: Brepols.

Chase, Michael. 2007. 'Did Porphyry Write a Commentary on Aristotle's Posterior Analytics? Albertus Magnus, Alfarabi and Porphyry on Per Se Predication'. In Peter Adamson (ed.), *Classical Arabic Philosophy: Sources and Reception*. London: Nifo Aragno, 21–38.

2008. 'The Medieval Posterity of Simplicius's Commentary on the Categories: Thomas Aquinas and Al-Farabi'. In Newton 2008, 9–29.

Chatti, S. 2016. 'Existential Import in Avicenna's Modal Logic'.

Clagett, M. 1959. *The Science of Mechanics in the Middle Ages*. Madison, WI: University of Wisconsin Press.

Clanchy, M. 1997. *Abelard: A Medieval Life*. Oxford: Blackwell.

Colish, M. 1990. *The Stoic Tradition from Antiquity to the Early Middle Ages*, two volumes, second edition. Leiden: Brill.

Conti, Alessandro. 1990. 'Ontology in Walter Burley's Last Commentary on the Ars Vetus'. *Franciscan Studies* 50: 121–176.

(ed.). 2013a. *A Companion to Walter Burley: Late Medieval Logician and Metaphysician*. Leiden: Brill.

2013b. 'Semantics and Ontology in Robert Kilwardby's Commentaries on the Logica Vetus'. In H. Lagerlund and P. Thom (eds.), *The Philosophy of Robert Kilwardby*. Leiden: Brill, 65–130.

Coppock, E. and Beaver, D. 2013. 'Principles of the Exclusive Muddle'. *Journal of Semantics* 31(3): 371–432.

Corbini, Amos. 2006. *La Teoria della scienza nel XIII secolo, i commenti agli Analitici secondi*. Tavarnuzze: ed. del Galluzzo.

Corti, Lorenzo and Bruun, Otto (eds.). 2005. *Les Catégories et leur histoire.* Paris: Vrin.

Courtenay, W. J. 2008. *Ockham and Ockhamism*. Leiden: Brill.

Crivelli, P. 2004. *Aristotle on Truth*. Cambridge University Press.

Cross, Richard. 2002. 'Gregory of Nyssa on Universals'. *Vigiliae Christianae* 56: 372–410.

Crubellier, Michel. 2014. *Aristote, Premiers analytiques (Organon III): Traduction et présentation par Michel Crubellier*. Paris: Flammarion.

Dahan, Gilbert and Rosier-Catach, Irène (eds.). 1998. *La rhétorique d'Aristote:Traditions et commentaires de l'antiquité au XVIIᵉ siècle*. Paris: Vrin.

D'Ancona, Cristina. 2005. 'Greek into Arabic: Neoplatonism in Translation'. In Peter Adamson and Richard C. Taylor (eds.), *The Cambridge Companion to Arabic Philosophy*. Cambridge University Press, 10–31.

De Haas, Frans A. J., Leunissen, Mariska and Martijn, Marije (eds.). 2011. *Interpreting Aristotle's Posterior Analytics in Late Antiquity and Beyond*. Leiden: Brill.

Denifle, H. 1889. *Chartularium Universitatis Parisiensis*. Paris: Delalain, I.

Denifle, H. S. and Chatelain, É. L. M. (eds.). 1889–1897. *Chartularium Universitatis Parisiensis: Sub auspiciis consilii generalis facultatum Parisiensium ex diversis bibliothecis tabulariisque collegit et cum authenticis chartis contulit*. Paris: Delalain.

De Rijk, Lambertus M. 1962–1967. *Logica modernorum*, two volumes. Assen: Van Gorcum.

1963. 'On the Curriculum of the Arts of the Trivium at St. Gall from c. 850–c. 1000'. *Vivarium* 1: 35–86.

1971. 'The Development of Suppositio Naturalis in Medieval Logic, I: Natural Supposition as Non-contextual Supposition'. *Vivarium* 9: 71–107.

1974. 'Some Thirteenth-century Tracts on the Game of Obligation'. *Vivarium* 12: 94–123.

1975. 'Some Thirteenth-century Tracts on the Game of Obligation II'. *Vivarium* 13: 22–54.

1976. 'Some Thirteenth-century Tracts on the Game of Obligation III'. *Vivarium* 14: 26–49.

1980. *Die mittelalterlichen Traktate de modo opponendi et respondendi: Einleitung und Ausgabe der einschlägigen Texte*. Münster: Aschendorff.

1982a. 'Semantics in Richard Billingham and Johannes Venator'. In A. Maierù (ed.), *English Logic in Italy in the 14th and 15th Centuries*. Naples: Bibliopolis, 167–183.

1982b. 'The Origins of the Theory of the Properties of Terms'. In N. Kretzmann, A. Kenny and J. Pinborg (eds.), *The Cambridge History of Later Medieval Philosophy*. Cambridge University Press, 161–173.

1985. 'Walther Burley's Tract *De exclusivis*: An Edition'. *Vivarium* 23: 23–54.

1986. 'Peter Abelard's Semantics and His Doctrine of Being'. *Vivarium* 24: 85–127.

1996. 'Burley's So-called *Tractatus Primus*, with an Edition of the Additional Quaestio "Utrum contradictio sit maxima oppositio"'. *Vivarium* 34: 161–191.

1999. *Johannes Venator Anglicus: Logica*, two volumes. Stuttgart: Friedrich Frommann Verlag.

Dod, B. 1982. 'Aristoteles latinus'. In N. Kretzmann, A. Kenny and J. Pinborg (eds.), *The Cambridge History of Later Medieval Philosophy*. Cambridge University Press, 45–79.

D'Ors, A. 1997. 'Petrus Hispanus O.P. Auctor Summularum'. *Vivarium* 35: 21–71.

Dronke, P. (ed.). 1992. *A History of Twelfth-Century Philosophy*. Cambridge University Press.

Duhem, P. 1906–1913. *Etudes sur Léonard de Vinci: Ceux qu'il a lus et ceux qui l'ont lu*, three volumes. Paris: A. Hermann.

1913–1959. *Le système du monde: Histoire des doctrines cosmoloqieus de Platon à Copernic*. Paris: A. Hermann.

Dutilh Novaes, Catarina. 2004. 'A Medieval Reformulation of the de dicto / de re Distinction'. In *LOGICA Yearbook 2003*. Prague: Filosofia, 111–124.

2005. 'Buridan's consequentia: Consequence and Inference within a Token-based Semantics'. *History and Philosophy of Logic* 26(4): 277–297.

2007. *Formalizing Medieval Logical Theories*. Berlin: Springer.

2008a. 'An Intensional Interpretation of Ockham's Theory of Supposition'. *Journal of the History of Philosophy* 46(3): 365–393.

2008b. 'Logic in the Fourteenth Century after Ockham'. In D. M. Gabbay and J. Woods (eds.), *Handbook on the History of Logic*, vol. 2: *Mediaeval and Renaissance Logic*. Amsterdam: Elsevier, 433–504.

2009. 'Medieval *Obligationes* as a Regimentation of "The Game of Giving and Asking for Reasons"'. In M. Palis (ed.), *LOGICA Yearbook 2008*. London: College Publications, 27–41.

2010a. 'Supposition, Theories of'. In H. Lagerlund (ed.), *Encyclopedia of Medieval Philosophy*. Dordrecht: Springer, 1229–1236.

2010b. 'Quantification, Theories of'. In H. Lagerlund (ed.), *Encyclopedia of Medieval Philosophy*. Dordrecht: Springer, 1093–1096.

2010c. 'Truth, Theories of'. In H. Lagerlund (ed.), *Encyclopedia of Medieval Philosophy*. Dordrecht: Springer, 1340–1347.

2011. 'Medieval *Obligationes* as a Theory of Discursive Commitment Management'. *Vivarium* 49: 240–257.

2012. 'Reassessing Logical Hylomorphism and the Demarcation of Logical Constants'. *Synthese* 185: 387–410.

2013. 'The Ockham-Burley Dispute'. In A. Conti (ed.), *A Companion to Walter Burley*. Leiden: Brill, 49–86.

Dutilh Novaes, C. and Spruyt, J. 2015. 'Those Funny Words: Medieval Theories of Syncategorematic Terms'. In M. Cameron and R. Stainton (eds.), *Linguistic Content: New Essays on the History of the Philosophy of Language*. Oxford University Press, 100–120.

Ebbesen, S. 1981a. 'Analyzing Syllogisms or Anonymous Aurelianensis III: The (Presumably) Earliest Extant Latin Commentary on the Prior Analytics, and Its Greek Model'. *Cahiers de l'Institut du Moyen-Âge Grec et Latin* 37: 1–20.

1981b. *Commentators and Commentaries on Aristotle's Sophistici Elenchi: A Study of Post-Aristotelian Ancient and Medieval Writings on Fallacies*, three volumes. Leiden: Brill.

1981c. 'Albert the (Great?)'s Companion to the Organon'. In J. P. Beckmann, L. Honnefelder and G. Jüssen (eds.), *Sprache und Erkenntnis im Mittelalters*. Berlin: Walter de Gruyter, 89–103.

1985. 'OXYNAT: A Theory about the Origins of British Logic'. In P. O. Lewry (ed.), *The Rise of British Logic*. Papers in Mediaeval Studies 7. Toronto: Pontifical Institute of Mediaeval Studies, 1–17.

1988. 'Concrete Accidental Terms: Late Thirteenth-Century Debates about Problems Relating to Such Terms as "Album"'. In N. Kretzmann (ed.), *Meaning and Inference in Medieval Philosophy*. Dordrecht: Kluwer, 107–174.

1990. 'Boethius as an Aristotelian commentator'. In Sorabji 1990, 373–391.

1996. 'Anonymi Parisiensis Compendium Sophisticorum Elenchorum: The Uppsala Version'. *Cahiers de l'Institut du Moyen-Âge Grec et Latin* 66: 253–312.

1998a. 'The Paris Arts Faculty: Siger of Brabant, Boethius of Dacia, Radulphus Brito'. In Marenbon 1998, 269–290.

1998b. 'Language, Medieval Theories of'. In E. Craig (ed.), *Routlege Encyclopedia of Philosophy*. London: Routledge, V, 389–404.

2003. 'The Trivium'. *Bulletin de Philosophie Médiévale* 52: 15–24.

2004. 'Where Were the Stoics in the Late Middle Ages?' In J. Zupko and S. K. Stange (eds.), *Stoicism: Traditions and Transformations*. Cambridge University Press, 108–131.

2007. 'The Traditions of Ancient Logic-cum-Grammar in the Middle Ages: What's the Problem?'. In Marenbon 2007, 136–152.

2008. 'Fragments of Alexander's Commentaries on *Analytica posteriora* and *Sophistici elenchi*'. In S. Ebbesen, *Greek-Latin Philosophical Interaction*. Aldershot: Ashgate, I, 187–202.

Ehrle, Franz. 1925. *Der Sentenzenkommentar des Peters von Candia*. Franziskanische Studien 9. Münster: Aschendorff.

Elamrani-Jamal, A. 1989. 'Allinus'. In *Dictionaire des philosophes antiques*, I, 151–153.

1995. 'Ibn Rušd et les Premiers Analytiques d'Aristote: Aperçu sur un problème de syllogistique modale'. *Arabic Sciences and Philosophy* 5(1): 51–74.

Élie, H. 1936. *Le signifiable par complexe*. Paris: Vrin.

El-Rouayheb, Khaled. 2009. 'Impossible Antecedents and Their Consequences: Some Thirteenth-century Arabic Discussions'. *History and Philosophy of Logic* 30: 209–225.

2010a. *Relational Syllogisms and the History of Arabic Logic. 900–1900*. Leiden: Brill.

2010b. 'Introduction'. In Khūnajī 2010, iii–lix.

2011. 'Logic in the Arabic and Islamic World'. In H. Lagerlund (ed.), *Encyclopedia of Medieval Philosophy*. Berlin: Springer, 686–692.

2012. 'Post-Avicennan Logicians on the Subject-matter of Logic: Some Thirteenth- and Fourteenth-century Discussions'. *Arabic Sciences and Philosophy* 22(1): 69–90.

2016. 'Theology and Logic'. In S. Schmidtke (ed.), *The Oxford Handbook of Islamic Theology*. Oxford University Press. URL http://www.oxfordhand-books.com/view/10.1093/oxfordhb/9780199696703.001.0001/oxfordhb-9780199696703-e-009 (last accessed 30 April 2016).

Erismann, Christophe. 2007. 'The Logic of Being: Eriugena's Dialectical Ontology'. *Vivarium* 45: 203–218.

2011. *L'homme commun*. Paris: Vrin.

Farge, James K. 1980. *Biographical Register of Paris Doctors of Theology 1500–1536*. Toronto: Pontifical Institute of Mediaeval Studies.

Ferrari, C. 2006. *Der Kategorienkommentar von Abū l-Faraǧ 'Abdallāh ibn aṭ-Ṭayyib: Text und Untersuchungen*. Leiden: Brill.

Fitzgerald, Michael. 2015. 'The "Mysterious" Thomas Manlevelt and Albert of Saxony'. *History and Philosophy of Logic* 36: 129–146.

Fleming, Brian. 1964. *Thomas de Bradwardine: Oxford Scholar, Royal Servant and Archbishop of Canterbury*. PhD thesis, University of Louvain.

Fortenbaugh, W. P., Huby, P., Sharples, R. W. and Gutas, D. (eds.). 1993. *Theophrastus of Eresus: Sources for His Life, Writings, Thought and Influence*. Leiden: Brill.

Frede, M. 1974. *Die stoische Logik*. Göttingen: Vandenhoeck and Ruprecht.

Frege, G. 1948. 'Sense and Reference'. *The Philosophical Review* 57(3): 209–230.

Fussenegger, G. 1954. '"Littera septem sigillorum" contra doctrinam Petri Ioannis Olivi edita'. *Archivum Franciscanum Historicum* 47: 45–53.

Gál, Gedeon and Wood, Rega. 1980. 'Richard Brinkley and His *Summa* Logicae'. *Franciscan Studies* 40: 59–101.

Gaskin, R. 2003. '*Complexe significabile* and Aristotle's *Categories*'. In J. Biard and I. Rosier-Catach (eds.), *La tradition mediévale des Catégories (XIIᵉ – XVᵉ siècle)*. Louvain: Peeters, 187–205.

2008. *The Unity of the Proposition*. Cambridge University Press.

Gätje, Helmut. 1982. 'Simplikios in der arabischen Überlieferung'. *Der Islam* 59: 6–31.

Geach, Peter T. 1980. 'Assertion'. In P. T. Geach, *Logic Matters*. Berkeley, CA: University of California Press, 254–269.

Georr, K. 1948. *Les Catégories d'Aristotle dans leurs versions syro-arabes*. Beirut: Dar el-Mach-req.

Gerogiorgakis, S. 2009. 'The Byzantine Liar'. *History and Philosophy of Logic* 30: 313–330.

Gilbert, Neil Ward. 1974. 'Ockham, Wyclif, and the "via moderna"'. *Miscellanea Mediaevalia* 9: 85–125.

Green, Romuald. 1963. *An Introduction to the Logical Treatise De Obligationibus, with Critical Texts of William of Sherwood [?] and Walter Burley*. PhD thesis, Katholieke Universiteit Leuven.

Green-Pedersen, Niels J. 1984. *The Tradition of the Topics in the Middle Ages*. Munich: Philosophia Verlag.

Guerlac, Rita. 1979. *Juan Luis Vives against the Pseudo-Dialecticians: A Humanist Attack on Medieval Logic*. Dordrecht: Reidel.

Guidi, M. and Walzer, R. 1940. *Uno Scritto Introduttivo allo Studio di Aristotele*. Rome: Bardi.

Gutas, Dimitri. 1993. 'Aspects of Literary Form and Genre in Arabic Logical Works'. In C. Burnett (ed.), *Glosses and Commentaries on Aristotelian Logical Texts*. London: Warburg Institute, 29–76.

1998. *Greek Thought, Arabic Culture: The Graeco-Arabic Translation Movement in Baghdad and Early 'Abbasid Society (Second–Fourth / Eighth–Tenth Centuries)*. London: Routledge.

2014. *Avicenna and the Aristotelian Tradition: Introduction to Reading Avicenna's Philosophical Works*, second edition. Leiden: Brill.

Hadot, Pierre. 1959. 'Un fragment du commentaire perdu de Boèce sur les Catégories d'Aristote dans le Codex Bernensis 363'. *Archives d'histoire doctrinale et littéraire du moyen âge* 43: 11–27.

1990. 'La logique, partie ou instrument de la philosophie'. In P. Hoffmann, I. Hadot and C. Luna (ed.), *Simplicius, Commentaire sur les Catégories*. Paris: Les Belles Lettres, I, 183–186.

Hamesse, J. 1986. 'Reportatio et transmission des textes'. In M. Asztalos (ed.), *The Editing of Theological and Philosophical Texts*. Stockholm: Almqvist & Wiksell, 10–26.

Hanke, Miroslav 2014. 'The Bricot-Mair Dispute: Scholastic Prolegomena to Non-Compositional Semantics'. *History and Philosophy of Logic* 35: 148–166.

Hansen, H. (ed.). 2012. *John Pagus on Aristotle's Categories: A Study and Edition of the Rationes super Predicamenta Aristotelis*. Leuven: Leuven University Press.

Hasnawi, Ahmad. 2001. 'Topic and Analysis: The Arabic Tradition'. In R. W. Sharples (ed.), *Whose Aristotle? Whose Aristotelianism?* Aldershot: Ashgate, 28–62.

2007. 'Boèce, Averroès et Abū al-Barakāt al-Baghdādī, témoins des écrits de Thémistius sur les Topiques d'Aristote'. *Arabic Sciences and Philosophy* 17: 203–265.

2008. 'Avicenna on the Quantification of the Predicate (with an Appendix on [Ibn Zurʿa])'. In S. Rahman, T. Street and H. Tahiri (eds.), *The Unity of Science in the Arabic Tradition*. Berlin: Springer, 295–328.

Hasse, D. N. 2014. 'Influence of Arabic and Islamic Philosophy on the Latin West'. In E. N. Zalta (ed.), *The Stanford Encyclopedia of Philosophy*, Fall 2014 edition. URL http://plato.stanford.edu/archives/fall2014/entries/arabic-islamic-influence/ (last accessed 30 April 2016).

Heim, I. and Kratzer, A. 1998. *Semantics in Generative Grammar*. Oxford: Blackwell.

Henry, Desmond P. 1964. *The De Grammatico of St. Anselm: The Theory of Paronymy*. University of Notre Dame Press.

Herzenberg, Caroline L. 2008. 'Medieval Era'. In S. Rosser (ed.), *Women, Science, and Myth*. Santa Barbara, CA: ABC-CLIO, 17–30.

Hodges, Wilfrid. 2010. 'Ibn Sīnā on Analysis: 1. Proof Search. Or: Abstract State Machines as a Tool for History of Logic'. In A. Blass, N. Dershowitz and W. Reisig (eds.), *Fields of Logic and Computation: Essays Dedicated to Yuri Gurevich on the Occasion of his 70th Birthday*. Lecture Notes in Computer Science 6300, Berlin: Springer, 354–404.

2012. 'Affirmative and Negative in Ibn Sīnā'. In C. Dutilh Novaes and O. T. Hjortland (eds.), *Insolubles and Consequences: Essays in Honour of Stephen Read*. London: College Publications, 119–134.

2013. (transl.). 'Avicenna, Shifa: Qiyas ii.4'. URL http://wilfridhodges.co.uk/arabic27.pdf (last accessed 30 April 2016).

2015. 'The Move from One to Two Quantifiers'. In A. Koslow and A. Buchsbaum (eds.), *The Road to Universal Logic: Festschrift for 50th Birthday of Jean-Yves Béziau*. Basel: Birkhäuser, I, 221–240.

Forthcoming. *Mathematical Background to the Logic of Ibn Sīnā*. URL http://wilfridhodges.co.uk/arabic44.pdf (last accessed 30 April 2016).

Hoenen, Maarten J. F. M. 2003. 'Via Antiqua and Via Moderna in the Fifteenth Century: Doctrinal, Institutional and Church Political Factors in the Wegestreit'. In Russell L. Friedman and Lauge O. Nielsen (eds.), *The Medieval Heritage in Early Modern Metaphysics and Modal Theory, 1400–1700*. Dordrecht: Kluwer, 9–36.

2011. 'Universities and Philosophy'. In H. Lagerlund (ed.), *Encyclopedia of Medieval Philosophy*. Berlin: Springer, 1359–1364.

Holtz, L., Baratin, M. and Colombat, B. (eds.). 2009. *Priscien: Transmission et refondation de la grammaire de l'Antiquité aux Modernes*. Turnhout: Brepols.

Horn, L. R. 1996. 'Presupposition and Implicature'. In S. Lappin (ed.), *Handbook of Contemporary Semantic Theory*. Oxford: Blackwell, 299–319.

2011. 'Only XL: The Assertoric Asymmetry of Exponibles'. In E. Cormany, S. Ito and D. Lutz (eds.), *Proceedings of Semantics and Linguistic Theory (SALT) 19*. New York: CLC Publications, 198–222.

Huby, Pamela. 2007. *Theophrastus of Eresus: Sources for His Life, Writings, Thought and Influence*, vol. II: *Logic*. Leiden: Brill.

Hugonnnard-Roche, Henri. 1992. 'Une ancienne "édition" arabe de l'Organon d'Aristote: Problèmes de traduction et de transmission'. In J. Hamesse (ed.), *Les des textes anciens problèmes posés par l'édition critique et médiévaux*. Louvain-la-Neuve: Univerdsité Catholique de Louvain, 139–157.

2003. 'Notices sur Aristote, La Poétique'. In R. Goulet (ed.), *Dictionnaire des philosophes antiques*, vol. *Supplément*. Paris: CNRS-Éditions, 208–218.

2004. *La Logique d'Aristote du Grec au Syriaque*. Paris: Vrin.

2013. 'Un Organon court en Syriaque: Paul de Perse versus Boèce'. In Brumberg-Chaumont 2013b, 193–216.

Hugonnard-Roche, Henri and Elamrani-Jamal, A. 1989. 'Aristote, L'Organon, tradition syriaque et arabe'. In R. Goulet (ed.), *Dictionnaire des philosophes antiques*. Paris: CNRS-Éditions, I, 502–528.

Ierodiakonou, Katerina. 2011. 'Logic, Byzantine'. In H. Lagerlund (ed.), *Encyclopedia of Medieval Philosophy*. Dordrecht: Springer, 695–697.

Iwakuma, Yukio. 1992a. ' "Vocales" or Early Nominalists'. *Traditio* 47: 37–111.

1992b. 'Twelfth-*Century Nominales*: The Posthumous School of Peter Abelard'. *Vivarium* 30: 97–109.

1993. 'The Introductiones dialecticae secundum Wilgelmum and secundum magistrum G. Paganellum'. *Cahiers de l'Institut du Moyen-Âge Grec et Latin* 21: 43–114.

2003. 'William of Champeaux and the *Introductiones*'. In H. A. G. Braakhuis and C. H. Kneepkens (eds.), *Aristotle's Peri Hermeneias in the Latin Middle Ages*. Turnhout: Brepols, 1–30.

Iwakuma, Y. and Ebbesen, S. 1992. 'Logico-Theological Schools from the Second Half of the 12th Century: A List of Sources'. *Vivarium* 30: 173–210.

Jacobi, K. 1988. 'Logic (ii): The Later Twelfth Century'. In P. Dronke (ed.), *A History of Twelfth Century Western Philosophy*. Cambridge University Press, 227–251.

Jardine, Lisa. 1988. 'Humanistic Logic'. In Charles B. Schmitt, Quentin Skinner, Eckhard Kessler and Jill Kraye (eds.), *The Cambridge History of Renaissance Philosophy*. Cambridge University Press, 173–198.

Johnston, Spencer. 2015. 'A Formal Reconstruction of Buridan's Modal Syllogism'. *History and Philosophy of Logic* 36, 2–17.

Kaluza, Z. 1988. *Les querelles doctrinales à Paris: Nominalistes et realistes aux confins du XIVe et XVe siecles*. Bergamo: Perluigi Lubrina.

1995. 'La crise des années 1474–1482: L'interdiction du nominalisme par Louis XI'. In J. F. M. Maarten, J. H. Hoenen, Josef Schneider and Georg Wieland (eds.), *Philosophy and Learning: Universities in the Middle Ages*. Leiden: Brill, 293–327.

1998. 'Late Medieval Philosophy, 1350–1500'. In Marenbon 1998, 426–451.

Kamp, H., van Genabith, J. and Reyle, U. 2011. 'Discourse Representation Theory'. In D. M. Gabbay and F. Guenthner (eds.), *Handbook of Philosophical Logic*. Dordrecht: Springer, XV, 125–394.

Kann, Christoph. 1993. 'Materiale Supposition und die Erwähnung von Sprachzeichen'. In H. Lenk and H. Poser (eds.), *Neue Realitäten. Herausforderung der Philosophie*, proc. XVI. Deutscher Kongreß für Philosophie. TU Berlin, 231–238.

2006. 'Medieval Logic as a Formal Science: A Survey'. In B. Löwe, V. Peckhaus and T. Räsch (eds.), *Foundations of the Formal Sciences*, vol. IV: *The History of the Concept of the Formal Sciences*. Studies in Logic 3. London: King's College Press, 103–123.

Kann, C., Loewe, B., Rode, C. and Uckelman, S. (eds.). Forthcoming. *Modern Views of Medieval Logic*. Leuven: Peeters.

Karimullah, Kamran. 2015. 'Unusual Syllogisms: Avicenna and Najm al-dīn al-Kātibī on per impossibile Syllogisms and Implication (luzūm)'. *Oriens* 43: 223–271.

King, Peter. 1991. 'Mediaeval Thought-Experiments: The Metamethodology of Mediaeval Science'. In T. Horowitz and G. J. Massey (eds.), *Thought Experiments in Science and Philosophy*. Savage, MD: Rowman & Littlefield, 43–64.

2004. 'Anselm's Philosophy of Language'. In Brian Davies and Brian Leftow (eds.), *The Cambridge Companion to Anselm*. Cambridge University Press, 84–110.

2005. 'William of Ockham: *Summa Logicae*'. In John Shand (ed.), *Central Works of Philosophy*, vol. 1: *Ancient and Medieval*. Chesham: Acumen, 343–374.

Klima, G. 2001a. 'Introduction'. In Buridan 2001, xxvii–lxii.

2001b. 'Existence and Reference in Medieval Logic'. In A. Hieke and E. Morscher (eds.), *New Essays in Free Logic*. Dordrecht: Kluwer, 197–226.

2004a. 'John Buridan and the Force-Content Distinction'. In A. Maierú and L. Valente (eds.), *Medieval Theories on Assertive and Non-Assertive Language: Acts of the Fourteenth European Symposium on Medieval Logic and Semantics*. Rome: Olschi, 415–427.

2004b. 'Consequences of a Closed, Token-Based Semantics: The Case of John Buridan'. *History and Philosophy of Logic* 25: 95–110.

2005. 'Nominalism'. In K. Brown (ed.), *Elsevier's Encyclopedia of Language and Linguistics*. Oxford: Elsevier, VIII, 648–652.

2006. 'Syncategoremata'. In K. Brown (ed.), *Encyclopedia of Language and Linguistics*, second edition. Oxford: Elsevier, XII, 353–356.

2009. *John Buridan*. Oxford University Press.

Klima, G. and Sandu, G. 1990. 'Numerical Quantifiers in Game-Theoretical Semantics'. *Theoria* 56: 173–192.

Kluge, E. 1973–1974. 'William of Ockham's Commentary on Porphyry: Introduction and English Translation'. *Franciscan Studies* 33: 171–254 and 34: 306–382.

Kneepkens, C. H. 1993. 'Orleáns 266 and the Sophismata Collection: Master Joscelin of Soissons and the Infinite Words in the Early Twelfth Century'. In S. Read (ed.), *Sophisms in Medieval Logic and Grammar*. Dordrecht: Kluwer, 64–85.

2003. 'Nam Defecatum Vas Quandoque Servat Amatum. Elementary Aids-to-Study: An Unconventional Access to Late-Medieval University Philosophy'. *Bulletin de philosophie médiévale* 45: 105–129.

2004. 'The "Via Antiqua" and the "Via Moderna" in Grammar: The Late Medieval Discussion on the Subject of the Sentence'. In A. Maierù and L. Valente (eds.), *Medieval Theories on Assertive and Non-assertive Language*. Florence: Olschki, 219–244.

Kneepkens, Corneille H. and Braakhuis, H. A. G. (eds.). 2003. *Aristotle's Peri hermeneias in the Latin Middle Ages*. Turnhout: Brepols.

Knuuttila, S. 1993. *Modalities in Medieval Philosophy*. London: Routledge.

1997. '*Positio Impossibilis* in Medieval Discussion of the Trinity'. In C. Marmo (ed.), *Vestigia, Imagines, Verba: Semiotics and Logic in Medieval Theological Texts (XIIth–XIVth Century)*. Turnhout: Brepols, 277–288.

2010. 'Medieval Commentators on Future Contingents in De Interpretatione 9'. *Vivarium* 48: 75–95.

2011a. 'Trinitarian Logic'. In H. Lagerlund (ed.), *Encyclopedia of Medieval Philosophy*. Berlin: Springer, 1335–1337.

2011b. 'Interpreting Medieval Logic and in Medieval Logic'. In Margaret Cameron and John Marenbon (eds.), *Methods and Methodologies: Aristotelian Logic East and West, 500–1500*. Leiden: Brill, 149–160.

2015. 'Medieval Theories of Modality'. In E. N. Zalta (ed.), *The Stanford Encyclopedia of Philosophy*, Fall 2015 edition. URL http://plato.stanford.edu/archives/fall2015/entries/modality-medieval/ (last accessed 30 April 2016.

Knysh. G. D. 1986. 'Biographical Reflections on Ockham'. *Franciscan Studies* 46: 61–91.

Kretzmann, N. 1970. 'Medieval Logicians on the Meaning of the Propositio'. *The Journal of Philosophy* 67: 767–787.

1982. 'Syncategoremata, Exponibilia, Sophismata'. In Norman Kretzmann, Anthony Kenny and Jan Pinborg (eds.), *Cambridge History of Later Medieval Philosophy*. Cambridge University Press, 211–245.

Kreztmann, N. and Stump, E. 1985. 'The Anonymous *De arte obligatoria* in Merton College M.S. 306'. In E. P. Bos (ed.), *Medieval Semantics and Metaphysics*. Aristarium Supplementa II. Nijmegen: Ingenium, 239–280.

Kretzmann, N., Kenny, A. and Pinborg, J. (eds.). 1982. *Cambridge History of Later Medieval Philosophy*. Cambridge University Press.

Lafleur, C. (ed.). 1997. *L'enseignement de la philosophie au XIIIe siècle: Autour du 'Guide de l'étudiant' du ms. Ripoll 109*. Turnhout: Brepols.

Lagerlund, H. 2000. *Modal Syllogistics in the Middle Ages*. Leiden: Brill.

2008. 'Assimilation of Aristotelian and Arabic Logic up to the Later Thirteenth Century'. In J. Woods and D. Gabbay (eds.), *Handbook of the History of Logic*, vol. 2: *Medieval and Renaissance Logic*. Amsterdam: Elsevier, 281–346.

2009. 'Avicenna and Tusi on Modal Logic'. *History and Philosophy of Logic* 30(3): 227–239.

Lagerlund, H. and Olsson, E. J. 2001. 'Disputation and Change of Belief: Burley's Theory of *Obligationes* as a Theory of Belief Revision'. In M. Yrjönsuuri (ed.), *Medieval Formal Logic*. Dordrecht: Kluwer, 35–62.

Lameer, Joep. 1994. *Al-Farabi and Aristotelian Syllogistics: Greek Theory and Islamic Practice*. Leiden: Brill.

Lawrence, C. H. 1984. 'The University in State and Church'. In J. I. Catto and R. Evans (eds.), *The History of the University of Oxford*, vol. I: *The Early Oxford Schools*. Oxford: Clarendon Press, 97–150.

Leader, D. R. 1989. *A History of the University of Cambridge*, vol. I: *The University to 1546*. Cambridge University Press.

Leff, G. 1968. *Paris and Oxford Universities in the Thirteenth and Fourteenth Centuries: An Institutional and Intellectual History*. New York: John Wiley & Sons.

Lenz, M. 2003. *Mentale Sätze. Wilhelm von Ockhams These zur Sprachlichkeit des Denkens*. Stuttgart: Franz Steiner Verlag.

Forthcoming. 'Between Things and Propositions. The Realism of Walter Burley and Walter Chatton'. In L. Cesalli and J. Marenbon (eds.), *Facts and States of Affairs*. Turnhout: Brepols.

Lewis, D. 1979. 'Attitudes De Dicto and De Se'. *The Philosophical Review* 88(4): 513–543.

Lewry, P. Osmund. 1978. *Robert Kilwardby's Writings on the Logica Vetus, Studied with Regard to Their Teaching and Method*. DPhil thesis, University of Oxford.

1981a. 'Robert Kilwardby on Meaning: A Parisian Course on the Logica Vetus'. In J. P. Beckmann, L. Honnefelder and G. Jüssen (eds.), *Sprache und Erkenntnis im Mittelalters*. Berlin: Walter de Gruyter, 376–384.

1981b. 'The Oxford Condemnations of 1277 in Grammar and Logic'. In H. A. G. Braakhuis, C. H. Kneepkens and L. M. de Rijk (eds.), *English Logic and Semantics from the End of the Twelfth Century to the Time of Ockham and Burley*. Nijmegen: Ingenium, 235–278.

1981c. 'Boethian Logic in the Medieval West'. In Margaret Gibson (ed.), *Boethius: His Life, Thought and Influence*. Oxford: Blackwell, 90–134.

Libera, Alain de. 1982. 'The Oxford and Paris Traditions in Logic'. In N. Kretzmann, A. Kenny, J. Pinborg (eds.), *The Cambridge History of Later Medieval Philosophy*. Cambridge University Press, 174–187.

1996. *La querelle des universaux. De Platon à la fin du Moyen Age*. Paris: Editions du Seuil.

2002. *La référence vide. Théories de la proposition*. Paris: Presses Universitaires de France.

Lohr, C. 1974. '*Supplementary Authors*'. *Traditio* 30: 119–144.

2010. *Latin Aristotle Commentaries*, vol. I.1: *Medieval Authors A–L*; vol. I.2: *Medieval Authors M–Z*. Florence: SISMEL Edizioni di Galluzo.

Lorenz, Sonke. 1996. 'Thomas Manlefelt (Maulefelt). Zu Leben und Werk'. In M. Kintzinger, S. Lorenz and M. Walter (eds.), *Schule und Schüler im Mittelalter*. Vienna: Archiv für Kulturgeschichte, XLII, 145–164.

Loux, Michael. 2011. *Ockham's Theory of Terms: Part 1 of the Summa Logicae*. Notre Dame, IN: St. Augustine's Press.

Luthala, Anneli. 2005. *Grammar and Philosophy in Late Antiquity*. Amsterdam: John Benjamins.

Lyons, M. C. 1982. *Aristotle's Ars Rhetorica. A New Edition with Commentary and Glossary*. Cambridge University Press.

Mack, Peter. 1993. *Renaissance Argument: Valla and Agricola in the Traditions of Rhetoric and Dialectic*. Leiden: Brill.

Madkour, Ibrahim. 1969. *L'Organon d'Aristote dans le monde arabe*, second edition. Paris: Vrin.

Magee, John. 1998. *Anicii Manlii Severini Boethii De Divisone Liber, Critical Edition, Translation, Prolegomena and Commentary*. Leiden: Brill.

Maierù, A. 1972. *Terminologia logica della tarda scolastica*. Rome: Edizione del'Ateneo.

1993. 'The Sophism "Omnis propositio est vera vel falsa" by Henry Hopton (Pseudo-Heytesbury's *De veritate et falsitate propositionis*)'. In S. Read (ed.), *Sophisms in Medieval Logic and Grammar*. Dordrecht: Reidel, 103–115.

Maierù, A. and Valente, L. (eds.). 2004. *Medieval Theories on Assertive and Non Assertive Language*. Florence: Olschki.

Makdisi, George. 1981. *The Rise of Colleges: Institutions of Learning in Islam and the West*. Edinburgh University Press.

Malink, M. 2013. *Aristotle's Modal Syllogistic*. Cambridge, MA: Harvard University Press.

Mallet, D. 1994. 'Le Kitāb al-Taḥlīl d'Alfarabi'. *Arabic Sciences and Philosophy* 4: 317–336.

Maloney, T. S. 2009. 'Who Is the Author of the Summa Lamberti?' *International Philosophical Quarterly* 49: 89–106.

Mandonnet, P. F. 1908–1911. *Siger de Brabant et l'averroïsme latin au XIIIme siècle*. Louvain: Institut Supérieur de Philosophie de l'Université.

Manekin, Charles H. 2011. 'Logic, Jewish'. In H. Lagerlund (ed.), *Encyclopedia of Medieval Philosophy*. Berlin: Springer, 697–702.

Marenbon, John. 1981. *From the Circle of Alcuin to the School of Auxerre: Logic, Theology and Philosophy in the Early Middle Ages*. Cambridge University Press.

1997. *The Philosophy of Peter Abelard*. Cambridge University Press.

(ed.). 1998. *Medieval Philosophy*. London: Routledge.

2000a. *Aristotelian Logic, Platonism and the Context of Early Medieval Philosophy in the West*. Aldershot: Ashgate.

2000b. 'Medieval Latin Commentaries and Glosses on Aristotelian Logical Texts, before c. 1150 AD'. In Marenbon 2000a, item II.

2000c. 'Alcuin, the Council of Frankfort and the Beginnings of Medieval Philosophy'. In Marenbon 2000a, item IV.

(ed.). 2007a. 'The Many Roots of Medieval Logic: The Aristotelian and the Non-Aristotelian Traditions'. *Vivarium* 45 (special issue).

2007b. Medieval Philosophy. An Historical and Philosophical Introduction, NY: Routledge, 2007.

2008. 'The Latin Tradition of Logic to 1100'. In Dov M. Gabbay and John Woods (eds.), *Handbook of the History of Logic*, vol. 2: *Medieval and Renaissance Logic*. Amsterdam: Elsevier, 1–81.

2011. 'Logic at the Turn of the Twelfth Century: A Synthesis'. In Irène Rosier-Catach (ed.), *Arts du langage et théologie aux confines des XIe-XIIe siècles*. Turnhout: Brepols, 181–217.

(ed.). 2013. 'La logique en Occident Latin'. In Brumberg-Chaumont 2013b, 173–192.

2014. 'Boethius's Unparadigmatic Originality and Its Implications for Medieval Philosophy'. In T. Boehm, T. Juergasch and A. Kirchner (eds.), *Boethius as a Paradigm of Late Ancient Thought*. Berlin: De Gruyter, 231–244.

Markowski, M. 1984. 'L'influence de Jean Buridan sur les universités d'Europe Centrale'. In Zénon Kaluza and Paul Vignaux (eds.), *Preuve et raisons à l'université de Paris: Logique, ontologie et théologie au XIVe siècle*. Paris: Vrin, 149–163.

1993. 'Die Rolle der Sophismata im unterricht der Krakauer Universität im 15. Jahrhundert'. In S. Read (ed.), *Sophisms in Medieval Logic and Grammar*. Dordrecht: Kluwer, 116–127.

Marmo, C. 1989. 'Ontology and Semantics in the Logic of Duns Scotus'. In U. Eco and C. Marmo (eds.), *On the Medieval Theory of Signs*. Amsterdam: John Benjamins, 143–193.

1990. 'Suspicio: A Key Word to the Significance of Aristotle's Rhetoric in Thirteenth Century Scholasticism'. *Cahiers de l'Institut du Moyen-Âge Grec et Latin* 60: 145–198.

Maróth, M. 1989. *Ibn Sīnā und die peripatetische 'Aussagenlogik'*. Leiden: Brill.

Martens, D. B. 2010. 'William Heytesbury and the Conditions for Knowledge'. *Theoria* 76(4): 355–374.

Martin, Christopher J. 1987. 'Embarassing Arguments and Surprising Conclusions in the Development of Theories of the Conditional in the Twelfth Century'. In

Jean Jolivet and Alain de Libera (eds.), *Gilbert de Poitiers et ses contemporains aux origins de la logica modernorum*. Naples: Bibliopolis, 377–401.

1991. 'The Logic of Negation in Boethius'. *Phronesis* 36: 277–304.

2001. 'Obligations and Liars'. In M. Yrjönsuuri (ed.), *Medieval Formal Logic*. Dordrecht: Kluwer, 63–94.

2004. 'Logic'. In Jeffrey E. Brower and Kevin Guilfoy (eds.), *The Cambridge Companion to Abelard*. Cambridge University Press, 158–199.

2009. 'The Development of Logic in the Twelfth Century'. In R. Pasnau (ed.), *Cambridge History of Medieval Philosophy*. Cambridge University Press, 129–146.

2010. '"They had added not a single tiny proposition": The Reception of the *Prior Analytics* in the First Half of the Twelfth Century'. *Vivarium* 48, 159–192.

2012. 'Logical Consequence'. In John Marenbon (ed.), *The Oxford Handbook of Medieval Philosophy*. Oxford University Press, 289–311.

2013. '*Instantiae* and the Parisian Schools'. In J. L. Fink, H. Hansen and A. M. Mora-Márquez (eds.), *Logic and Language in the Middle Ages*. Leiden: Brill, 65–84.

Mates, B. 1961. *Stoic Logic*. Berkeley, CA: University of California Press.

Meier-Oeser, Stephan. 1995. 'Signifikation'. In J. Ritter and K. Gründer (eds.), *Historisches Wörterbuch der Philosophie*. Basel: Schwabe, IX, 759–795.

1997. *Die Spur des Zeichens: Das Zeichen und seine Funktion in der Philosophie des Mittelalters und der Frühen Neuzeit*. Berlin: Walter de Gruyter.

2013. 'The Hermeneutical Rehabilitation of Supposition Theory in Seventeenth-Century Protestant Logic'. *Vivarium* 51: 464–481.

Miller. L. B. 1984. *Islamic Disputation Theory: A Study of the Development of Dialectic in Islam from the Tenth through the Fourteenth Centuries*. PhD dissertation, Princeton University.

1985. 'A Brief History of the Liar Paradox'. In R. Link-Salinger (ed.), *Of Scholars, Savants, and Their Texts*. New York: Peter Lang, 173–182.

Mitchell, O. 1983. 'On a New Algebra of Logic'. In C. S. Peirce (ed.), *Studies in Logic*. Boston, MA: Little Brown and Company, 72–106.

Monnoyer, J.-M. (ed.). 2007. *Metaphysics and Truthmakers*. Heusenstamm: Ontos.

Montague, R. 1974. *Formal Philosophy: Selected Papers by Richard Montague*. R. H. Thomason (ed.). New Haven, CT: Yale University Press.

Moody, Ernest A. 1967. 'Logic, History of: Medieval Logic'. In P. Edwards (ed.), *The Encyclopedia of Philosophy*. London: Macmillan, IV, 528–534.

Mora-Márquez, A. M. 2014. 'Martinus Dacus and Boethius Dacus on the Signification of Terms and the Truth-Value of Assertions'. *Vivarium* 52: 23–48.

Morscher, E. 1972. 'Von Bolzano zu Meinong: zur Geschichte des logischen Realismus'. In R. Haller (ed.), *Jenseits vom Sein und Nichtsein.*
Graz: Akademische Druck- und Verlaganstalt, 69–97.

    1990. 'Judgment Contents'. In K. Mulligan (ed.), *Mind, Meaning and Metaphysics:
The Philosophy and Theory of Language of Anton Marty.* Dordrecht: Kluwer,
181–196.

Movahed, Z. 2003. 'Ibn-Sina's Anticipation of the Formulas of Buridan and Barcan'.
In A. Enayat, I. Kalantari and M. Moniri (eds.), *Logic in Tehran.* Wellesley, MA:
A. K. Peters, 248–255.

    2010. 'De re and de dicto Modality in Islamic Traditional Logic'. *Sophia Perennis,*
2: 5–14.

Müller, I. von. 1897. *Über Galens Werk von wissenschaftlichen Beweis.*
Abhandlungen der königlichen Bayerischen Akademie der Wissenschaften,
philos.-philol. 20, 2. Munich.

Mulligan, K. 1989. 'Husserl on States of Affairs'. *Epistemologia* 12: 207–234.

Mulligan, K., Simons, P. and Smith, B. 1984. 'Truth-Makers'. *Philosophy and
Phenomenological Research* 44: 287–321.

Murdoch, J. E. 1991. 'Pierre Duhem and the History of Late Medieval Science
and Philosophy in the Latin West', in R. Imbach and A. Maierù (eds.), *Gli
studi di filosofia medievale fra otto e novecento.* Rome: Edizioni di storia e
letteratura.

Muskens, R. 1995. *Meaning and Partiality.* Stanford, CA: CSLI Publications.

Nauta, Lodi. 2007. 'Lorenzo Valla and the Rise of Humanist Dialectic'. In James
Hankins (ed.), *The Cambridge Companion to Renaissance Philosophy.*
Cambridge University Press, 193–210.

Newton, Lloyd A. (ed.). 2008. *Medieval Commentaries on Aristotle's Categories.*
Leiden: Brill.

Normore, Calvin. 1987. 'The Tradition of Medieval Nominalism'. In J. Wippel
(ed.), *Studies in Medieval Philosophy.* Studies in Philosophy and the History
of Philosophy 17. Washington, DC: CUA Press, 201–217.

    1999. 'Some Aspects of Ockham's Logic'. In Paul Vincent Spade (ed.), *The
Cambridge Companion to Ockham.* Cambridge University Press, 31–52.

Nortmann, U. 1996. *Modale Syllogismen, mogliche Welten, Essentialismus: Eine
Analyse der aristotelischen Modallogik.* Berlin: Walter de Gruyter.

Novikoff, Alex J. 2013. *The Medieval Culture of Disputation: Pedagogy, Practice,
and Performance.* Philadelphia, PA: University of Pennsylvania Press.

Nuchelmans, G. 1973. *Ancient and Medieval Conceptions of the Bearers of Truth
and Falsity.* Amsterdam: North-Holland.

Ottoson, Pen-Gunnar. 1984. *Scholastic Medicine and Philosophy*. Naples: Biblipolis.

Panaccio, Claude. 1999. *Le discours intérieur. De Platon à Guillaume d'Ockham.* Paris: Seuil.

2004. *Ockham on Concepts*. Aldershot: Ashgate.

2013. 'Ockham and Buridan on Simple Supposition'. *Vivarium* 51: 371–384.

Parsons, Terence. 2008. 'The Development of Supposition Theory in the Later 12th through 14th Centuries'. In D. M. Gabbay and J. Woods (eds.), *Handbook on the History of Logic*, vol. 2: *Mediaeval and Renaissance Logic*. Amsterdam: Elsevier, 157–280.

2014. *Articulating Medieval Logic*. Oxford University Press.

2015. 'The Traditional Square of Opposition'. In E. N. Zalta (ed.), *The Stanford Encyclopedia of Philosophy*, Summer 2015 edition. URL http://plato.stanford. edu/archives/sum2015/entries/square/ (last accessed 30 April 2016).

Pasnau, R. 1995. 'William Heytesbury on Knowedge: Epistemology without Necessary and Sufficient Conditions'. *History of Philosophy Quarterly* 12(4): 347–366.

(ed.). 2010. *The Cambridge History of Medieval Philosophy*, two volumes. Cambridge University Press.

Patterson, R. 1995. *Aristotle's Modal Logic: Essence and Entailment in the Organon*. Cambridge University Press.

Pérez-Ilzarbe, P. 1999. *El significado de las proposiciones: Jerónimo Pardo (†1502) y las teorías medievales de la proposición*. Pamplona: Ediciones universidad de Navarra.

2011. 'Disputation and Logic in the Medieval Treatises "De Modo Opponendi et Respondendi"'. *Vivarium* 49: 127–149.

Perini-Santos, E. Forthcoming. 'Explaining Away *complexe significabilia*: The Arguments of John Buridan'. In L. Cesalli and J. Marenbon (eds.), *Facts and States of Affairs*. Turnhout: Brepols.

Perler, D. 1992. *Der propositionale Wahrheitsbegriff*. Berlin: De Gruyter.

1993. 'Duns Scotus on Signification'. *Medieval Philosophy and Theology* 3: 97–120.

1994. 'Late Medieval Ontologies of Facts'. *The Monist* 77: 149–169.

Peters, F. E. 1968. *Aristoteles Arabus: The Oriental Translations and Commentaries on the Aristotelian Corpus*. Leiden: Brill.

Pinborg, J. 1967. *Die Entwicklung de Sprachtheorie im Mittelalter, Beiträge zur Geschichte der Philosophie und Theologie des Mittelalters: Texte und Untersuchungen 42/2*. Münster: Aschendorff.

1982. 'Speculative Grammar'. In Kretzmann et al. 1982, 254–270.

Pini, G. 1999. 'Species, Concept and Thing: Theories of Signification in the Second Half of the Thirteenth Century'. *Medieval Philosophy and Theology* 8: 21–52.

2001. 'Signification of Names in Scotus and Some of His Contemporaries'. *Vivarium* 39: 20–51.

2002. *Categories and Logic in Duns Scotus: An Interpretation of Aristotle's Categories in the Late Thirteenth Century*. Leiden: Brill.

Pironet, Fabienne. 1993. 'The *Sophismata Asinina* of William Heytesbury'. In S. Read (ed.), *Sophisms and Medieval Logic and Grammar*. Dordrecht: Kluwer, 128–143.

1995. 'Logique et droit au XIVe siècle'. In C. Bazán, E. Andujar and L. Sbrocchi (eds.), *Les philosophies morales et politiques au Moyen Age*, Proc. Ninth International Congress in Medieval Philosophy. New York, I, 548–554.

Pironet, Fabienne and Spruyt, Joke. 2015. 'Sophismata'. In E. N. Zalta (ed.), *The Stanford Encyclopedia of Philosophy*, Winter 2015 edition. URL http://plato.stanford.edu/archives/win2015/entries/sophismata/ (last accessed 30 April 2016).

Pourjavady, Reza. 2011. *Philosophy in Early Safavid Iran: Najm al-Dîn Mahmûd al-Nayrîzî and His Writings*. Leiden: Brill.

Pozzi, Lorenzo. 1990. *La Coerenza logica nelle Teoria Medioevale delle Obbligazioni: con l'edizione del trattato 'Obligationes'*. Parma: Edizioni Zara.

Qaramaleki, Ahad Faramarz (ed.). 2007. *Davāzdah risālah dar pārādūks-i durūghgū*. Tehran: Iranian Institute of Philosophy.

Quine, W. 1956. 'Quantifiers and Propositional Attitudes'. *Journal of Philosophy* 53: 177–187.

Rahman, S., Tulenheimo, T. and Genot, E. (eds.). 2008. *Unity, Truth and the Liar: The Modern Relevance of Medieval Solutions to the Liar Paradox*. Logic, Epistemology and the Unity of Science 8. Berlin: Springer.

Read, Stephen. 1991a. 'Descensus copulatim: Albert of Saxony vs. Thomas Maulfelt'. In J. Biard (ed.), *Itineraires d'Albert de Saxe: Paris-Vienne au XIVe*. Paris: Vrin, 71–85.

1991b. 'Thomas of Cleves and Collective Supposition'. *Vivarium* 29: 50–84.

(ed.). 1993. *Sophisms in Medieval Logic and Grammar*. Dordrecht: Kluwer.

1994. 'Formal and Material Consequence'. *Journal of Philosophical Logic* 23: 247–265.

2001. 'Self-Reference and Validity Revisited'. In M. Yrjönsuuri (ed.), *Medieval Formal Logic*. Dordrecht: Kluwer, 183–196.

2007. 'William Ockham's *The Sum of Logic*'. *Topoi* 26: 271–277.

2012. 'John Buridan's Theory of Consequence and His Octagons of Opposition'. In J.-Y. Beziau and D. Jacquette (eds.), *Around and Beyond the Square of Opposition*. Basel: Birkhäuser, 93–110.

2015. 'Medieval Theories: Properties of Terms'. In E. N. Zalta (ed.), *The Stanford Encyclopedia of Philosophy*, Spring 2015 edition. URL http://plato.stanford.edu/archives/spr2015/entries/medieval-terms/ (last accessed 30 April 2016).

Forthcoming. 'Robert Fland or Elandus Dialecticus?'.

Reicher, M. E. 2009. *States of Affairs*. Heusenstamm: Ontos.

Reisman, David C. 2013. 'The Life and Times of Avicenna: Patronage and Learning in Medieval Islam'. In P. Adamson (ed.), *Interpreting Avicenna: Critical Essays*. Cambridge University Press, 7–27.

Rescher, Nicholas. 1964. *The Development of Arabic Logic*. University of Pittsburgh Press.

Risse, Wilhelm. 1965. *Bibliographia Logica I: 1472–1800*. Hildesheim: Olms.

Rode, C. Forthcoming. 'States of Affairs as Mind-dependent and Intra-mental Complex Objects'. In L. Cesalli and J. Marenbon (eds.), *Facts and States of Affairs*. Turnhout: Brepols.

Rosenberg, S. and Manekin, C. 1988. 'Themistius on Modal Logic: Excerpts from a Commentary on the Prior Analytics Attributed to Themistius'. *Jerusalem Studies in Arabic and Islam* 11: 83–103.

Rosenthal, Franz. 1958. *The Muqaddima of Ibn Khaldun*. New York: Pantheon Books.

Rosier-Catach, Irène. 1983. *La grammaire spéculative des modistes*. Lille: Presses Universitaires.

(ed.). 2003a. 'Les syncatégorème'. *Histoire epistémologie langage* 25(II), (special issue).

Rosier-Catach, Irène. 2003b. 'Abélard et les grammairiens: sur le verbe substantif et la prédication'. *Vivarium* 41(2): 175–248.

2009. 'Sur le verbe substantif, la prédication et la consignification – Peri Hermeneias 16b20–25 dans les traductions et commentaires en latin'. In Suzanne Husson (ed.), *Interpréter le De interpretatione*. Paris: Vrin, 97–131.

2010. 'Grammar'. In Robert Pasnau (ed.), *The Cambridge History of Medieval Philosophy*. Cambridge University Press, 197–207.

2012. '"Vox" and "Oratio" in Early Twelfth Century Grammar and Dialectic'. *Archives d'histoire doctrinale et littéraire du moyen âge* 78: 47–129.

Russell, B. 2008. *The Problems of Philosophy*. Rockwell, MD: Arc Manor.

Rutten, Pepijn. 2005. '"Secundum processum et mentem Versoris": John Versor and His Relation to the Schools of Thought Reconsidered'. *Vivarium* 43: 292–336.

Sabra, A. I. 1965. 'A Twelfth-century Defence of the Fourth-figure of the Syllogism'. *Journal of the Warburg and Courtauld Institutes* 28: 14–28.

1980. 'Avicenna on the Subject Matter of Logic'. *Journal of Philosophy* 77: 746–764.

Schmutz, J. 2011. 'Verifactivum'. In I. Atucha, D. Calma, C. König-Pralong and I. Zavattero (eds.), *Mots médiévaux offerts à Ruedi Imbach*. Porto: FIDEM, 739–748.

Schöck, Cornelia. 2005. *Koranexegese, Grammatik Und Logik: Zum Verhältnis von Arabischer Und Aristotelischer Urteils-, Konsequenz- Und Schlußlehre*. Leiden: Brill.

Scott, Theodore K. 1966. *John Buridan: Sophisms on Meaning and Truth*. New York: Appleton-Century-Crofts.

Sharpe, Johannes. 1990. *Quaestio super Universalia*. A. D. Conti (ed.). Florence: Olschki.

Shiel, James. 1958. 'Boethius' Commentaries on Aristotle'. *Medieval and Renaissance Studies* 4: 217–244.

1990. 'Boethius' Commentaries on Aristotle'. In Sorabji 1990, 349–372.

Silva, J. F. 2011. 'Kilwardby'. In H. Lagerlund (ed.), *Encyclopedia of Medieval Philosophy*. Berlin: Springer, 1148–1153.

Smiley, T. J. 1973. 'What Is a Syllogism?' *Journal of Philosophical Logic* 2: 136–154.

Smith, B. 1989. 'Logic and the *Sachverhalt*'. *The Monist* 72: 52–69.

Smith, Robin. 1989. *Aristotle, Prior Analytics*. Indianapolis, IN: Hackett.

Sorabji, Richard (ed.). 1990. *Aristotle Transformed: The Ancient Commentators and Their Influence*. Ithaca, NY: Cornell University Press.

2004. *The Philosophy of the Commentators 200–600AD: A Sourcebook*, vol. 3: *Logic and Metaphysics*. Ithaca, NY: Cornell University Press.

Spade, P.V. (trans.). 1974. *Ockham's Theory of Terms: Part II of the Summa Logicae*. South Bend, IN: St. Augustine's Press.

1977. 'Roger Swyneshed's *Obligationes*: Edition and Comments'. *Archives d'histoire doctrinale et littéraire du moyen âge* 44: 243–285.

1978. 'Richard Lavenham's *Obligationes*: Edition and Comments'. *Rivista critica di storia della filosofia* 33: 225–242.

1979. 'Roger Swyneshed's *Insolubilia*: Edition and Comments'. *Archives d'histoire doctrinale et littéraire du moyen âge* 46: 177–220.

1980a. 'Robert Fland's *Obligationes*: An Edition'. *Medieval Studies* 42: 41–60.

1980b. *Peter of Ailly: Concepts and Insolubles*. Dordrecht: Reidel.

1982a. 'The Semantics of Terms'. In N. Kretzmann, A. Kenny and J. Pinborg (eds.), *The Cambridge History of Later Medieval Philosophy*. Cambridge University Press, 188–196.

1982b. 'Obligations: Developments in the Fourteenth Century'. In N. Kretzmann, A. Kenny, and J. Pinborg (eds.), *Cambridge History of Later Medieval Philosophy*. Cambridge University Press, 335–341.

1982c. 'Three Theories of *Obligationes*: Burley, Kilvington, and Swyneshed on Counterfactual Reasoning'. *History and Philosophy of Logic* 3: 1–32.

1988. 'The Logic of the Categorical: The Medieval Theory of Descent and Ascent'. In N. Kretzmann (ed.), *Meaning and Inference in Medieval Philosophy*. Dordrecht: Kluwer, 187–224.

1994. *Five Texts on the Mediaeval Problem of Universals: Porphyry, Boethius, Abelard, Duns Scotus, Ockham*. Indianapolis, IN: Hackett.

2007. *Thoughts, Words and Things: An Introduction to Late Medieval Logic and Semantic Theory*. URL http://pvspade.com/ Logic/docs/Thoughts,%20 Words%20and%20Things1_2.pdf (last accessed 30 April 2016).

2000. 'Why Don't Medieval Logicians Ever Tell Us What They're Doing? Or, What Is This, a Conspiracy?' URL http://pvspade.com/Logic/docs/Conspiracy. pdf (last accessed 30 April 2016).

Spade, Paul Vincent and Menn, Stephen. 2003. 'A Note on the Title of Walter Burley's *On the Purity of the Art of Logic*'. URL http://pvspade.com/Logic/ docs/BurlNote.pdf (last accessed 30 April 2016).

Spade, Paul Vincent and and Yrjönsuuri, Mikko. 2014. 'Medieval Theories of Obligationes'. In E. N. Zalta (ed.), *The Stanford Encyclopedia of Philosophy*, Winter 2014 edition. URL http://plato.stanford.edu/archives/win2014/en-tries/obligationes/ (last accessed 30 April 2016).

Speca, Anthony. 2001. *Hypothetical Syllogistic and Stoic Logic*. Leiden: Brill.

Spruit, L. 1994. *Species intelligibilis: From Perception to Knowledge*. Leiden: Brill.

Spruyt, J. 2011. 'Syncategoremata'. In H. Lagerlund (ed.), *Encyclopedia of Medieval Philosophy*. Berlin: Springer, 1241–1245.

2012. 'Peter of Spain'. In H. Lagerlund (ed.), *Encyclopedia of Medieval Philosophy*. Berlin: Springer, 1257–1261.

Strawson, P. 1950. 'On Referring'. *Mind* 59: 320–344.

Street, T. 2002. 'An Outline of Avicenna's Syllogistic'. *Archiv für Geschichte der Philosophie* 84: 129–160.

2004. 'Arabic Logic'. In D. M. Gabbay and J. Woods (eds.), *Handbook of the History of Logic*. Amsterdam: Elsevier, 523–596.

2005a. 'Fakhraddīn ar-Rāzī's Critique of Avicennan Logic'. In D. Perler and U. Rudolph (eds.), *Logik und Theologie. Das 'Organon' im arabischen und im lateinischen Mittelalter*. Leiden: Brill, 99–116.

2005b. 'Logic'. In P. Adamson and R. Taylor (eds.), *The Cambridge Companion to Arabic Philosophy*. Cambridge University Press, 247–265.

2010a. 'Avicenna's Twenty Questions on Logic: Preliminary Notes for Further Work'. *Documenti e studi sulla tradizione filosofica medievale* 21: 97–112.

2010b. 'Appendix: Readings of the Subject Term'. *Arabic Sciences and Philosophy* 20: 119–124.

2012. 'Medieval and Modern Interpretations of Avicenna's Modal Syllogistic'. In F. Opwis and D. Reisman (eds.), *Islamic Philosophy, Science, Culture, and Religion: Essays in Honor of Dimitri Gutas*. Leiden: Brill, 232–256.

2014. 'Afḍal al-Dīn al-Khūnajī (d. 1248) on the Conversion of Modal Propositions'. *Oriens* 42: 454–513.

2015. 'Arabic and Islamic Philosophy of Language and Logic'. In E. N. Zalta (ed.), *The Stanford Encyclopedia of Philosophy*, Spring 2015 edition. URL http://plato.stanford.edu/archives/spr2015/entries/arabic-islamic-language/ (last accessed 30 April 2016).

Forthcoming a. 'Avicenna: Logic'. In Ulrich Rudolph (ed.), *Grundriss Der Geschichte Der Philosophie. Philosophie in Der Islamischen Welt*, Basel: Schwabe.

Forthcoming b. 'Maragha Logic'.

Forthcoming c. 'Kātibī, Taḥtānī and the *Shamsiyya*'. In Kh. El-Rouayheb and S. Schmidtke (eds.), *The Oxford Handbook of Islamic Philosophy*. Oxford University Press.

Streveler, P. 1993. 'A Comparative Analysis of the Treatment of Sophisms in MSS Digby 2 and Royal 12 of the Magister Abstractionem'. In S. Read (ed.), *Sophisms in Medieval Logic and Grammar*. Dordrecht: Kluwer, 144–184.

Strobino, Riccardo. 2009. *Concedere, negare, dubitare: Peter of Mantua's treatise on obligations*. PhD dissertation, Scuola Normale Superiore Pisa.

2015 'Time and Necessity in Avicenna's Theory of Demonstration'. *Oriens* 43: 338–367.

Stump, Eleonore. 1982. 'Obligations: From the Beginning to the Early Fourteenth Century'. In N. Kretzman, A. Kenny and J. Pinborg (eds.), *Cambridge History of Later Medieval Philosophy*. Cambridge University Press, 315–334.

1985. 'The Logic of Disputation in Walter Burley's Treatise on Obligationes'. *Synthese* 63: 355–374.

1989. *Dialectic and Its Place in the Development of Medieval Logic*. Ithaca, NY: Cornell University Press.

Sylla, Edith. 1982. 'The Oxford Calculators'. In Kretzmann et al. 1982, 540–563.

2010. 'The Oxford Calculators' Middle Degree Theorem in Context'. *Early Science and Medicine* 15: 338–370.

Tabarroni, A. 1993. ' "Omnis phoenix est": Quantification and Existence in a New Sophismata-Collection' (MS Clm 14522). In S. Read, *Sophisms in Medieval Logic and Grammar*. Dordrecht: Kluwer, 185–201.

Tachau, Katherine. 1987. 'Wodeham, Crathorn and Holcot: The Development of the *complexe significabile*'. In L. M. De Rijk and H. A. G. Braakhuis (eds.), *Logos and Pragma*. Nijmegen: Ingenium, 161–187.

1988. *Vision and Certitude in the Age of Ockham: Optics, Epistemology, and the Foundations of Semantics, 1250–1345*. Leiden: Brill.

Tarski, A. 1983. 'On the Concept of Logical Consequence'. In A. Tarski, *Logic, Semantics, Metamathematics*, second edition. Indianapolis, IN: Hackett, 409–420.

Textor, M. 1996. *Bolzano's Propositionalismus*. Berlin: De Gruyter.

Thom, Paul. 1996. *The Logic of Essentialism: An Interpretation of Aristotle's Modal Syllogistic*. Synthese Historical Library 43. Dordrecht: Kluwer.

2003. *Medieval Modal Systems*. Aldershot: Ashgate.

2007. *Logic and Ontology in the Syllogistic of Robert Kilwardby*. Leiden: Brill.

2008. 'Logic and Metaphysics in Avicenna's Modal Syllogistic'. In S. Rahman, T. Street and H. Tahiri (eds.), *The Unity of Science in the Arabic Tradition*. Berlin: Springer, 362–376.

2010. 'Abharī on the Logic of Conjunctive Terms'. *Arabic Sciences and Philosophy* 20(1): 105–117.

2011. 'On Formalizing the Logics of the Past'. In Margaret Cameron and John Marenbon (eds.), *Methods and Methodologies: Aristotelian Logic East and West, 500–1500*. Leiden: Brill, 191–206.

2012a. 'Logical Form'. In J. Marenbon (ed.), *The Oxford Handbook of Medieval Philosophy*. Oxford University Press, 271–288.

2012b. 'Syllogisms about Possibility and Necessity in Avicenna and Ṭūsī'. In C. Dutilh Novaes and O. Hjortland (eds.), *Insolubles and Consequences: Essays in Honour of Stephen Read*. Milton Keynes: College Publications, 239–248.

2013. 'Robert Kilwardby on Syllogistic Form'. In H. Lagerlund and P. Thom (eds.), *The Philosophy of Robert Kilwardby*. Leiden: Brill, 131–162.

2016. 'Necessity in Avicenna and the Arabic Tradition'. In M. Cresswell (ed.), *The Logic of Modalities from Aristotle to Carnap: The Story of Necessity*. Cambridge University Press.

Thomsen Thörnqvist, Cristina. 2013. 'The "Anonymus Aurelianensis III" and Robert Kilwardby on the *Prior Analytics*'. In J. L. Fink, H. Hansen and A. M. Mora-Márquez (eds.), *Logic and Language in the Middle Ages*, Leiden: Brill, 185–198.

(ed.). 2014. '*Anonymus Aurelianensis III*' in *Aristotelis Analytica priora: Critical Edition, Introduction, Notes and Indexes*. Leiden: Brill.

Forthcoming. 'Bridging the Beginner's Gap: Apuleius, Boethius, and Porphyry on the Categorical Syllogism'. In Börje Bydén and Christina Thomsen Thörnqvist (eds.), *The Aristotelian Tradition: The Reception of Aristotle's Works on Logic and Metaphysics in the Middle Ages*.

Tkatsch, Jaroslaus. 1928–1932. *Die Arabische Übersetzung der Poetik des Aristoteles und die Grundlage der Kritik griechischen Textes*, two volumes. Vienna: Holder-Pichler-Tempsky.

Tweedale, Martin. 1976. *Abailard on Universals*. Amsterdam: North-Holland.

1988. 'Logic (i): From the Late Eleventh Century to the Time of Abelard'. In Peter Dronke (ed.), *A History of Twelfth-Century Philosophy*. Cambridge University Press, 196–226.

Uckelman, Sara L. 2010. 'Logic and the Condemnations of 1277'. *Journal of Philosophical Logic* 39: 201–227.

2011a. 'A Dynamic Epistemic Logic Approach to Modeling *Obligationes*'. In D. Grossi, S. Minica, B. Rodenhäuser and S. Smets (eds.), *LIRa Yearbook*. Amsterdam: Institute for Logic, Language & Computation, 147–172.

2011b. 'Deceit and Indefeasible Knowledge: The Case of Dubitatio'. *Journal of Applied Non-Classical Logics* 21(3/4): 503–519.

2012. 'The Reception of St. Anselm's Logic in the 20th and 21st Centuries'. In G. Gasper and I. Logan (eds.), *Saint Anselm of Canterbury and His Legacy*. Toronto: Pontifical Institute of Mediaeval Studies, 405–426.

2013. 'Medieval *Disputationes de obligationibus* as Formal Dialogue Systems'. *Argumentation* 27(2): 143–166.

2015. '*Sit Verum* and Counterfactual Reasoning'. *Vivarium* 53: 90–113.

Uckelman, S. L., Maat, J. and Katherina R. Forthcoming. 'The Art of Doubting in *Obligationes Parisienses*'. In C. Kann, B. Löwe, C. Rode and S. L. Uckelman (eds.), *Modern Views of Medieval Logic*. Leuven: Peeters.

Van der Helm, Alfred. 2014. *Thomas Manlevelt, 'Questiones Libri Porphirii'*. Leiden: Brill.

Van der Lecq, Ria. 2011. 'Modistae'. In H. Lagerlund (ed.), *Encyclopedia of Medieval Philosophy*. Berlin: Springer, 806–808.

Van Rijen, J. 1989. *Aspects of Aristotle's Logic of Modalities*. Synthese Historical Library 35. Dordrecht: Kluwer.

Versteegh, Kees. 1997. *Landmarks in Linguistic Thought III: The Arabic Linguistic Tradition*. London: Routledge.

Vittorini, Marta. 2013. 'Life and Works'. In Conti 2013a, 17–45.

Walzer, R. 1962. *Greek into Arabic*. Cambridge, MA: Harvard University Press.

Wei, Ian. 2012. *Intellectual Culture in Medieval Paris: Theologians and the University, c.1100–1330*. Cambridge Univeristy Press.

Weidemann, Hermann. 1979. 'Wilhelm von Ockhams Suppositionstheorie und die moderne Quantorenlogik'. *Vivarium* 17(1): 43–60.

Weijers, O. 1994. 'L'enseignement du trivium à la Faculté des arts de Paris: la quaestio'. In J. Hamesse (ed.), *Manuels, programmes de cours et techniques d'enseignement dans les universités médiévales*. Louvain-la-Neuve: Université Catholique de Louvain, 54–74.

Westerståhl, D. 1985. 'Logical Constants in Quantifier Languages'. *Linguistics and Philosophy* 8: 387–413.

Wilks, Ian. 2008. 'The Logical Theory of Peter Abelard and His Contemporaries'. In D. Gabbay and J. Woods (eds.), *Handbook of the History of Logic*, vol. 2: *Medieval and Renaissance Logic*. Amsterdam: Elsevier, 83–156.

Wippel, J. 1987. 'Thomas Aquinas's Derivation of the Aristotelian Categories (Predicaments)'. *Journal of the History of Philosophy* 25(1): 13–34.

Wisnovsky, Rob. 2004. 'The Nature and Scope of Arabic Philosophical Commentary in Post-classical (ca. 1100–1900 AD) Islamic Intellectual History: Some Preliminary Observations'. In P. Adamson, H. Baltussen and M. W. F. Stone (eds.), *Philosophy, Science and Exegesis in Greek, Arabic and Latin Commentaries*. London: Institute for Advanced Studies, 149–191.

Witt, C. and Shapiro, L. 2015. 'Feminist History of Philosophy'. In E. N. Zalta (ed.), *The Stanford Encyclopedia of Philosophy*. URL http://plato.stanford.edu/entries/feminism-femhist/ (last accessed 30 April 2016).

Yrjönsuuri, Mikko. 1993. 'Aristotle's Topics and Medieval Obligational Disputations'. *Synthese* 96: 59–82.

2000. 'The Trinity and *Positio Impossibilis*: Some Remarks on Inconsistence'. In G. Halström and J. Hintikka (eds.), *Medieval Philosophy and Modern Times*. Dordrecht: Kluwer, 59–68.

2001. 'Duties, Rules and Interpretations in Obligational Disputations'. In M. Yrjönsuuri (ed.), *Medieval Formal Logic*. Dordrecht: Kluwer, 3–34.

Zachhuber, Johannes. 1999. *Human Nature in Gregory of Nyssa: Philosophical Background and Theological Significance*. Leiden: Brill.

Zimmermann, F.W. 1976. 'Al-Farabi und die philosophische Kritik an Galen von Alexander zu Averroes'. In A. Dietrich (ed.), *Akten des VII. Kongresses für Arabistik und Islamwissenschaft*, 15–22 August 1974, Abhandlungen der Akademie der Wissenschaften in Göttingen, Phil.-Hist. Klasse, Dritte Folge, Nr 98, Göttingen, 401–414.

Zonta, Mauro. 1997. 'Fonti antiche e ledievali della logica ebraica nella Provenza del Trecento'. *Medioevo* 23: 515–594.

2011. 'About Todros Todrosi's Medieval Hebrew Translation of Al-Farabi Lost Long Commentary/Gloss-Commentary on Aristotle's Topics, Book VIII'. *History and Philosophy of Logic* 32(1): 37–45.

Zupko, Jack. 2003. *John Buridan*. University of Notre Dame Press.

Index